Career Counseling in P–12 Schools

•••••

Jennifer Curry, PhD, Certified School Counselor, teaches in the counselor education program at Louisiana State University where she is the coordinator of the school counseling program. Her educational background includes a bachelor of science degree from Western Kentucky University, a master's of education in human development counseling from Vanderbilt University, and a doctorate in counselor education from University of Central Florida. She has served as a professional school counselor in elementary, middle, and high schools. Her research interests include career and college readiness and school counselor development. She has presented her work nationally and internationally on a wide range of school counseling topics. Additionally, she has served as guest editor and editorial board member of ASCA's *Professional School Counseling* journal. Dr. Curry has also served on ASCA's delegate assembly and as the postsecondary vice president and president of the Louisiana School Counselor Association. She teaches all of the school counseling courses at Louisiana State University and integrates multisystemic career concepts in each course she teaches.

Amy Milsom, DEd, LPC-S, NCC, Certified School Counselor, teaches in the counselor education program at Clemson University and is the coordinator of Clemson's school counseling and clinical mental health counseling programs. She received a bachelor of arts degree in psychology, a master's of education in counselor education, and a doctorate in counselor education from Pennsylvania State University. Dr. Milsom has 20 years of experience in the counseling field as a counselor educator, a counseling supervisor, a middle and high school counselor, and provider of counseling services to children, adolescents, and college students. Her teaching experience includes a variety of counseling courses, including career counseling and numerous school counseling courses. A past editor of *Professional School Counseling*, Dr. Milsom has a strong record of peer-reviewed publications and editorial experience. Her research focuses on school counselor education and students with disabilities, with an emphasis on postsecondary transition planning and college readiness for students with disabilities.

Career Counseling in P–12 Schools

• • • • •

Jennifer Curry, PhD

Amy Milsom, DEd, LPC-S, NCC

SPRINGER PUBLISHING COMPANY
NEW YORK

Springer Publishing Company, LLC
11 West 42nd Street
New York, NY 10036
www.springerpub.com

Acquisitions Editor: Nancy Hale
Production Editor: Michael O'Connor
Composition: S4Carlisle Publishing Services

ISBN: 978-0-8261-1023-7
e-book ISBN: 978-0-8261-1024-4
Instructor's Manual ISBN: 978-0-8261-6421-6

Instructor's Materials: Qualified instructors may request supplements by emailing textbook@springerpub.com

14 15 16 17 / 5 4 3 2

The author and the publisher of this Work have made every effort to use sources believed to be reliable to provide information that is accurate and compatible with the standards generally accepted at the time of publication. The author and publisher shall not be liable for any special, consequential, or exemplary damages resulting, in whole or in part, from the readers' use of, or reliance on, the information contained in this book. The publisher has no responsibility for the persistence or accuracy of URLs for external or third-party Internet websites referred to in this publication and does not guarantee that any content on such websites is, or will remain, accurate or appropriate.

Library of Congress Cataloging-in-Publication Data
Curry, Jennifer (Jennifer R.), author.
  Career counseling in P-12 schools / by Jennifer Curry, PhD and Amy Milsom, DEd.
    pages cm
  Includes bibliographical references and index.
  ISBN-13: 978-0-8261-1023-7
  ISBN-10: 0-8261-1023-1
  ISBN-13: 978-0-8261-1024-4 (e-book)
  1. Career education—Curricula—Planning. 2. Counseling in elementary education. 3. Counseling in secondary education. 4. Vocational guidance. I. Milsom, Amy, author. II. Title.
  LC1037.C875 2013
  370.113—dc23   2013021403

Printed in the United States of America by Bradford & Bigelow.

For my parents, who taught me the importance of dreaming big, imagining possibilities, and not surrendering to limitations set by society or by myself.

To Emeric for love, support, encouragement, and the constant reminder that a life partnership is built on the day-to-day little things as much as major life moments.

To Gabby, the best writing partner I could ever have, for your unwavering support. Your love of life reminds me of how precious each opportunity truly is.

—Jennifer Curry

•••••

Contents

•••••

• • • • •

Preface

• • • • •

Our decision to write this book stemmed from our desire to provide school counselors with a resource that could help them easily conceptualize the career development needs of P–12 students and design relevant and meaningful career interventions. We wanted to develop a book that not only was practical but also pushed readers to be intentional in their work. Further, we believed it was important to respond to national initiatives that emphasize a focus on career and college readiness. The unique aspect of our book, compared to many other career counseling textbooks, is that we present a comprehensive, integrated, and practical approach to counseling specifically targeting career and college readiness in P–12 schools.

In this book we provide a review of developmental, ecosystemic, and career theories to inform relevant P–12 career and college readiness interventions. Given the variation that exists in the psychosocial, cognitive, and academic development of P–12 students, we review numerous developmental theories and assist readers in using them as a foundation to design sequential and developmentally appropriate career curricula and interventions. We also help readers understand the ecosystemic influences (e.g., family, school, community, society) on career development, and we discuss both why it is important to involve various stakeholders in career and college readiness initiatives and how to involve them. Finally, we provide readers with concrete examples of how to apply various career counseling theories when working with P–12 students.

We start this book with five foundational chapters in which we review current data and issues related to college and career readiness, career counseling preparation standards, cultural considerations, career assessment, and curriculum development. We then address career development and college readiness needs by grade level. Our focus in each grade level chapter is to help readers apply knowledge of theories and identify ways that multiple stakeholders can become involved in career and college readiness interventions.

We also provide concrete, practical examples, including case examples, to demonstrate the concepts we highlight for each theory.

We greatly enjoyed writing this book, but it was challenging at times for us to decide in which chapter to include certain information. In that vein, we encourage readers not to limit themselves to implementing career and college readiness interventions exactly as we outline them. Many of the activities and ideas we share could be applicable across numerous grade levels if modified to accommodate developmental differences. Also, P–12 students can benefit from repetition, so it never hurts to target something more than once. Our hope is that both pre-service and practicing school counselors find this book useful in helping identify career and college readiness needs and design developmentally appropriate interventions that are grounded in theory.

In addition to the textbook we have provided a guide intended to support instructors in developing a graduate level course on P–12 career and college readiness. This guide includes a sample syllabus that reflects the content of the textbook. We designed this sample course with a number of useful tools for each chapter including discussion questions, project-based activities, quizzes and essay questions, and social media that may be useful for teaching this course. These materials may also be additive to an existing course as supplemental materials. **The guide is available to qualified instructors by emailing textbook@springerpub.com.**

ACKNOWLEDGMENTS

We wish to acknowledge the help and support of Patrick Akos, Logan Chandler, Julie Coughlin, Tanya K. Dupuy, Ainsley Pellerin, and Jennie F. Trocquet.

Career Counseling in P–12 Schools

•••••

1

• • • • •

Ecosystemic, Developmental Career Education and Counseling in Contemporary P–12 Schools

• • • • •

Work should be an exciting blend of challenge and accomplishment that is engaging and meets the personal and professional growth needs of the individual. Beyond providing fiscal support, a person's chosen career ideally should provide mental stimulation, a creative outlet, an opportunity to contribute to society and the well-being of others, and feelings of personal value, pride, mattering, and mastery (Curry & Bickmore, 2012; Myers, Sweeney, & Witmer, 2000). When individuals make informed career decisions based on an assessment of aptitude, values, interests, and person–environment fit, they are more likely to be satisfied with their careers and be committed long term to their career choices.

To ensure students' future career success, contemporary schools need to offer diverse curricula and educational options that afford students opportunities to develop comprehensive skills and competencies to meet the demands of the 21st century workplace. As global economies, industry, and technology change, so must the preparation of students (Akos, Niles, Miller, & Erford, 2011). Johnson (2000) noted that employment in the future will include more contractual work, more temporary assignments, and decentralized work locations (e.g., site or field based, home office) rather than stable, long-term appointments. Thus, the future workforce must be more flexible, adaptable, and committed to lifelong learning as they approach postsecondary life (Johnson, 2000).

In discussing trends in higher education, Brock (2010) indicated that although access to higher education has greatly improved in recent years, success (measured by college retention and degree completion) has not improved. Demographically, postsecondary schools are more diverse than ever, but Brock (2010) discussed how most of that diversity is accounted for by enrollment at 2-year colleges and less selective institutions. Women now outnumber men at 4-year institutions, but women and individuals from minority populations are overrepresented at 2-year colleges. When considering college readiness, practitioners would be remiss if they neglected to identify the unique needs of populations like first-generation college students, English language learners (ELLs), students with identified disabilities, and students from lower socioeconomic backgrounds. Moreover, according to the National Poverty Center (using data from the U.S. Census Bureau) in 2010, more than 1 in 5 children in the United States live in poverty. Students living in poverty may have fewer familial resources to facilitate career and college readiness in the home. Therefore, school counselors need to be prepared to assist those students through equity-based programming. We will continue to examine the needs of these and other specific populations throughout this book.

Although many researchers, educators, and policymakers agree that college and career readiness are essential components of a P–12 education, there is no clear definition of what this means. Because the terms *career readiness* and *college readiness* are distinguishable from one another and nonsynonymous, one approach to defining them is to define them separately. Most of what has been written about college readiness focuses on readiness to succeed at 4-year institutions. Conley (2007) proposed that the construct of *college readiness* is multifaceted, with academic skills being only one component. He wrote that:

> The college-ready student envisioned by this definition is able to understand what is expected in a college course, can cope with the content knowledge that is presented, and can take away from the course the key intellectual lessons and dispositions the course was designed to convey and develop. In addition, the student is prepared to get the most out of the college experience due to a thorough understanding of the culture and structure of postsecondary education and the ways of knowing and intellectual norms that prevail in this academic and social environment. The student has both the mindset and disposition necessary to enable this to happen. (pp. 5–6)

College preparation expectations differ depending on whether students attend 4-year colleges, 2-year colleges, or vocational and technical schools. Aside from obvious academically related differences among 4-year, 2-year, and vocational/technical schools, Conley's definition of college readiness seems broad enough to apply to various types of post-secondary education. In essence, he suggested that on top of possessing requisite academic skills and higher-order thinking skills that enable students to retain and apply knowledge and skills, students do better when they have an idea of what to expect and are committed to developing the skills and knowledge to successfully navigate postsecondary school. We believe that better preparation for college via P–12 interventions could help to improve these success rates, and we discuss numerous interventions throughout this book.

In addition to college readiness, defining *career readiness* is of vital importance. According to the Association for Career and Technical Education (ACTE, 2010),

> Career readiness involves three major skill areas: *core academic skills* and the ability to apply those skills to concrete situations in order to function in the workplace and in routine daily activities; *employability skills* (such as critical thinking and responsibility) that are essential in any career area; and *technical, job-specific skills* related to a specific career pathway. (p. 1)

Regarding academics, the ACTE (2011) emphasized that basic math and English/language arts skills are critical for all students planning to enter the workforce. Additionally, ACTE noted collaboration, professionalism, ability to use technology, responsibility, flexibility, and problem solving as important employability skills.

Students who choose not to pursue college or technical school need to possess academic, employability, and technical skills upon high school graduation in addition to possessing basic job search knowledge and skills (e.g., fill out a job application, write a resume and cover letter, search for job openings, answer interview questions appropriately) to secure employment As mentioned, for students who do intend to pursue college, academic skills and employability skills will be necessary by graduation in order for them to be successful in college.

CURRENT TRENDS IN COLLEGE AND CAREER

Before we focus on interventions that can help students develop the skills and knowledge to be successful in college and careers, we want to provide an overview of what students do after high school. As we present the information that follows, you will see fairly consistent trends. Specifically, gaps in achievement and opportunity for minorities and individuals from lower socioeconomic groups are reflected in much of the data. These gaps unfortunately start during P–12 education and are demonstrated in high school matriculation data. According to the Census Bureau *Statistical Abstract of the United States* (2011), in 2009, 86.7% of citizens age 25 or older had completed a high school degree. However, high school graduation rates were reported at 88.2% for Asians, 87.1% for Whites, 84.1% for Blacks, and 61.9% for Hispanics. This is concerning as individuals without a high school diploma are at a disadvantage when it comes to career outcomes; they earn less and are more likely to be unemployed than high school graduates. We will explore this issue further.

College Attendance and Degree Attainment

According to a summary of U.S. Bureau of Labor Statistics (BLS) by Lacey and Wright (2009), by 2018 there will be an 18% increase in jobs requiring a master's degree, a 17% increase in jobs requiring a doctoral degree and a 30% decline in careers involving no postsecondary training (i.e., office and administrative support, production occupations). Carnevale, Smith, and Strohl (2010) reported that by the year 2018, the United States will need 22 million new college degree earners, but we will most likely be short by 3 million. The shortage will be based on an increase in the number of retirees coupled with the demand by employers to hire workers with higher levels of education and training. According to data presented by the Chronicle of Higher Education (2011), of people age 25 and older in 2010, approximately 40% had completed an associate's degree or higher and only 10.5% had completed a graduate or professional degree. Furthermore, of students enrolled in college, an estimated 40% attend community colleges, but for students whose families earn less than $40,000 annually, 50% attend community colleges. The information from Carnevale et al. coupled with these data suggest that an increase in people pursuing college degrees, and in particular advanced degrees, will be important for the future.

College attendance rates have increased in recent years. The Chronicle of Higher Education (2011) reported an overall average growth rate of 39% in undergraduate college enrollment (2-year and 4-year colleges) from 1999 to 2009; growth rates for enrollment in graduate school averaged 36%. Average growth rates for undergraduate enrollment were 93% for Hispanic students and 78% for Black students; growth rates for American Indians and Asians averaged 45%, and rates for Whites were the lowest at 24%. Despite increased college enrollment growth for Hispanics and Blacks, smaller percentages of minority students attend college. That is, the average college enrollment in 2009 was 41% of the U.S. population. For White students it was 45% while for Black and Hispanic students the rates were 38% and 28%, respectively. Carnevale et al. (2010) also noted that college education attainment continues to elude individuals from lower socioeconomic classes, with the greatest number of college graduates coming from the middle and upper classes.

According to the U.S. Census Bureau (2011), only 29.5% percent of U.S. citizens had attained a 4-year college degree. Four-year college degree attainment rates were reported as 52.3% for Asians, 29.9% for Whites, 19.3% for Blacks, and 13.2% for Hispanics (with intragroup differences identified among Cubans, Puerto Ricans, and Mexicans). Although we have no specific knowledge regarding the causes for these differences, numerous intrapersonal and environmental factors to be discussed later likely play important roles in the career and college success of these individuals.

We want to examine more specifically the concern expressed by Brock (2010) presented earlier in this chapter related to stagnant college success rates (i.e., retention and completion). In their longitudinal study of students attending and matriculating through college in 2008–2009, the National Center for Educational Statistics (NCES, 2011) revealed that 44% completed their bachelor's degree in 48 months, 23% in 49 to 60 months, and 9% within 61 to 72 months. A disheartening 24% did not finish within 72 months (6 years). Interestingly, approximately 30% of all students started their degrees at 2-year schools, and those who started at 2-years schools tended to take longer to complete their degrees (e.g., 50.6% of students who started at a 4-year school completed their degree in 4 years, compared to only 25.4% of students who started their degrees at 2-year schools).

Examining the data (NCES, 2011) more closely, as parental educational attainment increases, so did degree completion (e.g., 20% of students whose parents attained a high school diploma or less completed their degrees compared to 29.8% of students whose parents had a graduate or professional degree). Furthermore, the data suggested that Black and Hispanic students who completed their degrees tended to have parents with less education than did their White and Asian counterparts (e.g., approximately 38% of Black and Hispanic students reported parents having a bachelor's degree or higher, compared to approximately 60% of the White and Asian students). Black and Hispanic students also were more likely to have dependents than were White and Asian students.

The NCES (2011) data did not reveal the reason it takes some students longer than others to matriculate or why some students do not complete college at all. As mentioned previously, and based on the trends noted in the preceding, it seems likely that a number of intrapersonal and environmental factors affect long-term career and college outcomes for students. We will be discussing many of these factors throughout this book. One major concern, however, is that many students don't appear to be ready to do college level work.

In fact, college instructors estimate that up to 42% of college students are not adequately prepared by their high schools to meet college course expectations (Hart, 2005). Specifically, data pulled from the Chronicle of Higher Education's *Almanac of Higher Education 2011* (August 17, 2011) revealed that in 2011, only 25% of high school graduates who took the ACT were deemed ready for college coursework in all four content areas (English, math, reading, and science) based on their ACT scores. The percentage of students who achieved at or above the minimum college readiness scores was highest for Asian and White students (41% and 31%, respectively) than for American Indians (15%), Hispanics (11%), and Blacks (4%). Rates also were highest across all students in English and reading (66% and 52%, respectively) than they were in math (45%) and science (30%). While it is difficult to ascertain the exact reasons for these trends, one alarming concern noted by ACT in the executive summary of a policy publication on college readiness, *The Forgotten Middle* (2008), was that only 2 out of 10 eighth grade students are actually on track to take the courses in high school that will prepare them for college. In other words, many of our middle and high school students are not taking rigorous enough courses to prepare them for postsecondary education options. We revisit this problem throughout this book.

Career and Employment Outcomes

What happened to the students who did not graduate from high school or who did not attend college? According to an executive summary of the Georgetown University Center on Education and the Workforce report *Projections of Jobs and Education Requirements Through 2018* (Carnavale et al., 2010), individuals who do not attend some college and have only a high school diploma or less are mainly relegated to work in three main occupation clusters: food and personal services, sales and office support, and blue-collar employment. Additionally, just under 2% of women and 8% of men between the ages of 17 and 24 are actively involved in or are veterans of the military (Kelty, Kleykamp, & Segal, 2010).

Year 2010 employment data from the Bureau of Labor Statistics (BLS) (2011b) showed that a much larger number of individuals under the age of 25 are working than are attending college. Approximately 26% of all individuals age 16 through 19 are employed, with 25% of those employed full time. For individuals between the ages of 20 and 24, approximately 60% are employed, with 63% of those employed on a full-time basis. Differences exist when examining specific populations. For example, only 17.9% of individuals with disabilities between the ages of 16 and 19 were employed in 2009, as were 35.2% of individuals with disabilities ages 20 to 24 (BLS, 2010).

Some overlap exists, however, among people who are working and attending college. The BLS (2011a) reported that high school graduates who are not enrolled in college are more likely to be working than are those who are attending college (76.6% vs. 40%, respectively). Furthermore, part-time college students are more likely to be employed than are full-time college students (71.3% vs. 36.7%), and more students who attend 2-year colleges (52.4%) are working than are students at 4-year colleges (32%). Although data suggest that much of the younger workforce may be juggling college and work, a significant portion head straight into the workforce.

Of concern, a significant number of individuals age 18–24 are unemployed. According to the Bureau of Labor Statistics (BLS), employment population ratios are at an historic low for individuals between the ages of 16 and 24, from nearly 70% in 1990 to below 50% in July 2010. Of further interest, more males were unemployed than females, possibly due to shrinking employment in sectors that traditionally hire men (construction, manufacturing) versus those that hire women (education, health care). When race and ethnicity were considered, the results for employment of 16 to 24 year olds in the years 2007 to 2010 are even more concerning. Unemployment rates for Whites ranged from 9% to 16%, but they were 12% to 22% for Latinos, and 21% to 33% for African Americans.

With regard to career outcomes for college graduates, of those students completing their bachelor's degrees in 2008–2009, 84.1% were employed, but only 56.9% were employed in one, full-time job; all others were employed in one or more part-time jobs (NCES, 2011). This begets the questions: Were these individuals hired in their fields of study? What economic or systems issues are keeping more of them from securing full-time employment? Are students entering fields where there is projected growth and do they have employability skills when they graduate?

Another consideration, beyond employability issues, is that the disparity of earnings across ethnic groups, race, and gender persists.

According to an executive summary of Georgetown University's Center on Education and the Workforce, *The College Payoff: Education, Occupations, Lifetime Earnings* (Carnavale, Rose, & Cheah, 2011), women, African Americans, and Latinos continue to earn less than White and Asian males even when they have similar degrees (Tables 1.1 and 1.2).

FEDERAL INITIATIVES

As career and college readiness has gained importance in the U.S. educational discourse, federal policy has changed to give student development in these areas prominence. Although there are innumerable state, regional, and district level policies that should be considered when planning career interventions, we will focus on current federal initiatives that school counselors need to understand for effective practice. In

TABLE 1.1   Women's and Men's Lifetime Earnings by Educational Attainment

Degree Earned	Female Earnings ($)	Male Earnings ($)
Less than high school	797,000	1,103,000
High school diploma	1,117,000	1,500,000
Some college/no degree	1,327,000	1,802,000
Associate's	1,544,000	1,933,000
Bachelor's	1,939,000	2,593,000
Master's	2,321,000	3,145,000
Doctorate	2,857,000	3,466,000
Professional	3,010,000	4,033,000

Adapted from Carnavale et al. (2011).

TABLE 1.2   Lifetime Earnings by Educational Attainment Based on Race and Ethnicity

Degree Earned	Asian ($)	Latino ($)	African American ($)	White ($)
Less than high school	950,000	875,000	950,000	1,200,000
High school diploma	1,150,000	1,160,000	1,200,000	1,333,000
Some college/no degree	1,450,000	1,400,000	1,350,000	1,600,000
Associate's	1,650,000	1,550,000	1,500,000	1,750,000
Bachelor's	2,250,000	1,800,000	1,850,000	2,400,000
Master's	3,100,000	2,500,000	2,400,000	2,700,000
Doctorate	3,500,000	2,900,000	2,850,000	3,500,000
Professional	3,800,000	2,500,000	2,850,000	3,750,000

Adapted from Carnavale et al. (2011).

this section we highlight the No Child Left Behind Act, the Blueprint for the Reauthorization of the Elementary and Secondary Schools Act, the National Math and Science Initiative, and the Obama Administration's Winning the Future agenda.

No Child Left Behind Act

The No Child Left Behind Act of 2001 (NCLB; PL 107-110) was signed into federal law in January 2001 (U.S. Department of Education, 2004). The overarching goal of this legislation was to improve academic achievement and to focus attention on minority populations (e.g., second language learners, migratory children, children with disabilities) to help close the achievement gap. The most salient points of this law were: 1) increased accountability—specifically in relation to student proficiency in reading and math; 2) more choices for parents and students—students can change schools if the one they attend is deemed failing; and 3) putting reading first—all students should be competent readers by third grade. NCLB instituted a 12-year time frame for schools to close the achievement gap and have all students achieving at proficient levels (Martin & Robinson, 2011).

Blueprint for the Reauthorization of Elementary and Secondary Schools Act

According to the U.S. Department of Education's *A Blueprint for Reform: The Reauthorization of the Elementary and Secondary Education Act*, one major area of change in education policy under the Obama Administration is promoting greater high school graduation rates nationwide, along with expanding access to postsecondary options (e.g., junior college, 4-year universities, trade schools, and vocational training programs) through college and career readiness (U.S. Department of Education, 2010). Further, the current administration contends that one essential factor to attaining this formidable goal is focusing on rigor and achievement, particularly in low performing schools and in middle grades education (U.S. Department of Education, 2010). Other means to achieving this goal include: 1) raising standards for all students, 2) using assessments that align P–12 education with postsecondary standards, and 3) developing a more comprehensive, complete education where students are proficient in all academic areas (U.S. Department of Education, 2010). Other noted concerns in the Blueprint include more effective teaching, greater equity and access for all students, meeting the needs of diverse learners, promoting rigor, rewarding progress and success, and turning around low-performing schools.

Winning the Future Agenda

The Winning the Future agenda proposed by President Barack Obama is meant to strengthen the U.S. economy and global position by allocating funding and tailoring the U.S. budget to prioritize the areas of education, innovation, building, and reform. Included in the agenda are efforts to increase science, technology, engineering, and math (STEM) innovations, environmental sustainability, development and repair of infrastructure, and deficit reduction. In regard to education, the Winning the Future agenda is meant to propel educational success in the 21st century by increasing college access through maximizing Pell Grants (awarded to 9 million students), reforming K–12 school funding to reward successful schools with high standards and innovative practices, and preparing 100,000 STEM educators (an area of heightened growth in the educator sector).

The Winning the Future agenda relates to college and career readiness in terms of financial support (student Pell Grants) and the increased emphasis on STEM careers and STEM training (www.whitehouse.gov). In addition, emphasis is on a *complete education*, one in which students have demonstrated improved knowledge in all content areas (i.e., science, English, math, technology, environmental education, foreign language, and arts) and are afforded access to accelerated learning opportunities to promote postsecondary success. President Obama articulated methods to achieve these goals, including improving technology in teaching and learning, increasing data-driven accountability, offering more accelerated learning programs, and targeting high need districts (White House, 2011).

National Math and Science Initiative

According to the National Math and Science Initiative (NMSI, 2011) website, the United States is falling behind in STEM, a potential threat to our global standing. Based on data reported by NMSI, in a ranking of 31 countries by the Organization for Economic Cooperation and Development, students in the United States rank 15th in reading, 19th in math, and 14th in science. Furthermore, when it comes to science, only 29% of fourth graders in the United States are proficient; and even more astounding, only 18% of 12th graders are at or above the proficient level in science (NMSI, 2011). Major corporate sponsorship for this initiative comes from Exxon, the Bill and Melinda Gates Foundation, and the Michael and Susan Dell Foundation (NMSI, 2011). With so many potential career opportunities available, what makes STEM careers so critical? Who currently excels in STEM and how can we expand success to multiple populations?

STEM Careers, Women, and Minorities

Projections for STEM careers continue to show a great deal of growth and high demand for workers in these areas. This is no surprise given that the efforts in fields such as aeronautical engineering have made space travel and research possible, and have expanded our understanding of the complexities of our universe. Advancements in the frontier of sustainability engineering and the use of renewable energy sources (e.g., wind and solar power) hold promise for the health and integrity of our planet and the long-term needs of our growing population. Progress in the medical field in the treatment of illness and in understanding how the human body functions at a microscopic level have increased longevity and quality of life for millions of people.

The need for expertise in STEM areas is apparent, and long-term projections continue to show job growth in these areas and the need for a workforce to occupy these positions, in spite of economic recession and a loss of jobs in most sectors. For example, from July 2010 to July 2011, 299,000 jobs were added in the health care industry and 246,000 were added to professional and technical service industries (NCES, 2011). That same period saw drops or no growth in the areas of government employment, leisure, and hospitality. Moreover, recent data show that health and technical careers are the highest paid professions for individuals with bachelor's degrees (NCES, 2011). Yet, are students entering these professions?

According to the NCES (2011), 16.1% of 2008–2009 graduates majored in STEM areas. However, a demographic breakdown of this number proves concerning. In particular, 25.5% of college males and only 9.7% of college females majored in STEM areas. Differences in race were also present among STEM majors: 31.4% of Asian students enter STEM majors as do 16% of White students, 14.9% of Black students, and 12.3% of Hispanic students.

Many initiatives have been proposed to promote student interest and development in STEM areas, including the Race to the Top Fund where STEM is a priority in P–12 education, National Lab Day, and a plethora of grants for teachers, academics, counselors, and others to provide STEM opportunities for P–12 students. Moreover, corporate sponsorship of federal initiatives for STEM has grown to include prestigious donors such as the Bill and Melinda Gates Foundation, the Carnegie Corporation, Time Warner Cable, Discovery Communications, and The MacArthur Foundation (U.S. Department of Education, 2009). In this book, we look at ways to engage P–12 students in STEM education.

AN ECOSYSTEMS APPROACH TO P–12 CAREER DEVELOPMENT

Ecological and systems theories have become more prominent in recent years as both school-based professionals and researchers in many fields have begun to place greater appreciation on the role of family and community in the lives of P–12 students. In fact, school–family–community partnerships are frequently discussed in relation to addressing academic and behavioral concerns. We believe that two particular theories—Bronfenbrenner's *Bioecological Theory* and Young's *Career Concepts*—provide a strong foundation for conceptualizing when and how school counselors might involve a variety of stakeholders in their efforts to address college and career readiness.

Bronfenbrenner's Bioecological Theory

Urie Bronfenbrenner's Bioecological Theory (1977) is helpful in understanding the importance of students' environments on their preparation for college and career. In his theory, Bronfenbrenner indicates that a child's own biology is the most important environment that affects his or her development. Then, layers of environments (such as family, community, school, and society) interact to shape a child's development. These interactions become more complex as children develop increased cognitive abilities. As such, Bronfenbrenner supports the importance of choosing and implementing interventions that take into consideration a child's developmental level and involve individuals with whom the child interacts.

In describing the various environments that shape development, Bronfenbrenner defined multiple contexts including microsystems, mesosystems, exosystems, macrosystems, and chronosystems. *Microsystems* are the small environmental systems that exist in a child's immediate surroundings. Microsystems typically include a child's family, school, and neighborhood; the relationships that exist within microsystems are bidirectional, which is sometimes called reciprocity. For example, parental beliefs and actions are believed to affect those of the child, and vice versa. Bronfenbrenner indicates that the relationships that exist within microsystems are the most influential to a child. As such, we have chosen to devote a good amount of space in this text discussing the individuals who typically exist in a child's microsystems (e.g., parents, teachers, community members) and the roles they can and do play in shaping career development.

The remaining environmental layers described by Bronfenbrenner are important in relation to their indirect influence on children. *Mesosystems* are the interactions that occur between microsystems (e.g., communication between home and school); for example, the interaction between family members and school staff at a parent–teacher conference. *Exosystems* are the structures that interact with microsystems (e.g., resources available in a school, policies made by the school board). The *macrosystem* is comprised of the cultural beliefs and values held by a society. According to Bronfenbrenner, the macrosystem directly affects the exosystem, which directly affects the mesosystem. For example, societal values (macrosystem level) that reinforce the idea that only schools are responsible for preparing students for college and career may result in community microsystems feeling little obligation to offer career-related services or resources (exosystem level). Because the community has no resources or services, they would have no relevant structures in place and therefore no need to interact (mesosystem level) with the school. In a system like this, one might expect parents, teachers, and students to receive inadequate information or insufficient training in college and career readiness. School counselors may need to examine macrosystem level factors to understand how and why interactions at lower environmental levels occur as they do.

It could be argued that a mesosystem in which frequent communication and collaboration occurs among microsystems might be more desirable in relation to fostering career development than would a mesosystem in which there are few interactions (Milsom, 2007). With greater communication comes greater understanding of expectations. College and career transition can create challenges as new microsystems come into play. Diamond, Spiegel-McGill, and Hanrahan (1988) discussed Bronfenbrenner's theory specifically in relation to transitions for students receiving special education services. They indicated that "the transition process can be seen as one of expanding the child's immediate environments, which in turn results in a greater number of environments which must relate to each other within the mesosystem" (pp. 245–246). Students transitioning to college and career in essence eventually lose a familiar microsystem (e.g., public school system) and replace it with an unfamiliar one (e.g., college or employment setting). Milsom (2007) suggested that the more familiar a student becomes with an anticipated future microsystem, the more opportunities there are to develop the requisite knowledge, skills, and attitudes for success in that micro-system. It is likely that some skills and knowledge areas required for a successful transition to college or career may be unfamiliar to many students. In line with Bronfenbrenner's theory is the idea that students who have high school experiences that are similar to their anticipated college and career experiences should be fairly successful in their transition. An awareness of skill, knowledge, behavioral, and attitudinal components related to success in college and careers is critical for high school personnel in assessing student strengths and weaknesses in those areas. By planning ahead and allowing adequate time for students to develop new skills, school counselors and other stakeholders can help to "minimize the stress involved for children and their families and . . . maximize the chances of the child being successful in the new environment" (Kemp & Carter, 2000, p. 393). The development and maintenance of a collaborative mesosystem (to include communication with future microsystems) is in alignment with current thinking about school, family, and community partnerships. Figure 1.1 depicts the concentric circle of ecosystems.

FIGURE 1.1 Ecosystems

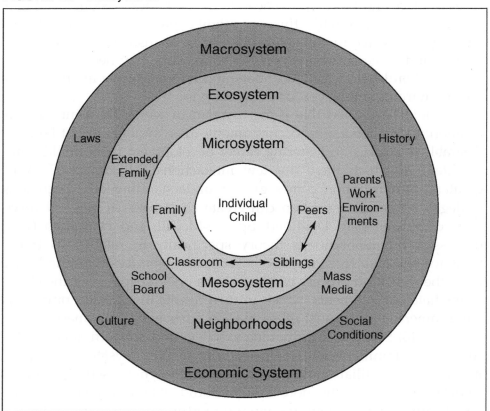

Young's Career Concepts

Young (1983) contended that while many career theories address developmental aspects of the individual, most fail to address the environmental contexts in which individuals live that influence career development. Using Bronfenbrenner's (1977) model, Young (1983) provided a framework for career counseling at each ecosystemic level that could help school counselors conceptualize a systems approach to intervention. For example, Young noted that at the microsystem level both family and school have a large impact on the individual. He highlighted five familial characteristics that interchangeably influence career development: 1) birth order, 2) early parent–child interaction, 3) the child's identification with parents, 4) the amount of contact the child has with parents, and 5) the child's perception of parent(s) influence. We will address each of these influences in subsequent chapters.

As previously mentioned, the school is also a microsystem that can hold great influence on career development, and Young (1983) explained that the school can exert two types of influence, *explicit* and *implicit*. The explicit influences at the school microsystems level include things that are directly done with the purpose of promoting career development, such as individual and small group counseling, career curriculum, and grade-level or school-wide career activities. The implicit influences at the school microsystems level include things that are indirect influences on student career development, such as integration of career in the educational curriculum, socialization experiences, access to extracurricular opportunities, and diversified course offerings that allow students to explore interests.

Other microsystems influences include peers and social support networks and, for many adolescents, workplace microsystems for seasonal and part-time employees. The positive developmental influences of part-time work on adolescents, according to Young (1983), include increased autonomy, realistic understanding of adult workplace expectations, and overall career knowledge. Negative career developmental influences of the workplace included decreased involvement with school, family, and peers (such as reduced participation in extracurricular activities like clubs and sports) and a focus in the workplace on task skills rather than higher order thinking skills. For example, for an adolescent working in a fast food restaurant, he or she may be trained to make fries and hamburgers but never understand the concepts of marketing (i.e., branding), the economic development of the fast food industry, and the reasons for safety requirements and industry regulation.

Young (1983) believed that multiple mesosystems influence students' career development: school to work transition, school to school transition, family and school interactions. These interactions can become very complex and may involve more than one mesosystem. For instance, in the transition from middle to high school, the family may be interacting both with the middle school teachers, counselors, and administrators and the same staff at the high school level. However, beyond these major mesosystem interactions, many small-scale mesosystem interactions impact career development, including career shadowing, field observations, field trips, and cross-age programming (e.g., older students providing mentoring or tutoring for younger students).

Exosystemic influences on career development appear to be prominent for many students. According to Young (1983), the exosystem influences include the social support network and employment of parents (especially maternal employment), family socioeconomic status, public policy, and social media. All of these systems can have positive and negative outcomes for the developing individual. For example, state policy requiring career education may be very helpful for students. However, financial constraints and budget cuts may make some career development programs vulnerable with the potential for being cut. Likewise, social media that promotes minorities and females in nontraditional roles (such as STEM careers) may promote career development (Choate & Curry, 2009). However, media that sexually objectifies women or stereotypes minorities may undermine career development. Another exosystem influence, according to Young (1983), is the impact child labor laws have on the amount and type of work exposure adolescents can have. Similarly, federal initiatives, such as those explored earlier in this chapter, are exosystem interventions based on cultural expectations of the importance of STEM careers and postsecondary success for students.

At the macrosystem level, work is an important aspect of each individual's unique identity in modern U.S. culture. According to Young (1983), the cultural aspects of education include social consensus on the purpose of education, work ethic, and job entitlement (in particular, a culturally decreasing work ethic coupled with an increasing expectation that jobs will be available), technological changes, and cultural changes in the belief that a person has one career for a lifetime. In 1983, Young projected that many of the cultural career expectations of the current generation of students growing up in a depression-free environment may be drastically altered with the advent of large-scale economic decline both in the United States and in global economies. Because we are currently living in an era of economic concern (10% unemployment), it is presumable that cultural shifts in career expectations regarding work ethic, job entitlement, and lifespan career transitions and change will occur.

HISTORICAL DEVELOPMENTS IN CAREER THEORY RELATED TO CHILDREN AND ADOLESCENTS

Numerous career development theories exist that guide the work of counseling professionals. However, we believe that school counselors can benefit most from a few specific theories for which practical application for children and adolescents is well documented. We have chosen in this text to highlight a number of individuals whose work provides a strong foundation for school-based career development interventions, and in the chapters that follow we will introduce their theories and articulate how their work relates to students in grades P–12. In this introductory chapter, however, we focus on four key career theorists: Frank Parsons, John Holland, Donald Super, and Linda Gottfredson.

Frank Parsons

It is commonly accepted that Frank Parsons, author of *Choosing a Vocation* (1909), is one of the most influential individuals in relation to career development. In his model, Parsons emphasized the importance of self-awareness, job awareness, and making logical job choices. He believed that people could be matched with jobs if they knew enough about themselves and about work requirements to determine if they would be a good fit for a particular job. His ideas served as the precursor to the trait and factor career theories that are so prominently used today in career counseling.

John Holland

Trait and factor theories emphasize finding a match between an individual's personality and a work environment. John Holland (1973) developed the *Theory of Vocational Choice*, one of the most practical and commonly applied career theories. He, like Parsons, believed that job success and job satisfaction result from a strong person–environment match. Of prominence in Holland's theory is what he describes as an individual's personality. He believes that a career personality emerges as a result of the interaction of inherent characteristics and the activities to which someone is exposed. The resulting personality is reflected in a person's interests, abilities, and values.

Holland developed a classification system, based on personality types, through which he is able to categorize people and occupations. In his theory Holland postulates that in order to be successful and satisfied,

FIGURE 1.2   Holland Codes

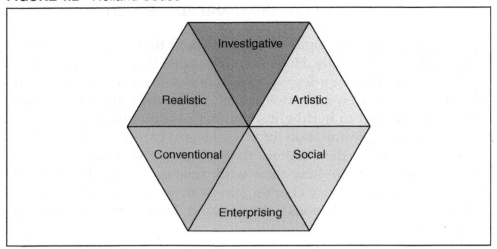

an individual needs to choose an occupation that is congruent with his or her personality. The six personality types are Realistic, Investigative, Artistic, Social, Enterprising, and Conventional. Holland displays these codes on a hexagon (Figure 1.2).

Realistic personalities interact with the environment by focusing on concrete and physical activities through which they can manipulate objects, tools, and machines. In contrast, *investigative* personalities interact with the environment by using their intellect. They prefer working with concepts and words. *Artistic* personalities interact with the environment through creativity, preferring to engage in activities like art, drama, and others that allow them to express themselves creatively. People who fall into the *social* personality type prefer to interact with the environment through use of their interpersonal skills. They like engaging in activities that allow them to interact with others. *Enterprising* personalities interact with the environment typically through activities that allow them to exhibit dominance and power over others and to experience recognition for their efforts. Finally, people who fall into a *conventional* personality type prefer activities for which they will receive approval from others. Their behaviors are expected and routine.

Through the identification of a Holland Code, the classification system captures the nuances that exist within people and occupations. The three-letter Holland Code (e.g., SAI) reflects the most prominent personality types exhibited by an individual or occupation. The first letter represents the most influential characteristics in describing an individual's career decisions; the second letter is the next most influential, and the third letter the third most influential. Holland indicates that the clarity of a person's identity is reflected in how well his or her personality code is differentiated and if the code is consistent. A personality code is well differentiated when the scores for the main personality types (i.e., Holland Code) are much higher than those for the remaining personality types. A consistent personality code is one that includes personality types that are adjacent on the hexagon (see Figure 1.2).

Assessment plays an important role in Holland's theory and the concrete application of his theory is likely what makes it so appealing to counselors. Holland's Self-Directed Search (SDS; see Chapter 4), an instrument that can be used to identify an individual's Holland Code, contains items that examine interests, abilities, and values. The self-report instrument has been validated for use with adolescents and adults. In Holland's Occupations Finder, occupations are categorized by Holland Code. Once individuals identify their Holland Code through the SDS, they can search the Occupations Finder to identify congruent occupations.

Donald Super

While trait and factor theories focus on identifying characteristics related to person–job fit, developmental theories focus on understanding career development across the lifespan. Donald Super's (1953) *Life-Span Life-Space Theory* is the most well-known developmental career theory. He explains that career choice results from a developmental process rather than from a one-time decision. He also believes that people may be happy engaging in more than one occupation. In his theory Super outlined five developmental stages (growth, exploration, establishment, maintenance, and disengagement) and explains that different career tasks occur throughout those stages. He also emphasized the importance of various life roles (e.g., child, worker, parent) on career development. Of most importance in Super's theory is self-concept, which consists of a person's view of themselves and their life situation. Super believes that career choices result from a person attempting to find work that fits his or her self-concept. As life roles change over time, naturally a person's self-concept will change, and therefore occupational preferences and choices may change over time.

Linda Gottfredson

In her *Theory of Circumscription and Compromise*, Linda Gottfredson (1981) explains how career aspirations develop over time, beginning in childhood. Similar to its role in Super's theory, self-concept plays a prominent role in Gottfredson's theory; she indicates that people usually choose occupations that are consistent with their self-concept. According to Gottfredson, self-concept consists of a social self (e.g., perceptions of sex, ability, and social status), and psychological self (e.g., values).

Gottfredson described a four-stage model of career development. The first stage, *Orientation to Size and Power*, typically occurs from ages 3 to 5. During this stage children develop the ability to picture themselves in adult roles. Their self-concept begins to develop but is limited to dichotomous views of self. During the second stage, *Orientation to Sex Roles,* children between the ages of 6 and 8 start to expand their knowledge of careers beyond those they see in their immediate family. They tend to become aware of careers to which they have frequently been exposed. Furthermore, during this stage children start to categorize people based on salient characteristics including sex and race, and these characteristics become prominent in their own self-concept; in particular, sex-typing becomes highly influential. In this sense, sex refers to the biological differences between males and females, whereas gender refers to the social or cultural differences between male and female identity. Both gender and sex matter to children in stage two. Stage three, *Orientation to Social Valuation,* typically occurs in the middle school years (ages 9–13). During stage three, children and young adolescents become aware of the existence of different socioeconomic levels and indicators of social status. They also develop an awareness of the connection between high-status jobs and increased educational requirements. Furthermore, they become keenly aware of their own academic abilities and social status, integrating those into their self-concept. The final stage, *Orientation to Internal, Unique Self,* is when adolescents are able to articulate their idealistic and realistic career aspirations.

A few key terms are critical to understanding Gottfredson's theory. Circumscription is the process of narrowing down or ruling out occupations. According to Gottfredson, individuals circumscribe occupations based on perceptions of their social self and perceptions of the accessibility of those occupations. During stages two, three, and four, occupations are ruled out when individuals do not perceive them to be consistent with their own sex, social status, or interests and abilities. Gottfredson describes the resulting list of occupations as the Zone of Acceptable Alternatives. She believes that once an occupation is circumscribed, reversing the process can be challenging but not impossible. A second important term, compromise, is when individuals give up occupations that are compatible for ones that are most accessible. According to Gottfredson, as people compromise they first consider their perceptions of sex type, then prestige, and finally interests.

COLLEGE AND CAREER READINESS SKILLS

The career theories we just reviewed emphasize the importance of self-awareness (knowing one's interests, aptitudes, values, and beliefs) and career awareness (knowing specific occupational training and skill requirements) so that meaningful career goals can be identified and pursued. Knowledge of the skills needed for success in college and career in general also can be important in helping students identify strengths and weaknesses and in helping counselors and other educators identify areas for intervention. As we discussed previously, 21st-century students need multiple skills to be successful in college and career. We talked about academic, employability, and technical skills, as well as important intrapersonal factors and dispositions. We want to look now at a few specific skills that all students, no matter what their career path, need to possess. These skills fall into six major categories: career exploration, social interaction and communication, higher order thinking, financial literacy, self-regulation, and employability.

Career Exploration Skills

As students enter the 21st-century workforce, it is most likely that their career paths will change multiple times. Students need to have the skills to explore various occupations, including having an understanding of how their own aptitudes, interests, and values impact overall career satisfaction and career decision making. Moreover, they also need to know how to comprehensively engage in career exploration tasks to access accurate information regarding the training required to enter an occupation, what a typical day on the job is like, what additional skill sets are required, what specialty areas exist within an occupation, average earnings/wages, and the projected outlook for the growth or decline of an occupation. To be able to find this information, students need to be provided opportunities to engage in activities such as completing career assessments, reviewing technical websites, engaging in job shadowing, and understanding interview protocols. Career exploration skills are more salient than ever as students are often exposed, via social media, to unrealistic careers. For example, many students may like the idea of entering the area of forensics as a result of watching crime scene investigation shows, however, careers are often inaccurately portrayed in such Hollywood creations. Being able to accurately explore a career allows students to develop a realistic view of the day-to-day realities of a particular occupation.

Social Interaction and Communication Skills

In addition to knowing how to explore a career, students need to have the skills to be successful in the workplace. There are myriad social and communication skills necessary for career success. Being able to work collaboratively with others as well as functioning autonomously are vital. Other skills include active listening, communicating effectively in writing, verbally, and electronically, compromising, managing conflict, and interacting effectively with a group (Sharf, 2006). Students also need to have self-awareness including their own values, cultural heritage, beliefs, and biases and how these may affect their interactions with others; most importantly, they need to have a true appreciation for diversity and a propensity for cultural sensitivity and positive affirmation of others (American School Counselor Association [ASCA], 2012; Holcomb-McCoy & Chen-Hayes, 2011).

Cognitive Skills

As suggested by Brock (2010) in his discussion of college readiness, students in the most basic sense need to possess cognitive skills that will enable them to retain and apply knowledge. We suggest that a continuum of cognitive skills would be important to assess when working on college and career readiness. At the most basic level, students need to possess the cognitive skills that would enable them to do things like focus their attention, concentrate on a task, and comprehend instructions. At a middle level, critical thinking skills would be required—the ability to identify problems and generate solutions. Finally, for students pursuing 4-year college degrees, higher-order thinking skills would be necessary to enable them to successfully engage in tasks like solving complex algebraic equations, writing fluent essays, and understanding scientific research methodology.

Financial Literacy Skills

Financial literacy may be defined as "possessing the skills and knowledge on financial matters to confidently take effective action that best fulfills an individual's personal, family and global community goals" (National Financial Educators Council, n.d.). For P–12 students, financial literacy skills related to postsecondary life include things such as learning how to create and manage a budget based on projected income and lifestyle, saving for college, and managing debt (e.g., credit cards, student loans, etc.). Related to budgets, all P–12 students can benefit from learning about financial matters that would relate to living on their own and supporting or contributing to a family. Understanding things like basic budgeting, mortgage rates, compound interest, and car loans can help them determine what they can and cannot afford based on their income. Learning how to manage debt also is important for all students, but particularly for students who need to take out loans to pay for their postsecondary education.

An estimated 66% of first-time bachelor's degree recipients borrowed to finance their education, with their average debt equaling $24,700 (National Center for Education Statistics [NCES], 2011). Skills to navigate the financial aid system (e.g., filling out a Federal Application for Student Aid [FAFSA]; exploring loan, scholarship, and other funding sources) can help students and their families develop a more realistic understanding of whether or not postsecondary school is possible. Currently, at least 13 states have scholarship programs that cover tuition and other costs for eligible students (Brandon, 2006). For example, Georgia's HOPE scholarship requires a high school GPA of 3.0 in a college preparatory curriculum, and it covers 100% of tuition and provides $300 for books (Brandon, 2006). Students and their families must understand the requirements for these scholarships by middle school so that they can make appropriate high school curricular choices. Furthermore, in order to determine what might be realistic financially, students and families also need to understand what expenses (e.g., residence hall fees, institutional fees, transportation costs, extracurricular activities, materials needed such as notebooks and laptops) the scholarships do and do not cover.

Self-Regulatory Skills

Self-regulation (Bandura, 1977) refers to the ability to set goals and manage behavior toward those goals. This is done by approximating consequences, determining the action required to meet a desired outcome, and evaluating one's abilities to successfully complete a desired behavior and reach a goal (Bandura, 1977). Self-regulation includes directing oneself in day-to-day activities with discipline, and it is a particularly important skill for facing challenges and being able to problem solve, break goals down into manageable tasks, and focus on task completion. According to Bandura (1986), mastery of any given task requires the minimal skills necessary to perform the task *and* feelings of efficacy in one's ability to effectively apply skills. Thus, in order for students to achieve in school and move through postsecondary training and career with success, they must possess the skills to set and attain goals as well as the belief that they can be successful.

Employability

Employability skills include those skills necessary to secure a position in one's chosen field. Skills such as developing a resume that accurately and effectively highlights one's achievements, writing a cover letter that distinguishes one from other job competitors, and confidently participating in an interview are all critical. Finding open positions in one's field and discerning the necessary qualifications for consideration of employment are also included in this skill set.

THE ROLES OF STAKEHOLDERS IN CAREER DEVELOPMENT

Who is responsible for promoting student college and career readiness? The obvious answer is the school counselor (ASCA, 2012); however, in today's educational environment, all educators are expected to play a role in assisting students to become college and career ready. According to a policy brief in the *Alliance for Excellent Education* (Miller, 2009), teachers must be prepared to teach to higher standards than ever before. Rather than just focusing on content, they also need to assist students in connecting academic content to career. Moreover, parents, administrators, and community partners all play a role in developing students' career awareness and potential. In this book, we highlight the role of the school counselor in assisting students' career growth while also looking at the counselor's role in fostering stakeholders' ability to promote student career development. We also focus on adult stakeholders we believe to be most consistently and directly involved in the child's career education: counselors, teachers, administrators, parents/guardians, and community partners.

Counselors

Counselors are positioned to promote student development in three specific areas: academic, career, and personal/social domains (ASCA, 2012). Through a comprehensive school counseling program, counselors design, implement, manage, and evaluate services to students and other stakeholders (i.e., parents, teachers, administrators, and community partners). In order to help all stakeholders understand the importance and purpose of a comprehensive career development approach in schools, it is important that school counselors involve these individuals in the coordination and development of the program (Niles & Harris-Bowlesbey, 2009). Moreover, career programming should be consistently delivered, based on measurable goals and objectives, and student outcomes evaluated. In this way, students receive quality services rather than piecemeal or sporadic interventions (ASCA, 2012; Niles & Harris-Bowlesbey, 2009). School counselors provide students with career knowledge, assessment, and skills; further, they assist students in understanding the connections between academics and the world of work. School counselors are trained to deliver the following career interventions for students and stakeholders: classroom lessons, small-group interventions, individual counseling and advising sessions, school-wide and grade-level career activities, faculty inservice, parent workshops, and community partner programs. Examples of all of these services are provided throughout this book.

Teachers

Teachers also play a pivotal role in student career development. Because students often question the need for academic knowledge (e.g., "Why do we have to learn algebra? I'm never going to use it!"), it can be helpful for teachers to introduce ways that academic content in the classroom relates to future career opportunities. Though career education has historically been the school counselor's role, many states are requiring teacher candidates to also demonstrate competency in developing student career and college readiness (Curry, Belser, & Binns, 2013). For instance, the South Carolina Department of Education, in order to align teacher preparation programs with the Education and Economic Development Act, states in the *Policy Guidelines for South Carolina Educator Preparation Units* that, in regard to the career curriculum, "all educator preparation units must provide assessment evidence to indicate that all educator candidates . . . possess the knowledge, skills, and disposition to integrate into the P12 curriculum" (2006, p. 13). However, many teachers may view the integration of career in the classroom curriculum as extra work. Therefore, it is important that teachers are provided with strategies to integrate career that are manageable and that engage students. In order to effectively do this, teachers need professional development opportunities to learn about technology and curriculum materials that can be used to integrate career in classroom instruction (Curry et al., 2013).

In this book, we explore how school counselors can provide teachers with such professional development and career education collaboration.

In addition, to proactively integrating career content into their classrooms, teachers should become aware of how their actions may encourage or discourage students from certain career options. They often are the first to identify students who possess aptitudes in certain areas or who have strong interests for certain subjects. With an appreciation for how their encouragement and support can make a difference in students' career aspirations, teachers can be intentional about how they work with students.

Administrators

Administrators play a major role in the types of programming that students receive. Effective principals and education leaders understand current policies and best practices, and know that career and college readiness is a critical component of P–12 education. Principals ensure that quality and rigor are maintained in the school's curriculum and work closely with the school counselor to promote the integration of career in the school's education agenda. The principal works to foster collaboration among teachers, parents, students, and the school counselor to improve students' access to rigorous course offerings, college planning, academic advisement, and assessment resources. Further, the principal and school counselor coordinate efforts to ensure that a comprehensive school counseling program is in place and utilized by all stakeholders.

Parents and Guardians

Families play a pivotal role in a child's career development. Indeed multiple family factors are correlated with college and career decision making including parents' education level (NCES, 2011), parents' educational expectations and support for the child, family socioeconomic status, and financial resources (Hossler, Schmit, & Vesper, 1999; Patton & Creed, 2007). Specifically, the higher the educational attainment of the parents, the more likely the child will earn a college degree. In a study of students attending college in the United States, 29.8% of students had a parent with a graduate or professional degree, 26.4% had a parent with a bachelor's degree, 23.7% had a parent with some postsecondary education, and 20.1% had a parent with high school education or less (NCES, 2011). Because parents convey family values about education, it is important that they understand their role in promoting postsecondary options for their children.

Most notably, it is important that school counselors and educators not assume that parents without postsecondary degrees do not value such experiences for their child. However, those parents may need more help assisting their children in navigating admissions, financial aid, registration, and so on; therefore, the resources they receive to do this are vital. School counselors also can educate parents about the ways in which they can promote interest in school, foster the innate talents their children possess, and provide opportunities for their children to explore careers.

Community Partners

Community partners play an invaluable role in student career development. They assist school counselors by providing insight on local workforce needs, providing student career mentorship, serving as career guest speakers, providing resources for career and technical fairs, and facilitating job-shadowing opportunities. Throughout this book we offer a variety of examples of how school counselors can engage community partners in career development initiatives.

HOW TO USE THIS BOOK TO PREPARE FOR P–12 CAREER DEVELOPMENT PROGRAMMING IN SCHOOLS

Developmental Overview

In each chapter of this book we present a holistic overview of the typical chronological ages present within the grade level under discussion. Children's social, physical, emotional, cognitive, and educational development are interrelated with and greatly influence career development (Gibson & Mitchell, 2006). Therefore, we begin each chapter with a review of the holistic developmental milestones and developmental tasks for the age group presented in that chapter. However, as an important caution to readers, it is critical to note that development is personal and continues throughout the lifespan, so the information presented in these chapters is general in nature and may not apply to each individual child. Indeed, development varies among children as rates of growth and personal factors (i.e., temperament, intelligence, support systems) are unique to each individual.

Sequential Career Development

In this book we use a sequential format. By this we mean that with each grade level we cover, we show the reader how student competence builds on prior learning in the areas of career knowledge and skills. For example, when learning math, a student is introduced to addition before multiplication. The same is true for career; each subsequent grade level will build on prior knowledge and skills.

Pedagogy, Grade Level Expectancies, Standards, and Curriculum Development

School counselors need to be able to develop a career curriculum to meet the needs of the population at the school they serve (ASCA, 2012). However, many school counselors do not have a background in education. Therefore, in this book we use a three-part approach to helping novice school counselors write curriculum: Bloom's Taxonomy, Grade-Level Expectancies (GLEs), and the ASCA Student Standards (2004). In counseling and education, pedagogy that paces higher cognitive development is often based on Bloom's Taxonomy. The taxonomy (see Chapter 5) denotes how learning begins with lower-level thinking (memorization, recognition, recall) and moves to more complex, higher-order thinking (proposing and using an evaluative criteria). All learning can be paced to higher-order thinking.

Other features of this book include how to use state-sponsored GLEs to design a career counseling curriculum. Examples of GLEs will be provided in each chapter. Additionally, we use a standards-based approach to career curriculum development. The ASCA Student Standards (2004) are used to assist school counselors in identifying grade level competencies and conceptualizing career development services. This book covers practical applications based on these standards for career services delivered by school counselors to include whole-school programs, grade-level programs, classroom presentations, small-group counseling, individual career counseling, individual planning/academic advisement, parent workshops, and faculty inservice on career related topics.

Samples Activities and Case Studies

Throughout this book we share examples of career development interventions that are empirically supported, grounded in theory, and/or have been successfully implemented in schools. Our examples reflect counselors' direct work with students (e.g., classroom and individual interventions) as well as their work for the benefit of or in collaboration with parents, teachers, and community partners. Many of the examples are suggested for a specific grade level or type of student, but could easily be adjusted for use with other populations. Further, given the cultural differences and variations possible within any school population, it is important that readers consider culturally sensitive career development practice (see Chapter 3).

SUMMARY

In this chapter we defined college and career readiness and the role of the school counselor in student career development. We reviewed federal initiatives that are impacting career development for students, particularly in the STEM areas, and looked at current trends in postsecondary enrollment and matriculation as well as in employment. We then discussed the type of skills students will need to be successful for the world of work and the importance of all stakeholders in promoting students' understanding of career. In the following chapters we will examine career education and planning by education levels for students in P–12 schools.

···❯ Test Your Knowledge

1. Explain how federal initiatives have impacted career development.
2. Based on the data and statistics shared in the beginning of this chapter, identify one or two specific populations you believe should be targeted in an effort to help close the achievement gap.
3. Compare and contrast the skills needed for career readiness with those needed for college readiness.

2
•••••

Professional Preparation
in Career Development
•••••

In any profession, basic knowledge and skills are requisite for an individual to competently engage in the tasks and responsibilities of that profession. Fortunately for those individuals who wish to engage in career development counseling in schools, a number of documents are available to provide guidance on the development of training and professional development programs. In this chapter we review competencies that school counselors need in order to effectively provide career counseling and development services in schools.

Before we review specific competencies, we provide a brief overview of the three documents that serve as the basis for the subsequent information.

1. *The National Career Development Association Minimum Competencies for Multicultural Career Counseling and Development* (NCDA, 2009). This document provides an overview of nine general competency areas for career counseling. It also emphasizes that career counseling must be provided to all individuals, regardless of their background, and that services should take into consideration the unique needs of individual clients. This document is available in Appendix A and the Guidelines section of the NCDA website (www.ncda.org).

2. *Career Counselor Assessment and Evaluation Competencies* (Krieshok & Black, 2009). This document was developed because of the importance of assessment and evaluation in effective career counseling. Competencies in eight areas are reviewed. A current version of this

document is available in Appendix B and the Guidelines section of the NCDA website (www.ncda.org).

3. *Council for Accreditation of Counseling and Related Educational Programs Standards* (CACREP, 2009). CACREP provides guidance for content to be covered in counselor education programs. Seven core content standards for career development are outlined. Also outlined are standards in areas that have relevance to career counseling (e.g., assessment, diversity). This document is available on the CACREP website (www.cacrep.org).

CAREER COUNSELING COMPETENCIES

This section contains information about numerous content and skills areas important for school counselors who will be addressing career development in P–12 schools. When applicable, we articulate some considerations that exist beyond the general competency area that are related to working specifically with a P–12 student population.

Knowledge of Career Theories

Just as counselors learn about a variety of general counseling and human development theories early in their graduate programs to help them conceptualize the issues their clients bring to them, they also should learn career counseling theories (CACREP, 2009; NCDA, 2009). Career counseling theories help to explain career-related thoughts and behaviors, and provide a framework for understanding students and developing interventions. Many career theories provide a lifespan perspective, which provides insight into how childhood career growth impacts lifelong career development. Further, knowledge of a variety of career counseling theories as well as the research related to those theories enables counselors and educators to select and use those that best fit the populations they serve. Operating from a theoretical framework allows school counselors and educators to be intentional in their work and to anticipate potential outcomes. It also allows them to identify and choose assessments that measure factors consistent with those theories. Throughout this text we review a variety of career counseling theories and discuss the ways in which they are applicable to students at various grade levels. We also review interventions and assessments that complement many of these theories.

Career Counseling Skills

Skills specific to career counseling have been deemed important enough to be included in the documents we mentioned previously (CACREP, 2009; NCDA, 2009). But what exactly are career counseling skills and how do they differ from basic counseling skills? Most counselors learn basic skills in individual and group counseling and consultation, collaboration, and referral, as well as skills related to working with diverse populations (see the discussion later in this chapter). They also learn skills in assessment and research (which we also discuss in more detail later). Further, graduate students in school counseling programs develop skills in classroom instruction, curriculum development, and lesson planning (see Chapter 3). All of these basic skills are relevant to career counseling. Specifically, it isn't that different skills are needed for career counseling; it is that counselors must be sure to develop and use all of those skills in their career-related work.

For example, a school counselor who feels very comfortable engaging in individual career and educational advising sessions (or *individual planning* activities as the American School Counselor Association [ASCA, 2012] would describe them) might slowly work her way through her caseload seeing one student at a time. If she felt more confident in her psychoeducational group counseling or classroom skills, she could approach her meetings on a larger scale via small-group or classroom-based interventions, allowing her to be more efficient in reaching all of the students. Similarly, the same school counselor might feel very comfortable consulting and collaborating with teachers and parents, but doesn't typically reach out to individuals or organizations in the community. Given the importance of connecting with businesses and educational institutions that ensure career and educational opportunities and connections are made available to students, this counselor ideally should work on developing her consultation skills.

Legal and Ethical Issues

What legal and ethical issues do counselors engaging in career-related work encounter that are different from those they experience doing any kind of counseling? Honestly, probably none in particular; they can encounter the same legal and ethical issues as they would with any kind of counseling with P–12 students. Again, it is more a function of making sure that counselors think about legal and ethical issues when providing career-related services in P–12 schools.

For example, issues related to confidentiality and not imposing one's values are very important to consider in career counseling. In an effort to be encouraging, a school counselor might be tempted to persuade a student to pursue college or might express an opinion about a student's occupational aspirations—the counselor is frustrated that the student is limiting his options and tells the student to aim higher because the student has strong potential to do well in college. The counselor also might say something to the student's science teacher, asking that teacher to encourage the student to consider science careers. Although good intentioned, these kinds of interactions do not align with ethical expectations related to confidentiality, promoting autonomy, and not imposing one's own values and beliefs.

Another ethical problem arises when parents and students have conflicting views about what students should be doing in the future. For example, the first author worked with a family that owned a hair salon and the parents wanted their only child to work at the salon after high school. The parents enrolled the child in a cosmetology program (a technical program offered at the high school) and the student became very distressed because she wanted to attend college and become a teacher. The school principal insisted that the child be registered for cosmetology in spite of her career interests because it was required that parents approve the student's coursework and they would not approve college-bound courses.

On the surface career-related issues may not seem as volatile as some of the more serious mental health concerns that counselors in schools encounter, but they may find themselves unintentionally loosening up on their professional obligation to treat the interactions as formal counseling sessions. That is, school counselors might believe it acceptable to share information obtained during a session with a student with the parent or a teacher without the student's consent. They also might feel more comfortable "giving advice" to that student about future plans. It is somewhat amazing how quickly counselors can disregard the beliefs and values of students and their families in these ways without even realizing they are doing it—basic counseling skills seem to go out the window. Despite good intentions to be helpful, counselors must remember that ethical and legal obligations apply as much to their use of interventions and services to address career development as they do to any other counseling services.

Similar to the ethical codes of other counseling organizations such as the American Counseling Association (2005) or the American School Counselor Association (2010), which target, respectively, counselors in general and school counselors, the *NCDA Code of Ethics* (2007) serves as a guide for career practitioners, addressing ethical expectations related to career counseling. Technically, ethical codes can only be enforced for people who are members of the organizations that developed them, and it is unlikely that everyone who provides career-related services in P–12 schools will become members of all of these organizations. Nevertheless, to protect the interests of students, it would benefit anyone who desires to serve as a career-related professional in a school setting to review the NCDA ethical code and make a best effort to adhere to the guidelines provided within.

Ability to Effectively Serve Diverse Populations

Picking up on the issue we just highlighted, school counselors providing career development interventions must be able to appropriately and effectively provide services to all individuals, no matter who they are (ASCA, 2010; CACREP, 2009; NCDA, 2009). Not only does doing so involve using skills and applying theories effectively with diverse populations, it also includes things such as choosing appropriate assessments (more information is given later in this chapter), having relevant resources, knowing when to make referrals, and using data to evaluate and identify student needs broadly.

School counselors learn the importance of collecting and disaggregating school data in order to identify similarities and differences among various populations. For example, they might track postsecondary school attendance data to examine the percentage of students who pursue 4-year versus 2-year colleges, breaking down the data by factors such as gender, ethnic groups, disability status, or students who would be first-generation college students. Other data they might examine could include choice of career cluster or results of ability or aptitude tests. Once they know the status of various subpopulations in their schools, they can then develop targeted interventions to try to ensure that everyone has access to the same resources, information, and opportunities to learn about themselves and careers, as well as to develop skills and knowledge in various areas.

It is important that school counselors be aware of specialized resources or services for diverse populations and have them available. For example, many students with disabilities need accommodations in order to fully participate in activities, complete school work, or take assessments, and school counselors cannot be expected to know how to address every student's need. They should, however, be able to identify others in the school or community who could become involved in facilitating the career development of these students. By partnering with special education teachers and vocational rehabilitation counselors, school counselors have a better chance of ensuring that the unique needs of students with disabilities are being considered during career planning. Also, by familiarizing themselves with the array of options available for students seeking postsecondary education (e.g., application fee waivers, summer orientation programs, supportive services designed for specific populations, etc.), school counselors can disseminate information and encourage involvement in these types of opportunities designed to help eliminate barriers.

General Knowledge of Assessment

Assessment is a critical component of career development work with P–12 students done by school counselors and educators. Before they develop interventions, these professionals must identify the needs of students and assessment can help in that regard. Further, assessment is an activity that informs student self-knowledge; students learn about themselves in relation to others and the world of work. In general, a basic working knowledge of assessment is necessary for school counselors and educators who are involved in some capacity with making decisions about assessments or who are working directly with assessment data in schools (CACREP, 2009; Krieshok & Black, 2009; NCDA, 2009). In the following we describe in more detail some important aspects of assessment that inform the knowledge and skills needed by school counselors and educators involved in career development and assessment in schools.

Knowledge of Factors Important for Choosing Assessment Methods
School counselors and educators must possess knowledge that will enable them to make informed decisions about which types of assessments would be most appropriate for any given situation (Krieshok & Black, 2009). This knowledge would include an awareness of the different types of assessment approaches that are available (e.g., formal versus informal), as well as the purposes, pros, and cons of using different approaches.

Knowledge of Assessments Instruments
Once school counselors and educators determine the types of assessments they want to use, they must narrow down their options. To do so, counselors must familiarize themselves with the array of career-related

assessments available (Krieshok & Black, 2009; NCDA, 2009). Knowledge of the factors that can be assessed (e.g., interests, values) as well as the different formats that are available (e.g., online, nonverbal, etc.) allows for comparison of the assessment tools against both student needs and school resources. Further, an understanding of aspects such as norm groups and language, reading, or developmental level is critical for identifying assessments that match the needs of students. In order to choose assessments that will provide meaningful data, school counselors and educators need to be able to understand and evaluate the psychometric properties (e.g., reliability, validity) of assessments. Finally, professionals involved in career assessment in schools must be able to identify assessments that they or others in their school are qualified to administer and interpret. In Chapter 4 we provide information about a variety of assessment tools commonly used with P–12 students.

Knowledge to Administer and Oversee School-Based Assessment

In a P–12 school, someone is responsible for ensuring that anyone involved in the administration of an assessment is prepared to administer the assessment, is aware of any standardized instructions that must be followed, and adheres to any protocol or policies regarding administration and confidentiality of assessment materials. The same importance should be placed on administering career-related assessments (Krieshok & Black, 2009). School counselors or educators responsible for overseeing the administration of career-related assessments, whether they are completed individually or in large groups, must be familiar with administration requirements and procedures so that they can enforce and monitor others who might be involved. They also should be familiar with policies and procedures for accommodating different learning styles and adhere to legal protections for students with Individual Education Programs (IEPs) and 504 plans.

Skills to Interpret and Summarize Assessment Data

As we discuss in Chapter 4, assessment without interpretation is meaningless; it is important to ensure that people know how to make sense of the results. As such, interpretation is an important competency area for school counselors and educators involved in assessment (Krieshok & Black, 2009). Not only should these professionals possess skills to explain assessment results to various groups (e.g., students, parents, teachers, or other stakeholders), they also should be able to adjust their explanations to accommodate language or other differences. The majority of individuals who will receive score reports will be unfamiliar with the terminology commonly used in assessment. It is the responsibility of school counselors and educators to avoid professional jargon, to use developmentally appropriate language, and to provide specific examples when possible to help ensure understanding.

In addition to being able to generally interpret and explain assessment results to others, school counselors and educators must be able to compile and analyze statistical summary data (Krieshok & Black, 2009). This involves being able to explain the school summary data that are provided along with individual student score reports and/or calculating and generating summary data. These types of data could include frequency distributions, measures of central tendency (e.g., mean, median), and variability (e.g., standard deviation), and might include the use of graphs and charts.

Evaluating Assessment Data

A final competency area that is important for school counselors and educators involved in career-related assessment is evaluation (Krieshok & Black, 2009). Career-related evaluation practices might involve helping a student make sense of what a number of different assessment results mean in relation to his or her future plans or choices. They also might involve the professional appreciating that results from a single assessment most likely are not sufficient for decision making as thorough, comprehensive evaluation really requires multiple and different data points. On a broader level, evaluation also can refer to the ability to examine summary data and make decisions about programs and services.

Career, Educational, and Labor Market Information

In order to ensure that students and their families are provided with the most current and accurate information, school counselors and educators must themselves stay abreast of career, educational, and labor market information (CACREP, 2009; NCDA, 2009). They also must ensure that they can provide this information to students in developmentally and culturally relevant ways. In order to do this, school counselors should examine a variety of available online and print resources (e.g., O*Net, Occupational Outlook Handbook, Bureau of Labor Statistics) and make a determination about which would be most useful and relevant to their populations. Similar to helping students and others interpret assessment results, school counselors and educators have a responsibility to make sure that career, educational, and labor market information are understandable to everyone; they should proactively reach out to share and clarify information and resources in these areas, ensuring that everyone has access to this information in some format.

Educational and Career Planning and Placement

CACREP (2009) identifies the importance of education and career planning and placement in relation to career development. This refers to the implementation of activities and services to assist students in developing future educational and career goals and to engage in activities to achieve those goals. The ability to educate students about decision making and goal setting is requisite for being able to help students figure out how to achieve their goals.

To assist with the latter, school counselors and educators must possess knowledge to help students navigate these areas—what is or is not required to achieve success in these different areas. Knowledge relevant to helping students navigate a number of educational milestones is important and includes: 1) the skills students need to succeed in high school and college, and how they can develop them; 2) the requirements for entering the career/vocational training program at the local high school; 3) high school graduation requirements; and 4) different college entrance requirements. It also would require that school counselors and educators possess knowledge of how to enter certain occupations—apprenticeship programs, job-shadowing opportunities, qualities desired by local business and industry, military options, and other training programs.

Collaboration skills are important as school and community connections are critical to successful educational and career planning and placement. School counselors and educators must rely on a number of other individuals to assist students in gathering information and navigating various systems outside of the school setting. School personnel ideally would work closely with military recruiters, college admissions representatives, and human resources personnel from local businesses. All of these individuals can share information directly with students or can serve as sources of information for counselors and educators. By frequently touching base with contacts in various educational and occupational settings, school counselors and educators can ensure they keep current about requirements and expectations that students should be aware of as they transition from grade to grade and from school to postsecondary settings.

Career Program Planning, Implementation, and Evaluation

Skills in program planning, implementation, and evaluation are the final competency area we will highlight, but by no means are these skills the least important. Endorsed by both CACREP (2009) and NCDA (2009), these skills actually encompass many of the competencies we have already discussed. Someone in a school or school district will be responsible for overseeing the career development services that all P–12 students receive and someone needs to be in charge of the big picture. Often the only "experts" in the school system when it comes to career development, school counselors might be very involved in overseeing the career-related services in their school or district, or might serve in an advisory capacity.

In any event, the individual responsible for career development planning must be able to generate a plan, which involves two major components: 1) conceptualizing the career development needs of the students at a particular school from a specific theoretical framework, and 2) choosing assessments and interventions that are both developmentally and culturally appropriate but that also match the theoretical framework. Collaboration with and input from others will be important, so here again, collaboration and consultation skills are critical. Although implementation of the programs and services will most likely involve more than one person, someone must be responsible for and capable of overseeing the implementation and management of services offered.

Finally, evaluation of career education programming and services is important in terms of monitoring the quality and effectiveness of those services. School counselors who receive training in the ASCA National Model (2012) learn to examine process, perception, and outcome data when they evaluate their work. Regarding process data, counselors might track the number of students who participated in a specific intervention (e.g., the number of students who attended a college fair) or who completed an assessment. They would examine those data by disaggregating it to examine across different groups. Next, counselors would gather and examine perception data. Perhaps they implement an opinion survey for parents or students, gathering feedback about how useful those groups thought a certain intervention was or how important an assessment was in helping them make future decisions. Finally, counselors would examine outcome data—graduation rates, the percentage of students who applied to or are starting a 4-year college, and so forth. Again, they would disaggregate these data to examine differences across various groups.

FIGURE 2.1 Career Program Planning, Implementation, and Evaluation Cycle

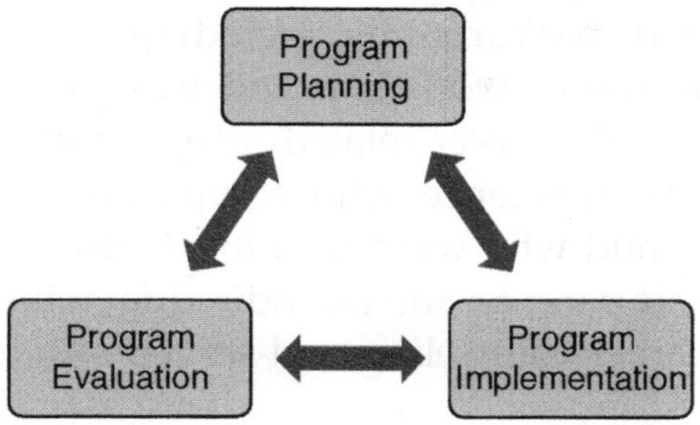

Program planning, implementation, and evaluation should be viewed as a cycle by school counselors and educators (Figure 2.1). Program planning, which includes the development of program goals, directs the implementation and evaluation of services provided. Feedback gathered during the implementation of services can influence decisions about which services to provide as well as how they were implemented, leading to potential changes to future program planning. Further, the experience of implementing the services might inform the direction or type of evaluation that occurs, either directly or indirectly, perhaps by opening up future program planning discussions. Similarly, overall evaluation data can inform decisions about program planning, such as determinations about which services will continue to be offered, new services that might be needed, or changes to the evaluation component. School counselors and educators involved in career development programming should be capable of participating fully in this type of process.

PREPARATION FOR PROVIDING CAREER DEVELOPMENT SERVICES IN SCHOOLS

By virtue of their educational backgrounds and training, school counselors generally possess the qualifications needed to develop, implement, and evaluate career-related counseling services in schools. In addition to numerous other courses, they usually have completed coursework in general counseling skills, career counseling, assessment, research/statistics, and multicultural counseling. Ongoing professional development in the area of career development is important to ensure that school counselors stay abreast of current trends in career counseling, assessment instruments, and programs available.

The backgrounds of other educators who are involved in career-related programs vary greatly. The authors have worked with individuals from a variety of backgrounds, including one administrator who completed a 3-day career workshop and was placed in charge of an entire school district's career-related programming; someone with a bachelor's degree in science who completed Career Development Facilitator training and who was hired to provide career interventions to students and their parents; and an individual who completed a graduate program in career counseling and served as a career counselor in a high school.

Each school or school district will differ in the types and qualifications of individuals available to provide career-related services to P–12 students. No matter their backgrounds, all of these individuals could seek opportunities to enhance their career-related knowledge and skills. They might do this through participating in professional development opportunities such as attending workshops or conferences, or they might pursue career-specific credentials. We discuss these two options in the following.

Professional Development and Credentials

Most professional positions within a school require the completion of renewal or continuing education credits in order to maintain eligibility to serve in that position. Fortunately for school employees, school districts typically offer, at no cost to their employees, various professional development seminars throughout the school year or during the summer. Sometimes school personnel can sign up for topics that interest them; other times everyone must attend a specific training session. Savvy school counselors and educators who are responsible for career-related programming will advocate for schools to provide professional development opportunities related to career and educational planning.

When opportunities are not available in-house, school counselors and educators can seek local or regional workshops. Colleges and universities occasionally offer workshops for counselors and educational consultants related to college admissions, choosing majors, or related topics. Local businesses, if asked, also may be willing to sponsor a speaker or offer seminars related to job trends or employability skills.

State and national conferences are always a good source of information. Although anyone can attend these conferences, registration rates tend to be higher for individuals who are not members of the organization sponsoring the conference. The ASCA and its individual state divisions hold annual conferences and one can always find career- and college-related sessions at those conferences. Labor market trends, career assessments, career interventions, and online resources are frequent session topics, usually presented by representatives of the organizations or companies that publish the resources, but often by school counselors who have tried-and-true programs to share. The National Career Development Association (NCDA) also holds an annual conference, as do many of its state divisions. Although the focus of these conferences goes beyond P–12 career development, school counselors and educators would likely find them beneficial for professional development purposes.

A number of other professional organizations also sponsor conferences that could offer relevant information for school-based career professionals. The Association for Career and Technical Education is an organization focused on preparing people for careers, as its name suggests. The National Association for College Admissions Counseling is an organization that focuses on sharing information to help professionals help students successfully transition to postsecondary education. The Council for Exceptional Children's Division on Career Development and Transition provides information and resources to individuals who want to help persons with disabilities successfully transition to college and careers. Most of these professional organizations offer numerous professional development opportunities beyond conferences, including informational resources on their websites, webinars, and special opportunities for members.

Finally, counselors may choose to acquire specific career counseling credentials. As we mentioned earlier in this chapter, a school counseling credential (i.e., certificate or license, depending on the state) typically reflects that someone has completed a graduate program that prepared them to engage in career-related work in schools. Although school counseling degree programs prepare graduates to address more than just career issues, one can feel confident in the career preparation of someone who is certified or licensed as a school/guidance counselor.

Nevertheless, someone might choose or be encouraged to acquire a credential such as the Global Career Development Facilitator (GCDF). A person who holds the GCDF credential has completed a minimum of 120 hours of training in career development and is qualified to provide career-related services in a variety of settings. Depending on the level of education a person has completed (ranging from high school diploma to graduate degree), he or she can receive the GCDF credential after accumulating varying levels of experience in career work. Offered by the Center for Credentialing in Education (CCE), individuals can seek training through online or in-person formats through a number of approved providers. Although the GCDF is typically a voluntary credential, some schools require it for individuals without a school counseling credential who are hired to provide career-counseling services in schools.

SUMMARY

In this chapter we discussed numerous issues related to the professional preparation of counselors who wish to provide career counseling in P–12 schools. We referenced a number of documents, reviewed a variety of competencies, and discussed options for professional development. Ethically, counselors are responsible for developing the skills and knowledge to effectively provide career development and counseling services to diverse populations.

···❯ Test Your Knowledge

1. Provide one example of how easily a counselor could impose his or her values during a career counseling session.
2. Name at least three professional organizations where a school counselor could seek professional development related to career counseling.

3
•••••

Cultural Considerations in P–12 Career Development
•••••

Although all students need career education and counseling, it is important to understand that some populations are more vulnerable to inequities in access to careers and college. Although the demographic landscape of the U.S. educational system has changed dramatically and will continue to do so, the disparities in educational and career success among various groups of students persist (i.e., the achievement gap). Moreover, many national trends have affected the job market for 21st-century students. For example, college affordability has decreased as the costs of tuition, room, and board have increased nearly 37% in 10 years (The Opportunity Agenda, 2010), greatly impacting college access for students from low socioeconomic backgrounds.

Because of increasing inflation rates, fluctuations in the stock market, concerns about financial sovereignty, and poor savings practices, many older Americans are not retiring at age 65. According to Ellis (2011), a reported 75% of Americans plan to work through retirement and 25% plan to work at least until the age of 80. This number appears to be confirmed by the U.S. Census Bureau (2010), as 6.7 million Americans over the age of 65 were still working as full-time employees. That number is expected to nearly double (to 11.1 million) by 2018 as the baby boomer generation reaches retirement age. With fewer positions opening up, getting quality, high-paying jobs becomes more competitive than it was for previous generations, so the future workforce must be well prepared with employability skills and requisite education experiences.

These economic concerns, coupled with slow job growth, make postsecondary preparation a pressing priority for school counselors. In this chapter we explore issues of inequity and barriers to postsecondary success for specific populations as well as cultural competencies for school counselors in promoting career and college readiness. We caution readers that the specific populations highlighted here are by no means exhaustive of the cultural considerations school counselors need to keep in mind. School counselors should consider the role of culture, ethnicity, race, gender, religion, socioeconomic status, sexual orientation, and other factors when designing career and college readiness interventions. We cannot comprehensively address all of these concerns; therefore, this chapter is meant to serve as an introduction to cultural considerations in career counseling and education. We highlight the career and college readiness of Latinos, African Americans, girls and women, Native Americans, and students with identified disabilities.

SPECIAL POPULATION CONSIDERATIONS

Hispanics/Latinos

The terms Hispanic and Latino are often used interchangeably; however, understanding the differences between them is important, as many educators and counselors are unsure of which term should be applied when referring to the populations they serve. In general, the term *Hispanic* refers to a region of origin, specifically regions that tend to be geographical locations that were historically occupied by, or conquered by, Spaniards; it is a term related to heritage, nationality, or lineage. Hispanic is the term most often used in federal documents (such as education and census data). However, some people prefer the term *Latino*, which refers to cultures of Latin America and is a term that may also encompass language and traditions. In this chapter we use both terms based on the language chosen by authors and researchers in the literature reviewed.

An important consideration for school counselors is that the Hispanic populations served in U.S. schools are vastly diverse. For example, a student from Venezuela who is first-generation in the United States and an English language learner is very different culturally from a student who is second generation, originating from Puerto Rico, and has always spoken English. The potential differences among students are highly complex, so although we present data that are aggregate for

Hispanic students as a whole in order to examine these populations in depth, we encourage school counselors to assess their school community and make an effort to examine and understand the cultural differences of the specific populations they serve. To provide a general overview of trends, however, we present aggregate data on Hispanic student achievement and college and career readiness.

Projections of growth in the Hispanic population are predominant. Specifically, the percent of the U.S. population that is Hispanic is currently estimated at 15.5%, but is expected to increase dramatically to over 24% by 2050 (U.S. Census Bureau, 2006). (See Figure 3.1 for projected Hispanic population growth rate.) Beyond the percentage of Hispanics in the U.S. population, the National Center for Education Statistics (NCES) reported that the number of Hispanic students in P–12 schools doubled between 1989 and 2009, and now comprises 22% of the total student public school population (U.S. Department of Education, 2010).

In spite of population growth, Hispanics continue to make markedly less reported income than their White counterparts. In particular, based on 2006 U.S. census data gathered through the *American Community Survey*, the median annual income for all males was $42,210, while Hispanic males earned a reported median annual income of $27,490. Similarly, the reported median annual income for all women was $32,649, yet it was only $24,738 for Hispanic women (U.S. Census, 2006).

Regarding Hispanic students, the Center for Education Policy (CEP, 2010) concluded that limited English proficiency, low parental education levels, and low family income compound educational difficulties faced by Hispanic students and become barriers to education and career

FIGURE 3.1 Projected Growth in U.S. Hispanic Population

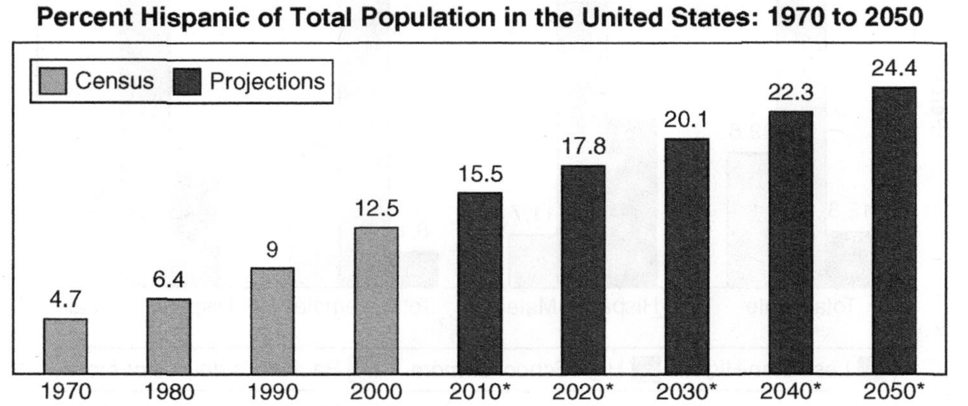

Percent Hispanic of Total Population in the United States: 1970 to 2050

Adapted from U.S. Census Bureau Data (2006).

success. Furthermore, poverty appears to be a pervasive and ubiquitous problem, with more than 25% of Latino students living below the poverty level and another 33% living near poverty level (U.S. Department of Education, 2008). These types of barriers often are reflected in the communities where Hispanic students live and the P–12 schools they attend. In particular, according to Hoover (2007), Latino students often attend P–12 education in districts with "limited rigorous course offerings, dilapidated school facilities, poverty . . ." (p. 33). Durodoye and Bodley (1997) noted that Latinos are underrepresented in talented and gifted programs but are overrepresented in special education.

Because of these and other challenges, a large number of Hispanic students are not successful in their pursuit of postsecondary education (Figure 3.2). As noted by Dolan (2008), many Hispanic students are first-generation students, and the majority that do go to college attend community colleges. Concerns enumerated by Dolan include Hispanic students having lower college persistence rates, lack of preparation for college course work necessitating remedial courses, and not enough adequate information about financial planning, developing effective study skills, or admission requirements and career preparation. Similarly, in

FIGURE 3.2 Educational Attainment of Hispanic Males and Females Compared to Total Population Males and Females

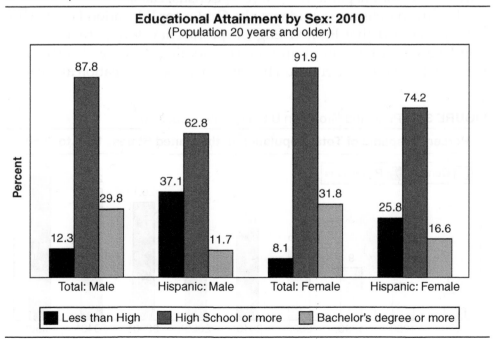

Educational Attainment by Sex: 2010
(Population 20 years and older)

Adapted from U.S. Census Bureau, 2006–2010 American Community Survey.

a qualitative inquiry of Latino students' college experiences, Taningco (2008) found that Latinos had general difficulty adjusting to college life and the academic demands of higher education.

Hoover (2007) contended that many Latino students feel underprepared and are uninformed about postsecondary options and college entrance requirements. However, in a qualitative, grounded theory study, Boden (2011) found different results. In the study, Latino, first-generation university students (seven) were interviewed about their perceptions of their own college preparedness. These participants reported feeling prepared and cited their understanding of academic skills, educational planning, guidance from a mentor, and their personal characteristics as precursors of successful college entrance and matriculation.

Boden's (2011) sample size was extremely small, and while participants felt prepared for college, research demonstrates that many Hispanic students are not. Indeed, it is possible that participants in Boden's sample felt prepared because they had no way to gauge their preparation against other students. As highlighted by Hoover (2007), however, admission to college and acquisition of scholarships largely depend on academic performance measured through GPAs and SAT or ACT scores. Based on these academic requirements, Hispanic students applying to college are at a pervasive disadvantage. For example, in regard to the ACT, national statistics indicate an average ACT score of 22.4 for Whites and an average ACT score of 18.7 for Hispanics (Strauss, 2011). This difference in ACT scores may reduce Hispanic students' ability to compete for early admission and academic scholarships. Moreover, according to Strauss, ACT scores for Hispanics did not improve between 2007 and 2011.

In a 2006 report, the Tomas Rivera Policy Institute provided an educational report on the current trends of access and achievement for education and career pathways for Latinos, particularly in advanced technology (Tomatzky, Macias, Jenkins, & Solis, 2006). The research was funded through a grant by the National Science Foundation (NSF) to investigate research and policy analysis pertaining to Latino students and technical careers. Given the importance and projected growth of science, technology, engineering, and mathematics (STEM) careers (see Chapter 1), it is critical that barriers to these careers are examined and that suggestions are made to improve educational practices that support Latino students' postsecondary success.

In the report, Tomatzky and colleagues (2006) noted that while Latinos constitute over 10% of the U.S. population, among scientists and engineers only approximately 3% are Latino. Of further concern, Latina women only accounted for 1% of scientists and engineers. When examining the types of occupations in which Hispanics work, the U.S. Census Bureau found that Hispanic males were largely employed in construction and maintenance, production and transportation, and service areas. Hispanic women were largely in sales and office occupations, followed by professional occupations, and then production and transportation (Figure 3.3).

In spite of overwhelming data suggesting that Latino students need equitable services to improve educational and career outcomes, and that they are performing significantly below Asian and White students on

FIGURE 3.3   Occupations Held by Hispanic Males and Females

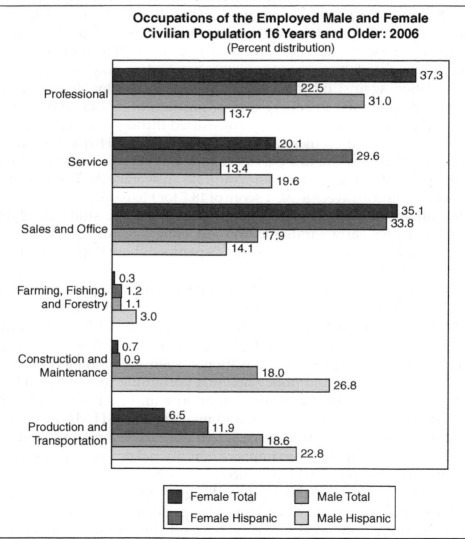

academic outcome measures such as ACT scores, there is some evidence that the achievement gap for Latinos has been narrowing since 2002 (Center on Education Policy [CEP], 2010). The CEP reported that since 2002, Latino students have had promising gains in both reading and math proficiency based on No Child Left Behind (NCLB) state measures of student outcomes. This growth may indicate that educational practices are creating an optimistic and promising future for Latino students, although more work needs to be done (CEP, 2010).

In considering the career and college readiness of Hispanic students, Durodoye and Bodley (1997) suggested that counselors must understand that there are traditional cultural values (e.g., strong allegiance to family) that may influence Hispanic students' career decisions. Moreover, according to Taningco (2008), family members may not always support a Latino student's decision to go to college for a variety of reasons, including misconceptions or biases about the following: gender stereotypes related to career goals, negative views of education loans, use of family money prioritized for things other than education, and pressure on students to earn an income immediately after high school. Other factors, such as oppression, discrimination, and prejudice, may have psychological consequences for Latino students, including lower self-esteem and self-efficacy, which in turn affect career aspirations and decision making (Durodoye & Bodley, 1997).

Given the unique cultural characteristics of Hispanic populations and the ongoing disparity in educational achievement, career development, and college readiness, school counselors need to continue to examine ways to promote Hispanic student access to postsecondary options. Ivers, Milsom, and Newsome (2012) conceptualized the academic and career needs of Latino students using Gottfredson's Theory of Circumscription and Compromise (2005) and offered suggestions for intervention to help improve school success. Target areas included identifying and involving Latino role models and mentors, providing information to students and parents about educational and career pathways, and increased communication between schools and families (including the use of translators).

Girls and Women

In a report issued by the Council of Graduate Schools, Bell (2011) noted that women are achieving at greater levels than ever before, surpassing men in graduate and doctoral degree admissions and matriculation. Lewin (2006) observed that women are graduating from college with more honors (i.e., cum laude, magna, summa), have higher GPAs, are more likely to make the Dean's list, and spend more time studying and preparing for class than their male counterparts. Yet, in spite of these gains in achievement, women continue to earn less than their male counterparts and men are still overrepresented in math and science careers. In particular, less than 25% of jobs in STEM areas are filled by women (U.S. Department of Commerce, 2011) in spite of the fact that women in those careers earn 30% more than women in non-STEM professions (Koebler, 2012).

Girls and STEM. In a survey conducted by the Society of Women Engineers, 75% of girls reported having no interest in science careers and generally expressed interest in entertainment, fashion, and helping fields (Roach, 2006). The disconnect between girls and STEM may be largely based on social factors including cultural stereotyping of careers and social media's promotion of limited, sexualized female identities (Choate & Curry, 2009). Diekman et al. (2010) found that when women opt out of science careers, it is often due to perceived incongruence of STEM majors and the communal goals that are socially promoted for women (i.e., working with and helping others). In their study, Diekman et al. (2010) reported that participants who held high communal goal beliefs were more likely to perceive STEM careers as self-promoting, individualistic, and success-driven careers. Further, the lack of an integrated belief system (e.g., "I can have a STEM career and reach my communal goals") was absent for many of the participating women. However, effective career exploration might have helped women reach that type of integration (e.g., "By becoming a civil engineer I can work with a team to help make my community safe by providing a sound infrastructure for us") and may actually improve girls' attitudes toward STEM pursuits (Diekman, Clark, Johnston, Brown, & Steinberg, 2011).

Stout, Dasgupta, Hunsinger, and McManus (2011) proposed that the stereotypes of STEM professions as male-dominated creates barriers for women entering those professions. Stout and colleagues proposed a stereotype inoculation model to promote STEM self-concepts for girls. One method they suggested was to expose girls to successful female role models in STEM professions. Additionally, the authors proposed that researchers and educators focus more on improving girls' STEM self-concepts than on improving test scores in the STEM domains.

Beyond a lack of role models and social reinforcement of communal goals for girls, research indicates that many girls are discouraged from pursuing STEM careers. For example, in the Bayer Facts survey

(Bayer Corporation, 2012), 4 out of 10 females and underrepresented minorities with careers as chemists or chemical engineers reported that they had been discouraged from pursing STEM studies or STEM careers at some point in their lives. Similarly, in a qualitative study, researchers found that school counselors had advised African American females to take lower rigor math and science classes in spite of their academic potential and interest in math and science (West-Olatunji et al., 2010). Further, women who enter college as STEM majors have lower persistence rates compared to males in STEM majors and are more likely to change majors (Griffith, 2010).

Researchers and scholars have proposed that there are many reasons why women may not pursue STEM careers, including self-efficacy, social encouragement to enter humanitarian and helping professions (psychology, teaching, counseling), and gender and cultural stereotypes that promote limited career aspirations (Diekman et al., 2010). Indeed, for women to fully commit to STEM careers and matriculate through postsecondary training, it is critical that they possess high career decision-making self-efficacy (CDMSE). In particular, CDMSE is affected by career maturity; that is, the degree to which an individual understands her career choice, including realistically understanding a typical day's work associated with an occupation, expected remuneration, training and education requirements, and personal values, aptitudes, and interests related to a given career choice. Interventions targeting those areas could help increase girls' self-efficacy beliefs.

Sexualization of Girls. One perpetual concern faced by girls and women is the sociocultural trend that establishes a limited, sexualized identity that compromises girls' self-concepts and career aspirations (Choate & Curry, 2009; Curry & Choate, 2010; Murnen, Smolak, Mills, & Good, 2003). This trend is pervasive across cultures and socioeconomic groups (Levin & Kilbourne, 2008). The pressure for girls to be thin and sexy is well documented, and may be evidenced in popular culture (i.e., magazines, television, movies, music). Even when women are portrayed in media as powerful and with exceptional careers, they are often tantamount to sexual objects or are shown to be obsessed with fashion (such as the ever-present stiletto heels) or talking frequently about men and sex (e.g., *CSI Miami, Pretty Little Liars, Keeping Up With the Kardashians*). These images of women impact the development of girls as the cultural expectation to be thin and sexualized may become a predominant concern for girls rather than academics or career and college readiness.

In a seminal work on self-objectification theory, Fredrickson and Roberts (1997) described what happens to girls when they are consistently exposed to sexualized images of women:

> Objectification theory posits that girls and women are typically acculturated to internalize an observer's perspective as a primary view of their physical selves. This perspective on self can lead to habitual body monitoring, which, in turn, can increase women's opportunities for shame and anxiety, reduce opportunities for peak motivational states, and diminish awareness of internal bodily states. (p. 173)

This self-objectification leads to reduced mental health, lower concentration and focus on major life tasks, obsession with appearance and body image, and reduced academic and career concentration (Curry & Choate, 2010). For strategies to combat the sexualization of girlhood, school counselors need to introduce a comprehensive approach (Choate & Curry, 2009). School counselors can help girls challenge stereotypes, develop media literacy skills, bolster self-esteem, and examine careers interests.

African Americans

African American students continue to achieve in secondary and postsecondary education at a much lower level than their White counterparts. For example, only 43% of African American males graduate high school on time compared to 71% of White males (Levin, Belfield Muennig, & Rouse, 2007). Additionally, by age 20, approximately 25% of African American males and 24% of African American females are high school dropouts, compared to 16% of White males and 9% of White females (Levin et al., 2007).

Although many factors contribute to between-groups differences in achievement, West-Olatunji, Baker, and Brooks (2006) noted that African Americans are expelled, suspended, or receive corporal punishment at rates far higher than other groups of students. The same authors observed that African American students, males in particular, are overrepresented in special education, are inordinately identified as emotionally disturbed, are underrepresented in gifted education, and are exposed to microaggressions, cultural hostility, and discriminatory practices in education settings that may be psychologically damaging. Goodman and West-Olatunji (2010) contended that many of the behaviors displayed by African Americans are misinterpreted as emotional disturbance or academic deficiency and may actually be the result of traumatic stress from living in systems of oppression and a hegemonic academy.

All of these factors can instill in African Americans a sense of inadequacy or low self-efficacy that, in turn, may lead to the exclusion or lack of equitable access to postsecondary success. For African Americans, not graduating from high school is compounded by subsequent social problems: significantly lower wages and yearly income throughout the lifespan, poorer health and higher mortality, higher stress, and greater risk of incarceration than their White counterparts (Levin et al., 2007; Muennig & Fahs, 2001; Raphael, 2004). According to Carty (2010), these differences are pervasive throughout the lives of African Americans, particularly African American males. Of the experiences of African American men, Carty stated,

> They have more trouble purchasing a home, have lower home values, have lower median incomes, own fewer businesses, and are less likely to be invested in a 401(k) retirement plan. Moreover, Black males are less likely than the general population to be employed, live above the poverty line, have a home computer with Internet access, or own a car. Health outcomes take into account death rates and life expectancy, lifetime health issues, and neonatal care and related issues. The prevalence of diabetes, homicide, and HIV are all higher among Blacks than Whites, and contribute to a difference in the age-adjusted death rate. Social justice factors highlight the heavy toll of incarceration and other interactions with the legal and criminal justice system. Black males are more likely to be murdered and/or to be the victim of a violent crime. (pp. 4–5)

Furthermore, African American students who graduate from high school and pursue a college degree often encounter challenges. For example, the national average for African American students on the ACT is 17, while it is 22.4 for White students (Strauss, 2011), which may limit access to early admissions and scholarships. Moreover, most African American students in college attend predominantly White institutions where they may experience a lack of support that results in less persistence and lower matriculation than White students (Lucas, 1993). In contrast, in a study of African American graduation rates in U.S. colleges and universities, Wright (2010) found that colleges and universities with Black cultural centers, high first-year retention rates, and a high number of student organizations were more likely to retain and graduate African American students.

Walker, Pearson, and Murrell (2010) studied differences between African American and White community college students and found that African American students relied more heavily on accessibility to faculty as a way of garnering academic support, learning about careers, and receiving career guidance, and mentorship. Additionally, Walker and colleagues (2010) found that counseling was critical for African American students who chose to talk to their community college counselors and advisors about topics like course registration, careers and majors, vocational interests, abilities, and aspirations. Walker et al. surmised that career exploration is a major task for African American community college students. Similarly, Lucas (1993) found that African American college students reported worrying about grades, time management, study habits, lack of information about careers, lack of knowledge regarding personal interests and skills related to careers, and poor career decision-making skills.

In addition to challenges related to postsecondary school attendance, African Americans tend to be underrepresented in careers high in prestige that command higher salaries (e.g., STEM careers; see Chapter 1). Potential reasons for African Americans not entering STEM careers include lack of exposure to STEM careers and a lack of access to rigorous high school courses (e.g., calculus, trigonometry, AP chemistry) that prepare them for college coursework. Also, compared to their White, middle-class peers, African American students also may lack financial resources to support activities such as attending summer space camp, participating in engineering clubs, or buying home chemistry sets where they could explore or develop interest in STEM areas.

A few researchers have recently examined factors that affect the educational and career experiences of African American students. Through a qualitative study, West-Olatunji et al. (2010) found that school counselors may lack the cultural competence to identify and utilize African American students' strengths and, therefore, view African American students' behaviors and academic potential through a deficit framework that could result in advising them toward less rigorous academic paths and lower career aspirations. Even when African American students are identified as gifted, it appears that their career aspirations are often lower than their White counterparts (Parris, Owens, Johnson, Grbevski, & Holbert-Quince, 2010). These researchers suggested that in order to support African American students in gifted programs, counselors need to assist them by acknowledging feelings of isolation, and address fears of being viewed as "acting White" or being different, heightened peer pressure, concerns about career access, and the need for career assessment and planning.

In addition to these types of systemic factors that affect African American students' educational and career decisions, cultural values also play a role. Specifically, Walker and Tracey (2012) found that Holland codes for social and enterprising careers (e.g., teacher, clergy, business leader) are given high prestige in African American communities, whereas in other cultural groups (Caucasian, Asian), careers that are investigative in nature (such as STEM) have higher social prestige. Walker and Tracey noted that African Americans tend to value careers that have social impact and promote community well-being (e.g., social or enterprising jobs). Further, Walker and Tracy believed that Afrocentric values (such as cooperation) may influence the perception of status that an individual places on a specific career (e.g., teaching may be viewed as a career that promotes community growth and development).

Improving African American Students' Access to College and Careers. To improve high school graduation rates and postsecondary success for African American students, many things can be done. To begin, counselors might use teacher inservice training opportunities to assist teachers in developing culturally responsive teaching practices (West-Olatunji et al., 2010). Curry (2010) suggested that counselors need to become aware of their own biases, and should consider how their language may be discriminatory or reflect cultural insensitivity (i.e., microinsults, microinvalidations). Ponec (1997) recommended that school counselors provide comprehensive college information, including presenting information about historically Black colleges and universities (HBCUs), incorporating collaborative and community activities with peers such as small-group guidance programs for career and college readiness, and providing mentorship opportunities between African American students and successful adult African Americans in various careers. For example, a school counselor at an all African American school in New Orleans takes eighth grade students on a yearly tour of HBCUs (i.e., Spellman, Moorehouse, Fisk) and the Alabama civil rights museum. African American leaders from the New Orleans community are invited to attend the trip with the students and to facilitate group discussions on African American college opportunities.

Another strategy for promoting African American students' success is the use of Rite of Passage programs (West-Olatunji, Sure, Garrett, Conwill, & Rivera, 2008). These programs focus on the strengths of minority youth, emphasize involvement in the community through service and leadership, and promote success skills such as self-control, creativity, moral development, problem solving, and academic skills. Other researchers have noted that including parents in career education opportunities (examples of how to do this are given throughout this book) is crucial to increasing African American adolescents' career self-efficacy (Alliman-Brissett,

Turner, & Skovholt, 2004). However, more research needs to be conducted to find programs that are efficacious in serving the career and college readiness needs of African American youth.

Native Americans

It is difficult to make many assumptions about Native American students, as the term Native American refers to many populations. For example, in 2011 the U.S. Department of the Interior, Bureau of Indian Affairs registered 564 tribal entities that were eligible to receive Bureau services (74 FR 40218). Each of these tribal entities are vastly different and geographically diverse (tribal groups are from Alaska, Hawaii, and the continental United States). Each has its own unique customs, language, and traditions and, therefore, making definitive conclusions about all populations is impossible. However, there are some definite patterns.

Native Americans experience higher unemployment rates than any other populations in the United States, and 31% of Native Americans live in poverty (Jackson & Turner, 2004). However, Shutiva (2001), citing research from Pavel and colleagues (1998), indicated that Native Americans are dramatically increasing their presence and achievements in higher education settings. According to Pavel, there was a 67% increase in Native American enrollment in colleges and universities from 1976–1994, and the number of awarded bachelor's degrees for that population grew 86% during that same time period. However, Wells (1997) pointed out that the graduation rate of Native Americans is around 25%, with only about 45% matriculating in college after the first year. In spite of poor high school and college matriculation rates, Brown and Lavish (2006) found that Native American students valued and ranked career and work as valuable and important.

Nevertheless, researchers have found that community and home/family hold more salience for Native American youth than do work or career (Brown & Lavish, 2006), an indication of the collectivist nature of many Native American cultures. Indeed, Long (1999) underscored how important it is for school counselors to understand that assisting a Native American student in career or college preparation may need to involve multiple family members, as postsecondary decisions may be made by the whole family for the individual. Moreover, the connection between the family, school, community, and tribe may be important to consider, particularly for students living on reservations. Though Long's assertion may be true for many Native American youth, the degree to which family and tribe need to be consulted may be largely determined by individual characteristics such as the individual's degree of acculturation.

Acculturation with tribal culture, or dominant White culture, may impact how much a Native American individual commits to tribal beliefs, values, and customs (Reynolds, Sodano, Ecklund, & Guyker, 2012).

Based on their qualitative study of Native American youth living on four different reservations, Hoffmann, Jackson, and Smith (2005) noted that Native American students living on reservations experience common career-related concerns. Specifically, the students in their study experienced a limited range of possible careers, academic difficulties, financial concerns, and family and peer pressure to remain on the reservation. More complex themes also emerged from their study, including the misperception by many males that jobs were plentiful and easy to attain and a lack of awareness, knowledge, or expressed concern about academic and career barriers.

In addition to general career concerns, transitions from high school to college may be significantly difficult for Native Americans, especially if they have to leave behind existing support systems. Moreover, many Native American students may not be equipped with the skills necessary to consistently achieve at college. Assisting Native Americans in finding colleges and universities that provide physical space where Native American students can meet with other Native American students and discuss and reflect upon their challenges, procure resources, and provide support for each other is crucial (Mihesuah, 2004).

Turner et al. (2006) asserted that an Integrative Contextual Model (ICM) of career development may be particularly salient with Native American adolescents. The authors contended that such a model provides a proactive approach that promotes positive adaptability and resilience. Specifically, they believe that utilizing an ICM can help Native American adolescents develop six vocational outcomes: 1) academic achievement, 2) positive self-efficacy expectations, 3) positive self-attributional styles, 4) vocational identity, 5) understanding of one's personally valued career interests, and 6) pursuit of one's life goals (Turner et al., 2006). In order to promote these outcomes, the authors identified six skills that must be taught to Native American youth: 1) career exploration skills, 2) person–environment fit skills, 3) goal-setting skills, 4) social and work-readiness skills, 5) self-regulation skills, and 6) consistent utilization of social support (for more information, see Turner et al., 2006).

Students With Disabilities

Currently, approximately 5.8 million students between the ages of 6 and 21 are eligible for and receive special education services in the United States (Education Week, 2011). Students are eligible for special education services if they meet criteria established under the Individuals with

Disabilities Education Act (IDEA) and have an emotional, mental, or physical disability. The 14 categories of disabilities recognized in IDEA legislation include: autism, deafness, deaf–blindness, developmental delay, emotional disturbance, hearing impairment, mental retardation, orthopedic impairment, specific learning disability, speech and language impairment, traumatic brain injury, visual impairment, multiple disabilities, and other health impairments (The Center for Public Education, 2009).

Of those students enrolled in special education programs, an estimated 61% have a learning disability or language/speech impairment (Education Week, 2011); very few have severe physical or mental disabilities (The Center for Public Education, 2009). The majority of students receiving special education services (95%) attend regular, public schools (NCES, 2011). It is beyond the scope of this chapter to cover all of the educational needs and disparities among students with identified disabilities or the challenges faced by these populations in educational environments. Additionally, although it is out of our purview here to highlight the special education process (i.e., identification, screening, notification and consent, assessment, eligibility determination, Individualized Education Program [IEP] development), we encourage readers to review this process to more fully understand the role of the school counselor in special education (Rock & Leff, 2011). Rather, our focus here is on college and career readiness for students with identified disabilities.

Postsecondary School. Indicating that many students with learning disabilities end up working in low paying jobs with few benefits and little job security, Dickinson and Verbeek (2002) suggested that completing postsecondary education could lead to greater career success for individuals with learning disabilities. Completion of a postsecondary degree can open up a vast array of options for students with disabilities. In college, students with disabilities experience the same challenges that students without disabilities face: academic demands, financial stress, balancing social life and work, and experiencing the transition to college life. However, Madriaga et al. (2010) reported that students with disabilities also face unique struggles in college related to their specific disabilities, including difficulty taking notes, hearing the instructor, reading and comprehending course materials, and gaining access to buildings/classrooms.

Since the passage of the Americans with Disabilities Act (ADA) in 1990 (PL 101-336), colleges and universities have experienced increasing enrollments of students with disabilities (Henderson, 1999). The implementation of college support services that arose as a result of the ADA is believed to have contributed to those increasing numbers (Flexer, Simmons, Luft, &

Baer, 2005). Students with identified disabilities now can receive any number of accommodations (e.g., extended time or distraction-free tests, scribes) from postsecondary institutions in order to level the playing field.

Despite increased college enrollments, postsecondary education gaps still exist between students with and without disabilities. Wagner, Newman, Cameto, Garza, and Levine (2005) reported that within 2 years of graduating from high school, 10% of students with disabilities and 12% of students without disabilities have attended community colleges. Further, Wagner et al. reported that approximately 6% of students with disabilities versus 28% of students without disabilities attended 4-year colleges. The U.S. Department of Education (as cited in Janiga & Costenbader, 2002) reported that since 1989 only 53% of students with disabilities either had completed their postsecondary degree or still were enrolled, as compared to 64% of students without disabilities.

Through her research, Milsom (Milsom & Deitz, 2009; Milsom & Hartley, 2005) identified a number of factors relevant to college success for students with disabilities. In addition to the college and career readiness skills relevant for all students (see Chapter 1), other important factors include 1) knowledge of one's disability, or disability self-awareness, 2) knowledge of the ADA of 1990, specifically regarding personal rights and responsibilities as well as postsecondary school responsibilities for providing accommodations, and 3) self-advocacy skills. Limited research, however, has specifically examined these factors in relation to college success. In one somewhat dated study, Dalke (1993) found that disability self-awareness was a characteristic of students with disabilities who were successful in college.

Little research exists connecting specific skills to college success for students with disabilities; likewise, research regarding effective interventions targeting the areas listed previously is limited and dated. Further, most of the empirically supported interventions were conducted with students after they graduated high school. Three interventions with high school students worth examining (Aune, 1991; Milsom, Akos, & Thompson, 2004; Phillips, 1990) all included strong psychoeducational components focused on the students' developing self and college awareness.

Career Preparation. For students with disabilities who are not planning to pursue college, other postsecondary preparation is necessary and should be considered a priority. Such preparation may include filling out a job application, writing cover letters and resumes, developing interviewing skills, and participating in life skills training (i.e., creating a budget, balancing a checkbook, learning to navigate public transportation, securing housing)—skills relevant to any students who will be seeking employment right after high school. For many students with disabilities, this preparation also might involve connecting them to vocational rehabilitation personnel who can help them secure competitive employment.

Research shows that in many instances, career development interventions designed for students who have more severe disabilities tend to focus on occupational choice rather than on broad career development issues like career and self-exploration (Rumrill & Roessler, 1999). Wadsworth, Milsom, and Cocco (2004) emphasized the importance of helping students with disabilities make meaningful career choices, which means involving students with disabilities and their families in all of the career development interventions provided to other students. Although the way career development activities are approached might vary depending on the cognitive or physical abilities of students with disabilities, every student in school deserves the opportunity to choose his or her future: "Having a career does not mean being placed in a job but having the opportunity to make choices" (Hagner & Salomone, 1989, p. 154).

ADVOCACY AND EQUITY IN P–12 CAREER COUNSELING AND EDUCATION

Examining Personal Biases

To develop critical consciousness and become a stronger advocate for equity for all students in the areas of college and career readiness, it is important first to consider one's own biases (Bailey, Getch, & Chen-Hayes, 2007; Durodoye & Bodley, 1997; Gibson & Mitchell, 2008; Holcomb-McCoy & Chen-Hayes, 2011; Remley & Herlihy, 2007). Thinking about personal biases and limitations will allow counselors to be more open to understanding the perspectives of others and the barriers that exist within the school and community context for certain groups of students. It is recommended that all school counselors continue to receive supervision and feedback throughout their careers, and that supervision should include personal reflection, an examination of one's own values, and an honest self-appraisal of areas where cultural sensitivity and growth need to be cultivated.

Understanding Patterns in School Data

Consistent with the ASCA National Model (2012), school counselors should use data to identify inequities in educational achievement and

EXHIBIT 3.1
Critical Data Elements for School Counselors
to Review and Disaggregate

AP Course Enrollment
ACT Scores
Attendance Reports
Curriculum Track (e.g., General, College Prep, etc.)
Disciplinary Reports
Dropout Rates
End of Course Test Results
Extracurricular Activity Participation
Gifted Education Enrollment
Grade Level Retention and Promotion Data
Grades and Grade Point Averages
Parent Education/Income Data
SAT Scores
Special Education and 504 Eligibility
Standardized Test Scores

should work collaboratively with other professionals to improve student outcomes. Exhibit 3.1 includes a list of critical data elements that a school counselor could review in order to identify educational disparities between groups of students, and potential barriers to success for specific groups. This list is not meant to be exhaustive, as school counselors are encouraged to use databases that exist in their school districts and to actively collect data to drive curriculum changes and student success.

Best Practices for Supporting College Preparation Options for At-Risk Students

Multiple strategies have demonstrated evidence for supporting college preparation and academic achievement for low socioeconomic status, first generation, and minority students. Some school-based practices that school counselors can promote include 1) providing adequate and diverse course offerings, 2) providing teacher inservice (i.e., cultural competence training, postsecondary preparation and options), 3) creating professional learning communities for faculty to research and discuss cultural concerns, 4) developing engaging and intense course curricula, and 5) increasing rigorous course offerings such as college preparatory, accelerated, honors, advanced placement, and dual enrollment opportunities (Center for the Study of Education Policy, 2005). When school counselors lack information about certain diverse populations, they should seek additional training and supervision when possible, and also should locate local experts or *cultural brokers* (i.e., individuals who, based on their knowledge and understanding of the culture of the families, can help to bridge the gap between family and school) who can help them develop knowledge and skills to effectively assist these groups of students. Exhibit 3.2 illustrates how a school counselor took the initiative to gather and share information about an unfamiliar cultural group at her school.

EXHIBIT 3.2

Example of a School Counselor Using Data to Identify a Concern and Learning About an Unfamiliar Culture Before Intervening

Mrs. Chandler, a new ninth grade school counselor at Burlington High School, ran grade reports during the first 9 weeks of the school year in order to identify any students who were falling behind in their coursework and were at risk of failing. After compiling and reviewing data, she noticed that nearly all of the Kurdish girls in ninth grade had low to failing grades in the majority of their courses (the Kurdish are a group of Iranian people, predominantly Muslim, who fled Iraq during Saddam Hussein's regime due to persecution). Mrs. Chandler's school had a significant population of Kurdish students (15% of the school's overall population) because the city in which she lived had a nonprofit organization that had assisted the Kurdish in political exile from Iraq.

   Mrs. Chandler decided to consult with Mrs. Stewart, the ninth grade algebra teacher to find out why this group of students had such low grades. Mrs. Stewart stated that, in general, the Kurdish girls were not turning in any of their homework. At the ninth grade team meeting, it was confirmed that this was true in other courses as well; yet, the Kurdish boys *were* turning in their work. One teacher, Mr. Simms, noted that he had asked a particularly

(continued)

EXHIBIT 3.2 *(Continued)*

bright female Kurdish student why her homework was not completed, and stated that she replied, "I can't do it at home. I have to cook and watch my little sisters." Before assuming that this one student's statement indicated anything about this pattern among all of the girls, Mrs. Chandler requested that Mr. Huertas, the 10th grade counselor, investigate to see if there was a similar pattern in 10th grade report data, and there was.

Deciding that having a better understanding of Kurdish culture might be important, Mrs. Chandler and Mr. Huertas contacted the local Islamic center and were granted a meeting with the imam, a local Muslim leader. At their meeting, the imam explained that for some Islamic groups, their beliefs exclude girls from education. He explained that because they are legally obligated in the United States to register and enroll their daughters in school, they do so, but culturally, these families believe that girls need to learn domestic responsibilities to fulfill their future duties as wives. So, when the daughters come home each day from school, their domestic responsibilities and domestic training are the priority. He also noted that Kurdish families most likely are not preparing their daughters for postsecondary options, but they are generally okay with their daughters receiving college and career information as part of their U.S. education. The imam also cautioned the school counselors that Kurdish Muslims are distinctly different from other groups of Muslims.

After meeting with the imam, Mrs. Chandler and Mr. Huertas delivered a faculty inservice where they discussed what they had learned and had teachers brainstorm different ways to assess work in class rather than using homework as the primary assessment of student knowledge. The teachers decided to use more collaborative in-class projects and in-class writing assignments in lieu of homework grades for the Kurdish girls. Additionally, the administration scheduled a time to have the imam come speak with the faculty and answer questions about how to better serve Muslim students and families in the Burlington High School community. Although the counselors in this case example found some answers for how to work with the Kurdish population in their school, they were left with many questions such as: What type of career education is culturally appropriate for the Kurdish girls in our school? How do you work with the family of a Kurdish female who wants to go to college?

Designing Targeted Intervention Programs

Durodoye and Bodley (1997) encouraged systemic, small group, and one-on-one interventions to promote career and college readiness for high risk groups. They encouraged counselors to disseminate accurate and consistent information about STEM careers, assist students with resume-building and interviewing skills, provide students with mentors and role models, and promote culturally sensitive teaching practices. Although it may not be possible to always find adult role models or mentors within the community, seeking role models who inspire students in their respective interests is important. For example, in a qualitative study of Latinos in STEM careers conducted by the Tomas Rivera Policy Institute (2008), one successful Latino engineer noted that his interest in science began when he learned about the first Latino astronaut who had traveled in space, Dr. Franklin Chang-Diaz.

SUMMARY

In this chapter we highlighted some of the cultural considerations that school counselors must make when implementing career counseling and education services. Although the information covered here is not exhaustive, it is meant to illustrate some of the systems issues affecting the academic and career development of specific populations. School counselors are encouraged to 1) become aware of their biases, 2) use data to identify group differences, 3) develop professional learning communities about culturally relevant practice within their school communities, and 4) consult with experts on culturally sensitive practices with specific groups.

⋯❯ Test Your Knowledge

1. Consider a population in your community that you don't know much about. How could you learn more about the customs, traditions, and values of that group?
2. Explain the relationship between historical racial oppression and the current trends in career and college readiness for African American youth.
3. In what ways can school counselors increase STEM opportunities for students from low socioeconomic families?

4
• • • • •

P–12 Career Assessment and Evaluation
• • • • •

What is assessment? Why is it important? What does it look like for students across P–12 grades? In this chapter we review the purpose of assessment in P–12 career education and counseling, as well as important considerations for choosing and interpreting career assessments. We also review various types of assessments relevant to career counseling in P–12 schools. Before we jump in, however, we set the stage by clarifying these two important terms. The National Career Development Association (NCDA, 2009) defines *assessment* as:

> the systematic gathering of information for decision making about individuals, groups, programs, or processes. Assessment targets include abilities, achievements, personality variables, aptitudes, attitudes, preferences, interests, values, demographics, beliefs, and other characteristics. Assessment procedures include, but are not limited to, standardized and nonstandardized tests, questionnaires, inventories, checklists, observations, portfolios, performance assessments, rating scales, surveys, interviews, card sorts, and other measurement techniques. (p. 2)

Evaluation refers to "the collection and interpretation of information to make judgments about individuals, programs, or processes that lead to decisions and future actions" (NCDA, 2009, p. 2).

Assessment and evaluation are both important in the career-counseling process and complement each other. Assessment is critical to evaluation; without assessment data, counselors would have nothing to evaluate. Further, assessment without evaluation is meaningless. Why gather information only to do nothing with it? Schools sometimes get caught in the trap of collecting assessment data, but not always using that data to transform education and counseling practices. For example, a school counselor may collect data that show that only 25% of graduating seniors at the school are taking the ACT before their senior year. In order to increase that percent, the counselor may need to inform parents and students about the benefits of taking the ACT earlier in high school.

Another example occurred when the second author worked in a high school that encouraged all students to take the Armed Services Vocational Aptitude Battery (ASVAB) because it was offered at no cost. But, the school had no plans for formally using the results and the school counselors did not have time to meet with all students regarding their results. Although the ASVAB results were used by military personnel in making decisions about possible occupations for those students who were going to enter the military, the school counselors only occasionally were able to engage other students in discussions about their results and how they might inform career decision making. Was it worthwhile for students to take that test?

School counselors often are the only professionals in schools who have knowledge and skills related to career counseling and development. School districts usually employ administrative personnel with expertise in assessment and evaluation, but their focus often is on school accountability and accreditation with an emphasis on academics. School counselors should work closely with these individuals to make decisions about district-wide career assessments. In Chapter 2 we reviewed a number of important career counseling competencies. With regard to assessment, school counselors also should remember their roles as leaders and advocates and take a proactive approach to ensuring that school-wide career assessment is meaningful and purposeful.

Purpose of Career Assessment

For over 100 years, guidance workers and counselors have engaged in career assessment. Frank Parsons (1909) introduced the *trait-and-factor* approach that serves as a basis for much career counseling and assessment today. A number of career counseling theories were developed based on this approach, but today, the most widely used trait-and-factor approach is that of Holland (1973, 1997). We introduced Holland's theory briefly in Chapter 1 and review it further in some of the grade level chapters in this book. We also cover various assessment tools based on Holland's approach later in this chapter and some grade level chapters.

The main goal of a trait-and-factor approach is to help people identify possible future occupations—a very relevant goal for students in P–12 schools. In general, a trait-and-factor approach suggests that by knowing oneself and knowing occupational requirements and characteristics, a person can make an informed decision by looking for a match between self and occupation. Such assessment data are critical to gaining self- and occupational awareness. Parsons' three-part trait-and-factor approach involves: 1) gathering information about self, 2) gathering information about the world of work, and 3) applying a decision-making process to make an occupational choice. Common target areas for self-assessment include abilities, interests, values, and personality styles; we present assessments related to these target areas later in this chapter. Results from these kinds of assessments can be used to help students identify occupations that might or might not match their personal characteristics. For example, for a student whose aptitude test results show strengths in math and spatial skills, a counselor might suggest that student explore occupations in Holland's realistic personality type.

Other career counseling theories provide guidance to help school counselors identify specific P–12 student career development needs, design relevant interventions, and determine appropriate target areas for assessment. Based on *developmental career counseling theories* such as those of Super (1980) or Gottfredson (1981, 2002, 2005), school counselors might examine how ready an individual is to engage in various career counseling tasks or identify what factors are informing their career interests and behaviors. With this in mind, assessment results can be used as a foundation for determining what types of interventions might or might not be relevant for a particular student. For example, a counselor might want to start by implementing activities to help a student whose assessment results indicate limited knowledge of occupations develop a greater awareness of the world of work.

School counselors adhering to *learning-based career counseling theories* like those of Krumboltz, Mitchell, and Jones (1976), Lent, Brown, and Hackett (1994), or Peterson, Sampson, and Reardon (1991) would assess things such as beliefs, self-efficacy, and perceived barriers in order to better understand how career-related decisions are being made. Results from assessments targeting these areas can be used to identify where to focus career intervention. For example, if a student's assessment results showed that she was not very motivated to explore careers or that she did not believe she could succeed in college, then a counselor could develop interventions to explore those issues or challenge faulty thinking. Throughout this book we discuss many of these theories as they relate to P–12 students, and assessments relevant to these theories are presented later in this chapter.

Career assessment is particularly important during the initial process of choosing an occupation or career path as it can help counselors identify occupations that students might like or might excel. Assessment data also can help explain why some students struggle with career decision making or why they limit their options. Because the focus of this book is to help school counselors and educators working with students who will be making initial career decisions, we are limiting our discussion of assessment to issues most relevant to working with P–12 students. In the section that follows, we discuss factors that school counselors and educators should consider when choosing career assessments.

CHOOSING CAREER ASSESSMENTS

In Chapter 2 we discussed important competencies related to career assessment and evaluation, and we want to emphasize the importance of having qualified individuals making decisions about career assessments and administering and/or interpreting career assessments. Resources such as *A Counselor's Guide to Career Assessment Instruments* (Whitfield, Feller, & Wood, 2009) that contain information about and critiques of a variety of career assessments can be useful to school counselors. In this section we review factors that should be considered when choosing career assessments.

Reliability and Validity

Reliability and validity arguably are two of the most important things to consider when choosing an assessment. *Reliability* refers to how stable or consistent the assessment is in measuring a construct, and *validity* indicates whether or not an assessment measures what it intends to. Information about the psychometric properties of an assessment, including reliability and validity data, generally can be found in the technical manual or user's guide that accompanies the assessment. We do not have space in this book to review psychometric properties of assessments in detail, and most readers should have or will cover these topics in an assessment or appraisal course. Needless to say, school counselors and educators want to feel confident that the time and money they put into purchasing, administering, and interpreting assessments are well spent. They need to be able to guarantee that the results will be meaningful, and using assessments that have proven reliability and validity is a good way to start.

Norms

Norms help school counselors determine whether or not a particular assessment is appropriate for their students, and information about norm groups should be included in an assessment's technical manual and/or the assessment summary reports the school receives. The norm group reflects the individuals who participated in the early development, or piloting, of an instrument. It also includes the group(s) for whom an assessment has been determined valid through additional research.

For example, an assessment instrument might initially be piloted with a group of 10th-grade students from a suburban area outside a large city in the Northeastern part of the United States. The initial norm group would reflect the characteristics of this specific population: Let's say it included males and females, students with a variety of disabilities, and a majority of White students from middle to upper-middle class families. This group of students is not representative of most places in the United States, so an assessment that is normed on this group would have limited applicability to most schools. Over time, the individual who developed the instrument piloted it with other populations, including students from rural and urban areas, from low socioeconomic status families, from diverse racial and ethnic groups, and from different grade levels. Information was now available regarding the applicability of the assessment to a much broader group of students. Assuming no major differences or concerns were noted regarding its use, the assessment would now be appropriate for a larger set of schools throughout the United States because the norm group is representative of their populations.

School counselors and educators should be mindful about choosing assessments in relation to norm groups, especially as school populations change over time. If a particular school's population shifts dramatically over the course of a few years, an assessment instrument that the school has successfully used for many years may become relevant only for a specific subgroup of the school. Further, as more and more research is conducted with assessments, information about their norms changes. It is important that someone in the school keeps abreast not only of changes in the school's population, but also of the information that is available about the assessments they are using.

Usefulness for Diverse Populations

Choosing an assessment that is appropriate for diverse populations means examining information about a number of factors, including norm groups (see the preceding), age level, reading level, and other factors. Some instruments have different versions designed for use with different age groups, and others have versions in multiple languages. With the growing population of second-language learners in the United States, especially students who speak Spanish, ideally school counselors and educators should be looking for career materials that are available in English as well as Spanish, or other languages as needed. Students will not always tell the counselor when they don't understand a question; they often just fill in answers to avoid drawing attention to themselves. If students have difficulty reading or understanding assessment materials, but do not express these concerns, then counselors have no way of knowing if their scores or results are valid.

Considering the content of an assessment is important in determining its relevance for various populations. To do this, school counselors and educators should try to make sure that they choose instruments for which cultural bias is not evident, and examining norms data is a useful way to do this. Further, school counselors might review any pictures that are used to ensure that they are representative across diverse groups as well as represent individuals in nontraditional careers. They also can review sample test items to determine if bias in language use or terminology is present. Additionally, reading reviews and critiques of assessments specifically in relation to their appropriateness with diverse populations is an important way to gather information about an instrument's appropriateness for various groups.

Finally, some instruments offer alternative formats to accommodate different learning styles. Although most career assessments require reading and answering questions by hand or on a computer, a few of the assessments we list in the following involve the use of pictures or videos, which is useful for students with low reading or comprehension levels. Other assessments permit accommodations for individuals with disabilities, such as responding verbally, having unlimited time, or using a scribe or test reader. School counselors and educators want to ensure that all students have an opportunity to be accurately assessed via whatever instruments are used, and consideration of these kinds of factors is important.

Cost, Time, and Ease of Administration

Assessment is a common practice in schools, especially as it relates to academics. Achievement tests, end of course or end of grade tests, aptitude tests, advanced placement tests, and so on, are used to help monitor student academic progress and allow schools to show how they are, or are not, meeting various standards. Given the amount of time that students spend in school taking tests, and the money and time it takes faculty to administer and interpret them, school counselors and educators absolutely need to take cost and time into consideration when choosing career assessments. Fortunately a variety of options exist for assessing factors related to career development.

Regarding cost, some of the comprehensive, online systems that we describe later in this chapter can be the most cost effective for schools, as they include multiple assessments as well as access to supplemental information. A school district can sometimes purchase access to those kinds of systems at a lower cost than if they purchased individual assessment instruments. Further, some states supplement the cost of online systems or have their own (e.g., South Carolina Occupational Information System [SCOIS]), which allows anyone in the state to access at no cost via a username and password.

Online career guidance systems may not be the most appropriate choice for every school. In some instances, schools might want to assess factors that are not covered in those online systems (e.g., career beliefs, self-efficacy), or they might prefer to use assessments that have certain psychometric properties. In those instances, school counselors and educators must weigh their options and prioritize based on availability of resources, student needs, and other factors. Availability of space and staff to administer assessments are important considerations as well.

Purpose

As we discussed earlier in this chapter, there are multiple potential purposes of career-related assessments. School counselors and educators must consider their main goal in working with students on career development. Do they want to focus on students' self-exploration or self-awareness? If so, then assessments that focus on interests, abilities, personalities, or values might be most useful. Do they want to identify student needs, readiness for change, or figure out where students are developmentally? If any of those areas reflect their goal, then assessments that focus on factors like beliefs, attitudes, or self-efficacy would be most appropriate. In the next section we review a variety of career assessment instruments that can be used with school-age students, broken down by target areas.

CAREER ASSESSMENTS

Assessments can be either formal or informal, and both types can be of benefit to school counselors and educators. In this section we present formal assessments by categories focusing on different target areas, and review some common informal assessments. The career assessments presented in this section are listed alphabetically within each category.

Formal Assessments

Formal assessments are considered *formal* because they have been developed through a scientifically rigorous process. These kinds of assessments are standardized; they rely on consistency by having specific instructions for administration, scoring, and interpretation. Formal assessments also have reliability and validity data, and usually a norm reference group for results comparison. These assessments range in price, type of administration, and scoring, but most are designed for large group administration.

Ability and Aptitude Assessments

Armed Services Vocational Aptitude Battery (ASVAB). Published by the Department of Defense (2004) and used to determine which types of military occupations individuals are eligible to pursue. The ASVAB is a multi-aptitude test with eight subscales (arithmetic, auto and shop information, general science, electronics information, math knowledge, mechanical comprehension, paragraph comprehension, and word knowledge). The battery takes approximately 3 hours to complete either in person or online. It is appropriate for students in grades 10 to 12.

Campbell Interest and Skill Survey (CISS). Published by Pearson Assessments (1992). The CISS is an assessment that measures self-reported interests and skills in seven broad scales (adventuring, analyzing, creating, helping, influencing, organizing, and producing) that are broken down further into 25 categories. The survey takes approximately 30 minutes to complete and can be administered individually or in a large group. It is appropriate for use with adolescents aged 15 and up.

Differential Aptitude Test (DAT). Published by Pearson Assessments (1990). The DAT is an assessment that measures eight types of aptitudes grouped in three broad categories: cognitive skills (verbal reasoning and numerical ability), perceptual skills (abstract reasoning, mechanical reasoning, and space relations), and language and clerical skills (spelling, language usage, and clerical speed/accuracy). The test takes approximately

3 hours and is usually administered in large groups. Different forms of the assessment target students in grades 7–9 or in grades 10 to 12.

Self-Directed Search (SDS). Published by Psychological Assessment Resources, Inc. (Holland, 1994). The SDS is an assessment that measures self-reported interests and skills and presents results in the form of Holland Codes. The self-assessment takes approximately 20 minutes to complete, can be self-scored, and can be administered individually or in a large group as well as online. Different forms of the assessment target students in middle and high school.

Attitudes, Beliefs, and Readiness Instruments

Career Beliefs Inventory (CBI). Published by Mind Garden, Inc. (Krumboltz, 1994). The CBI is an assessment consisting of 96 items that are rated on a Likert scale. A total of 25 subscales are reported under five main categories: Changes I Am Willing to Make, Efforts I Am Willing to Initiate, Factors That Influence My Decisions, My Current Career Situation, and What Seems Necessary for My Happiness. The CBI can be administered individually or in groups and it is appropriate for use with students in grades 8 to 12.

Career Decision Making Self-Efficacy Scale (CDSE). Published by Mind Garden, Inc. (Taylor & Betz, 1983). The CDSE includes items that address how confident someone is to make career decisions. Items reflect five broad areas including 1) self-appraisal, 2) gathering occupational information, 3) selecting goals, 4) making plans, and 5) solving problems. Long (50 item) and short (25 item) versions are available. The instrument can be administered individually or in groups and is appropriate for high school students.

Career Development Inventory (CDI). Published by Consulting Psychologists Press (Super, Thompson, Lindeman, Jordaan, & Myers, 1984). The CDI is an 80-item assessment that identifies four aspects of career maturity: career planning, career exploration, decision making, and world of work information. The assessment takes approximately 1 hour to complete and can be administered individually or in groups. It is appropriate for use with high school students.

Career Thoughts Inventory (CTI). Published by Psychological Assessment Resources, Inc. (Sampson, Peterson, Lenz, Reardon, & Saunders, 1996). The CTI is an assessment consisting of 48 items, with results presented in three scales: commitment anxiety, decision-making confusion, and external conflict. The assessment takes approximately 15 minutes and is usually administered individually. It is appropriate for use with high school students.

College-Going Self-Efficacy Scale (CGSES). (Gibbons & Borders, 2010). The CGSES measure beliefs about college attendance and persistence. The instrument consists of 30 items and can be administered individually or in groups. It is designed for use with middle school students.

My Vocational Situation (MVS). Published by Consulting Psychologists Press (Holland, Daiger, & Power, 1980). The MVS is an assessment that identifies factors that affect career decision making. The three main factors assessed via the 18 items of this scale include 1) lack of vocational identity, 2) lack of information or training, and 3) barriers. The assessment can be administered individually or in groups, and it is appropriate for use with high school students.

Interest Inventories

Campbell Interest and Skill Survey (CISS). See the description in the Ability and Aptitude Assessments section.

Pictorial Inventory of Careers (PIC). Published by Talent Assessment, Inc. (2000). The PIC requires students to rate how much they like certain occupations after watching short video segments of people at work. The 17 subscales include agricultural, business (data processing, marketing/sales, and secretarial), communications–art/graphics, electrical/electronics, engineering technology, environmental services, food services, health services, protective services, science and laboratory, service–barber/cosmetology, service–personal and industrial (construction, mechanical, and metal trades). The PIC takes approximately 22 minutes to complete and can be administered individually or in groups. It is designed for use with middle and high school students as well as individuals with disabilities. The PIC also can be used with individuals who have limited English-speaking skills.

Reading-Free Vocational Interest Inventory-2 (R-FVII:2). Published by Elbern Publications (2000). The R-FVII:2 requires students to indicate how much they like certain occupations by circling pictures of individuals in different work settings. The 11 interest areas measured include animal care, automotive, building trades, clerical, food service, horticulture, housekeeping, laundry service, materials handling, patient care, and personal service. The R-FVII:2 takes approximately 20 minutes to complete and can be administered individually or in groups. It is designed for use with students aged 13 and up who have a diagnosis of mental retardation or learning disability, but it can be used with any students who might benefit from a nonverbal assessment.

Self-Directed Search (SDS). See the description in the Ability and Aptitude Assessments section.

Strong Interest Inventory (SII). Published by Consulting Psychologists Press (2004). The SII is an assessment that measures self-reported interests. Results are present in relation to six occupational themes (realistic, investigative, artistic, social, enterprising, and conventional) as well as by basic interest scales, occupational scales, and personal style scales. The test takes approximately 45 minutes to complete, and can be administered individually or in large groups as well as online. The SSI is designed for students aged 14 and up.

Personality Assessment

The Myers-Briggs Type Indicator (MBTI). Published by Consulting Psychologists Press (Briggs & Briggs Myers, 2004). The MBTI is an assessment that measures personality traits across four dimensions: extraversion/ introversion, sensing/intuition, thinking/feeling, and judging/perceiving. The assessment takes approximately 30 minutes to complete, and can be administered individually or in a large groups as well as online. The MBTI is appropriate for use with high school students.

Values Assessment

Life Values Inventory (LVI). Published by Applied Psychology Resources (Brown & Crace, 2002). The LVI is a 42-item assessment that asks students to rate both the strength and the importance of numerous values. The 14 values assessed by the LVI include: achievement, belonging, concern for the environment, concern for others, creativity, financial prosperity, health and activity, humility, independence, interdependence, objective analysis, privacy, responsibility, and spirituality. The assessment takes approximately 20 minutes to complete, can be administered individually or in groups, and is appropriate for use with high school students.

Comprehensive, Online Systems

Career Key (Jones, 2009). This system is appropriate for use with students in middle and high school and is based on Holland's theory. Students complete the online interest inventory and receive ratings by Holland Type (RIASEC). Within the system they can explore occupations, career clusters, and college majors. Information is also available regarding how to choose a career and a college major.

DISCOVER. Published by ACT (2011). The DISCOVER system is appropriate for use with middle and high school students. It offers ACT's UNIACT interest inventory as well as skill and values assessment—all self-report. After completing all or some of the inventories, students receive results related to career clusters and the world of work map. Within the system students can search occupational information and college majors.

EXPLORE. Published by ACT (2012). EXPLORE is designed for students in grades 8 and 9. It offers assessments in English, math, reading, and science as well as a career exploration component. Results are provided in relation to how scores on the assessments align with benchmarks for college readiness. Students also are provided information about possible careers related to interest areas they identified.

Kuder Career Planning System. The Kuder system (2006) offers options for elementary (Kuder Galaxy—career exploration), and middle and high school students (Kuder Navigator—interest, skills, and values assessments). The Kuder Navigator assessments produce results in the form of percentile ranks for each of the 16 National Career Clusters (NASDCTEc, 2012): 1) agriculture, food, and natural resources, 2) architecture and construction, 3) arts, audio/visual technology, and communication, 4) business management and administration, 5) education and training, 6) finance, 7) government and public administration, 8) health science, 9) hospitality and tourism, 10) human services, 11) information technology, 12) law, public safety, corrections, and security, 13) manufacturing, 14) marketing, 15) science, technology, engineering, and mathematics, and 16) transportation, distribution, and logistics. The Kuder interest and skills assessments can be completed in approximately 20 minutes and are appropriate for use with students in grades 7 to 12. With the Kuder system, students can create portfolios and explore college and career information.

Informal Assessments

Informal assessments are just that—informal. They usually do not have reliability or validity data to support their use, they do not come with comparison norms, there are no specific ways that results must be interpreted, and they usually allow for flexibility in use, administration, and scoring. These types of assessments can be desirable to schools because they tend to be free or inexpensive, do not require assessment booklets to be purchased, require limited materials, and can be used creatively. In the following we discuss some of the more common informal assessments used in schools.

Card Sorts. Card sorts can be used in career counseling to help students identify occupational or college major interests (e.g., *Missouri Occupational Card Sort*—Hanson, Johnston, Krieshok, & Wong, 2012), values (e.g., *Career Values Card Sort*, Knowdell, 2005), or other areas. Just as the name suggests, card sorts rely on a set of cards with words or pictures on one side and a longer description or related information on the other side. In counseling, students would be asked to organize the cards in some manner, often into piles labeled Like, Dislike, and Unsure, or Like Me, Not Like Me, or Not Sure. Because card sorts are informal assessments, there is no right or wrong way to use them. Counselors can be creative in how they have students organize the cards.

Typically, once piles are sorted, students are asked to go through and further sort each pile however they want or based on some suggestion made by the counselor. For example, a student might say that she wants to sort cards with college majors she likes based on how much she knows about them. The counselor might encourage her to sort the majors she says she dislikes in the same manner, and could follow up with discussion about majors she ruled out but didn't really know much about. A follow up activity could be having her research some of the unfamiliar majors from all of her main categories.

Options for using card sorts are unlimited, and most card sort sets come with suggestions for use. An important aspect of using card sorts is examining the process—how students feel as they are sorting or what they are thinking as they are sorting. Students can use card sorts independently, but while it might be less stressful for them to sort without someone watching, they may miss out on processing their experience. Counselors who ask students to use card sorts on their own should consider providing a worksheet, like the one in Exhibit 4.1, that the student could complete (with instructions provided in advance) and bring in for discussion later. Additionally, some of these card sorts (e.g., Knowdell's) actually come with worksheets so students have a copy of their values rankings to store in a portfolio.

Career Genograms. Career genograms are commonly used in counseling to explore family relationships, composition, and patterns. In career counseling, genograms or family tree activities can be useful tools for examining career and educational trends throughout a person's family (Gibson, 2012). Typically, students would be asked to start by listing themselves, then adding relatives to the extent the counselor deems relevant. For example, elementary students might just include parents and grandparents, where high school students might include aunts and uncles, great grandparents, cousins, and so on. Then they would be

EXHIBIT 4.1
Card Sort Worksheet

1. Which main categories did you use to sort your cards?
   Like/Dislike/Unsure
   Very Important/Not Important/Not Sure
   Like Me/Not Like Me/Not Sure
   Definitely/Absolutely Not/Not Sure
   Other . . . please list your categories
2. Explain how you sorted within each main category.
   _____
   _____

3. In the space below, list the cards that were easy for you to sort.
   What made them easy? What were you thinking or feeling at the
   time? How did you finally decide?
   _____
   _____

4. In the space below, list the cards that were difficult for you to sort.
   What made them difficult? What were you thinking or feeling at
   the time? How did you finally decide?
   _____
   _____

5. In the space below list the cards you ended up with as your
   final choices, and indicate why you kept them. How certain are
   you about your final choices?
   _____
   _____

6. What next steps do you plan to take based on completing this
   activity?
   _____
   _____

7. Why is it valuable to consider your values when choosing a career?
   _____
   _____

asked to indicate the occupations represented by each person and also
perhaps the level of education they completed. This kind of activity can
easily be adapted to meet the needs of all students—using pictures and
templates for younger students or those with cognitive deficits, and perhaps allowing older students to create their own formats.

In reviewing career genograms, counselors have the flexibility to focus on whatever seems relevant for the student. When used as part of a classroom activity, school counselors might have a specific set of questions to help students make sense of what they learned; it could be as simple as asking, "How similar are your career and educational goals to those of your family?" It is important to remember that P–12 students may or may not feel comfortable sharing their family work history with their peers, so if used in large group settings, school counselors and educators should find ways to help all students benefit without making them share aloud. An easy solution is to use worksheets that can be collected, so students who want to share in class can do so, but others can have private follow-up sessions later as relevant.

Career genograms often require the involvement of families, as many students may not be familiar with the employment or educational history of their relatives. We see this as one of the benefits of this kind of activity, although it is important to realize that some students will have difficulty gathering information from their families. The authors have found it helpful to send a letter home to parents/guardians explaining the purpose of the activity and providing suggestions for how they can discuss with their child/adolescent their family work history. For example, counselors might encourage families to share what they know about how decisions were made by different people, what expectations family members did or did not have for them, whether or not people worked in occupations that they truly enjoyed, or what barriers might have existed for them to pursue certain occupations or types of education.

Sometimes family involvement leads to unplanned information that benefits students. The second author worked with a 10th-grade student who discovered through this activity that one of his distant family members had attended college and everyone else found work with high school degrees. He said that when his mother helped him complete the genogram and pointed this out, she told him that she really hoped he could be the next one to go to college. Until that point, he had not been aware that she felt that way—they never really talked about school or work. He had wanted to go to college but didn't think his family cared, so he wasn't planning to go.

Follow-up activities are important when using genograms, and they will depend on why the genogram was initially used and what information was gathered. For example, with elementary students who might be asked to simply identify what their parents and grandparents do, a follow-up activity might be for them to learn more about the occupations of their family members by interviewing at least one person about his or her job. The high school student in the previous example might be encouraged to explore occupations that require a college degree given that he had not considered them before. School counselors and educators can think of endless possibilities for taking students beyond the information they put into their genograms.

To help young students who are not familiar with some of the occupations held by family members, a relevant activity is to create a paper doll that goes to work with the family member. The doll is designed and decorated by the child. The child then gives the paper doll to the family member who takes the doll to work and takes pictures of the doll engaging in work tasks. For example, a parent who is an auto mechanic would take a picture of the paper doll in the auto shop, possibly pretending to work on a car. Similarly, a student who has a parent who is a nurse may have pictures of the paper doll in the hospital taking someone's blood pressure. The teacher could make a video montage of all of the paper dolls in the class at "work" and the class gets to see many different work environments and what types of work occur in each.

Career Style Interview (CSI). The CSI (Savickas, 2005) is grounded in the Theory of Career Construction (see Chapter 13). Savickas believes that while objective data obtained from formal assessments are important, subjective data that reflect personal experiences are equally important, as they help to explain how students make sense of things in their lives. The CSI allows counselors to examine students' experiences and to help them identify patterns and themes that might suggest possible future career paths.

The CSI is an informal assessment, meaning that it does not need to be completed in a specific or consistent manner. Nevertheless, Savickas (2005) provides a structure for gathering and making sense of the information gleaned from the interview. Ideally, in completing the interview, students provide information about the following: role models, favorite books and magazines, favorite hobbies, favorite and least favorite school subjects, favorite quote or motto, ambitions and parent's ambitions for them, and an important choice or decision they made and how they made it. Information gathered is used to collaboratively identify themes or patterns (see Chapter 13 for an example of what this "interpretation" looks like).

As with other informal assessments, counselors using the CSI should take advantage of opportunities to process information with students and expand their discussion and insight. For example, Savickas (2005) suggested that when identifying role models, counselors ask follow-up questions such as "What do you like or respect about this person?" or "Why did you identify his or her as your role model?" Follow up questions related to school subjects might help to examine aspects of those subjects or classes that the student enjoys or does not enjoy. The main goal for such processing is to better understand the student's choices and decisions as that information will inform the interpretation and identification of themes.

In addition to costing nothing and being very flexible (the interview can be completed over a number of sessions or all at once—there is no timeframe), another benefit of the CSI is its adaptability. It can be completed in numerous ways, verbally or by using pictures. The second author successfully has used the CSI by having students create collages in which they represent each topic area, or by drawing or bringing in pictures to reflect some of their responses. Follow-up discussion of the collage items can be done the same way as in an interview. This author also has had students complete the interview during a session, as well as have them take a worksheet home and then meet to review responses. School counselors should consider the developmental needs and personal styles of students when determining the most effective format and timeframe for completing the CSI.

USING ASSESSMENT RESULTS: EVALUATION

Choosing and administering career-related assessments is only half the picture—it's what is done with the assessment data that really matters. This is not an assessment textbook, so we want to just briefly address a few important considerations for interpreting and using assessment data.

Considerations for Interpreting Assessment Data

1. **Examine data from multiple assessment tools.** No one single assessment tool should be used to make a determination about a student's future. On any given day in any given situation, a student may or may not have been at her best. Further, some students respond better to one type of assessment versus another. Data collected over a number of different instruments will likely be more reliable in reflecting that student.

   In addition to having multiple data points from which to make determinations about future options, school counselors and educators should consider the benefits of using different types of assessments. A combination of formal and informal instruments assessing the same factor can be useful in comparing and contrasting results and looking for themes or patterns. Also, assessments targeting different areas (e.g., interests, skills) can be combined in order to more comprehensively assess a student.

2. **Interpret results accurately.** Each assessment has its own unique score report or instructions for interpretation, and school counselors and educators must ensure that they are accurately making sense of results. Given the variety of ways that assessment data are reported, it is imperative that the individuals reviewing and explaining the results understand concepts such as correlations, standard scores, percentile ranks, stanine scores, and grade equivalents. Further, in order to help make meaning of the results, school counselors and educators need to understand how to read norms tables and expectancy tables.

3. **Ensure that students understand their results.** Do not leave students on their own to make sense of the results. Both of the authors have had experience working with students who jump to conclusions about what their results "are telling them" to be or do. Often, students want tests to give them answers. It is up to us to help them realize that assessment results are helpful in identifying factors such as strengths, weaknesses, or things to consider, and that future plans and decisions should be made with that information in mind. Handing students their assessment results without explanation or follow up can quickly lead to misperceptions and inaccurate assumptions on their part. Just because instructions and interpretations might be included as part of an individual student's summary report doesn't mean that the student will understand them or read them carefully. Verbal explanations and follow-up discussions can be very important to ensure accurate understanding by students as well as their parents or guardians.

Using Assessment Data for Program Planning

While individual student assessment results are beneficial to students, school counselors and educators should consider the benefits of examining student data for the purposes of informing program planning. For example, if a school counselor administered an interest inventory and, through summary data, learned that the majority of student interests fell into five specific career clusters, perhaps the counselor could initiate a discussion about the possibility of offering elective courses or supplemental learning opportunities related to those areas. Or, if through an assessment the counselor learned that students do not feel confident in their abilities to access career information, supplemental educational or information sessions could be implemented in order to better prepare students and their families to engage in career exploration activities.

An important skill for school counselors (ASCA, 2012) is to examine data, and specifically to disaggregate data. By breaking results down into various groups (e.g., ethnicity, disabilities, first-generation college students), school counselors can identify any populations that might need more support. Efforts to close the achievement gap can be facilitated by evaluating assessment data—without knowing what differences exist or in what areas they exist, school counselors and educators cannot effect change.

Subsequent to student assessment and results interpretation, school counselors should be prepared to share their findings. By reporting findings to the counseling advisory council, administration, parents, or other stakeholders, school counselors can garner support for program planning in response to student outcomes. To use an example from the beginning of the chapter, if a school counselor learns that only 25% of students at the school take the ACT before their senior year, the counselor may choose to design an intervention to increase the number of students taking the ACT in their sophomore and junior years and may report this information to the school principal and the counseling advisory council. Together they may decide that a classroom lesson plan highlighting the benefits of early ACT participation is necessary and that they should send out a letter to parents explaining the importance of taking the ACT early. In this way, data are being used to drive decision making and interventions. Following these interventions, the school counselor would continue to monitor ACT participation for sophomores and juniors to determine if there is an increase or not.

SUMMARY

In this chapter we discussed the importance of assessment and evaluation in P–12 career education and counseling. When considering which assessment instruments to choose for their schools, counselors should be familiar with psychometric properties (e.g., validity, reliability), normed populations, potential content and language biases, as well as how the assessment can be administered or modified to appeal to various learning styles or students with learning disabilities. We also cautioned readers to comprehensively consider the time, cost, and purpose of assessments given to students to ensure that the assessment is worthwhile. We reviewed numerous formal and informal assessments that can be used in P–12 settings and offered tips on interpreting results and using assessment and evaluation data for program planning. In the grade level chapters that follow, we will refer to many of the assessments listed in this chapter.

···❯ Test Your Knowledge

1. Name at least one assessment that you could use to assess each of the following: 1) values, 2) interests, 3) abilities, and 4) beliefs.
2. Explain why counselors would want to consider using a combination of formal and informal assessments.
3. Why are norm groups important?
4. Clarify the difference between reliability and validity.

5
•••••

P–12 Career Curriculum Development
•••••

Developing and delivering a core counseling curriculum are essential tasks for school counselors and a direct service component of the American School Counselor Association's (ASCA) National Model (2012). Jalongo and Isenberg (2004) defined curriculum as "the pathway of education; it is what children actually experience in schools from arrival to departure and reflects the philosophy, goals, and objectives of the program, classroom, or school district" (p. 185). According to Graves (1996), a curriculum that is well designed engages students through active learning, a process that involves both *action* and *reflection. Action* occurs through directly interacting with "people, materials, events, and ideas" (p. 4) and *reflection* occurs when students are asked to construct knowledge about those interaction experiences in a way that is relevant and meaningful. Curriculum should be rigorous, establishing high expectations for all students, while also being culturally relevant (Jalongo & Isenberg, 2004).

With all of this in mind, curriculum development can be a daunting task for new school counselors who may be unsure of how to design or write curricula. A further concern is that stakeholders may question the need for career development activities, especially if career development takes time away from the core academic curriculum, particularly for elementary students, since many adults may not understand the need for career interventions in primary grades (Niles & Harris-Bowlsbey, 2009). In this chapter, we explore critical issues in curriculum development including curriculum foundations, developing objectives, choosing interventions and writing lesson plans, implementing the curriculum, and evaluating outcomes.

CHOOSING A CURRICULUM FOUNDATION

As noted by Niles and Harris-Bowlsbey (2009), one major barrier to successful career development interventions is that the curriculum is often patched together rather than being a cohesive, systematic program throughout P–12 grades. For example, at a conference one middle school counselor recently told the first author how difficult it is for her to know what the sixth grade students in her school understand about career, as she has no idea what career interventions they were given in elementary school. This lack of cohesive, formal planning among and between school levels (elementary, middle, and high schools) means that students may be given duplicate information (i.e., learning the same information about career clusters in both elementary and middle school) or miss information at one level that they are expected to know (i.e., being asked to choose a college in their junior year when they haven't had any career exploration and therefore don't know what postsecondary training they need).

To avoid some of these problems, it is important that school counselors within districts and school clusters co-plan curricula. Further, Brown (2012) noted that school counselors will want to gain administrative support before designing and implementing the career curriculum in order to allocate time for co-planning curricula across schools and to ensure that teachers will support time away from core curricula for career development. Additionally, school counselors should garner input from the guidance advisory council and base curricula decisions on school and district data, national and state standards, and grade-level expectations in order to provide a foundation for success. In this section, we provide an overview of how school counselors can use standards-based curriculum and grade level expectations to begin the process of designing career guidance curricula.

Creating a Standards-Based Curriculum

The *ASCA Student Standards* (ASCA, 2004) gives school counselors a framework for identifying the skill and knowledge competencies that students need to develop in personal/social, career, and academic domains. It is up to individual schools to determine which of these standards are most relevant for students in their buildings. Some standards might be covered and assessed multiple times and in different ways across grade levels. Other standards might be addressed only once.

In order to effectively use standards for curriculum development, these authors suggest that school counselors should: 1) read all of the standards thoroughly, 2) identify, by grade, what students need to know, 3) write curriculum objectives, 4) design assessments to measure student learning, 5) design lesson plans, 6) deliver lesson plans and assess student learning, 7) share assessment results with the guidance advisory council, and 8) use assessment results to plan future guidance instruction. The *ASCA Student Standards* (2004) for student career development can be found in Table 5.1.

TABLE 5.1 The ASCA Student Standards, Competencies, and Indicators for Student Competence (Career Domain)

Standard A: *Students will acquire the skills to investigate the world of work in relation to knowledge of self and to make informed career decisions.*

C:A1 Develop Career Awareness

C:A1.1	Develop skills to locate, evaluate and interpret career information.
C:A1.2	Learn about the variety of traditional and nontraditional occupations
C:A1.3	Develop an awareness of personal abilities, skills, interests, and motivations
C:A1.4	Learn how to interact and work cooperatively in teams
C:A1.5	Learn to make decisions
C:A1.6	Learn how to set goals
C:A1.7	Understand the importance of planning
C:A1.8	Pursue and develop competency in areas of interest
C:A1.9	Develop hobbies and vocational interests
C:A1.10	Balance between work and leisure time

C:A2 Develop Employment Readiness

C:A2.1	Acquire employability skills such as working on a team, problem solving, and organizational skills
C:A2.2	Apply job readiness skills to seek employment opportunities
C:A2.3	Demonstrate knowledge about the changing workplace
C:A2.4	Learn about the rights and responsibilities of employers and employees
C:A2.5	Learn to respect individual uniqueness in the workplace
C:A2.6	Learn how to write a resume
C:A2.7	Develop a positive attitude toward work and learning
C:A2.8	Understand the importance of responsibility, dependability, punctuality, integrity, and effort in the workplace
C:A2.9	Utilize time- and task-management skills

Standard B: *Students will employ strategies to achieve future career goals with success and satisfaction.*

C:B1 Acquire Career Information

C:B1.1	Apply decision-making skills to career planning, course selection, and career transition
C:B1.2	Identify personal skills, interests, and abilities and relate them to current career choice
C:B1.3	Demonstrate knowledge of the career-planning process
C:B1.4	Know the various ways in which occupations can be classified
C:B1.5	Use research and information resources to obtain career information
C:B1.6	Learn to use the Internet to access career planning information
C:B1.7	Describe traditional and nontraditional career choices and how they related to career choice
C:B1.8	Understand how changing economic and societal needs influence employment trends and future training

(continued)

TABLE 5.1   The ASCA Student Standards, Competencies, and Indicators for Student Competence (Career Domain) (*Continued*)

C:B2 Identify Career Goals

C:B2.1	Demonstrate awareness of the education and training needed to achieve career goals
C:B2.2	Assess and modify their educational plan to support career goals
C:B2.3	Use employability and job-readiness skills in internship, mentoring shadowing, and/or other work experience
C:B2.4	Select coursework that is related to career interests
C:B2.5	Maintain a career planning portfolio

Standard C: *Students will understand the relationship among personal qualities, education, training, and the world of work.*

C:C1 Acquire Knowledge to Achieve Career Goals

C:C1.1	Understand the relationship between educational achievement and career success
C:C1.2	Explain how work can help to achieve personal success and satisfaction
C:C1.3	Identify personal preferences and interests influencing career choice and success
C:C1.4	Understand that the changing workplace requires lifelong learning and acquiring of new skills
C:C1.5	Describe the effect of work on lifestyle
C:C1.6	Understand the importance of equity and access in career choice
C:C1.7	Understand that work is an important and satisfying means of personal expression

C:C2 Apply Skills to Achieve Career Goals

C:C2.1	Demonstrate how interests, abilities, and achievement relate to achieving personal, social, educational, and career goals
C:C2.2	Learn how to use conflict management skills with peers and adults
C:C2.3	Learn to work cooperatively with others as a team member
C:C2.4	Apply academic and employment readiness skills in work-based learning situations such as internships, shadowing, and/or mentoring experiences

Reprinted with permission from ASCA (2004).

NATIONAL CAREER DEVELOPMENT GUIDELINES

The National Career Development Association (NCDA) developed a standards framework known as the National Career Development Guidelines (2008) for a curriculum that focuses on the areas of personal social development (PS); educational achievement and lifelong learning (ED); and career management (CM) (see Appendix D). This framework, similar to ASCA's, describes potential content and indicators of competence. Moreover, according to Niles and Harris-Bowlesbey (2009), the NCDA guidelines can be used in multiple ways. For example, they can be used as a framework to design needs assessments, review and modify an existing career program/ curriculum, and determine gaps in student career competencies. The guidelines also can be helpful as teachers review and integrate career information in their core content and pedagogy, and as school counselors set goals and objectives (i.e., student learning targets) for which they will be accountable.

Grade Level Expectations

Some states have developed their own grade level expectations (GLEs) for the core counseling curriculum. For example, Missouri's Comprehensive Guidance Program underscores content standard GLEs for personal/social, career, and academic competencies (Missouri Center for Career Education, 2006). These GLEs assist school counselors in identifying what students should know, or be able to do, in a specific domain by the end of a grade. As an example, Table 5.2 demonstrates Missouri's GLEs for K–2 students in the career development domain. The first grade GLEs in the section of Table 5.2 titled, "Applying Employment Readiness Skills and the Skills for On-the-Job Success," state that at the end of first grade, students should be "able to identify and develop personal, ethical, and work habit skills needed for school success." Given this outcome expectation, school counselors can set objectives and design classroom lessons that will facilitate development of this skill. (The Missouri GLEs for grades for K–12 can be found in Appendix C.)

WRITING CURRICULUM OBJECTIVES

After reviewing standards and determining which are wanted or needed as a foundation for their curriculum, school counselors should develop learning objectives, by grade, for the career curriculum. It is important to understand that these objectives need to be developmental and sequential. In other words, the exact same objective should not be written for kindergarten, first, and second grade. Rather, each grade would have a distinct set of learning objectives for career development. Moreover, objectives should be written such that outcomes are specific and measurable. In this section we review key concepts for writing effective curriculum objectives.

Bloom's Taxonomy

Benjamin Bloom's *Taxonomy of Educational Objectives* (i.e., Bloom's taxonomy) is a seminal work that has been informative to education practitioners in constructing curricula (Bloom, Engelhart, Furst, Hill, & Krathwohl, 1956). Based on the psychology of learning and developmental theories, Bloom's taxonomy is designed to help educators make conscious choices about how

TABLE 5.2   Missouri Comprehensive Guidance Program Content Standards Grade Level Expectations (GLE) for K–2 Career Development

Concept	GLE: Kindergarten	GLE: Grade 1	GLE: Grade 2
Big Idea 7: CD 7 Applying Career Exploration and Planning Skills in the Achievement of Life Career Goals			
A. Integration of Self-Knowledge into Life and Career Plans	a. Identify likes and dislikes at home and school.	a. Identify strengths and interests at home and school.	a. Identify new activities and interests to explore.
B. Adaptations to World of Work Changes	a. Identify workers in the school and in families related to the six career paths.	a. Identify workers in the local community related to the six career paths	a. Identify the academic skills necessary for workers in the six career paths.
C. Respect for All Work	a. Recognize that all work is important.	a. Explain the importance of jobs in the family and school.	a. Explain the importance of jobs and workers in the community.
Big Idea 8: CD 8 Knowing Where and How to Obtain Information About the World of Work and Postsecondary Training/Education			
A. Career Decision Making	a. Identify roles and responsibilities of family members in the world of work.	a. Identify and compare roles and responsibilities of workers within the school.	a. Identify and compare roles and responsibilities of workers within the community.
B. Education and Career Requirements	a. Identify the skills family members use in their work.	a. Identify the skills needed by workers in the school.	a. Identify the skills needed by workers in the community.
Big Idea 9: CD 9 Applying Employment Readiness Skills and the Skills for On-the-Job Success			
A. Personal Skills for Job Success	a. Identify personal and ethical skills needed to work cooperatively with others in a group at school.	a. Identify and develop personal, ethical, and work habit skills needed for school success.	a. Identify personal, ethical, and work habit skills needed for workers in the community.
B. Job-Seeking Skills	a. Identify helper jobs that are available in the classroom.	a. Understand how helper jobs are assigned in the classroom.	a. Identify and apply the steps to obtain helper jobs within the classroom.

Based on the Missouri Center for Career Education (2006).

the educative process unfolds and challenges students' thinking. That is, educators should expect that students will be able to engage in more advanced ways of thinking about various concepts as they develop and, therefore, activities and assessments should match where students are developmentally.

According to Bloom et al. (1956, p. 25), the following four questions should be considered and used as a guide in developing curricula:

1. What educational purposes or objectives should the school or course seek to attain?
2. What learning experiences can be provided that are likely to bring about the attainment of these purposes?
3. How can these learning experiences be effectively organized to help provide continuity and sequence for the learner and to help the learner in integrating what might otherwise appear as isolated learning experiences?
4. How can the effectiveness of learning experiences be evaluated by the use of tests and other systematic evidence gathering procedures?

Bloom's taxonomy is meant to help educators organize, developmentally, a curriculum that addresses the aforementioned questions by graduating learning experiences in a systematic, hierarchical order. The original taxonomy objectives were revised by a group of cognitive psychologists to reflect modern learning. Today, the following are Bloom's taxonomy learning objectives: 1) remembering, 2) understanding, 3) applying, 4) analyzing, 5) evaluating, and 6) creating. An explanation of each objective is provided in Table 5.3, and the hierarchical nature of Bloom's revised taxonomy is represented in Figure 5.1.

TABLE 5.3 Taxonomy of Educational Objectives and a Description of Each for the Revised Bloom's Taxonomy

Objectives and Descriptions From the Revised Bloom's Taxonomy
Remembering: Remembering is the ability to recall, recognize and retrieve information that has been previously learned. Defining, memorizing, and repeating information are all included in this objective.
Understanding: Understanding is the construction of meaning from graphs, data, charts, written and oral language. Students demonstrate understanding by interpreting, summarizing, comparing and explaining information.
Applying: Applying a theory to a problem, particularly in a new way, implementing a procedure.
Analyzing: Breaking information into parts, developing an understanding of how each part works, how it works compared to other parts, and how each part contributes to the whole, differentiating and organizing information.
Evaluating: Reviewing and critiquing information base on standards or specific criteria.
Creating: Putting together or reorganizing elements into a new pattern to create a functional whole, generating, producing.

FIGURE 5.1   Taxonomy of Revised Education Objectives From Most Concrete to Most Abstract

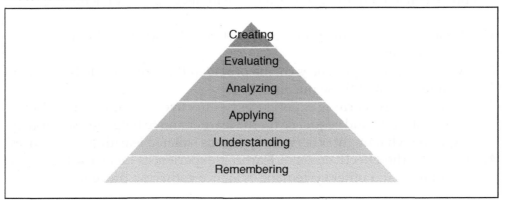

Writing Measurable Objectives

Curriculum objectives should be established for the school counseling program at the beginning of each year and developed based on data (e.g., from needs assessments, from previous year's assessments). These objectives ideally should cover all three of the ASCA domains—career, personal/social, and academic. Educators at state and district levels often refer to objectives by a variety of terms (e.g., student learning targets), but all of those terms refer to what we want students to know or be able to do in relation to a specific content area.

When writing career curriculum objectives, it is important that school counselors be as specific as possible. By doing so, the objectives provide an indication of what the school counselor will do and what outcomes are expected as a result. In order to have developmentally appropriate objectives, counselors should write separate objectives for each grade level. We recommend the ABCD method of writing objectives proposed by Heinrich, Molenda, Russell, and Smaldino (1996). The ABCD method consists of including the following elements in each objective: **(A)** the *audience* element denotes who is the intended learners; **(B)** the *behavior* element indicates what you expect the learner to be able to do, and it should be observable; **(C)** the *condition* element describes the specific circumstances or context in which the learning will occur; and **(D)** the *degree* is the amount of mastery the learner will achieve. Table 5.4 provides examples of career curriculum objectives written with the ABCD method for elementary, middle, and high school.

Upon writing the objectives for the career curriculum, school counselors should then proceed to choose evaluative measures to determine desired student outcomes. Thus, after developing and writing program objectives, school counselors would then identify relevant evaluations for each objective as well as choosing interventions (including writing lesson plans).

TABLE 5.4 Sample Career Curriculum Objectives for School Counseling Programs

Grade Level	Sample Curriculum Objective
Third Grade	At the conclusion of a unit on career clusters, third grade students will be able to identify the career clusters that specific careers belong to 80% of the time.
Seventh Grade	At the conclusion of a classroom lesson on career values, 85% of seventh grade students will be able to list five personal values they have related to career.
Eleventh Grade	At the completion of two classroom lessons on writing effective scholarship essays, 80% of eleventh grade students will be able to identify four components of a well-written scholarship essay.

CHOOSING INTERVENTIONS AND WRITING LESSON PLANS

As previously mentioned, prior to designing and delivering lesson plans, school counselors should review state and national standards, including GLEs, determine what students need to know by grade level, write curriculum objectives, and choose assessments. After engaging in these curriculum-planning activities, school counselors can begin to design lesson plans. In this section we describe how the choice of interventions and activities can help to increase student maturity, and we provide the reader with considerations for creating student learning experiences.

Increasing Career Maturity

One of the most important and desired outcomes of career guidance, education, and counseling is that students gain career maturity throughout their time in P–12 education. The concept of career maturity came from Super (1980), and is described by Sharf (2006, p. 180) as having five distinct components:

1. Orientation to vocational choice, which deals with concern about career choice and using occupational information
2. Information and planning about a preferred occupation; that is, the specific information that the individual has about the occupation he or she intends to enter
3. Consistency of vocational preference, concerned not only with stability of an occupational choice over time, but also with its consistency within occupational fields and levels
4. Crystallization of traits, including seven indices of attitudes toward work
5. The wisdom of vocational preference, which refers to the relationship between choice and abilities, activities and interests

To comprehensively increase students' career maturity, it is essential that the counseling curriculum reflect an underlying theoretical framework (i.e., Gottfredson, Holland, Super, etc.), that the school counselor chooses interventions that are theory- and evidence-based, that the counseling curriculum addresses student standards for career and college preparation (e.g., ASCA, 2004), and that the counseling curriculum is evaluated for effectiveness. Moreover, the counseling curriculum should be culturally responsive, appeal to a variety of learning styles, and should be developmentally appropriate. We discuss each of these concerns in this section.

Culturally Responsive Curriculum

Effective and appropriate curriculum is culturally relevant, supporting students' home culture and language while also assisting students in navigating the culture of the school (Jalongo & Isenberg, 2004). A culturally relevant curriculum supports diverse learners in three ways: 1) by accepting, valuing, and welcoming all students *and their families,* 2) accommodating different learning styles through varied teaching strategies, and 3) encouraging students to have personal pride in their culture and to use cultural knowledge to motivate children by increasing self-esteem, self-knowledge, and an appreciation for others (Jalongo & Isenberg, 2004). Further, a culturally responsive curriculum promotes cultural understanding, awareness, acceptance of other cultures, and sensitivity to others.

When designing a culturally responsive curriculum, school counselors should choose culturally relevant materials (e.g., books, pictures, music) that reflect and value the unique cultural lives and languages of all students. A truly culturally responsive career curriculum includes much more than lesson plans that reflect an appreciation of diversity. Indeed, school counselors must remember that all students have potential. In order to encourage all students, it is critical that students are given access to a counseling curriculum consistently throughout P–12 education and that diverse academic courses are offered in every school environment that are both rigorous and challenging to students.

Addressing Learning Styles and Multiple Intelligences

Alexander (2000) noted that information is received in particular ways by each individual. Specifically, Alexander organized learning styles into three major categories that can be considered when developing an instructional or training plan: 1) visual learners, who prefer seeing pictures, graphs, charts, PowerPoints, props and videos; 2) auditory learners, who prefer hearing instructions and explanations; and 3) kinesthetic learners, who prefer hands-on opportunities to learn, such as role plays, science experiments, and math labs. Howard Gardner (1983) is credited with expanding Alexander's work through the development of the concept of multiple intelligences. In his seminal work, *Frames of Mind: The Theory of Multiple Intelligences,* Gardner explained that individuals have different learning styles and that instruction should reflect these multiple styles in order to engage all students. Table 5.5 contains a list of intelligences and provides a description of each.

TABLE 5.5 Gardner's Multiple Intelligences

Type of Intelligence	Characteristics
Linguistic Intelligence	Individuals with natural mastery or expertise in language. Individuals with linguistic intelligence use language for communicative and expressive purposes. For example, an individual with a natural ability to understand words and use them such as writing poetry. Students with this learning style may enjoy activities like writing career stories.
Logical-Mathematical Intelligence	Individuals with this learning style enjoy learning information through reasoning, abstraction, mathematics, and scientific investigation. Students with this learning style may enjoy exploring careers through technology.
Musical Intelligence	Gardner noted that musical talent is the first type of intelligence to emerge. Individuals with this type of intelligence may use songs or rhythm to remember information, have a propensity toward playing musical instruments, singing, or composing music. Students with this learning style may enjoy careers in the music industry and may enjoy alternative learning techniques, such as writing a career rap song.
Bodily-Kinesthetic Intelligence	Individuals with this learning style enjoy movement such as sports, dance, and other physical activities. Students with this learning style learn better when they are moving and may enjoy career exploration games that involve physical activity (i.e., career baseball, career safari).
Spatial Intelligence	Individuals with this learning style have strong visual observation skills and are often artistic. Students with this learning style may like career exploration activities that include drawing careers, creating career genograms, mapping career clusters, and other artistic/visual activities.
Interpersonal Intelligence	Individuals with this learning style generally enjoy social pursuits and collaborative and team work activities. Students in this category may enjoy creating career skits, interviewing people, and classroom career discussions.
Intrapersonal Intelligence	Individuals with this learning style are very reflective and introspective. They may prefer working alone and enjoy analyzing their own thoughts and perceptions as they are effective contemplators. Students in this category might enjoy reading career information, taking assessments and reflecting on the results, and doing individualized exploration activities.
Naturalistic Intelligence	Individuals with this learning style enjoy learning in natural environments, growing and nurturing animals and plants. Students in this learning category may enjoy career exploration with natural elements. For example, students with this type of intelligence might enjoy activities like learning about agricultural careers if they get an opportunity to actually interact with elements (i.e., taking a field trip to a farm and feeding animals).

Adapted from Gardner (1983).

Grounded in Theory and Developmentally Appropriate

In order to design meaningful and relevant career development lessons, school counselors should have in-depth knowledge of theories of child and adolescent development. In the subsequent chapters, we provide an overview of holistic development related to career growth including social/emotional, cognitive, physical, and cultural development concepts, and continue to connect career and college readiness activities to developmental and career theories. Proposed grade level interventions are based on the work of various theorists, including Bourdieu (1977), Gottfredson (1981), Holland (1997), Bandura (1977), and Super (1980), to name a few.

The Well-Written Lesson Plan

After completing a review of standards, writing the counseling program's curriculum objectives, choosing assessments, and considering culture, development and theory, the school counselor is ready to write (or choose) lesson plans. A wealth of free and downloadable lesson plans are available online (e.g., see Missouri Center for Career Education, www.missouricareereducation.org). However, before acquiring lesson plans written by others, school counselors should ensure that the selected lesson plans adequately address the standards and objectives of their specific school counseling program.

Components of a Well-Written Lesson Plan. A well-written lesson plan includes, at minimum, six core components: 1) standards, 2) objectives, 3) materials, 4) detailed instructions, 5) summary, and 6) evaluation. At the beginning of the written lesson plan, school counselors should indicate the *standards* that they are using in forming the lesson. This may include standards from the ASCA Student Standards(2004), the NCDG (2008), and applicable state standards or GLEs upon which the lesson is based. The *objectives* of the lesson plan should also be listed; these specific objectives should align with the school program objectives and should articulate what skills or knowledge students should acquire at the completion of the lesson or learning unit. The *materials* section includes any supplies necessary for delivering the lesson plan including markers, paper, worksheets, puppets, and so forth. In the *detailed instructions* section of the lesson plan, the school counselor lists step-by-step directions for delivering the lesson to students. The *summary* section denotes how the school counselor will wrap up the lesson and provides closure instructions such as reflection questions, follow-up activities for the teacher to implement, and suggestions for practicing newly acquired skills or knowledge. Finally, the *evaluation* component includes assessments that measure whether or not the specific objectives of the lesson plan have been met. For an example of a lesson plan containing these six key components, please see Exhibit 5.1.

EXHIBIT 5.1
Sample First-Grade Lesson Plan

Title of Lesson: Jobs I Like at Home and School

Outcome: a) Students will be able to name strengths, indicate interests, and explain the importance of jobs at home and at school; b) students will have some knowledge of different jobs they do at home and at school.

American School Counselor Association Student Standards:

- Career Development Domain
  Standard A: Students will acquire the skills to investigate the world of work in relation to knowledge of self and to make informed career decisions.
- Personal/Social Domain
  Standard A: Students will acquire the knowledge, attitudes and interpersonal skills to help them understand and respect self and others.

Competencies/Indicators:

- C:A1.3: Develop an awareness of personal abilities, skills, interests, and motivations
- PS:A1.10 Identify personal strengths and assets

Missouri Grade Level Expectations:

- CD.7.A.01.a.i: Identify strengths and interests at home and school
- CD.7.C.01.a.i: Explain the importance of jobs in the family and school

Learning Objective: After completing the lesson, all students will be able to identify at least one of their strengths and one of their interests on the *My Strengths and Interests* worksheet.

Materials:

- Classroom job chart
- Flip chart
- Markers
- *My Strengths and Interests* worksheet

Introduction: The following are some essential questions to keep in mind during the lesson:

- Why are children expected to do jobs at home? Why are students expected to do jobs at school?

(continued)

EXHIBITS 5.1
Sample First-Grade Lesson Plan *(Continued)*

- Why do people need to have jobs at home or school?
- What are some important jobs that people do at home and in your classroom?
- What would happen if people didn't have jobs?

Developmental Learning Activities:

1. Look at the classroom job chart. Name each job, and ask the students to give a "thumbs-up" if they would like to do that job. Ask the students, "Which jobs would you do well in the classroom? Are there some jobs that you like to do more than others?"
2. Summarize what the students have said, noting the jobs that students have mentioned as the jobs they would do the best.
3. Tell the students that things we can do really well are call strengths.
4. Ask the students, "What is an interest?" Does an interest have to be a strength of a person? Is there a difference between strengths and interests? The classroom jobs you gave a "thumbs-up" rating are things that you are interested in doing.
5. Ask the students to form a circle. The counselor says, "This is our *Strength and Interest Circle.*" Ask each student to tell about one strength and one interest they have at school and at home. Give some examples if necessary.
   a. My strength is helping others in my family
   b. I'm interested in reading books at school
   c. I'm interested in learning about new things
6. On the flip chart, write *Our Jobs at Home.* Create a home job chart using suggestions from the students. The counselor will write the suggestions on the flip chart.
7. Name each job and ask the students to give you a "thumbs-up" if they like the job. Ask a few of the students to tell you what they like about those jobs. After reviewing the list, make the connection between what they like to do/what they're interested in doing and what they are good at doing.
8. Look at the two job charts (classroom and home). Ask the students which jobs are important. What would happen if we didn't have classroom jobs? What would happen at home if people didn't do their jobs?
9. Summarize the lesson by stating that people have different strengths and interests, and these strengths and interests help them do their jobs well. ALL jobs are important to help our homes and school run smoothly.

(continued)

EXHIBITS 5.1
Sample First-Grade Lesson Plan *(Continued)*

10. Hand out the *My Strengths and Interests* worksheet. Have each student write their name on the worksheet and fill it out to the best of their ability. Collect the sheets at the end of the lesson.

Evaluation/Assessment: Students will be given the *My Strengths and Interests* worksheet (please see Exhibit 5.2) to complete at the end of the lesson. If the students are able to identify at least one strength and one interest, the learning objective has been met.

Followup: When the teacher assigns classroom jobs, the teacher might reinforce the strengths and interests that students are bringing to those tasks.

Adapted from Missouri Comprehensive Guidance Programs

EXHIBITS 5.2
My Strengths and Interests Worksheet

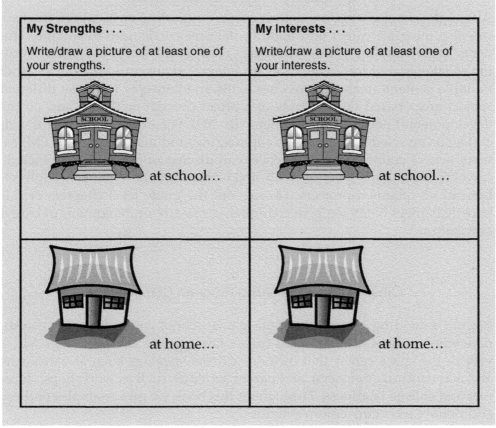

My Strengths . . .	My Interests . . .
Write/draw a picture of at least one of your strengths.	Write/draw a picture of at least one of your interests.
at school…	at school…
at home…	at home…

IMPLEMENTING THE CURRICULUM

Prior to implementing the curriculum and classroom lesson plans, Brown (2012) suggested that school counselors consider the following: 1) What types of materials and resources are needed to effectively deliver the program (e.g., games, assessments)? 2) How can technology be used to deliver or enhance the guidance curriculum? 3) What aspects of the career curriculum can be infused in classroom education in existing content units? 4) How can parents be included in the curriculum?

The answers to these questions will be school specific and, as is evidenced throughout this book, it is not necessary for school counselors to buy a lot of expensive curriculum books and materials. However, if counselors have a budget and can buy some materials they should do so with intentionality. For example, there are expensive career exploration software programs that can be purchased but there are many free technology resources that may serve similar purposes (e.g., Occupational Outlook Handbook, Drive of Your Life, O*Net, California Career Zone).

Classroom Curriculum Integration

Although school counselors deliver career counseling curriculum, teachers can also integrate career education in the core curriculum to enhance students' understanding of how academics relate to the world of work. According to Jalongo and Isenberg (2004), an integrated curriculum joins together multiple content areas and "teaches skills and concepts from the different subject areas based on the study of a broad concept or theme, and on the developmental needs of the learners" (p. 203). For example, given the federal focus on science, technology, engineering, and mathematics (STEM) careers, school counselors and teachers can discuss opportunities to include career information in science, math, and technology classrooms through collaboratively planned projects. Throughout the grade level chapters of this book (Chapters 6–14), we give examples of classroom integration of career curriculum.

Other School Counseling Program Components

Beyond providing classroom lesson plans, school counselors also coordinate whole school activities (i.e., career fairs), grade level activities (i.e., a visit to the space center that includes careers speakers such as astronauts and aeronautical engineers), and parent activities such as workshops on career and college readiness. Throughout this book we give examples of these additional career curriculum activities.

EVALUATING OUTCOMES

As noted by Carter and Curtis (1994), ongoing evaluation (i.e., at the end of lessons or units), allows for immediate feedback. By evaluating student performance on curriculum objectives, school counselors can determine if students are gaining competence in career development based on knowledge and skills learned through the guidance curriculum. Second, if evaluations are thoughtfully created, then the act of providing evaluation feedback can be a learning and reflection experience for students (Carter & Curtis, 1994). Finally, student outcome evaluation data are important for determining the success of program objectives and for determining future plans of action.

Choosing Evaluation Methods

The method that is used to evaluate a lesson will depend on a number of factors, including the developmental level of the students as well as their learning styles. In Table 5.6 we revisit the curriculum objectives we presented

TABLE 5.6 Sample Career Curriculum Objectives and Evaluation Methods

Grade	Sample Curriculum Objective	Sample Evaluation Methods
3rd	At the conclusion of a unit on career clusters, third grade students will be able to identify the career clusters that specific careers belong to 80% of the time	1. Students will complete a test in which they match a list of careers to a list of clusters or students place pictures of individuals in careers under the appropriate cluster headings (Bloom's *remembering* objective)
		2. Students will create a collage in which they visually place career cards in clusters and demonstrate an understanding of how those careers fit together (Bloom's *understanding* objective)
7th	At the conclusion of a classroom lesson on career values, 85% of seventh grade students will be able to list five personal values they have related to career	1. Students will create a picture in which they represent the five personal values that arose as strongest influences based on their assessment results (Bloom's *understanding* objective)
		2. Students will submit a written list of their personal values, including a brief explanation of how they might influence their career choices (Bloom's *applying* objective)
11th	At the completion of two classroom lessons on writing effective scholarship essays, 80% of 11th grade students will be able to identify four components of a well-written scholarship essay	1. Students will produce a scholarship essay that contains the four components (Bloom's *applying* objective)
		2. Students will critique an essay based on the four components (Bloom's *evaluating* objective)

earlier in this chapter. Beside each objective, we offer a couple of ways that it could be evaluated. In the first example for third grade, you can see two different methods for assessing the same *remembering* objective—the picture option could be beneficial for individuals with lower reading skills or for students who are visual learners. The same approach could be used for learning objectives at any grade level.

Sharing Results and Making Decisions

Data collected should be shared with major stakeholders annually. The school counseling advisory council, comprised of community members and school personnel, generally agree upon the objectives of the career guidance curriculum at the beginning of the school year. If outcomes do not meet expectations set by the objectives, the advisory council can be helpful in determining why outcome targets were not reached and how the program plan might be altered in the future to meet objectives. Conversely, if projected outcomes were met then the advisory council can celebrate these findings and begin to plan new objectives for the following year (ASCA, 2012).

Other ways that the school counselor can make outcomes known is through marketing within the school and in the larger community. For example, one school counselor at an inner city school shared with the first author that she includes outcomes of the school counseling program in the morning announcements at her school when it seems appropriate to do so. She gave the example of the results of a career fair that over 90% of the ninth grade class attended. After the fair, nearly 100% of attendees were able to write down three careers that they had learned about during the fair that they would like to know more about. She also shared that increases in college admissions and commitment for seniors, increases in the number of students taking honors courses, and number of scholarships are things she reports to the local paper for publication each spring. School counselors may also want to give the results of career program evaluation in administrative team meetings, parent workshops, and faculty inservice days.

SUMMARY

In this chapter, we highlighted key aspects of career curriculum development. Creating curriculum interventions can be a complicated process for beginning school counselors and involves understanding and managing many pieces of information. Specifically, to effectively design career curriculum school counselors should review state and national standards and GLEs, write measurable and specific objectives, choose assessment methods, develop and deliver classroom lesson plans, and evaluate student outcomes.

···❯ Test Your Knowledge

1. Pretend to be an elementary school counselor. Write a rationale for why you should implement a grades P–5 career curriculum for your school. Make sure the rationale is no longer than one page.
2. Imagine you are a middle school counselor in a very diverse school. Your school is 35% African American, 35% Hispanic, 20% Asian, and 10% Caucasian. How might you include diversity in a classroom unit on personal values related to career exploration?
3. Explain how you might evaluate the following career objective for ninth grade, "At the completion of a career exploration unit, 80% of ninth grade students will be able to write a five-paragraph research essay on a career of their choice."

6

• • • • •

Career Education and Counseling for Grades P–1: Career Exposure

• • • • •

At a research university, in a graduate-level research course in education, students were asked by a guest lecturer "At what age should career counseling and education begin?" The students (who represented a wide range of fields including higher education, curriculum and instruction, and education leadership) voted and overwhelmingly said either late high school (junior and senior year) or in the first year of college. Out of a class of 23, only two of the graduate students indicated that elementary school was the appropriate time to begin such exploration. It was apparent that the majority of graduate students in the class knew little about the developmental nature of career growth for P–12 students. In this chapter, we explore the early elementary years and how career education can positively impact academic success and open postsecondary options, even for very young students.

CAREER DEVELOPMENT, COUNSELING, AND EDUCATION FOR PreK, KINDERGARTEN, AND FIRST GRADE

The American School Counselor Association's (ASCA's) National Model (2012) and federal initiatives such as the National Math and Science Initiative (2011) and the Obama Administration's Reauthorization of the Elementary and Secondary Schools Act (2010) all underscore the importance of career and college readiness for all students. Historically, attention to career development for students in PreK, kindergarten, and first grade has been minimal, yet studies show that young children can realistically understand careers and need career education in order to connect academics to the world of work. Development of career-related social and thinking skills (such as critical thinking and problem solving) begins early in life as well.

In this chapter, we use Gottfredson's career theory and Young's (1983) ecosystemic career development concepts to illustrate how school counselors can design practical and fun career development activities for PreK, K, and first grade students. Additionally, we explore stakeholder education related to career development for parents, teachers, and community partners. Using developmentally appropriate play techniques coupled with grade level expectations (GLEs) and student competencies, we examine how to effectively design and implement PreK, K, and first grade career activities for large-group guidance as well as grade-level activities.

DEVELOPMENTAL OVERVIEW

In order to effectively implement career education and counseling in PreK, K, and grade 1, it is important to consider the overall development of children at those grade levels. What follows is a general overview of child development and how each area of development connects to career growth. Please note that this overview is general and may not apply to every child.

Psychosocial and Socioemotional Development

According to Erikson (1963), children between the ages of 3 and 5 are in the psychosocial stage known as *initiative versus guilt*. During this time, the main psychosocial task is to actively explore one's environment and to develop a sense of control over physical surroundings. Therefore, children in this age group are very active, inquisitive, and, because of their natural curiosity (Sharf, 2006), love to play in the world of fantasy. They are beginning to engage with other children, although much of their play is still side-to-side rather than face-to-face play (particularly in PreK), and the major influence in the life of children in this age group is predominantly the family unit.

Around the transition period from kindergarten to first grade, children begin to enter the stage of *industry versus inferiority* (Erikson, 1963). The focus in this stage is on children learning and mastering academic tasks; students are continually learning new information and, particularly in today's educational environment, are tested to demonstrate their competence. Students who excel at tasks gain self-confidence while those who do not often develop feelings of inferiority (e.g., poor self-concept). These positive and negative feelings can greatly affect future career outcomes as well as overall self-esteem. Teachers and counselors may begin to notice some children in PreK, K, and first grade starting to have negative thoughts about themselves, having doubts about their likability or attractiveness, or worrying that they are not smart enough. Self-esteem can be built through helping children have success experiences and assisting them in recognizing their unique strengths.

During the early elementary years, two major feelings develop that contribute to socioemotional development: shame and guilt. Shame comes from feeling humiliated, while guilt comes from feeling badly about hurting another person (Belsky, 2007). While shame can foster unhealthy socioemotional development, guilt may be essential to ensuring that children learn that other peoples' feelings matter. Learning to care about the feelings of others, but not be consumed by focusing on others, is an important skill. Further, Belsky identified an orientation toward prosocial tendencies as an important part of socioemotional development. Prosocial behavior is described as "behavior intended to benefit another" (Eisenberg et al., 1999, p. 1360). Prosocial behaviors may include comforting others, using manners, sharing, engaging in cooperative work or play, exhibiting kindness, and displaying empathy for others (Belsky, 2007; Simmons & Sands-Dudelczyk, 1983) and are largely formed during early elementary years. In the context of career and college readiness, socioemotional maturity is a critical element for developing effective relationships in college and in the workplace.

One final socioemotional skill that is critical during this developmental period is emotional regulation (Belsky, 2007). Emotional regulation becomes possible as children gain self-awareness and self-control. According to Belsky, emotional regulation includes learning to manage feelings and deal appropriately with emotions—neither having externalizing (e.g., inappropriate outbursts, fighting, demanding, controlling behaviors, or acting out aggressively toward others) nor internalizing (e.g., timidity, self-consciousness, unmanageable anxiety) tendencies. Children with emotional regulatory capacities display balanced emotion that is appropriately expressed given their circumstances. So, a child with positive emotional regulation skills who falls down may cry but is consolable and, once comforted, resumes normal activities. Conversely, a child with poor emotional regulation skills who falls down may cry but may also get up and, in a fit of rage, hit others who are nearby or blame others for falling down. Emotional self-regulation is important for success in both college and career because of the need to get along with others in collaborative group work as well as deal with stress, anxiety, and conflict.

Cognitive Development

According to Jean Piaget (1977), children in PreK, K, and first grade are generally in the cognitive stage of development known as *preoperational thought*. During this stage, children have difficulty conceptualizing time (such as the future) and, therefore, may have difficulty projecting what their future lives may be like, including considering what careers they may want. This does not mean, however, that they can't think about and learn about careers.

Children in this stage generally do not display logical, linear thought and are often very egocentric. *Egocentrism* in regard to preoperational thought refers to the child's lack of understanding that other people have worldviews or perspectives that differ from their own (Belsky, 2007). Children at this age may display thought influenced by fantasy, or magical thinking, and can have some difficulty discerning what is real or not; children in preoperational thought literally believe that what they see is real (Belsky, 2007).

Learning for children at this stage of cognitive development requires that adults delivering instruction are excellent scaffolders, meaning that they break down content into smaller, more manageable pieces of information, give students lots of opportunities to practice what is learned in order to achieve mastery, and give students autonomy to direct some learning activities (Belsky, 2007). According to Vygotsky (1978), children use a working memory where they actively process information based on prior learning or discard information that is not necessary to remember. Adults can help children improve their memory capacities by incorporating activities that involve repetition and practice. These skills are highly necessary for future academic success.

Children can begin problem-based learning at this age and their natural curiosity lends to this type of learning. For example, students in one preschool class had a garden where they were growing carrots. A number of the students and a teacher noticed that some of the carrots were being eaten. The teacher had the class think about what kind of animal might eat carrots and how they could find out for sure who was eating the carrots. The class hypothesized that a rabbit was eating their carrots. They also had a parent agree to install a motion video camera that could film the culprit eating the carrots. They later discovered it was a raccoon! This kind of hands-on learning is ideal for young children.

Other considerations for addressing the learning needs of young children include using contextual learning strategies (e.g., using examples that are familiar to students) and providing interactive and experiential learning opportunities where students can manipulate and interact with objects and tap into their need for fantasy and creative play. Counselors can be most effective when they meet students where they are developmentally, starting with familiar concepts, then exposing them to new ideas through activities that allow them to discover. Overall, students at this age are very active learners. Career play is very appropriate and can easily be integrated in classroom career instruction. We will explore career play techniques later in this chapter.

Moral Development

According to Kohlberg (1981) most children in PreK, K, and first grade are in the preoperational stage of moral development and, therefore, judge actions as either right or wrong based on the consequences of the action. In short, if the person committing the action gets punished, then students in this stage of development would believe the action was wrong. Two forces of thought are predominant in preoperational moral development: 1) obedience and punishment characterized by deference and respect to authorities, and 2) self-interest–driven behavior characterized by behavior that benefits the self. For this reason, students at this age are impressionable and may show interest mainly in careers held by their parents, teachers, and other adults they want to please rather than based on career knowledge or exploration.

Students in grades PreK to grade 1 also are vulnerable to integrating judgments about careers based on the perspectives of family or other adults. Indeed, according to Kohlberg (1981), children in this developmental period have an orientation to obedience and make choices based on what is denoted as right and wrong from the authorities in their lives. It is very common for students at this age to tattle on their peers if they see them breaking a rule. Likewise, they may have very rigid beliefs about which careers are acceptable and which are not, particularly based on gender roles. They also might categorize careers as "good" or "bad"; for example, being a police officer may be perceived as a "good" career and being a sanitation worker may be perceived as a "bad" career based on judgments the students have internalized from their family or from gender and social status socialization.

Gender

In early elementary school, children's preoperational cognitive development leads to a tendency to categorize people, including by gender. In PreK, K, and grade 1, students have very concrete views of what men and women should look like, how they should act, and what roles are appropriate. Much of this comes from socialization in the family where children are often given sex-typed toys and their parents/guardians treat them in sex-typed ways. For example, girls may be given play dishes, a kitchen set, and a doll for gifts, whereas boys may receive tools, cars or trucks, and building blocks. This type of gender socialization can have a lasting impact throughout the lifespan (Ivey, Ivey, Myers, & Sweeney, 2005).

According to Belsky (2007), "once children understand which basic category (girl or boy) they belong in, they selectively attend to the activities of their own sex" (p. 193). By early elementary school, many students have begun to play with same-sex friends primarily, have received gender-type reinforcement from family members, and understand that their sex is a permanent characteristic (can't be changed by chance). These differences manifest in play and school through common behavior patterns; in general, girls are more collaborative while boys are more competitive, girls are usually calmer while boys experience greater excitability, and boys seek group dominance in play while girls display nurturance (Belsky, 2007). Finally, gender matters in career decision making for early elementary students. In the next section we review Gottfredson's theory and just how predominant sex typing is in the career development of children.

RELEVANT CAREER THEORY FOR PreK, K, AND FIRST GRADE STUDENTS: GOTTFREDSON AND YOUNG

Gottfredson's Theory of Circumscription and Compromise

Historically, school systems have introduced career development activities for students in high school. This approach is incredibly problematic, according to Gottfredson's (1981) theory, because children and adolescents have already been circumscribing (i.e., narrowing) their career options since early elementary school. Recent support for Gottfredson's theory came from a study of elementary children conducted by Auger, Blackhurst, and Wahl (2005), where they found that by fifth grade, many students had already circumscribed their career aspirations and self-limited their career options. Indeed, it appears that circumscription begins around the age of 6. This finding underscores the need to continually work on broadening students' understanding of career and existing postsecondary options throughout P–12 education. In this chapter we focus on Stage 1: *Orientation to Size and Power* and Stage 2: *Orientation to Sex Roles,* as these are the predominant stages of career development for children in grades PreK–1.

According to Sharf (2006), Gottfredson's Stage 1: *Orientation to Size and Power* refers to how children begin to understand that their world is different from the world of adults. They realize that there are limits to what they can do because of their size and power; for example, a child may see that his father owns a lawn care company where he has to run lawn equipment such as mowers, weed eaters, and edgers. The child realizes that the work his father does takes strength and height that the child does not have. So, although the child understands that the tools used for lawn care are part of the father's work, the child also believes that he is too small or weak to do that type of work.

As children get chronologically older (around the age of 6), they enter Stage 2: *Orientation to Sex Roles.* Once this occurs, they begin to develop a strong sense of sex-typing, which dictates which careers are tolerable for girls and which are tolerable for boys. This boundary can be very definitive, and adults must be intentional and deliberate in order to challenge sex-type assumptions. We will explore this stage more fully in the next chapter as it affects second and third graders comprehensively.

In spite of children's career assumptions, there is reason for optimism, according to Gottfredson (1981, 2002). Specifically, she notes that children can be encouraged to reconsider their career choices by being given formative new experiences that challenge career sex types. When school counselors understand how to do this effectively, they may increase student perceptions of possible career options.

Young's Career Concepts

As previously mentioned in Chapter 1, and according to the National Poverty Center (2011), in the United States one in five children under the age of 18 live in poverty. With this in mind, school counselors have to consider how the systems in which children live may affect their understanding of careers. Students living in poverty may have fewer opportunities for exploring academic interests or exposure to events and places that stimulate future career decision-making processes. For example, students living in poverty may not have access to museums, galleries, or travel. Young (1983) asserted that an ecosystemic approach to career development was critical, and this may be especially true for elementary school students, as their parents and teachers are so influential in their lives. Additionally, teachers and parents may not have received career education as young children and may be unsure of how or why they should help their early elementary school-aged children explore careers. Thus, considering how to engage teachers and parents within the scope of a comprehensive school counseling program to promote college and career readiness is important, and we will address this concern more fully later in this chapter. Beyond considering Gottfredson's and Young's work with small children, school counselors must also have an understanding of how to integrate play techniques in career education for elementary students.

PLAY TECHNIQUES AND CAREER DEVELOPMENT FOR P–1 STUDENTS

Play is the natural language of children and is the manner in which children communicate (Landreth, 1982). Play is used by children to explore and experiment; therefore, it is a critical learning tool and part of the process by which children can understand their own thoughts, feelings, ideas, and behaviors (Frank, 1982; McMahon, 1992). Play is a means for promoting formative cognitive development (Yawkey & Diantoniis, 1984). Further, McMahon (1992) contended that play may be one of the best learning mediums for children with learning difficulties or disabilities. Through the manipulation of play materials, all children resolve conflicts, practice new behaviors, and engage the world around them. Additionally, children use play to understand the functions of things in their environment (Caster, 1984). For instance, when playing with building blocks (such as Legos, Tinker Toys, or Lincoln Logs) children learn about building and construction. Similarly, children playing with tools and a tool bench become oriented to the use of those tools as they begin to explore how they are used in the real world (e.g., a hammer is used for pounding). Using play techniques to engage children can help adults in schools develop relationships through establishing mutual positive affect, reacting with warmth and empathy to the child, conveying caring and nurturance, and developing rapport through eye contact and verbal and nonverbal behaviors (Wettig, Franke, & Fjordbak, 2006). Therefore, play is a very functional approach for school counselors to use in teaching young children, particularly PreK, K, and first grade students, about career and real world success skills.

Some might ask if play therapy should be used by school counselors. And if so, what kinds of play? Structured? Guided? Unstructured? According to Nelson (1982), there are many uses of play in therapy, yet not all types of play therapy may be appropriate for elementary school settings due to the nature of the environment and the intended use in learning. For example, play therapy has been used in the treatment of severe sexual abuse for young children, but this type of counseling is most likely out of the scope of competence of school counselors and an inappropriate use of service delivery time; therefore, this type of play therapy should be referred to a specialist (ASCA, 2012). For the purposes of this chapter we are focusing on large-group, structured, and directed play in PreK to first grade classrooms for the purpose of engaging students to learn about careers. Although many elementary school counselors may have received some training in play techniques in their graduate programs, they are not required to be registered play therapists and most do not have advanced training in play therapy techniques. Thus, the interventions we discuss in the following require little specific training and could be reasonably and ethically initiated by most school counselors. We will review some basic principles of play as they relate to career exploration.

The Nature of Play and Learning. According to McMahon (1992), play allows children to take risks through imagination, a key benefit of the fantasy nature of play. In terms of career, children are allowed to explore possibilities through the creativity and autonomy afforded in play in spite of the realities in which they live. Applied to careers, children can explore the world of an astronaut (space toys), an archeologist (dinosaurs and digging), or a safari guide (toy animals and vehicles) even if these opportunities are not accessible through their home or immediate surroundings. Equally important, during play children can step out of expected gender roles; girls can be construction workers and boys can learn to be cooks and caregivers. This exact realm of play, fantasy and exploration, may be the initial way in which career circumscription (Gottfredson, 1981) might be combatted for very young children (grades PreK–1). McMahon (1992) also pointed out that play comes without the risks associated with the real world; in terms of play and career exploration in schools, children can be or do anything without being told "you are not capable of that." They can play the role of a doctor, a scientist, or the president without the reminders of social stigma, gender roles, or low social expectations. Truly, children may be free to explore the careers they wish to explore if school counselors and teachers create the expectation that play is autonomous. Explorative play can be integrated in the classroom through the use of career centers where students have access to dress-up and play items associated with careers. Students can visit these centers when they have completed their classwork and during structured breaks.

Play can also be integrated in the core counseling curriculum. Ericksonian play therapy (named after Milton Erickson) uses an approach that may be particularly helpful in schools due to the limited amount of time the school counselor has in each classroom. In the Ericksonian approach, two layers of communication are occurring, known as parallel communication or *refraction* (Marvasti, 1997). We will use puppets as the medium to illustrate the concept. In this type of play, the counselor introduces children to a metaphorical problem similar to the child's own problem or issue needing resolution. In regard to career, in order to promote career awareness and decision making self-efficacy, a school counselor may introduce a puppet to children during a classroom lesson. In the following case, this activity is used at the culmination of a classroom unit on careers to help students with application of prior knowledge. The puppet's dilemma is that she doesn't know about careers and so the students will be teaching the puppet what they have learned and will help the puppet make career decisions. In doing so, the students' learning will be reinforced, resolving confusion about careers and career decision making. Exhibit 6.1 gives an example of the use of puppets as a play technique with a group of kindergarten students.

EXHIBIT 6.1
An Example of Refraction in a Kindergarten
Classroom Career Lesson

Counselor: Okay, students, today I have a very special guest for you to meet. Her name is Sally. (Counselor holds up puppet.) Oh, no! Sally looks sad. (Puppet is slouching, looking down.) Sally, what's wrong?

Puppet: In my class my teacher said we are going to be learning about careers, but I don't know what a career is.

Counselor: Sally, the students in this class have also been learning about careers. Maybe the students would like to help you. Students, would you like to help Sally? (Students say yes—loudly.)

Puppet: Oh, thank you so much. (Sally looks up.)

Counselor: Great. Okay, who can tell Sally what a career is?

Student 1: It's like something you want to do when you grow up. Kind of like work only you plan to do it.

Counselor: Thank you, something you do when you grow up, something planned.

(continued)

EXHIBITS 6.1
An Example of Refraction in a Kindergarten
Classroom Career Lesson (Continued)

Student 2: And you are trained to do something. You might go to college or be trained by someone to do a career.

Student 3: Ummm . . . my dad . . . works in an office. And my mom works at a school as a teacher. That is their careers.

Student 4: It's work you like to do.

Counselor: Thank you all. Sally, does that help?

Sally: I think I understand that career is something that a person chooses and plans to do, it requires training beyond school, and it is something that a person likes and wants to do. Is that right?

Students: Yes!

Sally: But I don't know what I want to be when I grow up! I don't even know what choices I have!

Counselor: Well, Sally, that's okay. Many girls and boys are unsure of what they want to be when they grow up. Students, how many of you are unsure of what you want to be? (Some students raise hands.)

Puppet: Golly! I thought I was the only one!

Counselor: Students, what have we discussed about careers that might help Sally?

Student Responses: Careers in your neighborhood.

Counselor: Good answer! Yes, we talked about Community Helpers. What were some examples of community helpers?

Student Responses: Mail carrier, fire fighter, police officer, day care worker.

Counselor: Well these students are great listeners, Sally, because we did talk about all of those. What other types of career things have we talked about this year?

Students: Your family's careers. What your mom or your granny or your uncles and people like that do . . . what their career is. We also talked about our likes and dislikes.

Counselor: Oh my! I can tell you all have been really listening. I definitely think we can help. Sally, let's start by talking about the careers you see in your neighborhood . . .

By helping the puppet (Sally), students are integrating and applying prior career learning and are also beginning to use the career language they are developing (Pellegrini, 1984). The material the students suggest to the counselor to help Sally solidifies salient information they have acquired and demonstrates that they are internally thinking through developmentally appropriate strategies for career decision making, a skill they are just starting to learn and a key piece of developing career maturity. Through a fun and engaging activity, the counselor is helping the students use what they know to resolve a parallel conflict.

Counselors also can use play in early childhood education to allow students to explore a career. An example of this happened when a group of PreK teachers and the school counselor took PreK students to the local fire department for a tour and fire safety tips at the end of a unit on community helpers. The students were all given plastic fire safety helmets and honorary firefighter badges. The children were given 20 minutes of play time in the field area beside the fire house to play firefighters with the real firefighters. Through the use of an obstacle course and their new gear, the students were guided through a simulated fire field where they got the chance to experience the role of a firefighter, regardless of gender. A digital photograph of each child was taken and printed at school on a sheet of paper that said: "What I learned about firefighters." Each child was assisted by his or her teacher and teacher's aide in writing a sentence about what they learned at the firehouse. In this way, students were integrating imitative role play (playing the firefighter) and symbolic meaning (words to describe what they learned) in order to continue to develop a lexicon for career with a conscious understanding of career roles (Pellegrini, 1984). At the end of the day each child was sent home with a fire safety coloring and workbook for their families with instructions for parents about talking to their child about fire safety in their home, how to call 911, and community helper careers.

THE SCHOOL COUNSELOR AND CORE COUNSELING CURRICULUM

During PreK, K, and first grade there are some essential career, academic, and personal social skills that are essential to postsecondary success. Most importantly, many students may not know anything about what careers are or even have a language to discuss careers in PreK. The core counseling curriculum should focus on the major tasks of beginning to understand career. Specifically, by the end of first grade, students should be able to: 1) recognize careers and how they are different from jobs, 2) be able to identify community helpers, 3) be able to use career language, 4) demonstrate positive attitudes toward self, others, school opportunities, and feelings of competence, and 5) be able to articulate likes and dislikes (Missouri Center for Career Education, 2006).

Additionally, when students have been given opportunities to learn about careers in PreK and kindergarten, they are often ready to learn about tools of the trade for careers. For example, students can start to recognize that doctors use stethoscopes, firefighters use a water hose, musicians use instruments and sheet music, and carpenters use hammers and saws. By the end of first grade they can understand that people use different tools to perform specific work, that work occurs in a variety of locations, and that various types of occupations require different clothes (i.e., a nurse wears scrubs).

In developing the career counseling curriculum, school counselors should consider several pieces of information including ASCA Student Standards (ASCA, 2004), grade level expectations (GLEs), and needs assessment and critical data for the population at the specific school where they work. To begin, ASCA delineates the standards for student competence in the area of career; that is, the knowledge, skills, and awareness students need to competently explore, prepare for, and choose a career path. GLEs are used to help counselors develop curricula by spelling out the sequential and developmental tasks for each grade. As noted in Chapter 5, the Missouri Center for Career Education (2006) has published GLEs that counselors can use in designing a career curriculum. Table 6.1 provides the Missouri GLEs for kindergarten and first grade.

TABLE 6.1 Missouri Career GLEs for Kindergarten and First Grade

Concept	Kindergarten	First Grade
Integration of Self-Knowledge Into Life and Career Plans	Identify likes and dislikes at home and school.	Identify strengths and interests at home and school.
Adaptations to World of Work Changes	Identify workers in the school and in families related to the six career paths.	Identify workers in the local community related to the six career paths
Respect for All Work	Recognize that all work is important.	Explain the importance of jobs in the family and school.
Career Decision Making	Identify roles and responsibilities of family members in the world of work.	Identify and compare roles and responsibilities of workers within the school.
Education and Career Requirements	Identify the skills family members use in their work.	Identify the skills needed by workers in the school.
Personal Skills for Job Success	Identify personal and ethical skills needed to work cooperatively with others in a group at school.	Identify and develop personal, ethical, and work habit skills needed for school success.
Job-Seeking Skills	Identify helper jobs that are available in the classroom.	Understand how helper jobs are assigned in the classroom.

Based on the Missouri Center for Career Education (2006).

Helping students achieve these major tasks is critical to early career development and should be guided by the school counselor who has expertise in career development. As noted in Chapter 5, curriculum development is a critical role for school counselors and writing lesson plans is an important task.

It is important that school counselors consider how they evaluate student learning outcomes and be flexible because of early elementary students' level of reading comprehension. Often counselors must be creative to ensure that they are accurately evaluating student knowledge in a developmentally appropriate way. With early elementary students, counselors may want to consider having students use matching and other recognition activities. For instance, as previously mentioned, by the end of first grade students can realistically understand the tools that go with specific occupations. Imagine that a school counselor had written the following outcome objective for a lesson on "Tools of the Trade" using the ABCD method highlighted in Chapter 5: *At the completion of this lesson, 80% of first grade students will be able to accurately match tools to specific occupations four out of five times.* For the lesson, the school counselor has 30 toy tools (e.g., plastic hammer). After explaining tools of the trade, the school counselor hangs pictures of careers around the room. Students are placed in dyads and are given two or three "tools" per dyad. They are asked to place their tools by the careers they match. Next, the school counselor and the students discuss each picture, which tools match each picture, and how the tools are used in each specific career. After the lesson the school counselor could give the students a worksheet with five pictures of occupations being performed (i.e., teacher, firefighter, doctor, construction worker, artist). Opposite of the occupations are pictures of five instruments (i.e., hammer, water hose, paint palette, stethoscope, chalk). Students are asked to draw a line from the "tool" to the matching career. The school counselor is assessing whether or not 80% of students can get four out of five correct to evaluate student learning for this activity.

Delivering the core counseling curriculum is a critical role for elementary school counselors. However, implementing the career curriculum in P–12 schools is not the responsibility solely of the school counselor. In the following we discuss the important roles that various stakeholders play in students' career development.

IMPORTANCE OF STAKEHOLDERS

Parents/guardians, extended family members, and other adults are highly influential in the lives of PreK, K, and first grade students. Helping stakeholders develop awareness and knowledge of careers can foster positive communication and interaction about careers between adults and kids. Through collaboration and consultation, providing faculty inservice training, offering parent workshops, and developing a comprehensive career curriculum, school counselors are well positioned to assist stakeholders in becoming more aware of the needs of their children/students as well as the roles they all can play in students' career development.

Stopping the Dream Squasher

Adults often have the inclination to promote what they perceive to be realistic career options for children rather than allowing kids to simply explore. In other words, they may intervene to stop students from imagining or discussing careers that they perceive as being difficult to attain or undesirable in some way. For example, the first author was at a family's home when their 6-year-old son brought out a play guitar and began strumming and screaming "I'm a rock star!!! Yeah, yeah, yeah . . . I'm a rock star!!!" The father laughed and said, "I hope not, that means you'll be starving or eating cans of ravioli for the rest of your life." Most of the adults in the room laughed at the father's joking cliché about the starving artist. However, it is important for parents to realize that a natural interest their child may have could be linked to many careers, and that within career clusters there may be many lucrative careers and opportunities for gainful employment. Although the child in this example may not have had a true aspiration to be a rock star (he was simply playing at the time), there is room to discuss careers even in the context of ordinary play. For example, careers in the music industry go well beyond rock star to include music producers, technicians, talent scouts, signing agents for record labels, videographers, promoters, and disc jockeys, among others. Helping parents expand their vocabulary and understanding of careers gives them a common language to discuss careers with their children. Also, providing concrete examples of the subtle and not-so-subtle ways they might squash their children's dreams may encourage them to monitor their reactions.

A similar scenario happened with the first author (an elementary school counselor at the time) and a first grade teacher. The teacher had students in her classroom write down on a piece of paper what they wanted to be when they grew up. Five of the boys in the class wrote down "football player" (it may be contextually important to note that this occurred the week of the Super Bowl). The teacher was frustrated and began to tell kids what a poor career choice football is and how most people don't become professional athletes. The teacher came to the counselor later and shared her frustration and exasperation about what she perceived to be poor choices. The first author then encouraged the teacher to help students explore related areas of work to professional sports, including sports journalists, reporters, physical therapists, marketers, trainers, coaches, and others. By assisting the teacher in understanding how to link students' interests with a broader range of career opportunities, the author was hopefully able to intervene against future incidents of dream squashing!

Working With Teachers to Integrate Careers in Classroom Curriculum

Teachers play an integral role in student academic and career development. To begin, teachers influence students' understanding of how classroom instruction relates to careers and the world of work, provide meaningful learning opportunities for students both in and out of the classroom, and influence the positive work habits and attitudes students develop (Curry, Belser, & Binns, 2013). Yet, many teachers may not have received training in how to integrate career content into their existing curriculum, so we begin by discussing career faculty inservice for early elementary teachers.

Faculty inservice for early elementary teachers. When teachers are asked to integrate career information in the education curriculum, they may feel hesitant due to the overwhelming demands placed on them already from high stakes testing and other measures of accountability. However, when school counselors demonstrate that integrating careers is a natural adjunct to the existing curriculum and does not require an extraordinary amount of time, teachers may be more open. Illustrating the infusion of careers for teachers is critical and can be done through faculty inservice programs, team meetings, or one-on-one consultations. Sample faculty inservice activities could include: how to find quality guest speakers for career development, finding out about careers through technology (e.g., demonstrating *O-Net* and the *Occupational Outlook Handbook* online), connecting their content to the world of work, or providing information about science, technology, engineering, and mathematics (STEM) careers and STEM content, and so forth.

Developing positive work habits and work attitudes. Beyond assisting teachers with how to integrate career information within the academic curriculum, school counselors can help teachers emphasize workplace success skills. Work habits and work attitudes begin to develop very early in life. These habits include organization, community and social responsibility, cooperation, sharing, appropriate participation, and emotional self-regulation. Students can learn to enjoy and appreciate the importance of work and community through classroom interactions. One kindergarten teacher described how she worked to promote community and social responsibility in her classroom. She stated that she had weekly assignments for each child (such as being line leader, pushing chairs in under desks, collecting papers, and organizing materials) and that these responsibilities allowed each child to try a different role each week while always contributing to the organization of the classroom.

Meaningful academic opportunities that promote careers. Beginning early in their school careers, students need to understand how the content they are learning is related to the world of work. By giving students opportunities to practice hands-on learning, teachers promote student understanding of what they can do with what they are learning. School counselors should encourage teachers to do this and explain why it is helpful. One important way to do this is to develop community partnerships so that students have career development support from professionals and workers in the community. For example, at one elementary school, the school counselor and first grade teaching team collaborated on a science unit on weather. The students learned about weather patterns, seasonal changes, temperature readings, and precipitation. At the end of the unit the school counselor arranged for a field trip to the local news channel (community partner) where students met a meteorologist and learned about hurricanes. Later, when they came back to school, they drew weather pictures and set up their own weather lab in the classroom where they did daily precipitation and temperature readings, noted the weather patterns and changes, and used the Internet to record the 3-day weather outlook. Each morning, one student played weather reporter and gave the results to the class, giving each child a chance to practice the role of meteorologist. Exhibit 6.2 gives another example of an activity that links academic content and career education.

EXHIBIT 6.2
Sample Activity to Connect Academic Content
and Career Learning Opportunity

During a health sciences unit, the kindergarten classes at Great Oaks Primary were given information on personal hygiene (e.g., the importance of proper handwashing). As one of the unit lessons, the kindergarten teachers and school counselor collaborated to have a dentist and a dental hygienist (community partners) come to the school to talk about the importance of brushing and flossing teeth. The dentist brought models of human teeth and demonstrated the correct way to brush teeth and the students practiced brushing the models' teeth using tooth brushes provided by the dentist. During the presentation the dentist and dental hygienist explained what they do each day at work. They described how they work together and what their individual roles are when a patient comes for a visit; additionally, they showed the students the types of tools they use to do their jobs. They also told the students what they can expect if they come to the dentist to get their teeth cleaned. At the end of the day each students was given a bag containing a coloring book about going to the dentist, a letter home to parents about what they had learned about oral hygiene and dental careers, a small tube of toothpaste, a child-size toothbrush, and a sample of dental floss.

Parent Engagement Activities

As previously mentioned, parents are a critical component of student career development. Fortunately, there are many ways to engage parents in career development activities in the early elementary years. In this section, we focus on practical strategies for including parents and assisting them in career education and curriculum, including communicating with parents about careers, financial literacy training, and school-based activities that promote learning and career.

Communicating with parents about careers. Developing a culture of career and college readiness in the school begins with including parents. Communicating about careers and suggesting home-based strategies for career development is a crucial role for school counselors. A comprehensive approach to disseminating this type of information may be best for communicating with parents. For example, many school counselors have websites, but given the current poverty and unemployment rates in the country, a substantial number of parents may not have a computer or Internet access. Those who don't may miss out on important information if it is only disseminated online. Therefore, including a career corner in the school's newsletter, asking local newspapers and news reporters to highlight career and college readiness events, and advertising through parent–teacher associations and parent–teacher conferences are all helpful ways of reaching out to ensure information is accessible to all parents. School counselors should not underestimate the power of using news media; indeed, the local news and newspaper often enjoy running stories about positive things happening in the community.

Financial literacy training. Although many states have begun to give college tuition waivers through various programs to promote postsecondary entrance and attendance, not everyone qualifies for those programs. Also, financial literacy is crucial for children's postsecondary success, whether they attend college or not. Learning to manage a budget, save money, and plan for financial difficulties are crucial skills to lifelong financial health and stability. Many parents may be in need of information either to manage their own finances, to help teach their children how to manage money, or to know what options they have to save for their children's future. As an outreach activity, schools can partner with a local bank or credit union to offer free educational workshops on all of those topics.

At one elementary school the school counselor has an account manager from a local credit union speak at a parent night once a year. The account manager also comes to the school once per semester and parents can schedule time to talk one-on-one during that time about long-term college savings plans. By conveying the importance of thinking and planning ahead, school counselors may help families realize their children can have more opportunities than they initially thought. During one such meeting, a family shared a unique strategy for saving money. The family was going through a lot of financial difficulty (father lost his job) and the family was living on just the mother's income. So, each week, the parents had their children cut coupons from the newspaper, and for each coupon used, the family put the saved money into a college fund. So even though their income was limited, the parents continued to save money for college. Opportunities such as parent workshops can allow families to share their creative ideas for saving.

Including parents in school-based career learning opportunities. Just as students need a common language to discuss careers, helping parents develop the language of careers can promote career communication at home. Offering a workshop on the importance of career development would allow school counselors to provide parents with relevant information and language. Moreover, by creating opportunities for parents to participate in learning activities with their children, school counselors and teachers can model how to integrate career information into learning activities and can deliver important career development concepts to both children and their parents. Exhibit 6.3 provides a sample parent–student activity that illustrates a way to promote student learning and career development.

EXHIBIT 6.3
Sample First Grader–Parent Activity

At Windy Hills Elementary, the first grade teaching team developed a classroom unit on plant science. Students learned about the differences between flowers, plants, vegetables, and trees. They also learned about the conditions plants need to live: soil with nutrients, water, and sunlight.

At the end of the unit, parents were invited to participate with their children in a plant science night at the school. Funding for the night was provided by a local Lowe's Home Improvement store (community partner) and the Parent–Teacher Association at Windy Hills. Parents and children first met in their child's classroom for a 10-minute review on plant science. Afterward, each family was asked to go out into the school yard and pick five different leaves. They brought the leaves to the gym where tables were set up so that the leaves could be sorted by categories: oak, palm, maple, grass, and so on. Students learned that all trees have unique leaves. At each table a teacher or teacher's aide helped them categorize their leaves and talked about what the tree does for the leaf and what the leaf does for the tree.

After the leaf collection and category activity, parents and students sat in the bleachers as the school counselor showed a quick video with pictures and descriptions of careers related to plants (gardener, lawn care worker, greens keeper, farmer, and horticulturist). Parents and

(continued)

EXHIBIT 6.3 *(Continued)*

children then went to the cafeteria where displays were set up. The displays were designed by and set up by fifth grade students. Each display had a picture of a type of plant and a career. For example, one display had a picture of a farmer with a wheat crop. Each child who visited that display received a wheat cracker. The next display had a farmer with an orchard, and each child visiting received a slice of apple. The next was a picture of farm hands picking walnuts (students each got a walnut to taste). In all, 30 displays that demonstrated a plant and a plant career were set up. Not all had food; for example, the greens keeper display had a miniature golf hole (borrowed from a local mini golf course!).

At the end of the night, courtesy of Lowe's Home Improvement store, each student and parent were given a small pack of flower seeds and a small plastic pot. Instructions were given on how to grow them, and families were sent home to begin their own plant science experiment. This family science night did not cost the school or families any money and was well received by all who attended.

SUMMARY

In this chapter we have highlighted career development and education opportunities specifically for PreK, K, and first grade students. As elaborated, students in this age group are beginning to explore the world around them through play and interaction with other students, teachers, parents, and counselors. This is an essential time to begin career development, as students are influenced by their social environments and are developing their own conceptions of their strengths and limitations applied to careers. In particular, we reviewed Gottfredson's first two career development stages and examined the integration of play techniques in career curriculum. We continue to look at the role of the school counselor and the development of comprehensive career training in the next chapter with a focus on second and third grade.

···❯ Test Your Knowledge

1. What is refraction?
2. In what ways have you seen children play out careers?
3. What keeps parents or teachers from helping PreK to grade 1 children explore careers?

7

•••••

Career Education and Counseling for Grades 2 and 3: Career Play and Exploration

•••••

Students in second and third grade are naturally inquisitive, energetic, and are developing their own unique personalities, interests, and attitudes. However, school counselors may be unsure of how to help students at this age develop career-related skills and connect academics to the world of work. Therefore, it is critical to remember that the objective of career exploration in elementary schools is to expand student options rather than to push students to make forgone conclusions that limit their career choices (Herr, Cramer, & Niles, 2004). We begin this chapter by highlighting the unique developmental aspects of middle childhood.

DEVELOPMENTAL OVERVIEW

The areas of physical, psychosocial, social, cognitive, and cultural development have a large impact on students' career development and understanding of the world of work. As with early childhood development, in middle childhood context matters, and systems influences should be taken into consideration. Specifically, the family continues to play a primary role in influencing the exploration of options for both college and career (Herr et al., 2004). In this section we explore developmental milestones of middle childhood as they influence career growth, but wish to note that although there are general patterns of development, children progress at their own pace. We also acknowledge that many factors that are beyond the scope of this chapter (e.g., chronic anxiety, learning disabilities, mental health concerns) could emerge that would affect students' development.

Physical Development

Children in second and third grade are generally between the ages of 7 and 9, and these are unique ages in regard to physical development, particularly as it relates to self-concept. Specifically, by the time children get to second grade, they generally have highly developed motor skills. There are two types of motor skills: gross and fine. *Gross motor skills* involve large muscle movements (e.g., running, jumping, climbing) and are necessary for athletic success in most sports. *Fine motor skills* involve small, coordinated movements necessary for painting, coloring within lines, printing, and writing in cursive (Belsky, 2007), and lend to artistic endeavors. These skills become important to self-concept because they affect student success in sports and art, two socially valued skill sets. Because students in this age group can compare and contrast their skills with other children, they may feel insufficient or insecure when they assess their skills to be below those of their peers, especially if the lack of skill has a social consequence. For example, students with poor motor skills may lack athletic talent and may not be chosen (or may be chosen last) to participate in sports teams.

Moreover, differences in physical development and skills become apparent in relation to academic course work as well as in ancillary classes such as physical education and art. Students who excel in these areas may experience significant gains in academic self-concept while those who fall behind may suffer from lower self-concept. Their self-concept, in turn, may impact students' willingness to put forth effort in related future endeavors. Thus, a student who is unsuccessful at climbing a rope in gym class may also feel anxious about trying other activities that involve arm strength (pull ups, push ups, etc.) due to self-consciousness at the prospect of failing the physical task in front of others.

Although this may not seem like a significant concern to adults, it is crucial to consider how these types of day-to-day accomplishments or lack thereof, impact students' self-concept, particularly with regard to psychosocial development (see more on this in the following section). Further, students may receive affirmation or support from adults for various skills that may then influence their self-concept related to tasks where those skills are utilized. For instance, a second grader told the first author, "I'm really good at art." The author asked the student, "What does it mean to be 'really good at art'?" The student replied, "My mom says I'm good at it and she hangs up my pictures at home."

Psychosocial and Social Development

Students in second and third grade are most likely in Erikson's (1963) stage of psychosocial development known as *industry versus inferiority*, which generally begins around the age of 6 and ends around the age of 12. During this stage, the main task is for the children to develop a sense of accomplishment through competence in academics and other socially valued activities (depending on the context, these could include sports, art, and music). Students who are successful gain confidence, positive academic self-concept, and the support and encouragement of adults. As a result, they may be more open and curious about career exploration as future options may seem more attainable (Niles & Harris-Bowlsby, 2009). Children who don't develop competence in valued activities begin to have a sense of inferiority and feelings of doubt about their abilities. They may also experience social humiliation, alienation, and lower academic self-concept.

Two critical developments can occur at this stage. The first development is *task attempt*. Students who experience a sense of accomplishment and industry may continue to attempt new tasks, including tasks they are unfamiliar with or those they fear they may not successfully complete. The opposite may occur for students who don't have a sense of accomplishment or an expectation of being successful. For example, a second grade teacher was frustrated by a student who sat day-after-day without doing any work in class. No matter how much encouragement the teacher provided, the student didn't try. The teacher referred the student to the school counselor. When asked why he didn't do his class work the student shrugged and stated, "I'm dumb. I don't know how." The student believed he could not be successful and, therefore, it was pointless to even try; he had resigned himself to failure.

Children who internalize their failures can develop learned helplessness, a condition where they believe that they are absolutely helpless to overcome a situation (such as academic difficulties). Learned helplessness leads to low task attempt, as students believe there is no point in even trying (Belsky, 2007). The primary way to combat learned helplessness is to give children opportunities for efficacy building through small, planned accomplishments (Bandura, 1986).

The second key development at this age is *internal motivation*. As students begin to develop positive feelings of personal accomplishment and competence, they require fewer external motivators. Although many schools have incentive programs such as Accelerated Reader programs, where students can earn prizes for reading books, students actually need fewer incentives as they become successful and gain confidence in their abilities.

Social tasks second and third graders are developing include: 1) an understanding of social norms, 2) complex, collaborative play, 3) friendships based on trust and emotional support, and 4) an understanding of how to navigate conflict. All of these social skills are critical to building a foundation of future workplace social skills such as collaboration, conflict resolution, and appropriate boundaries for social versus workplace conduct. In addition, children ages 7 to 9 need to be able to pick up on social cues (e.g., when it is appropriate to laugh, the normal cadence of a conversation, sharing, taking turns, etc.). Students who have trouble with social norms may act immature for their age, use inappropriate humor, monopolize conversation or play, and be bossy or overly aggressive.

Regarding future career and workplace relationships, the middle childhood tasks of developing friendships based on trust and support and learning to deal with conflict are critical tasks. Children in second and third grade often form secret clubs or groups where they have a password or secret handshake and club information. These kinds of activities are attempts to socially organize, share secrets, build trust, and foster support; all of these skills are essential to navigating workplace social structures. However, although developmentally appropriate, these kinds of activities can cause hurt feelings for children who are excluded and lead to feelings of low self-worth. Additionally, complex play can lead to more conflicts and arguments as children have to learn to navigate roles within the social structure of play groups. Although it is tempting for adults to become involved in resolving these issues, it is important to note that students need the opportunity to develop and practice conflict resolution skills that they will put to use in their future roles in the workplace. We explore these in depth later in this chapter.

Finally, play also changes at this time as children become more collaborative and their play begins to resemble complex social functions. One example is that children need to learn to lose games with grace. Children who cannot do this may become aggressive (sore loser) or may begin to cheat in order to win. Learning to lose without compromising one's self-esteem or blaming others is an important social development. More so, students need to be able to learn from their mistakes and improve in future endeavors, and this is an important aspect of future career success (e.g., how to accept and integrate feedback).

Cognitive Development

Although students in second and third grade may still be in the stage known as *preoperations* (see Chapter 6), they are likely transitioning to the *concrete operations* stage of cognitive development (Piaget, 1977). Students may still exhibit egocentrism and may continue to display thought that is largely influenced by fantasy and magical thinking (Belsky, 2007). However, in second or third grade, concrete thinking begins to emerge as children develop a more realistic understanding of the world. One task that children can perform in the concrete operations stage is *reversibility*, or an understanding that the stages of the problem-solving process can be worked backward, or in the opposite direction. For example, during a maze activity with a third grade class, the first author noticed that some of the children worked the maze from the end point backward to the beginning point. This skill is an essential foundation of future problem-solving work. When it comes to tasks of conservation, children in concrete operations can *decenter*, or focus on the whole picture and multiple aspects of a problem, rather than focusing on one small detail at a time (Belsky, 2007). This ability sets the stage for students to develop more complex skills needed in the workforce.

Other important cognitive skills that students begin to develop include *class inclusion*, the ability to understand that a category can include multiple subcategories, and *seriation*, or the ability to group objects based on some type of principle or characteristic (Piaget, 1965). For example, a second grade child might group a bunch of toy animals by places where these animals would live in the wild (e.g., ocean, jungle, the desert). These two cognitive skills are especially useful in career education in middle childhood as students begin to understand the relationships between specific careers and the common characteristics of careers in a career cluster.

Students in the early stages of concrete operations are becoming more complex in their understanding of patterns, measurements, and the transformation of various materials (liquids, solids, gases). For example, in middle childhood most kids understand that water is a liquid, ice is a solid, and steam is a gas, but that the chemical properties of the substance are the same (H_2O). During this stage, students begin to practice new behaviors for academic success, including the use of executive functions—actions used to promote memory. Examples include 1) rehearsing information (children may repeat material in order to retain it) such as through the use of flash cards or via oral recitation of vocabulary words and songs to remember facts, 2) demonstrating selective attention or a focus on relevant detail, 3) practicing self-control, such as controlling the impulse to shout out an answer in class, and 4) organizing through anticipation (e.g., a student determining what materials he will need for a class project) (Belsky, 2007). All of these skills are critical for academic success even in postsecondary institutions.

Most importantly, children in concrete operations (Piaget, 1977) gain self-awareness (Harter, 1999), which affects how they perceive themselves in relation to others and the ideals set by society. This self-awareness greatly contributes to psychosocial development in the stage of *industry versus inferiority* (Erikson, 1963), as they compare their successes, or lack thereof, with their peers. The development of all of these skills is critical for academic success and, subsequently, career success, as these skills will be useful for understanding and completing job-related tasks in the future. Students who struggle to develop these skills may need to receive remediation through the school counselor or teachers through services such as study skills groups.

Gender and Culture

Gender and culture begin to exert a stronger influence in middle childhood as children begin taking greater notice of things like media, social class, and race. These influences begin to shape and impact students' career growth and development. For example, students in second and third grade may circumscribe their career aspirations and expectations based on cultural contexts and restrictive, negative stereotypes (Herr et al., 2004). We covered culture and gender in Chapter 3 but wish to reiterate that influences from both highly impact students in middle childhood in regard to career development. Specifically, even when barriers to postsecondary success are removed for marginalized groups, the internalization of discriminatory and prejudicial realities can manifest as self-limiting, a condition the theorist Bourdieu termed "habitus" (Connolly, 1998, p. 17). In other words, negative, lived experiences shape our future expectations and behaviors even when circumstances of our social world change and permit more positive outcomes (Connolly, 1998).

RELEVANT CAREER THEORY

As previously mentioned in Chapters 1 and 6, an ecological perspective (Bronfenbrenner, 1979) of children's career development takes into consideration the developing individual within multiple contexts. In this section we review theoretical concepts that are relevant to career counseling and education for second and third grade students. Both theories we review herein propound significant ecological frameworks.

Bourdieu

In middle childhood, the impact of culture greatly influences career development. The theorist Bourdieu (1977) highlights three major concepts that should be considered when conceptualizing student career growth and development within systems contexts: habitus, field, and capital. As previously mentioned, *habitus* refers to the internalization of experiences that shape our future beliefs and actions. In regard to culture, habitus can refer to the internalization of social discourse, prejudice, discrimination, and oppression about race, gender, sexual orientation, religion, and other individual characteristics. Specifically, these internalized experiences become habitualized thoughts and behaviors (Connolly, 1998). When it comes to careers, children can habituate low social expectations for postsecondary academic and career success.

   The term *capital* is used by Bourdieu to describe the limited goods and resources of a society and how they are distributed based on social status, social relationships, and dominant discourse (Connolly, 1998). Bourdieu (1977) described four types of capital: 1) economic or financial, 2) cultural, referring to the legitimacy of a person's knowledge or behavior, 3) social, referring to resources gained through significant connections with others, and 4) symbolic, referring to a person's prestige. All four of these relate to career development. For example, social capital can influence an individual's ability to gain entrance into prestigious schools or programs, or to gain highly competitive employment through networking (i.e., it's not what you know, it's who you know). Although capital largely is a result of the culture and family to which an individual is born, some capital can be attributed to certain individual characteristics. For example, females who fit social ideals for beauty (thin, attractive) may gain capital. Likewise, males who fit social ideas for athleticism may also gain capital. Children begin early in life to recognize signs that they do or do not have capital, and they begin to attempt and struggle to gain capital—part of the habitus process.

The term *field* is used by Bourdieu (1977) to describe the context in which capital occurs. Specifically, something that is highly socially valued in one context may not be in another. For example, traditional and socially valued feminine characteristics (e.g., having a sense of style) may make a girl popular among other girls. However, boys displaying the same characteristic, stylishness, may become ostracized by other boys. Another example of an attribute that may be context specific is a personal sense of humor.

These three terms—habitus, capital, and field—are important for understanding academic and career development. Connolly (1998) noted that schools are a type of field and that what constitutes capital within different school fields varies, particularly in regard to masculine and feminine characteristics. So while in one school field it may be highly socially valued for individuals to be able to read music and play an instrument, in other school fields individuals may not gain, or could even lose, capital for such skills.

It can be difficult for students to appreciate that the academic or career activities they are engaging in will only increase their capital if those activities are within the realm of what is deemed socially desirable in the contexts in which they live. What is most notable in regard to student development in second and third grade is that much of the focus on capital comes from meeting the requirements of socialized gender roles (see the following discussion of Gottfredson's theory). Therefore, combatting gendered notions and careers should be a primary focus in designing curriculum and career interventions for second and third graders. Specifically, helping students to recognize that there are many ways to be successful and that different contexts demand different skills is important to the task of broadening their interests.

Gottfredson's Theory of Circumscription and Compromise

Gottfredson's Stage 2: *Orientation to Sex Roles* occurs from about ages 6 to 8, and according to Sharf (2006), children in this stage often believe they are a member of the superior gender (e.g., girls rule!). Because children in middle childhood are concrete thinkers, they are often very dualistic in their thinking. As such, they begin to develop a tolerable sex-type boundary of occupations that are acceptable for girls and those that are acceptable for boys. For example, a boy may perceive that nurses should be girls and, therefore, that occupation is not a tolerable consideration for him. During this time, it is important to have role models and examples of individuals in nontraditional roles. For example, teachers can be provided with coloring sheets representing people in nontraditional careers to use on occasions when students have extra time in class before the next academic activity. By intentionally displaying the colored pages around the classroom, teachers can provide subtle reminders that people can work in nontraditional careers.

THE SCHOOL COUNSELOR AND CORE COUNSELING CURRICULUM

The career counseling curriculum is an essential component of a comprehensive program (American School Counselor Association [ASCA], 2012). In order to provide the best possible career development curriculum, school counselors should consider the academic and personal skills that students will need to be successful after high school. An overarching focus in these grades should be career exploration. Moreover, school counselors should use grade level expectations (GLEs) and standards to determine age appropriate career competencies for second and third grade students. See Table 7.1 for the Missouri Center for Career Education GLEs for second and third grade.

TABLE 7.1 Missouri Career GLEs for Second and Third Grade

Concept	Second Grade	Third Grade
Integration of Self-Knowledge into Life and Career Plans	Identify new activities and interests to explore.	Identify and apply the steps to setting short-term, long-term, personal, and educational goals.
Adaptations to World of Work Changes	Identify the academic skills necessary for workers in the six career paths.	Compare and contrast the academic skills required of workers in the six career paths.
Respect for All Work	Explain the importance of jobs and workers in the community.	Recognize the contributions made by all workers to the school and community.
Career Decision Making	Identify and compare roles and responsibilities of workers within the community.	Explain what workers do and need to know in various careers.
Education and Career Requirements	Identify the skills needed by workers in the community.	Gather information regarding training and education for a variety of careers.
Personal Skills for Job Success	Identify personal, ethical, and work habit skills needed for workers in the community.	Compare personal, ethical, and work habit skills needed for school success with those of workers in the community.
Job-Seeking Skills	Identify and apply the steps to obtain helper jobs within the classroom.	Identify and apply the steps to obtain helper jobs within the school.

Based on the Missouri Center for Career Education (2006).

SCHOOL COUNSELING INTERVENTIONS

Findings from a qualitative study by Blackhurst, Auger, and Wahl (2003) revealed that by fifth grade, most of the participants in their study had an inaccurate understanding of the preparation needed for particular jobs. They also found that fifth grade students had a limited ability to distinguish among postsecondary options (technical school, community college, university). These results support the need to help students in middle elementary grades (second and third) to explore careers, learn about preparation requirements for careers (including college or vocational and technical training), and be exposed to postsecondary options.

School counselors should focus on ways to engage students in the career curriculum by making activities fun, engaging, and meaningful. Given their developmental level, the activities should provide opportunities for students to gain feelings of confidence in their abilities and to challenge their preconceived ideas. We provide numerous examples in the following.

Career Exploration Activities

To engage students and explore careers, the first author (an elementary school counselor at the time) used a lot of games. One example was at the end of a career exploration unit; she worked with the art teacher to create a lake in the middle of a classroom. The school counselor designed a lake using blue butcher paper and the art teacher had students use time in art class to create fish using construction paper, glitter, markers, and glue. The fish were laminated and a paper clip was added to each one. The counselor then created fishing poles using dow rods, yarn, and a magnet. The game was called "Fishing for Careers" and as students caught a fish they had to answer career-related questions. Here are a few sample questions:

1. Name three careers from the hospitality and tourism cluster.
2. Name two types of scientists.
3. How much education is required to be a teacher?
4. What does an architect do?
5. True or False? A woman can be a construction manager.
6. True or False? A man can be a ballet dancer.
7. Name a career where workers use math.
8. Name two careers where workers do a lot of writing.
9. List two work habits a farmer needs.

When students didn't know answers they were allowed to use one life line (other students in the class). This game was very popular and kids, teachers, and parents all asked for the return of "Fishing for Careers" each year. Once the materials were designed and the questions were created, the game was very easy to use each year. This type of activity is appropriate because it is creative, engaging for students, and helps them gain confidence in their career knowledge. Further, the questions can be created to challenge students' gender and cultural stereotypes, increase career knowledge, and help them to better understand the relationships between careers and academics. School counselors can tailor the questions for different age groups (PreK, kindergarten, grades 1, 2, 3, 4, and 5) and use the same materials.

Based on student cognitive development in middle childhood (e.g., seriation, the ability to categorize and subcategorize), students in second and third grade are ready to be introduced to career clusters. Students' natural curiosity lends to career exploration, and students in second and third grade love to use multiple media to play through career exploration. Using puzzles or art activities to draw and include careers that are within clusters is a fun way to help students visually map the relationships among careers.

For example, the first author provided students with a worksheet that had 20 careers illustrated. The students would use crayons to draw lines connecting the careers in the same cluster. For example, if there were illustrations of careers on the page that were in the information technology cluster, then students would use a designated color, such as blue, to circle those careers on their sheet and then draw a line connecting those careers together. Then, using a designated color, like yellow, students would circle all of the careers in agriculture, food, and natural resources and draw a line connecting those careers. Where older students might be capable of articulating or discussing in detail the different career clusters, having younger students recognize and match careers based on similar characteristics using active strategies is a developmentally appropriate way of engaging them.

Career Language

Popular media for teaching career guidance curriculum to elementary students include storytelling and role playing (Herr, Cramer, & Niles, 2004), both of which are excellent for building career vocabulary and beginning to explore careers. Truly, school counselors can choose many creative games and should work to make learning fun and engaging. The more students are exposed to careers, the more career language they will use. Increasing students' vocabulary related to careers can start with breaking down broad career areas into specific occupations (e.g., science careers, like doctor, can be broken down into specifics such as cardiologist and dentist). Other career terms and postsecondary terms that could be introduced include career clusters, college, university, and technical school.

Interpersonal Skills and Career Development

As noted in Chapter 1, changes to the U.S. economy have necessitated changes to how the future workforce is trained. According to a study by Barker and Satcher (2000), school counselors recognize the need to consistently provide skills training that promotes career competency equitably among college-bound and work-bound students. Indeed, the skills needed for both may be more similar than disparate. Specifically, beginning in elementary school, students should be comprehensively prepared for all potential postsecondary options through the development of academic, social, and work-related skills.

According to Greene (2006), technical skills and education are no longer sufficient for career success, as many employers now seek individuals with more advanced "soft skills" that may include communication skills, being a team player, generating solutions and problem solving, and demonstrating self-understanding and awareness, cultural sensitivity, positive manners, and workplace etiquette. As discussed previously, these are all things that students in grades 2 and 3 are capable of working on. Therefore, we review opportunities for promoting social skills that will allow students to be successful in postsecondary life.

Collaborative groups and team building. Within classrooms during counseling activities or in small-group counseling, students can learn the skills of working as a team. Giving students the opportunity to set goals in small groups and to work together to achieve those goals is an excellent start toward workplace camaraderie and collective efforts for success. Activities that involve problem solving and a whole-group effort are especially helpful. An example of this occurred in a third grade classroom where a school counselor and classroom teacher put students into groups of four. Groups were given Tinker Toys and building blocks and instructed to create the highest tower they could. After the activity, the teacher and school counselor processed with the students what teamwork skills they used (listening to each other, trying multiple ways of completing the task) and discussed careers related to the activity (e.g., architecture, construction, and engineering).

Conflict resolution. Any elementary school counselor can testify to the difficulty experienced by students in middle childhood who are learning to navigate play in groups. Friendship conflicts are frequent as children learn to handle disagreements in everyday discussions. Conflict resolution, cultural sensitivity and awareness, and communication and active listening skills are necessary for future workplace success and should be introduced by second grade. School counselors can do this through the provision of classroom lessons addressing these skills. There are many different curricula available for this type of activity. However, we suggest school counselors consider best practices for implementing these types of pro-social skills and conflict resolution curricula. For example, the *Enhancing Relationships in*

School Communities project (Wertheim, Freeman, & Trinder, 2012) was formulated with the following principles in mind: 1) administrator support and buy-in are critical to the success of any program or initiative, 2) teachers must take ownership in order to help students use the conflict resolution skills after they learn them, 3) there should be professional development available to teachers and staff on conflict resolution strategies being taught to students, and 4) sufficient time has to be given to students to learn and practice the conflict resolution skills. School counselors can visit the ASCA website to view the catalog of resources (curriculum, games) available for purchase for teaching the skills mentioned here.

IMPORTANCE OF STAKEHOLDERS

As mentioned in previous chapters, engaging stakeholders in students' career development is critical to ensure that students get a comprehensive introduction to career exploration. As is noted in the ASCA *National Model* (2012), collaboration is a key theme of school counseling and is vital to the implementation of a successful career development curriculum. Although we have discussed integrating career education within the classroom curriculum through collaboration with classroom teachers, in previous chapters we have not explored the role of specialty faculty in promoting careers. In this section we focus on ways in which specialty faculty can be included in a comprehensive school counseling program's career development curriculum.

Specialty Faculty

Specialty, or related arts, faculty in elementary schools generally teach ancillary classes that are meant to enrich student learning in the areas of physical education, library and media studies, art, music, and foreign languages. The curriculum offered by specialty faculty can be particularly useful to assist children in learning about diverse career opportunities. However, like classroom teachers, specialty faculty may have had very little training in career education and development and may need support and encouragement from the school counselor in order to effectively integrate career information. Moreover, students who have fantasy occupational aspirations (e.g., professional athlete, rock star, model, actor/actress) may benefit from a more realistic understanding of related careers. This is especially true given that students, boys in particular, who have fantasy occupation aspirations as professional athletes in third grade continue to have the same aspirations by sixth grade (Helwig, 1998). Just as school counselors provide classroom core counseling curriculum instruction, they can also work with specialty faculty to integrate career education in ancillary classrooms. See Exhibit 7.1 for an example.

EXHIBIT 7.1
Third Grade Sports Careers Unit

Mrs. Callahan, an elementary school counselor, was conducting a career exploration unit with third grade students and was concerned about the number of students (particularly males) who were displaying an interest in becoming professional athletes. During a third grade classroom lesson, students were asked to draw a career that they were interested in and over half the boys in the class drew a picture of a football player. Mrs. Callahan was concerned that focusing on athletics was self-limiting and an unrealistic career choice for most students. Indeed, she knew that the majority of students would not become professional athletes and she wanted them to embrace other options; however, she did not want to discourage student interest in athletics. Therefore, she decided to collaborate with the physical education (PE) teacher, Mr. Jackson, to develop a sports careers unit.

Mrs. Callahan and Mr. Jackson worked collaboratively to develop a unit on sports careers, relying on Mrs. Callahan's knowledge of careers and Mr. Jackson's knowledge of sports. In the first lesson, students were introduced to the many careers related to professional athletics including: athletic trainers, coaches, physical therapists, medical staff, sports managers/administrators, ticket sales, photographers/camera and film technicians, marketing staff, retail sales, sports reporters, and facilities management. Students were put in small groups where they discussed and wrote a list of responsibilities and skills for each of these careers.

In the second lesson, Mrs. Callahan and Mr. Jackson set up five centers and the students rotated through in small groups of five spending 10 minutes at each center. At the centers they learned more about careers and completed a related activity. The centers were staffed by volunteers and teacher's aides. See Table 7.2 for a list of the centers, careers included at each center, and activities students completed at each center.

For the third and final lesson, the students, under the direction of Mrs. Callahan and Mr. Jackson, were randomly assigned one of the careers they had learned about in the last few weeks. Role plays included helping an injured athlete (sports medicine), training the team (coaching), selling merchandise and tickets, photography and reporting, and statistics. As the final activity, students selected three careers related to professional athletics that they found interesting and wrote two sentences about each.

TABLE 7.2 Third Grade Sports Career Unit Centers

Center	Careers Covered	Activities
Center 1: Sports Training	Sports trainers and coaches	A sports trainer was at this center and did a demonstration with volunteers of strength-training activities and regular workouts.
Center 2: Sports Medicine	Physical therapy, injury prevention/treatment, sports improvement, and fitness	A sports therapist was there with a model of a human leg and students practiced wrapping a sprained ankle.
Center 3: Sports Marketing	Ticket sales, retail, branding, public relations	A speaker from the local NFL retail store talked about merchandise and team branding. Students were given a paper with the outline of a jacket. Students were able to design a jacket with their favorite team logo.
Center 4: Sports Reporting	Photo journalism, televised reporting, film technicians	A member of the sports reporting team at a local news station was the speaker at this center. Students watched a 30-second clip of a sports play and practiced reporting the play in a microphone. Their reports were recorded on video and they viewed them later.
Center 5: Sports Administration	Facilities management, accounting, team management, statistics, scouts	One of the statistics keepers from a local university basketball team was the speaker for this center. Students practiced watching a 2-minute basketball clip and using a spreadsheet to record attempted baskets, scored points, fouls, and foul shots.

In the example, the school counselor used students' natural and socially constructed interest in athletics to foster career exploration; the collaboration with Mr. Jackson allowed both professionals to use their strengths to promote student career understanding beyond professional athletics.

Academic Subject Teachers

Teachers have an opportunity to exact a strong influence on student career development in second and third grade, particularly in the areas of academic and social skills development. School counselors can work collaboratively with teachers to design classroom lessons that encourage career exploration opportunities.

Academic growth. School counselors can provide students with developmentally appropriate academic skills instruction, and teachers can reinforce these skills in the classroom. Using the American School Counselor Association (ASCA) Student Standards (2004) as a foundation, students in second and third grades should learn to write academic goals and monitor their progress toward those goals (initiating self-regulatory behavior). Students in these grades also need to learn personal organization skills, use a planner, manage homework and supply materials, and develop homework, test-taking, and study-skills strategies. These skills are essential to college and career readiness in that organization, planning, and goal setting are critical to success in higher education and the workplace. School counselors can develop lesson plans that address these skills and co-facilitate instruction with classroom teachers. Classroom teachers, in turn, will be able to reinforce the skills in the classroom on an ongoing basis.

Social growth. To promote the development of prosocial skills, school counselors should encourage teachers to include collaborative and group work assignments for second and third grade students. Further, school counselors can provide classroom lessons on conflict resolution strategies and communication skills, and teachers can reinforce these skills in day-to-day interactions with students. School counselors also can foster social development through the collaborative implementation of positive behavior programs and character education throughout the school, which support personal responsibility as well as civic and social interest.

Career growth. As mentioned in Chapter 6, school counselors can work with teachers to integrate career information in the classroom. Because students in second and third grade can understand career clusters, it can be fun and engaging to include clusters with academic content (see Exhibit 7.2). During classroom lessons, school counselors can introduce all of the career clusters and help students understand the relationships between careers. Most importantly, school counselors need to continually help teachers infuse career in the educational agenda.

Parent Engagement Activities

As noted in Chapter 6, parents are the greatest influence on student career development in early and middle childhood; therefore, including parents is a necessary and desirable way to promote student career growth (ASCA, 2012; Herr et al., 2004). Indeed, career development that includes parents is crucial. Evidence of this comes from findings of a longitudinal study of students, beginning in second grade (Helwig, 1998). According to Helwig, parents were a major influence on students' career development throughout childhood, adolescence, and early adulthood. Therefore, he suggested that parents should be included in career activities and given the tools and resources to assist their children in career growth and decision making. Specifically, students from low socioeconomic status (SES) families (a determination based on family income, prestige of parents' occupations, and parent education level) are more likely to have lower educational attainment and lower occupational status than their higher SES peers; this is a generational problem that may be in part due to the fact that the parents of low SES students may be unable to

EXHIBIT 7.2
Second Grade Health and Safety Unit With Careers

Mr. Denton, an elementary school counselor, worked with Mrs. Norton, a second grade teacher, to design a career clusters game to go with a health and safety unit. In the unit, Mrs. Norton covered topics such as food safety, nutrition, food groups, personal hygiene, illness, and injuries. Mr. Denton and Mrs. Norton collaborated to design one career-related assignment for the unit. Students were given a homework assignment that included reading a paragraph about the health sciences career cluster and a link to a list of careers in health sciences (www. worldwidelearn.com/career-planning-education/health-sciences/ index.html). Each student was asked to choose a career from the list of health science careers. With their parents' help, students were asked to do the following:

1. Choose a career from the health sciences career cluster list.
2. Describe what people with this career do in two sentences.
3. Write one sentence about the kind of training or education that is necessary for this career.
4. Write one sentence about how people with this career help others to be healthy.
5. Write one sentence about why or why not you might like this career.

Although this was a short homework assignment, it helped students connect what they were learning in their academic unit with the world of work and reinforced technology, research, and writing skills.

offer career guidance due to a lack of knowledge about career development or how to guide their children through career and college readiness tasks (Shaffer, 2009). This is why including parents is so critical, so that they can also develop skills necessary to support and guide their children. It is important to note that regardless of a family's socioeconomic status, all parents should be invited to participate in career development activities.

According to Amundson and Penner (1998), parents who aren't given a rationale for exploring careers with their child or don't possess the skills to assist their child's career development may be prone to push their own personal preferences for their child (e.g., parents deciding the child needs to be a doctor or others pushing their child into manual labor jobs). As noted by Amundson and Penner, increasing parental involvement in career development activities promotes a positive parent–child relationship and greater family communication. Parents may wonder how to help students connect academic instruction and careers, a skill they can be taught by school counselors and teachers. Moreover, given the current federal initiatives for science, technology, engineering, and mathematics (STEM) careers, it is important to recognize the role of parents for encouraging student interest in the STEM areas. Because many parents may not possess knowledge of STEM careers or may not feel confident about their math or science skills, an educational approach is warranted (see Exhibit 7.3 for example).

EXHIBIT 7.3
Third Grade Parent and Student Math Night

Once a month at Norcross Elementary School, the school counselor, Miss Sanchez, would meet with each grade-level team to discuss any student concerns such as academics and behavior and to coordinate and plan grade-level activities. During one such meeting with the third grade team, the teachers disclosed that students were struggling with understanding many of the math concepts being taught in a new unit on metric to fraction conversions. One of the teachers, Mr. Nelson, stated that he asked the students when they might use fractions at home and none of them had an answer. Another teacher suggested that they could have a math day at school and focus on math activities. Miss Sanchez suggested instead that they have a parent and student math night. The team decided to do this and the parent–teacher association (PTA) agreed to sponsor the event.

The Math Night was scheduled for a Thursday evening and a local pizza parlor supplied a pizza dinner for the families. Parents and children ate in the cafeteria where they were introduced to the evening's activities. The counselor did a short presentation on math-related careers (engineering, accounting, actuary) and then each family was given a ruler, a worksheet, and a conversion sheet. Families took measurements and then worked on converting (e.g., inches to centimeters). For the culminating activity, all of the students and parents got to play the role of bakers. Each family was given a calculator and instructions on how to convert decimals to fractions to get the measurements needed to make no-bake cookies. Teachers were available to answer questions and found that many parents revealed that they had forgotten some of the math skills reviewed. At the end, all of the families enjoyed a tasty treat.

As a result of the math night, teachers reported that students were more enthusiastic about fractions and measurements. Several of the teachers noted that students appeared to be turning in more homework and that math homework scores seemed to be higher. The teachers attributed this to parents feeling more efficacious to help students with math conversions and students feeling more excited about math.

As illustrated in the math night example, including parents is an important way to improve student STEM performance and to help families connect academics and the world of work. Other ways to include parents are to conduct workshops that focus on labor market information, training requirements for a diversity of careers, and how to access current career information using up-to-date technology (Amundson & Penner, 1998). Other family night activities for second and third graders could include financial literacy (how to help your child understand money and develop a simple budget), planning and goal setting, and providing academic enrichment for children.

The latter, academic enrichment, is an important topic to cover before long breaks (such as summer vacation). This presentation ideally should include a focus on local, community-based opportunities such as public library reading programs, sports camps, summer learning programs through zoos or museums, visiting local farmers markets, and camps or programs for specialty training such as music, art, and theater. If it is possible, having local donors and business partners support scholarship funds for enrichment programs is a great way to ensure all students have equitable access to such programs.

SUMMARY

In this chapter we discussed the developmental milestones of middle childhood and student career development. We highlighted relevant career theory with a special emphasis on Bourdieu and Gottfredson in regard to the influence of culture and gender. We reviewed the importance of a multisystemic approach to career counseling in comprehensive school counseling programs and focused attention on specialty faculty, classroom integration, and parent engagement activities.

···❯ **Test Your Knowledge**

1. How does lack of success in elementary school academics impact students' career development?
2. How does the sexualization of girlhood affect girls' self-concept related to career?
3. What gendered messages do students receive in schools that may increase their propensity for Orientation to Sex Roles based on stereotypes?

8

• • • • •

Career Education and Counseling for Grades 4 and 5: Preparing for the Middle School Transition

• • • • •

Throughout this book we have maintained the critical importance of beginning career education and counseling in early childhood and of consistently promoting career development throughout the P–12 years. Yet, as alleged by Watson and McMahon (2008), it is important to note that career development practices by elementary school counselors still largely lack a comprehensive, integrated, and holistic approach. As previously mentioned (Chapter 1), much of the career literature and education for school counselors is based on theories that address adolescent and adult career development, rather than that of children (Porfeli, Hartung, & Vondracek, 2008). Although research on children's career development has begun to emerge, there is often no theoretical framework consistently applied to practice (Schultheiss, 2008). For this reason, we have utilized Gottfredson, Young, and Bourdieu to frame middle childhood career development in this text. In this chapter we add Bandura's Social Learning Theory to expand the theoretical framework to tailor career counseling and education interventions for fourth and fifth grade students.

DEVELOPMENTAL OVERVIEW

Fourth and fifth graders (generally between the ages of 9 and 11) are at the end of childhood and are transitioning to early adolescence (preteens). According to Havighurst (1972), several developmental tasks should be achieved before the adolescent transition. Some of these tasks include developing the physical skills to successfully participate in sports and games, building a positive attitude toward self, developing interpersonal skills, becoming tolerant and accepting of others, developing academic skills in core areas, and achieving a sense of independence. The development of these tasks occurs within many contexts (e.g., family, school, church, community) and various factors affect individuals' growth. In this section we cover physical, social, cognitive, and gender development. However, we again caution that not all students will move through developmental stages at the same pace, and it is outside the scope of this book to review all developmental trends and possibilities.

Physical Development

Physically, students in fourth and fifth grades are undergoing the initial changes associated with transitioning to early adolescence. Specifically, the development of secondary sexual characteristics may begin to emerge as preteens begin the physical changes associated with puberty. According to Belsky (2007), there appears to be a drop in the age of puberty, with girls beginning menarche younger than in previous generations, sometimes as early as late elementary school. This change in the onset of puberty and secondary sexual characteristics may be attributed to major changes in lifestyle; in particular, nutrition appears to be the principal underlying variable (Belsky, 2007).

As these physiological changes occur, pre-teens' brains also are changing because of the impact of hormones on the functioning of neurotransmitters. Changes in mood and increased emotionality often result. It is important for adults to recognize these changes and to help students develop strategies for emotional self-regulation and for reducing emotional reactivity—skills they will need for maintaining positive working relationships in their careers. It is also important to identify students who are having difficulty navigating these changes, as manifested by feelings of self-consciousness about their bodies and/or displaying embarrassment about changes in their appearance. Students struggling with body image concerns may need extra support (small group or individual counseling) in order to continue to have a positive self-concept, a critical dimension of positive career development.

Psychosocial and Socio-Emotional Development

In late childhood, children are most likely still in Erikson's stage of *industry versus inferiority*, and are continuing to resolve issues related to competence in academics, athletics, and other socially valued activities. By late childhood and early adolescence, social relationships, primarily peer friendships, are based on mutual interests and the peer group becomes a socializing force for what is normal and acceptable. In particular, social acceptance and popularity are based on social characteristics, "such as friendliness, a moderate degree of assertiveness, a sense of humor, and competence in valued activities" (Ferguson, 1970, p. 143). Popularity and social acceptance can serve to bolster self-concept and this, in turn, can impact career development. Moreover, the development of meaningful and intimate friendships can promote empathy for others (Ferguson, 1970), which may lead to an increase in pro-social behaviors such as compassion, kindness, forgiveness, and gratitude (Shaffer, 2009). All of these characteristics and behaviors are important for developing future workplace relationships.

Cognitive Development

Fourth and fifth grade students most likely continue to be in Piaget's (1977) stage of *concrete operations*, as discussed in Chapter 7. The cognitive tasks of conservation, decentering, and seriation become more solidified and are used by children with greater consistency as they apply these skills to day-to-day learning. Additionally, children are being introduced to more complex functions; for example, in fourth and fifth grades, math students are introduced to the relationships of proportions, ratios, fractions, and decimals. Further, as previously noted in Chapter 7, students in middle childhood begin to use information processing to promote their own memory (i.e., use of rehearsal and selective attention).

By late childhood, the cognitive functions associated with memory require that students have opportunities to use multiple strategies, and, by doing so will find strategies that are most helpful to them. Belsky (2007) asserted that parents can practice these strategies with children at home to help them identify responsibilities and expectations and remember what they need to do to meet those expectations. For example, parents might ask their children to articulate the daily tasks they need to complete (e.g., chores such as feeding the dog or washing dishes). Through using this type of rehearsal activity, children begin to develop an understanding of personal responsibility and how to keep track of what they need to do, an important step in developing self-regulatory behavior (see Bandura, discussed in the following), which is a necessary skill for workplace success. Further, in order to promote positive self-concept, it is important to help students at this age begin to understand that everyone has unique gifts and talents that they can use to become better learners and workers.

Gender

As fourth and fifth grade students become more immersed in popular culture, the influences of macrosystems become more pronounced. In Chapter 7 we highlighted Gottfredson's (1981) Stage 2: *Orientation to Sex Roles*, and it is important to underscore that the continued effects of gendered socialization are strong in the late elementary years. In many ways, social pressures for gender ideals increase as preteens view social media, listen to music, and begin to notice trends and patterns of how other males and females dress, act, respond, and which actions bring social value.

As proposed by Choate and Curry (2009), problems resulting from the sexualization of girlhood are noticeable in 21st century schools. Girls begin to self-objectify in middle childhood, and there is an increased ruminative pattern of self-objectification in late elementary and early middle school. According to the American Psychological Association's *Task Force Report on the Sexualization of Girls* (2007), the negative mental health impact (e.g., anxiety, depression, negative self-concept) on girls based on sexualization can lead to lower academic achievement, career expectancy, and decreased career aspirations (Choate & Curry, 2007).

Beyond the sexualization of girlhood, there are gendered social inductions for males as well. According to Kimmel (2005) male bravado and overconfidence promoted in social media stereotypes for boys increase risk-taking behaviors, violent reactions, and inauthenticity as boys are forced to display emotions that are not congruent with their true feelings (i.e., appearing tough, aloof, uncaring). These behavior patterns lead boys to experience more disruptive behaviors in school, suspensions, grade level retention, lower grades, referrals for psychological screenings, ADHD diagnoses, and other negative consequences (Kimmel, 2005). Indeed, Kimmel stated, "Boys see academic success itself as a disconfirmation of their masculinity" (2005, p. 241) based on traditional stereotypes that the ideal male has great athletic prowess and is unemotional and disinterested in academic pursuits.

This "boy code" as noted by Kimmel (2005) results in boys displaying more anger (as is socially promoted) and less compassion, empathy, and vulnerability (socially sanctioned). The consequences for long-term career development are that boys are left still needing to develop critical skills (e.g., academic, positive interpersonal communication, relationship building) for future workplace success. Therefore, school counselors need to be aware that gender socialization should be addressed throughout the school curriculum, and career curriculum in particular, by challenging stereotypes and traditional roles with consistency and deliberation (Choate & Curry, 2009; Curry & Choate, 2010).

RELEVANT CAREER THEORY

In this section, we review career theories and concepts important to the future career success of fourth and fifth grade students. We introduce two of the most important cross-theoretical concepts: self-regulation and career self-efficacy. Our review starts with an in-depth look at Social Learning Theory (Bandura, 1977).

Bandura's Social Learning Theory

Albert Bandura, the originator of Social Learning Theory, has contributed greatly to how we conceptualize life tasks related to career development

(Bandura, 1977). In his theory, Bandura propounds three major constructs pertinent to understanding the development of career efficacy: reciprocal determinism, self-regulation, and efficacy expectancy.

Reciprocal Determinism. Bandura (1977) proposed that reciprocal determinism exists among cognitive, behavioral, and environmental factors. He contended that the interactions of this trifecta, not just one facet, impact the individual as variant sources of influence, depending on circumstances and context. Bandura further believed that the relationship among these factors was not a function of unidirectional operation, but rather, "interlocking determinants" (p. 10) (see Figure 8.1).

As noted by Bandura (1977), the environment may support positive growth for individuals or it may inhibit optimal development. The individual's behavior may reciprocally influence the environment through positive or negative impact. Further, characteristics of the individual (cognitive, affective, and physiological) also interact with the environment and behavior to shape circumstances (Bandura, 1977). In other words, students are influenced by the environments they are in (school, family, community) and also by the way they cognitively process information (person) and react to it (behavior). In this way, students influence the environment as well as the reactions other people have to them. For this reason, children must learn to

FIGURE 8.1   Behavior, Cognition, and Environment as Interlocking Determinants. Adapted from Bandura (1977).

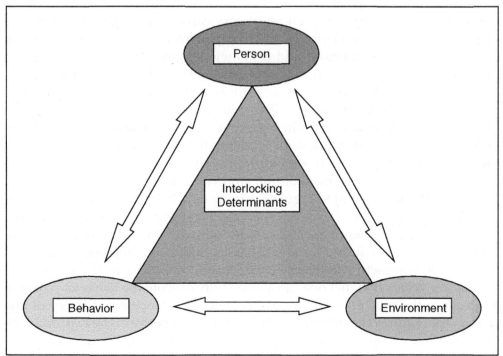

regulate all of these aspects (thoughts, emotions, and behaviors) in order to move toward goals.

Self-Regulation. Based on the theoretical assumptions of Social Learning Theory (Bandura, 1977), self-regulation (sometimes referred to in professional literature as self-management or self-monitoring) is an individual's ability to plan and manage his or her own behavior toward successfully reaching a goal. To fully comprehend self-regulation, it is critical to conceptualize how it is generated and maintained. Self-regulation stems from individuals envisioning potential courses of action, judging their ability to produce the actions necessary for desired outcomes, and then setting goals and taking action (Bandura, 1977). An example of this type of behavior comes from marathon runners who have to manage their behavior (nutrition intake, sleep/rest, consistent training) in order to successfully complete the task of running an endurance race.

Self-regulation is important for future career success, as students need to learn to set goals and engage in behaviors that will assist them in progressing toward those goals. In the workplace, employees may be expected to complete large-scale or long-term projects that require breaking the projects into small, manageable tasks and determining a timeline for completing tasks. Beyond project-based work, in the average workplace employees are expected to self-manage their behaviors to produce results in line with their employer's expectations. Self-regulation is a learned skill that can be taught in the day-to-day operations of fourth and fifth grade education, and we provide some examples later in this chapter of how teachers and parents can help students develop this skill.

Individuals with strong self-regulatory capacity also have the ability to regulate emotions appropriately and to cope effectively with stress. Coping by attempting to understand and acknowledge one's emotions during distressing events has been found to be significantly linked to lower trait anxiety, lower depressive symptoms, and positive adjustment (Stanton, Parsa, & Austenfeld, 2002). All of these positive outcomes of emotional self-regulation promote workplace success as they improve the mental health of individuals. School counselors can work with students through a personal/social curriculum to develop strategies to appropriately express emotions and learn how to accept support in overcoming stress (Stanton et al., 2002).

Self-Efficacy. Pivotal to regulating one's own behavior, individuals must be able to estimate outcomes of their actions. These expectations, referred to by Bandura as efficacy expectancies, include approximating consequences, identifying the action required for any behavior, and evaluating one's abilities to successfully complete a desired behavior (Bandura, 1977). An efficacy expectation is "the conviction that one can successfully execute the behavior required to produce the outcomes" (Bandura, 1977, p. 79). Competent mastery of any given task requires the minimal skills necessary to perform the task and feelings of efficacy in one's ability to effectively apply the skills (Bandura, 1986).

According to Bandura (1977), self-efficacy—a person's determination about his or her ability to be successful—affects the degree of effort an individual will put forth in overcoming difficult or arduous circumstances. When people believe they are competent, they are more likely to undertake challenging tasks. Evidence of this can be seen in any classroom as students who believe they cannot do a particular assignment may not even attempt to do the work assigned. According to Bandura (1977), "perceived self-efficacy not only reduces anticipatory fears and inhibitions but, through expectations of eventual success, it affects coping efforts once they are initiated" (p. 80). The relationship between efficacy and coping through stress was underscored by Fernandez-Ballesteros, Diez-Nicolas, Capara, Barbaranelli, and Bandura (2002) when they suggested that, "unless people believe they can produce desired outcomes and forestall undesired ones through their actions, they have little incentive to act or to persevere in the face of difficulties" (p. 108). Consequently, a sense of efficacy about a given task promotes persistence toward meeting a goal.

Therefore, self-efficacy prompts people to pro-action, and fosters the ability to endure stress for greater quantities of time in order to achieve some goal or to perform some desired behavior. Thus, students with greater academic and career efficacy may persist in school even when they struggle, as they perceive they are capable of eventual success. Conversely, students who don't think they will be successful in career pursuits may see no reason to take more rigorous courses, and may show a decreased commitment to academics. Therefore, building student academic and career efficacy is an important task for elementary school counselors to undertake before students transition to middle school.

Sources of Efficacy Expectancy. According to Bandura (1977), there are four main sources of efficacy expectations: 1) performance accomplishments, 2) vicarious experiences, 3) verbal persuasion, and 4) emotional arousal. Bandura labeled these hierarchically based on each source's dependability as an influence on efficacy. The strongest dependent contributor is performance accomplishments and the least is emotional arousal.

Performance accomplishments (Bandura, 1977) are the most dependable source of efficacy expectation because they are based on the lived experience of the individual. For example, for students to envision their ability to become a scientist, being able to partake in activities that scientists do (e.g., lab work, field experiences) is critical. The more success individuals experience in related activities and tasks, the greater will be their efficacy for mastery of increasingly difficult competencies. The converse is also true: If individuals experience repeated failure, then they are at risk of producing lower efficacy expectations.

Vicarious experience was the second most dependable producer of efficacy expectation. Bandura (1977) stated that "seeing others perform threatening activities without adverse consequences can create expectations in observers that they too will eventually succeed if they intensify and persist in their efforts" (p. 81). For this reason, career role models are important. When students see people similar to themselves (based on race, gender, socioeconomic background, religious affiliation, English Language Learners, etc.) being successful in a given occupation or activities related to that occupation, they are more likely to assess that they also could be successful in that occupation.

Verbal persuasion (Bandura, 1977) includes encouragement or prompting, such as exhortation and suggestion; it is the third most dependable source of efficacy expectancy. Bandura ascertained that this type of efficacy would be short-lived at best, especially if the individual experiences disconfirmation of competence. For example, some students internalize negative feedback much more easily than they do positive feedback. No matter how many people comment on their strengths or express confidence in their abilities, those students only recall the one person who said they had no chance of making it, and they make decisions with that one person's input in mind.

The last of the sources of efficacy expectancy is *emotional arousal*. Emotions are often perceived by individuals as indicators of the amount of stress they are able to endure or how capable they are of completing a task. For example, some people might interpret emotional reactions of fear, anxiety, and nervousness (normal emotions in new or stressful circumstances) as indicators that they cannot handle the task at hand. This negative labeling may spark a cyclical reaction according to Bandura (1977): "Because high arousal usually debilitates performance, individuals are more likely to expect success when they are not beset by aversive arousal than when they are tense, shaking, and viscerally agitated" (p. 82). For example, students undertaking a new academic task (such as fourth and fifth graders learning about ratios) may mistakenly attribute their anxiety about undertaking the task as an inability to successfully complete the task.

Finally, Bandura (1977, 1986) contended that efficacy beliefs differ on three dimensions. The first is *magnitude*, based on the simplicity versus the complexity/difficulty of the task being considered. The second dimension is *generality*. Generality is the degree to which efficacy beliefs are specific to given tasks or if they broadly encompass other life arenas or competencies. The third dimension is *strength*. The stronger an efficacy belief, the less impact disconfirming circumstances will have, and the greater effort one will exert to master challenges. Conversely, individuals with low self-efficacy discontinue or decline efforts if they are met with failure (Bandura, 1986).

While self-efficacy may be the impetus for the bridge from cognition to action, it may also serve other purposes. According to Masten and Reed (2002), self-efficacy is a personal characteristic predictive of "good adaptation in the context of risk" (p. 82) and promoting self-efficacy may mitigate risk factors and improve resilience. Bandura, Barbaranelli, Caprara, and Pastorelli (1996) stated that self-efficacy may impact individual development and adaptation. Maddux (2002) maintained that self-efficacy beliefs are critical for psychological adjustment and physical health, as well as competency-based pursuit behaviors—such as those necessary for a successful work life. Maddux further enumerated many benefits of self-efficacy. To begin, strong self-efficacy beliefs promote and encourage exploration—a skill critical to one's sense of agency and career development. Also, self-efficacy beliefs have been found to assist in self-regulation toward goal attainment by influencing the types of goals an individual chooses. Self-efficacy beliefs also lead to more effective problem solving, better utilization of personal and cognitive resources, lower depression, increased coping strategies (Maddux, 2002; Fernandez et al., 2002), and improved academic functioning (Bandura et al., 1996).

Gottfredson's Theory of Circumscription and Compromise

Students in fourth and fifth grades are in Gottfredson's (1981) Stage 3: *Orientation to Social Valuation*. Students in fourth grade begin to view themselves from a third-party perspective. This means they are noticing how valued they are by their peers, who have social capital (Bourdieu, 1977) as manifested by popularity, prestige, and status symbols. According to Sharf (2006), students begin to notice the types of clothes their peers are wearing as well as the size and expense of their and others' homes, cars, and so on. In fourth and fifth grades, students also begin to recognize the social value of the careers of family members, to understand which careers will be accepted by their families, and to circumscribe career choices that they perceive as above or below their own social position.

One aspect of social valuation that is important for school counselors to pay attention to is that students begin to place a value on how hard certain occupations are (i.e., perceived difficulty). Generally, the harder the occupation is perceived to be, the more social value it is assigned. For example, students rate being a doctor as very hard and highly valued; therefore, students who don't view themselves as intelligent (self-concept) or don't believe they have the ability to learn what is needed to become a doctor (self-efficacy) may eliminate such a career choice as beyond their abilities. For this reasons, students can benefit from opportunities to experience first-hand the activities related to highly valued or "difficult" careers so that they can experience success, build self-efficacy (performance accomplishment), and then envision themselves in these kinds of occupations.

Young's Career Concepts

By fourth and fifth grades, peers are beginning to gain prominence in their importance and influence on each other, and this is true even in relation to career development. For example, an elementary school counselor asked one fifth grade classroom of students what careers they were interested in, and a popular young man raised his hand and said, "sportscaster." Immediately following, about five other boys in the class raised their hands and gave the same answer. Students with prestige and social capital begin to gain leadership in the classroom and other students begin to follow.

Regarding careers, as was noted in Gottfredson's (1981) Stage 3, the social value assigned to careers by students can evolve largely based on their peer group in the classroom (Young, 1983), and that peer group is influenced in general by the larger community in which they all live. For this reason it is important that school counselors continue to give students individual reflection time and activities that allow them to consider their own career interests and aptitudes. So, although working in small groups with peers during classroom instruction is desirable, school counselors should also ensure that students get some personal reflection time to think about careers. Further, Young (1983) underscored the ongoing importance of parents and family in career exploration and decision making. Thus, school counselors need to support parent–child activities to promote career development. Specifically, parents need to be offered opportunities to consistently engage in career conversations with their children through structured offerings that foster parent understanding of career exploration and parent–child engagement.

Super's Life-Span/Life-Space Approach

Although we discuss Super's theory in greater detail in subsequent chapters, we do wish to highlight Super's (1980) nine concepts or activities of childhood career development that foster career development through personal awareness and career decision making. These concepts are: 1) curiosity, 2) exploration of oneself or environment, 3) information that promotes awareness of the importance of career information, 4) key figures or career role models that play a meaningful role in a child's life, 5) a child's personal interests, 6) locus of control, 7) time perspective that aids in student awareness of the need to plan, 8) self-concept, and 9) planfulness or an understanding of the importance of planning.

Super's concepts were investigated through qualitative inquiry by Schultheiss, Plama, and Manzi (2005). Forty-nine urban elementary students participated in the study (writing assignments using open-ended career development questions as prompts) and data revealed that overwhelmingly, students' writings reflected the importance of Super's concepts in career development. The only one of the nine concepts missing from the data was curiosity. Schultheiss et al. reported that fourth and fifth grade students in their study described career exploration activities in the classroom, connecting learning to work, and exploring careers through play. Regarding self-concept, participants in the study were able to identify interests, abilities, and activities they found enjoyable. Further, students were able to express an internal locus of control (belief that they had control over their own behavior and future), key figures in their career development, conceptions of work, time perspective and the importance of planning, and decision-making processes.

These findings underscore the importance of understanding and identifying markers of career development and career maturity. School counselors should consider Super's concepts and ask themselves, "Are the students at my school displaying, consistently, that their career decision making and maturity include these concepts?" Throughout this chapter we continue to place an emphasis on programming, such as core counseling curriculum designed using ASCA (2004) standards and Missouri Center for Career Education's (2006) grade level expectations (GLEs) that promote career maturation for fourth and fifth grade students.

THE MIDDLE SCHOOL TRANSITION

The transition to middle school can seem like a predominantly academic milestone for students, but the impact of this transition on career development is critical. Students prepared for the academic rigor of middle school are more likely to be academically successful in their middle grades education. Specifically, students and their parents/guardians need to be well informed of the available options for course work, encouraged to register for the most rigorous classes they are capable of taking, and prepared for the differences in their daily routine as they move from elementary to middle school. Most notably, it is important to prepare parents, guardians, and teachers to provide supportive guidance and to promote student academic and career efficacy (Hall, 2003) during this adjustment period. Although personal/social issues are also very important during this transition, our discussion focuses on academic and career interventions.

THE SCHOOL COUNSELOR AND CORE COUNSELING CURRICULUM

According to Niles and Harris-Bowlesby (2009), by the end of elementary school students should have gained several basic career development skills including: "self-knowledge, skills for interacting with others, basic skills in educational and occupational career exploration, awareness of the relationship between work and learning, basic skills to understand and use career information, awareness of the importance of personal responsibility and good work habits, and awareness of the career planning process" (p. 322). If school counselors approach career development through a comprehensive, systematic approach, including multisystems stakeholders (ASCA, 2005), then by the time students reach the fourth and fifth grades, they should

TABLE 8.1 Missouri Grade Level Expectations for Career Counseling Curriculum

Concept	Grade Level 4	Grade Level 5
Integration of Self-Knowledge into Life and Career Plans	Compare interests and strengths with those of workers in the local community.	Compare interests and strengths with those of workers in the global community.
Adaptations to World of Work Changes	Identify school and community resources available for exploration of the six career paths.	Describe occupational changes that have occurred over time within the six career paths.
Respect for All Work	Recognize the contributions of all jobs to the community.	Describe the self-satisfaction that comes from completing a work responsibility.
Career Decision Making	Relate current student learning to each of the six career paths.	Compare and contrast the roles and responsibilities of workers within the six career paths.
Education and Career Requirements	Outline the training and educational requirements for a variety of careers.	Compare and contrast the training and educational requirements for a variety of careers.
Personal Skills for Job Success	Demonstrate personal and ethical skills needed to work with diverse groups of people.	Apply personal, ethical, and work habit skills needed for success in any school or work environment.
Job-Seeking Skills	Identify the components of a portfolio.	Identify the skills needed to develop a portfolio.

Based on the Missouri Center for Career Education (2006).

be equipped for deeper career exploration. Once again, we suggest that the Missouri Center for Career Education (2006) GLEs offer a guide for designing fourth and fifth grade career guidance curriculum (see Table 8.1.)

Career Exploration, Technology, and Interests

If students have been adequately introduced to career clusters and the relationships among careers in the second and third grades, then they will be ready by the fourth and fifth grade to learn the process of exploring individual careers. In order to develop career decision-making self-efficacy, that is, feeling that they can successfully engage in the tasks of exploring and deciding on a career, students have to gain relevant experience (performance accomplishment) in varied career exploration activities (Gushue, Scanlan, Pantzer, & Clarke, 2006). Utilizing technology for career exploration, students can be introduced to sources that will assist them in better understanding careers they are interested in and how to use these tools to explore careers on their own (e.g., Occupational Outlook Handbook online, O*Net). In Exhibit 8.1 we illustrate a culminating guidance activity, using a framework based on Missouri

EXHIBIT 8.1
The Student Career Fair

Mr. Butler, an elementary school counselor in an inner city school, West-dale Elementary, had completed a five-lesson career unit with fifth grade students. In the unit, students learned introductory career exploration skills using technology, the components of a resume, how to determine the educational and training requirements for a career, and how to write a cover letter for a job that highlights personal characteristics and values related to a career. Although the students were at a beginning level in all of these skills, Mr. Butler wanted them to apply the skills to further solidify their knowledge and understanding. Mr. Butler considered hosting a career fair, but it was difficult to get community partners and parents to participate in these types of activities at his school.

Mr. Butler consulted with the fifth grade team. They decided to have a student-led career fair. Students were allowed to choose a career and they were given 2 weeks to create cardboard trifolds to present their career findings to the rest of the fifth grade. Mr. Butler was able to get the trifolds and other materials necessary for the project through Office Depot, a local community partner with the school. Students mounted multiple career exploration artifacts on the trifold. Each trifold contained a picture of someone performing a work task associated with the career, a fact sheet about the daily responsibilities of the career, a sheet with education requirements and salary, and a student resume and cover letter designed for the career. Other artifacts included drawings or construction paper cut outs that represented tools of the trade. For example, one student, Clarissa, studied the career of a zookeeper. She had a picture of a zookeeper with a zebra, a fact sheet, a sheet with career education requirements for a zookeeper, and multiple artifacts attached to the trifold (cutouts of animals, a packet of bird seed for feeding birds, and pictures of animal habitats). Students set up their trifolds in the gym and each class took turns presenting their career trifolds to the entire fifth grade. Students and teachers love the career fair and Mr. Butler continues to host it each year.

Center for Career Education (2006) GLEs, Niles and Harris-Bowlesby's (2009) student competencies, and technology that a school counselor can use to let students explore career skills and develop efficacy.

Based on the example in Exhibit 8.1, Mr. Butler used the Missouri Center for Career Education (2006) GLEs and competencies proposed by Niles and Harris-Bowlesby (2009) to design a curriculum to enhance student skills and knowledge about career exploration. Then, based on his desire to help the students' apply their new knowledge (promoting career exploration efficacy through performance accomplishment), he had the students design their own career fair. The activity promoted student career exploration efficacy and self-regulation behaviors. Specifically, because students had to complete multiple tasks over time as well as develop a way to present their projects using the trifold and other materials, self-regulation was necessary to successfully complete the task (setting a goal and breaking it down into smaller, manageable tasks). Although Mr. Butler didn't have the parent and community resources at his disposal for a more traditional career fair (adult speakers and demonstrations), he used the resources available in his school community to meet the comprehensive career needs of his students.

IMPORTANCE OF STAKEHOLDERS

Parents and teachers continue to exert a large influence on fourth and fifth grade students and, therefore, should continue to be an integral part of a comprehensive career counseling curriculum.

Promoting Student Self-Regulation in the Classroom. It is important that by fourth grade, students are able to keep their own daily agenda, write down tasks to complete for each day, and organize their materials in the classroom. Teachers can assist students by allotting 5 to 10 minutes at the beginning of each day to help them get their materials organized. Moreover, students need to learn the skills of effective note taking, outlining ideas before writing, and creating plans to follow for long-term projects. By doing so, the foundation is being laid for strong self-regulatory behavior. Further, students who accomplish these tasks will likely receive positive reinforcement through improvement in their grades, and this performance accomplishment may increase efficacy expectancies in future academic endeavors as they learn to implement success skills and strategies. By increasing student self-regulation and efficacy, teachers are effectively preparing students for future career success.

Collaborating With Teachers

Collaborating with teachers is critical to the successful integration of careers into the classroom curriculum (ASCA, 2012). Based on the Missouri Center for Career Education (2006) GLEs (Table 8.1.), there are numerous student career competencies that teachers could integrate into the education curriculum with the assistance of the school counselor. Specifically, in fourth and fifth grades, students need to be able to reflect on the positive feelings associated with completing work responsibilities, to demonstrate the skills for working with diverse groups of people, to apply personal, ethical, and work habits to the school environment, and to relate academic learning to career paths.

Moreover, teachers and counselors can consider alternative and creative methods for exposing students to opportunities to explore and experience careers. One way to do this is through peer and cross-age programs. Most often when people think of peer and cross-age programs they may imagine peer tutoring, mentoring, and conflict resolution. However, an example of an afterschool enrichment program for fifth grade students (see Junior Engineers in Exhibit 8.2) exemplifies how teachers collaborated with the school counselor in a cross-age program to expose students to exploring the work (performance accomplishment) of the field of engineering.

EXHIBIT 8.2
The Junior Engineers Club

Mr. Thompkins, an elementary school counselor was contacted by Mr. Donaldson, a high school physics teacher who was the club sponsor for an Engineering Club at the high school. The Engineering Club met once a month at the high school and had recently decided that they wanted to develop a cross-age program to introduce younger students to engineering as a service learning project. They decided to provide the opportunity to fifth graders interested in engineering, and they decided to call the group the Junior Engineers Club. Mr. Thompkins agreed to co-sponsor the club.

All fifth grade students were invited and 18 decided to participate. A fifth grade teacher, Mrs. Simmons, also attended in order to get ideas for integrating engineering in the future fifth grade curriculum for all students. The group met once a month. For each meeting, a different structural design was introduced. For example, during the first meeting, high school students presented a PowerPoint® of the structural components of pyramids and showed pictures of ancient and modern-day pyramids. High schoolers presented the strengths of the pyramid's design. Afterward, club members learned to sketch a design of a pyramid three dimensionally, and then used different materials to create pyramids using what they learned (wood blocks, Styrofoam blocks, and Legos®). Other designs that were explored in subsequent months included columns (Roman design), arches, cubes, foundations, and supports.

The high school Engineering Club enjoyed working with the fifth graders and the partnership continues today. Additionally, Mrs. Simmons was able to integrate some of the activities into the regular fifth grade curriculum and eventually wrote a small grant ($1,200) to purchase the materials needed to develop engineering projects. Today, the Junior Engineers Club explores more complex engineering feats such as bridges, roads, and towers.

The example in Exhibit 8.2 demonstrates how a cross-age program was used to expose students to engineering. The Junior Engineers Club gave students specific content knowledge, engineering role models (the older students), and an opportunity to experience the work of engineers (performance accomplishment), all of which are important for developing feelings of efficacy in one's ability to successfully become an engineer. Infinite possibilities exist for the types of clubs that could be started in elementary school. Clearly, such clubs have existed at the high school level for a long time (e.g., Future Farmers of America); yet, based on the importance of developing career-related efficacy (Bandura, 1977), teachers and counselors can consider creating these opportunities for younger students.

Although science, technology, engineering, and mathematics (STEM) careers have gained importance in recent years, there are many forums in which other types of careers can be examined, including those in fine arts (i.e., drama, music, visual arts, painting, writing, poetry, dance). For example, in Exhibit 8.3 we review a fourth grade project demonstrating how fine arts, business, and economics were combined to allow students to become exposed to a wide range of careers.

As illuminated in Exhibit 8.3, students were allowed to explore a variety of roles in entertainment and business. In this way, multiple intelligences (Gardner, 2004) were used and students were able to bring their own strengths and interests to the activity. By having students write their reflective essays and discuss their views on the project afterward, the school counselor and teachers promoted student awareness of their skills, interests, and feelings of efficacy related to the project (running a coffee shop). Additionally, by experiencing the various roles, the students were given an opportunity for performance accomplishment (Bandura, 1977) in managing a small business, the result of which may be increased efficacy expectancy for careers in business and marketing. Of additional importance, parents were invited to participate, an intentional strategy for increasing family involvement in career development.

Parent Engagement

As we discussed earlier in this chapter, by middle school, peers become a predominant influence in each other's lives (Young, 1983). However, for fourth and fifth grade students, parents continue to play a paramount role in career development and need to be included in ongoing career education and exploration opportunities. Based on Bandura's Social Learning Theory (1977), one very important topic to cover with parents of fourth and fifth grade students is how to help their kids become better self-regulators. As the demands of homework increase and students become more involved in extracurricular activities, students need to become better organized, manage their time, and learn how to break projects down into doable tasks. Some fun ways to do this at home include letting kids co-plan family activities like vacations. Families

EXHIBIT 8.3
Fourth Grade Coffee House and Fine Arts Night

At LaGrange Elementary School, the fourth grade classes offer a quarterly (once every nine weeks) Coffee House Night for parents, grandparents, and other special guests. For each quarter a different fourth grade class runs the coffee shop. Students take turns playing different roles in the coffee shop (cashier, server, marketing director, menu developer, pastry baker, coffee barista, dishwasher, purchasing manager, etc.) and they are responsible for all of the preparation necessary under the supervision of their teacher, teacher's aides, and a few parent volunteers. This preparation includes marketing through the development of materials (flyers/brochures) and communication (developing letters of invitation and business emails).

Parents come to the coffee shop and order from a simple menu (pastries, coffee, tea, water) while the fourth grade classes perform entertainment. Parents can walk through a gallery with art produced by students in art class (pencil drawings, watercolors, oil pastels), and students read poetry, short stories, perform short skits, dance, and play instruments. Income generated from the Coffee House funds materials and supplies needed for future Coffee House Nights and fourth grade field trips.

Additionally, the Coffee House Nights give students a chance to learn about how a business is run. The students have to prepare the Coffee House (decorate the cafeteria), develop a purchasing list (purchases are made by a parent volunteer), take orders, give change, deduct expenses from money generated to fund future coffee nights, and serve parents. In addition they get to practice displaying art, designing an "art gallery," and performing music and written arts. Students experience various roles hands-on. At the conclusion of each class's running of the Coffee House, they categorize the different jobs by career clusters and write a short essay on "What It's Like to Run a Coffee Shop." After completing the essay, the school counselor and teacher co-facilitated a classroom guidance follow up where students discussed how they felt about the Coffee House Night. In small groups, students discussed what they liked or didn't like about running a coffee shop, what they learned from the activity, what skills or talents they had to contribute to running the coffee shop, and how confident they felt that they could run a coffee shop (or other business venture) in the future.

do not have to start with a large project like a vacation; planning a family game night will also help children practice the same skill set.

After implementing a parent workshop that promoted ways for parents to help their middle school students develop self-regulatory skills, the first author received a call from a fifth grade parent who implemented the suggestions. The parent, who had twin fifth graders, had her children plan the dinner menu for two nights per week. She had her kids write down what they wanted to serve for dinner, figure out the ingredients needed, and write a grocery list. She then issued a budget for each dinner and the kids had to shop and meet the budget (sometimes choosing generic options or making substitutions if necessary). When it came to cooking, the children prepared the food by following a recipe and if they didn't have a recipe they wrote out the steps to follow to create the dish they were making (for example, the steps for making pizza). During the phone call, the first author suggested to the mother that she tie this activity to her children's career development by having the kids come up with a list of careers where they could use the skills they were learning. The kids did this activity at home and the mother was amazed by the variety of careers the kids thought of (bank teller, sports manager, chef, grocery manager, etc.). Some months later, the mother told this author that her children were up to planning dinner four nights per week, something they enjoyed and their mother was proud of! Many parents are not aware of the simple ways that they can facilitate their child's development. Simply by recognizing this need and following through with education as well as concrete ideas, school personnel can help parents become active partners in their child's career development.

THE FIFTH TO SIXTH GRADE TRANSITION

The fifth to sixth grade transition constitutes one of the most important academic transitions for P–12 students. Most often, students enter a new school building (middle school) often on a separate campus than previously attended for elementary school. Students may feel fearful and concerned about the social system they are entering and how their experiences will differ from what they have experienced in elementary school.

Partnering With Middle School Personnel

As an elementary school counselor, the first author compiled a portfolio of all academic, personal/social, and career activities students had completed in their K–5 experience (Curry & Lambie, 2007). This portfolio was given to the middle school counselor to ensure that the middle school counselor knew what kinds of ASCA Student Standards (2004) had been promoted and what competencies the students had demonstrated in elementary school. Because the middle school counselor met with the elementary counselor and received these materials, she was able to provide continuity in career education and counseling by not duplicating the same content and experiences. Besides communicating about the counseling curriculum, there are many ways that elementary and middle school counselors can collaborate to promote a successful transition for fifth grade students moving to middle school.

The Middle School Field Trip. One great way to prepare students and introduce them to middle school is to have the school counselor and fifth grade teachers take the students on a field trip to the middle school. During the visit, students can meet with a panel of middle school students for a question-and-answer session. The middle school students can serve as role models and can help to assuage many of the fifth grade students' fears (e.g., fears about switching classes in the time between class periods, using lockers, homework). The middle school counselor can share suggestions for fifth grade students about what types of skills they would need to be successful in middle school, being specific to highlight self-regulation skills (homework strategies, note taking, organizing homework materials) and the types of resources offered to assist students in being successful (e.g., before and after school tutoring, small group counseling, study skills summer institute).

Engaging Parents in the Fifth to Sixth Grade Transition. It is incumbent upon elementary school counselors to assist students and their parents in preparing for the fifth to sixth grade transition. As previously mentioned, classroom presentations aimed at preparing students for the ambiguity of adjusting to a new school and new expectations are very important. It is equally important to assist parents and one way of doing so is through parent workshops. The first author, while running a focus group for parents in a local school district, found that parents were shocked by the changes as their students moved from elementary to middle school. Things parents listed as surprising were the amount of homework, expectations for students to be self-directed and self-regulating, differences in how much communication they received from classroom teachers (they received significantly less as the students went from one teacher to six teachers), and the difficulty of assignments (parents felt unsure of how to help their children as they were unfamiliar with the content).

An optimal way to conduct workshops for parents regarding the fifth to sixth grade transition is to have the elementary and middle school counselor co-facilitate and answer questions. Potential topics for these workshops are listed in Table 8.2.

TABLE 8.2 Potential Topics for Parent Workshops on Middle School Transitions

Title of Workshop	Material Covered
Helping Your Child Prepare for Middle School Academics	Getting organized, study skills, and homework strategies
Helping Your Child Connect Career Goals to Middle School Academics	Career clusters, paths, and the middle school education agenda
Talking to Your Child About Difficult Topics	Sex, drugs, etc.
Harder Classes or Straight As? Which Should You Choose?	Introduction to the importance of rigor as post-secondary and career preparation instead of the assured "A"
Increasing the Middle Schooler's Responsibilities at Home: How Much Should You Expect?	Helping parents recognize chores that are appropriate and how to help students become increasingly responsible

SUMMARY

In this chapter we provided an overview of salient developmental milestones on student career development (physical, cognitive, social, and gender), and focused on career theory specific to fourth and fifth grade students. Of upmost importance, we took an in-depth look at Bandura's (1977) Social Learning Theory as it pertains to the development of self-regulation behaviors and the promotion of efficacy expectancies for future career success. We discussed the Missouri GLEs for student career development and explored ways to integrate career theory concepts in the guidance curriculum. We underscored the importance of a multisystem approach to comprehensive career counseling (parents, teachers) and expanded this to include the middle school counselor. Finally, we focused on the importance of the fifth grade transition to middle school for future academic and career success.

···❯ **Test Your Knowledge**

1. Define career self-efficacy.
2. Define efficacy expectancy. What are the three dimensions of efficacy beliefs?
3. Give three to four examples of self-regulatory behaviors that are age appropriate for fourth or fifth grade students at home and at school.
4. How is self-regulatory behavior related to academic success? Future career success?

9

•••••

Career Education and Counseling
for Grades 6 and 7: Career and Self-Awareness

•••••

Adolescence was described by G. Stanley Hall (1904) as a time of storm and stress, a description that underscores the turbulent nature of vast changes experienced by youth in the transition from childhood to adulthood. Yet Hindley (1983) asserted that much of the turmoil of the adolescent experience depends on prior learning, support, and environmental factors that either promote or inhibit the individual's ability to cope with the stressors brought about by growth, change, and development in the adolescent years. The ambiguity of adolescence—balancing the desires of childhood with the impending responsibilities of being an adult—helps make adolescence an ideal time for exploration, contemplation, and hope for many life possibilities. In this chapter we review developmental concepts, career theory, counseling curriculum, and the involvement of stakeholders in career education and counseling for sixth and seventh grade students.

DEVELOPMENTAL OVERVIEW

Although there are notable patterns of development in adolescence, it is an incredibly complex period of growth (Hindley, 1983). In this section we cover major changes in physical, cognitive, psychosocial, social, and cultural development in the adolescent years. As always, we caution readers to be aware that each student is unique and that characteristics and patterns discussed here may not apply to every individual.

Physical Development

Adolescence is a time of unparalleled physical changes, including the development of primary and secondary sexual characteristics, growth spurts (e.g., skeletal/muscular changes, changes in body proportions, strength), physical coordination, hormonal and neurochemical changes, motor skills, and mechanical abilities (Ausubel, 1954). Most importantly, as noted in Chapter 8, these physical changes are important when considering career growth and development as they can have an enormous impact on self-concept based on body image and evaluations of self from a social perspective. The impact on self-concept may be particularly salient during adolescence given the social capital credited to individuals based on physical attributes. An example given by Crow and Crow (1965) is that males who attained greater height and strength than their peers experienced greater social prestige (popularity) and personal adjustment.

Another important consideration for future career development is the impact of hormones and physical changes that affect personality, temperament, and other aspects of personal expression (e.g., self-consciousness). An example of this was noted by the first author during her work as a middle school counselor helping a seventh grade male with anger management concerns. The student stated, "Nothing's really different at home or school, it's just me, I suddenly started feeling angry all the time." Although the anger experienced by the student may have been due to a variety of potential factors, the anger might have also been brought about by the introduction of increased hormones, such as testosterone, that were affecting the student's affective responses to stressors.

As was mentioned in Chapter 8, students learn to regulate their emotions and behaviors by gaining self-control. Doing so can be difficult for students in early adolescence, especially because they are going through a great magnitude of change that impacts every aspect of their lives, from sleep patterns to social interactions. Emotional self-regulation and the ability to express oneself appropriately is part of the preparation adolescents must have for the world of work, and this can be a challenging task as they undergo dramatic physical changes.

Cognitive Development

According to Crow and Crow (1965), numerous characteristics emerge in adolescence that create the composite of intelligence and are considered markers of mental maturation: verbal comprehension, word fluency, mathematical abilities, spatial relations, memory, perceptual abilities, and reasoning. During adolescence, successful students demonstrate the ability to adapt to the demands of the educational environment by developing skills to concentrate, utilize imagination and creativity, memorize, and problem solve (Crow & Crow, 1965). Piaget (1969) maintained that there are multiple intellectual transformations with salient characteristics in the stage of *formal abstract* thought, which begins around the age of 11 or 12 and reaches equilibrium around the ages of 14 or 15. These characteristics include the ability to: 1) manipulate thoughts rather than just objects, 2) project into the future (e.g., understand long-term consequences of behavior), 3) formally reason based on a hypothesis, propositional operations (based on logic), reversibility by inversion, or reciprocity (e.g., algebraic equations), 4) synthesize information, and 5) generate experimentally formulated hypotheses.

Hindley (1983) acknowledged that major changes in cognitive functioning have implications for how individuals conceptualize the world and social concerns as well as how moral thought, reasoning, and behavior are manifested. For example, the ability to empathize with others, demonstrate compassion, and develop altruistic thoughts and behavior are largely based on cognitive development (Eisenberg, Miller, Shell, McNalley, & Shea, 1991). In this way, social maturation and development of positive interpersonal relationships are related to cognitive development. Further, the development of these cognitive skills helps sixth and seventh grade students apply logic and reasoning to how they conceptualize careers and project future actions necessary for workplace success.

Psychosocial Development

According to Erikson (1963), students entering adolescence are transitioning from the stage of *industry versus inferiority* to the stage of *identity versus role confusion.* Many things go into identity formation, including a sense of awareness about one's interests, strengths, weaknesses, and beliefs. The *identity versus role confusion* stage can be a difficult time for students and their families as adolescents may begin to differentiate from the views and beliefs of their families, which can cause strain on the family system (Bowen, 1976). According to Bowen, when students have low differentiation from their family of origin, they are overly dependent on their family members' acceptance of their choices and, therefore, have difficulty making decisions based on their individual preferences, thoughts, and beliefs. During the *identity versus role confusion* stage, students also begin to view themselves through a third-party perspective and begin to evaluate their social status and capital (Bourdieu, 1977) based on their social interactions with others. Low social capital and status can injure young adolescents' self-concept as their perceived weakness, low status, and lack of popularity may become predominant in their view of self.

Havighurst (1972) expanded on Erikson's theory and reported that the stage of *identity versus role confusion* is a very active time for youth and has specific challenges that include planning for one's future. This planning requires an understanding of oneself, one's future goals, and the consequences of behavior as it applies to the future. Further, based on Havighurst's (1972) conceptualization, positive identity formation in adolescence is dependent on the following tasks:

1. Achieving new and more mature relations with age mates of both sexes
2. Achieving a masculine or feminine social role
3. Accepting one's physique and using the body effectively
4. Achieving emotional independence from parents and other adults
5. Preparing for intimate relationships and family life
6. Preparing for an economic career
7. Acquiring a set of values and an ethical system as a guide to behavior—developing an ideology
8. Desiring and achieving socially responsible behavior

Students may vary in the amount of time it takes to master the tasks suggested by Havighurst, as individual development and system supports both play significant roles in how adolescents navigate these tasks.

Other theorists also have contributed to an expanded understanding of Erikson's stage of *identity versus role confusion*. Specifically, James Marcia (1987) proposed identity statuses to describe how individuals explore the possibilities of their adult lives, including their future careers. Marcia (1987) concluded that there are two major tasks that comprise the achievement of identity: 1) actively exploring future options and 2) committing to an identity. Marcia identified four *identity statuses* that comprise the relationship between these two tasks.

The first identity status is *identity diffusion,* where adolescent neither have explored future options nor committed to an identity. Adolescents in this status often seem withdrawn, resigned, and unmotivated; they are without a plan and may seem as though they are drifting through life with no future goals. The second identity status is *identity foreclosure*. In this status, adolescents have committed to an identity, but did so without exploration, which may result in unhappiness later in life. For example, a school counselor asked a middle school student what types of careers she was interested in exploring. The student said, "I think I'll be an orthodontist like my dad." Her dad then interrupted and said, "It would be crazy for her to do anything else. I am an orthodontist, my father was an orthodontist. She can be one and inherit our practice." Although the student may be happy with other possible future careers, she has committed to being an orthodontist before taking the time to explore other options. The third status Marcia (1987) proposed is *moratorium*. In this status, students are actively exploring options but have not committed to a career. This is an ideal status for sixth and seventh graders as they can be thinking critically about their future and keeping their options open. The fourth status, *identity achievement*, occurs after students have fully and critically considered their future options and then committed to an identity.

Beyond the stage of *identity versus role confusion* (Erikson, 1963), other social and emotional changes begin to occur in early adolescence. According to Crow and Crow (1965), changes to adolescent physical and cognitive development lead to greater ability to understand self and personal feelings, and adolescents are more expressive of a wide range of emotions including anxiety, worry, jealousy, and fear. Adolescents also may appear to be moody; for example, students who have been previously happy and well-adjusted may seem melancholy or display a lack of interest in other people and activities. It is important for middle school counselors to recognize emotional reactivity and heightened behavioral changes that accompany the physical maturation of adolescents and how it may become problematic in the classroom. Helping adolescents to develop self-control and other self-regulatory behaviors rather than having emotional outbursts is important for their future workplace success.

As adolescents begin to develop a sense of understanding about others and relationships with others, they may become more open to self-exploration and defining "who am I" (Hindley, 1983, p. 40). Indeed, the ability to understand other people and to understand others' perspectives helps students become more aware of their own interests, dispositions, and aptitudes related to career.

Gender/Culture

Havighurst (1972) proposed that many development tasks, such as sexual maturation, occur across cultures; however, he noted that many developmental tasks are culture specific. Yet Havighurst (1972) pointed out that the complexity of career growth and development is based on social expectation and opportunity. For example, in more primitive and agrarian societies, youth may only have one career option (farming). Within the contemporary U.S. culture, there are myriad differences based on community and environmental factors for what is expected of adolescents. Likewise, there are tremendous variations in the opportunities perceived to be available by youth.

Most importantly, in middle school, students generally want to fit in and feel accepted. However, during this time, cultural (e.g., being Muslim in a primarily Christian community) and individual differences (e.g., sexual orientation or gender expression, disability) may cause students to stand out and gain negative attention from peers. Helping students feel comfortable with who they are and teaching all students to be welcoming of differences are critical to their future career development.

CAREER THEORY AND DEVELOPMENT

A focus on career development is crucial in early adolescence. As noted by Ausubel (1954), although each adolescent may have an "apparent preoccupation with the immediate and often esoteric activities of his interim peer culture, the adolescent's primary goals are really predicated upon inclusion in the adult world" (p. 437). Ausubel (1954) contended that as adolescents develop formal abstract thought and patterns of thinking about issues with greater complexity and depth, they develop an initial understanding of the dynamic relationship between career choice and multiple factors such as personal economic needs, social status (prestige) of specific occupations, special talents and abilities, perceived intelligence, interests, and economic urgency (i.e., financial considerations of college or technical training versus immediate income). Interest, motivation, and maturity also become largely influential in early adolescents' career aspirations and career expectancies. Therefore, previous aspirations may not be stable over time (Ausubel, 1954), as many emerging factors substantially persuade the individual's career choices. Most importantly, career development in early adolescence is largely influenced by self-concept and an awareness of one's own interests, abilities, values, and aptitudes. In short, knowing oneself is the key to early adolescent career growth. In this section we review theories that speak specifically to the career needs of early adolescents.

Gottfredson's Theory of Circumscription and Compromise

Similar to students in fourth and fifth grade, students in grades 6 and 7 are most likely in Gottfredson's career development Stage 3: *Orientation to Social Valuation*. As stated in Chapter 8, students in this stage begin to consider which careers are within or outside of their tolerable level boundary. In other words, students will circumscribe careers that are, in their evaluation, either socially beneath or socially above them. Adolescents also may have heightened preoccupation with status and status symbols, a developmental milestone of understanding their own social capital and positionality. This can be exemplified in daily activities at school (e.g., students paying attention to the brand names of each other's clothing). A school counselor in an economically disadvantaged inner city school was asked by a sixth grade student, "What kind of home do you live in?" The counselor, confused, asked, "What do you mean?" The student replied, "Like a trailer or apartment, a house or something?" The student followed the question by stating, "I'm not trying to be nosy I just didn't know what kind of homes counselors can afford." This is an example of linking status (the type of home) to occupation (counselor).

Although a focus on material things may seem unrelated to career development, this focus is a sign that students are considering the social value of things and people—a definitive measure that they are entrenched in Gottfredson's Stage 3. The important thing for school counselors to remember is that students in the stage of orientation to social valuation need opportunities to challenge, through exploration, their tolerable level boundary. In other words, career exploration may decrease self-circumscription of career options.

Holland's Theory of Vocational Choice

John Holland's career theory (1973, 1997), known as *Theory of Types*, encompasses six different categories that represent individuals' self-perceived competencies and interests. The six types created by Holland (1973) are an amalgamation of the interaction among a person's heredity (or biological traits), interests, self-perceived competencies, and dispositions (personality traits, sensitivity to environmental influences, values, perceptions of self and world, and self-concept). Holland himself acknowledged that many factors influence the expression of a person's type: ethnicity, race, religion, sexual orientation, socioeconomic status, and more. Therefore, the types provide a guide, not absolutes, for career exploration.

As mentioned in Chapter 1, the six Holland types are: realistic, investigative, artistic, social, enterprising, and conventional. A description of the six different Holland types can be found in Table 9.1. By having students complete one of Holland's assessments (e.g., the self-directed search [SDS]; see Chapter 4), school counselors can help students narrow down career exploration to sets of careers that may fit them as individuals.

Because Holland's theory begins with an assessment of a person's interests and aptitudes, it is ideal for middle school students because they love learning about themselves. Moreover, Holland's theory is very useful in helping students to critique how they might enjoy certain work environments and daily tasks. As noted by Sharf (2006), most individuals will have more than one Holland type (generally a combination of up to three); this may be particularly true for individuals exposed to a variety of environments and activities (e.g., extracurricular activities, hobbies, athletics, travel).

In a study of middle school students using structural equation model analysis, Turner, Conkel, Starkey, and Landgraf (2010) found that males tended to have greater realistic interests and females had greater artistic and social interests. More gender differences emerged in the study, including females capitalizing on their skills and abilities and more actively preparing for their future career plans than males. Males, on the other hand, were more assertive and desired to create their own career opportunities and were more apt to use instrumental support. These findings suggest that continuing career exploration, increasing self-awareness, and increasing students' perceptions of career options that are not rigidly bound by gender are critical in elementary and middle school career counseling programming.

Young's Career Concepts

As discussed in previous chapters, Young (1983) highlighted the vital role of parents in adolescent career development. He particularly highlighted the dynamics of the parent–child relationship including: parent–child interaction, identification with parents, adolescents' perception of parental

TABLE 9.1   Holland Types

Type	Description	Possible Careers
Realistic	Prefer activities that are practical in nature including manipulation of tools, machinery, objects and animals. Some careers in this field require physical strength. Does not enjoy therapeutic or educational activities.	Farmer, surveyor, electrician, roofer, auto mechanic, painter
Investigative	Prefer to investigate physical, biological and cultural phenomenon through observation, symbolism, and systematic processes with strong scientific and mathematical competence. Does not enjoying selling, leadership, or persuading, people or repetitive activities.	Chemist, biologist, anthropologist, medical technologist, geologist
Artistic	Prefers creative activities such as fine arts (e.g., sculpting), performing arts (e.g., drama, music), dance, and creative writing. Does not enjoy repetitive activities or highly structure, ordered activities.	Stage director, choreographer, actor/actress, interior decorator, musician
Social	Prefers activities that encompass working with others to train, educate, develop, enlighten, or cure in order to help others reach a goal. Does not enjoy mechanical or scientific activities.	Nurse, counselor, teacher, speech therapist, social worker, religious worker
Enterprising	Prefers activities that include manipulating others to attain economic gain or organizational change. Does not enjoy observational, symbolic activities.	Producer, sports promoter, salesperson, manager, business leader, buyer
Conventional	Prefer activities that include interpretation of data, record keeping, filing materials, organizing written and numerical data. Does not enjoy ambiguous, unstructured, and exploratory activities.	Bookkeeper, accountant, financial analyst, cost estimator, banker

Adapted from Holland (1973, 1997); Jones (2011); Niles & Harris-Bowlesby (2009).

influence, and amount of contact with parents. Because of these relationship dynamics, intentional inclusion of parents in career and postsecondary exploration is an important component of the school counselor's career curriculum. According to Young, Paseluikho, and Valach (1997), parents need to co-construct career goals with their children through meaningful dialogue that promotes shared interests, values, and emotions.

Young and colleagues (1997) contended that emotions in career conversations are demonstrative of the level of adolescent career motivation and cognitive appraisal of self (i.e., self-concept related to career). Specifically, they found that emotion in parent–adolescent career conversations promoted career action. It is presumed that this connection exists because language (in this case, conversation) provides a primary medium for adolescents to conceptualize and negotiate career goals, construct personal meanings related to career, and determine the purpose of career-related work in their lives (Young et al., 1997). When parents and adolescents are given the opportunity to participate in career conversations as part of a deliberate and planned component of the comprehensive school counseling program, then families can support adolescents in career problem solving, planning, and decision making. Through such conversations, adolescents and parents can be given a chance to explore the adolescent's feelings related to career development.

MIDDLE SCHOOL COLLEGE AND CAREER READINESS

As was highlighted in Chapter 1, low college graduation rates have extensive personal and social costs. More importantly, the demand for college degrees is growing. It is estimated that there will be a shortage of at least 3 million individuals with postsecondary degrees by 2018 (Carnevale, Smith, & Strohl, 2010). Although not every student will go to college, it is important that stakeholders are aware of the skills that students need so that college can remain an option. According to the California College Board, these skills include participation in a rigorous high school curriculum and the development of skills in 1) higher-order thinking, 2) studying and researching, 3) reasoning, 4) problem solving and analyzing, 5) writing, and 6) understanding college and career options, including college admissions and financing (Mijares, 2007). If these skills are important in high school, what career education and training are critical in middle school to prepare students for a rigorous high school curriculum?

Throughout this book we propose a multisystemic approach to career and college readiness. It is important to underscore that parents, teachers, administrators, and community partners all play a vital role in the career development of middle school students. For example, Orthner (2012) identified benefits (including increased school engagement, higher performance on end of grade tests in math and reading, fewer unexcused absences and disciplinary referrals) among students whose teachers used *CareerStart*, an instructional strategy designed to help students connect academics to careers. CareerStart emphasizes a whole-school approach, including parent and community involvement, to improve school engagement and achievement. In the next section we highlight how school counselors can address the career development needs of sixth and seventh graders through a comprehensive curriculum and a multisystems approach.

THE SCHOOL COUNSELING CURRICULUM

The school counseling career education curriculum in middle school should be centered on helping students explore their personal fit with careers by examining their interests, aptitudes, dispositions, and values related to career. The curriculum also ideally should help build students' career decision making self-efficacy (e.g., *The Career Horizons Program*; see O'Brien, Dukstein, Jackson, Tomlinson, & Kamatuka, 1999). We begin in this section by including the Missouri Center for Career Education (2006) Grade Level Expectations for sixth and seventh grade students (Table 9.2). We also want to call readers' attention to the importance of including technology and assessment in the comprehensive career curriculum to expose students to many possible options that are personally suited for them (i.e., focus on person–environment fit). Remember, middle school students love to talk about themselves and think about who they are, and that makes developing the career curriculum particularly fun.

TABLE 9.2   Missouri Grade Level Expectations for Career Counseling Curriculum

Concept	Grade Level 6	Grade Level 7
Integration of Self-Knowledge into Life and Career Plans	Use current interests, strengths, and limitations to guide individual career exploration.	Use current interests, strengths, and limitations to guide career exploration and educational planning.
Adaptations to World of Work Changes	Recognize the career path concept as an organizer for exploring and preparing for careers now and in the future.	Be aware of occupations and careers as they relate to career paths, personal interests, and aptitudes.
Respect for All Work	Identify males and females in nontraditional work roles.	Recognize the relevance of all work and workers, and their existence in a global society.
Career Decision Making	Evaluate career and educational information resources.	Utilize career and educational information to explore career paths of interest.
Education and Career Requirements	Compare different types of postsecondary training and education as they relate to career choices.	Utilize a variety of resources to obtain information about the levels of training and education required for various occupations.
Personal Skills for Job Success	Assess and analyze personal, ethical, and work habit skills as they relate to individual student success.	Utilize information about personal, ethical, and work habit skills to enhance individual student success.
Job-Seeking Skills	Develop a resume of work experiences for home and school.	Identify and demonstrate basic job seeking skills of interviewing and completing applications.

Based on the Missouri Center for Career Education (2006).

Assessment in Middle School Career Counseling

School counselors should use assessment to help middle school students discover the skills, aptitudes, interests, and values they hold that may impact their fit with potential careers. Although we covered various assessments in Chapter 4, we highlight a few in this section that are particularly useful in sixth and seventh grade classroom career guidance lessons. The activities we share can be helpful for promoting self-exploration and moving adolescents from diffusion and foreclosure to moratorium (Marcia, 1987), where they can actively begin to question who they are in relation to their future career choices.

Values card sort. Richard Knowdell's Career Values Card Sort (2005) can be used effectively with sixth or seventh grade students, as they are capable of understanding values they hold related to potential careers. The Knowdell Career Values Card Sort is a deck of cards with each card listing a value related to careers (e.g., team work, creativity, problem solving) and an explanation of the value.

The first author, when using the values card sort activity with students, would place students in small groups seated in a circle. Each group was given one deck of cards and one student was the dealer. The dealer gave each student six cards and students were asked to place the cards in order from the thing they valued most in a future career to the thing they valued least. Then the group discussed their values and why they chose what they chose and how it relates to careers. The Knowdell Career Values Card Sort comes with activity sheets that the students filled out as they went. The sheets gave students a chance to think about the values they chose and to reflect on their own personal preferences of values related to careers. Students were then asked to remove the card they ranked as most valuable and give it to the student sitting on their right in the circle. Then they re-ordered their cards to integrate the new card they just received. As a follow up activity, the English teacher had each student write a reflection on the things they value in a future career. Students reported enjoying this activity and the discussions in the small groups were generally lively. In addition, the cards gave students a chance to broaden their career values vocabulary.

Career genogram. According to Gibson (2012, 2005), the career genogram activity is one way to have students examine the influence of their family members and other significant adults on their career choice. It also can help them identify ways that their interests may be different from those of family members; remember, according to Erikson (1963) and Bowen (1976), adolescents are exploring their own individual beliefs and values and how they resemble or differ from those held by their family of origin. If a school counselor has not facilitated a genogram activity previously, he or she can access instructions from Gibson (2005, p. 358). In addition to filling out the genogram, Gibson (2012) recommends that students be provided with questions to ask family members that will deepen their knowledge, such as: 1) What

FIGURE 9.1   Ainsley's Career Genogram

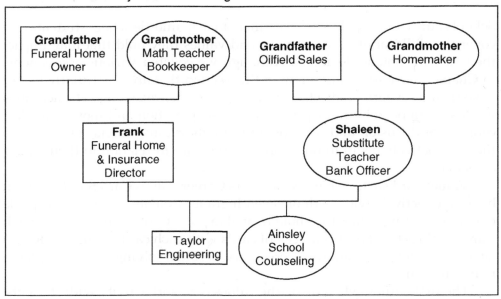

influenced family members' career decisions? 2) Who influenced their career decisions? and 3) At what age did they decide on their career choice? Another question that could be asked that would link academics, career, and postsecondary options is about the type of training or education that was needed for the career each family member is in. Figure 9.1 includes an example of Ainsley's career genogram (Ainsley is a student wishing to become a school counselor).

Based on this genogram, some questions that could be posed to Ainsley that may help her see the similarities and differences between her career choice and those of her family members' include: Who in your family has a career that is similar to the career you have chosen? (In Ainsley's case, she may choose her mother, a substitute teacher.) How is his/her career similar to the career(s) you are considering? (Both involve working with children in an education setting.) Whose career is different? (Ainsley's father, a funeral director.) What similar characteristics or values exist between your career choice and the career choices of your family members? (Ainsley may identify similar characteristics of kindness or compassion.) How has your family influenced your career decisions? In what ways have you chosen your own career path?

ENGAGING STAKEHOLDERS

Johnson (2000) reported results of a study conducted with sixth and ninth grade students. Only about half of the students in the study could identify a skill needed for career success. More alarming, approximately 88% of the participants "reflected little or no awareness of how the skills, knowledge, or attitudes learned in the subject coursework might relate to future employment" (Johnson, 2000, p. 269). However, Johnson (2000) also reported that sixth grade students found schoolwork more useful to their careers than did ninth grade students, an indication, according to Johnson, of students' feelings of increasing discontentment with their school experience between the sixth and ninth grade years. Therefore, sixth and seventh grade teachers have an important task in keeping students engaged in academics and connecting academics to career. Indeed, nearly every middle school teacher and counselor has heard students say about various content, "Why do I have to learn this? I'm never going to use it!" This feeling that the information being learned is not useful or applicable to students' lives may leave students feeling disengaged, frustrated, and unmotivated to learn. The *CareerStart* (Orthner, 2012) program is one evidence-based way to help students feel more engaged in school. Lesson plans and suggested activities are provided, but teachers are encouraged to scaffold lessons to cater to their specific populations. In the following, we identify other options.

Teachers

Middle school teachers have the opportunity to engage middle school students in learning. Curry, Belser, and Binns (2013) highlight numerous ways that middle school teachers can integrate career-related information in the education curriculum. For example, a middle school counselor, Mr. Braxton, met with all of the seventh grade math teachers at Rock Creek Middle School. He explained that he would be introducing students to math careers every quarter in their math class and that he would like to coordinate this with the seventh grade math teachers. Each quarter, the math teachers and Mr. Braxton met to discuss what types of math activities were being covered and how these might relate to careers. One example occurred after a unit on measurements (i.e., mass, volume, perimeter, circumference). Mr. Braxton and the seventh grade math teachers completed a lesson on careers where math measurements are used (e.g., chemist, engineer, construction worker, architect). Students were then given an opportunity to discuss in small groups what they found challenging or interesting about the math skills learned in the unit and which, if any, of the related careers were of interest to them. Mr. Braxton did this with every math class each quarter and teachers reported that students seemed to take a greater interest in learning math skills as a result.

Moreover, there may be some evidence that career knowledge and maturity may result in positive student outcomes. For example, Legum and Hoare (2004) conducted a study with urban, at-risk middle school students. They divided the participants into control and experimental groups. Participants in the experimental group received a 9-week career intervention program that linked academics to careers; the control group received no intervention. At the end of the study there were no major statistical findings between the control and experimental groups in academic outcomes, but several qualitative changes were reported. Teachers were interviewed at the completion of the groups, and they identified positive changes in the students attending the experimental group at the end of the study including gains in self-esteem, academic achievement, academic motivation, participation in class, and more willingness to attempt class work. Teachers did not notice similar changes in the control group (Legum & Hoare, 2004). This study only lasted 9 weeks; therefore, what is not known is whether or not a longer and more systematic intervention would have a definitive and significant academic impact.

The major consideration based on Legum and Hoare's (2004) study is that career exploration may help students to feel more engaged in the educational agenda of middle school (motivation, willingness to attempt class work, classroom participation), making career curriculum integration a worthwhile task for teachers. Further, there are many ways to include teachers, and it is most important to point out that much of the career and college readiness curriculum infusion does not require large amounts of time from teachers. Often, short quantities of time devoted to career (when done with frequency and consistency over time) may be effective. Orthner (2012) found positive results from core academic subject teachers implementing 10 lessons per year. In Exhibit 9.1 we share an example of how a school counselor and teacher can integrate a brief intervention.

Parents

Hall (2003) described the nuanced and complicated relationship between individuals' families and their career choices. One major factor creating this dynamic is that students who choose careers that are out of their family's perceived level of prestige (aiming too high or too low based on the perception of family members) are at emotional risk. In other words, students may suffer emotional consequences (e.g., stated disapproval or anger from parents) for making a decision that family members do not agree with (Hall, 2003). For example, one school counselor conducted a career session with a parent and student. The student was adamant about becoming a music major and the father, an accountant, told the student that if she wanted a career in music she would have to move out and pay for college herself. The father followed up by stating that if the student chose "a real major" he would support her and pay her way through school. In this way, the father was exerting an emotional and economic sanction for his disapproval of the student's career choice. The emotional, fiscal, cognitive, and social investments parents make in raising their children can lead them to have highly emotional reactions when discussing careers with their children.

EXHIBIT 9.1
College Colors Day at Highland View Middle School

A middle school counselor, Mr. Burnett, delivered a classroom lesson on career exploration and postsecondary options. He found that many students did not understand the differences between universities, community colleges, and technical schools, and he wanted to do more to promote student awareness of postsecondary institutions and the types of degrees or training certificates they offer. More importantly, he thought students needed this information more consistently and that it should become a continuous part of the academic curriculum.

Mr. Burnett devised a plan with the help of his school counseling advisory committee (American School Counselor Association [ASCA], 2005), which they introduced at a faculty inservice on career and college readiness. The advisory committee collected information on universities, colleges, community colleges, and technical schools in their state and in all surrounding states in the region. At the beginning of each 6-week period, every teacher was given a postsecondary institution to present in each of their classes (each teacher taught six classes and had one planning period) on a day designated as *College Colors Day*.

On *College Colors Day*, teachers wore the colors of the postsecondary school they were assigned to present. In each of their six classes they gave a 5-minute presentation including: types of programs/degrees offered, number of students attending, strengths of the school (such as arts, specific degrees, job placement), highlights about the town in which the school is located, and so on. Every 6 weeks the teachers were all given a different postsecondary institution with information to present on *College Colors Day*. Students were exposed to information about seven different postsecondary options each *College Colors Day*. By the end of the year they had heard about 42 different options, and discussions of postsecondary education became a more regular part of the academic discourse of the school.

As previously mentioned, Young and colleagues (1997) noted the importance of career communication and emotions between parents and their middle school children in developing positive career action. Usinger (2005) conducted a 5-year longitudinal, interpretive study of seventh grade students in low-achieving schools and how they constructed their academic and career aspirations. Usinger focused on the parent/guardian role in this process. Based on her findings, Usinger asserted that parents need opportunities to reflect on their own career disappointments, regrets, triumphs, and insights. By including parents in career education and by creating opportunities for them to consider their own growth and development, the career counseling process can include the family system in a meaningful and relevant way. Usinger also highlighted the importance of parents discussing their own struggles and how they have overcome them in order to role model personal success for their children and also demonstrate that everyone has their own personal struggles. These kinds of conversations can become increasingly important, and deeper, as students in middle school contemplate their futures. Moreover, based on a study by Turner and Lapan (2002), perceived parent support was a predictive factor in students' career self-efficacy as it accounted for 29% to 43% of total unique variance in career self-efficacy for a sample of middle school students, more evidence of the impetus to include parents. Other career skills that parents and students both need during the middle school years include how to effectively explore careers using technology, understanding education and labor market trends, and how to reduce the impact of socially constructed gender types for careers (Amundson & Penner, 1998; Turner & Lapan).

Literature provides some suggestions of career interventions for parents and students that school counselors can review before designing their own programs (e.g., Parent Involved Career Exploration [PICE]; see Amundson & Penner, 1998). However, before beginning to implement any parent-involved career curriculum, we suggest accurately identifying the career needs of the school population served through a needs assessment (ASCA, 2012). See Exhibit 9.2 and Table 9.3 for an example of a school counseling program activity designed to include parents.

EXHIBIT 9.2
The Career Conversation Workshops

Mr. Drexler, a middle school counselor, decided to provide seventh grade students and their parents with an opportunity to have career conversations as part of a large-scale career and college readiness program Mr. Drexler was implementing at Grove Middle School. Although students were receiving career education curriculum in their courses, Mr. Drexler also designed three parent–student workshops for family career exploration (one in September and two in October). He also partnered with a local counselor educator, Dr. Shelton, to collaborate and design the workshops. Dr. Shelton's school counseling graduate students were volunteers who helped with the parent night programs (nine volunteers in all). Three total workshops were provided lasting 2 hours each with homework assignments for the parents and students in between.

(continued)

EXHIBIT 9.2 (*Continued*)

For the first program, parents and students were given an introduction to career and college readiness and the types of tasks they will need to complete from 7th through 12th grade. Then, parents and students were given a brief introduction to active listening (including videos with good and bad examples) and positive communication skills. Parents were then asked to discuss three questions with their children (taking turns with both adults and students answering each question): 1) If you could have any career in the world, what would it be? 2) What gifts or talents do you have to bring to the workplace? 3) What skills do people need to be successful in the workplace? After parents and their children discussed these questions, they came together in groups (facilitated by the school counseling graduate students) to discuss their answers. Homework was assigned at the end of the workshop; the assignment was to fill out a worksheet exploring one career on the Occupational Outlook Handbook website and answer the questions on the worksheet.

For the second program, parents and students were reminded of active listening and positive communication skills, then all were introduced to family and individual values. Dr. Shelton provided a brief developmental overview of how family values do influence youth, but also how students begin to develop their own unique value systems as they get older. Parents and students were given a list of 48 values (see Table 9.3) that may impact the fit between an individual and his or her career. Then, pictures of individuals working were posted on a screen and the parents and their child discussed the possible values that a person in that work might have that fit with that career. For example, when looking at a picture of a female firefighter, parents and students looked at the careers value list (Table 9.3) and came up with three to five values that a person with the career of firefighter might have (e.g., team work). Next, students and parents each chose three careers of interest to them (one of which they had explored in their homework assigned at the last session), and discussed what values they have that might be a fit for that career. They also talked about things they valued that may not be a fit. For example, one parent stated that a dream job of his was rock star but that he has strong family values and touring/being on the road would not be a fit. Finally, everyone was placed in groups (facilitated by the school counseling graduate students) and discussed values portrayed in social media and how those values may be confusing to people as they consider careers. In one group a mother mentioned that women

(continued)

EXHIBIT 9.2 *(Continued)*
The Career Conversation Workshops

are often portrayed in clerical/secretarial roles or as housewives (she named several TV shows and commercials). She was bothered by this as these portrayals didn't reflect the values she was trying to teach her daughter about being a leader. She stated, "My daughter can be a CEO of a company. I don't want her to feel she can only be the CEO's assistant or wife." The homework assignment for the second workshop was to watch television together and count and list the number of careers seen in a specific show. The parent and student then filled out a worksheet about the values associated with each career and if the career was portrayed in a realistic, stereotypical, or nontraditional way (careers that are portrayed out of gender type, such as male nurses).

In the third parent and child career workshop, parents and students were given specific information about the types of career exploration assessments and activities that students would experience throughout the remainder of seventh grade (from October to May). Parents and students were reminded of communication and active listening skills, then they were asked to answer the following questions:

Parents: What do you wish you knew when you were making career and college decisions for yourself? What career might you have today if you had received the best possible information?

Students: What career concerns do you have today? As you think about the future, what three careers are of most interest to you?

In the final activity, students and parents co-created a collage about what they had learned about and what their wishes were for the student's future career (magazines were provided by a local distributor). Everyone was put in small groups and the school counseling graduate students facilitated the final discussions and presentations of the career collages.

The parent workshop in Exhibit 9.2 illuminates some of the suggestions for student career development provided by Turner and Lapan (2002): having parents and students engage together in activities that reduce career gender typing (such as co-viewing media and improving media literacy skills to question stereotypes) and developing career exploration skills (e.g., considering values related to careers and using technology to explore and answer questions about a specific career). Moreover, the career conversations in the example provided a structured opportunity for parents and students to discuss careers in a meaningful way.

TABLE 9.3 Career Values Chart

Intellectual Status	Diversity	Independence	Make Decisions
Friendships	Excitement	High Earnings	Affiliation
Stability	Change and Variety	Team Work	Moral Fulfillment
Competition	Power and Authority	Honesty and Integrity	Fast Pace
Public Contact	Influence People	Physical Challenge	Adventure
Work Under Pressure	Location	Fun and Humor	Family
Challenging Problems	Precision Work	Collaboration	Status
Time Freedom	Security	Tradition	Recognition
Aesthetics	Job Tranquility	Artistic Creativity	Steep Learning Curve
Predictability	Spirituality	Feeling Competent	Practicality
Help Society	Work Alone	Creative Expression	Work–Life Balance
Supervision	Knowledge	Community	Fame

SUMMARY

In this chapter we reviewed developmental concepts and career theory relevant to comprehensive career planning with sixth and seventh grade students. In particular, we highlighted Marcia's identity statuses and the importance of students learning about themselves in relation to their future careers (values, beliefs, dispositions). We highlighted how pre-adolescence and early adolescence are times of growth where students come to understand how their individual preferences may be similar to, or different from, their family of origin (Bowen) and how school counselors can help them explore these similarities and differences (career genogram, parent–student career conversations). In summary, middle school is a time of vast changes and growth, and the perfect opportunity to promote student understanding of their future career and college options.

••❯ Test Your Knowledge

1. What tasks are involved in the development of positive identity formation (consider Erikson, Havighurst, and Marcia)?
2. In what ways is self-concept related to career development for sixth and seventh grade students?
3. What are the goals of career assessment measures for sixth and seventh graders? In other words, what types of knowledge or insights should they gain?

10
••••

Career Education and Counseling for Grade 8: High School Transition Planning

••••

The eighth grade is typically when students are expected to make important choices regarding their futures. In many states, students must decide by the end of their eighth grade year what curriculum they want to follow in high school. Although they are referred to by various descriptors (e.g., courses of study, tracks, academic paths), the curricula from which students must choose typically reflect long-term college and career plans. For example, students might choose a vocational or technical curriculum that would prepare them to search for a job, enter the military right after high school, or attend a technical training program (e.g., culinary arts). Conversely, students may choose a college preparatory curriculum that would enable them to pursue postsecondary training at a 2- or 4-year college, or they might choose a rigorous honors or advance placement (AP) curriculum that would enable them to competitively pursue 4-year college degrees. Because of differing math, science, and foreign language requirements, among other things, students who choose a less rigorous curriculum may be limited in postsecondary school options should they decide later on that they do want to attend college; moreover, they may have to take remedial courses (such as algebra) or prerequisite courses (such as foreign languages) once in college in order to catch up with their collegiate peers. On the other hand, students who choose an honors college preparatory track may find that they took on more than they were ready for academically, and their grades may suffer accordingly.

Clearly, choosing a high school curriculum requires a lot of thought. Preparing for the transition to high school and the corresponding decisions that must be made also require a keen awareness both of self and of careers. Furthermore, knowledgeable school counselors and a collaborative approach involving families, teachers, and community members can help to ensure a smooth high school transition process. Middle or junior high school personnel must be familiar with high school requirements and expectations, and parents must be involved in helping to make these important curricular decisions. In this chapter we discuss student readiness for high school and focus on collaborative efforts to help students make the transition from eighth to ninth grade.

DEVELOPMENTAL OVERVIEW

The typical eighth grade student, who has progressed through school in a traditional manner, is age 13 or 14. Although we acknowledge that students vary immensely in their development at any age, we highlight below some of the more common developmental characteristics of students in eighth grade. Later we discuss appropriate interventions based on these developmental considerations.

Psychosocial Development

According to Erikson (1963), students in eighth grade would fall into the *identity versus role confusion* stage. Adolescents struggle to identify who they want to be now and in the future—both as people in general (e.g., beliefs, values) and in relation to their future career role. Students in this stage need opportunities to explore and try out new things so they can figure out what they like and don't like, as well as in what areas they possess strengths and weaknesses. Part of the challenge with developing a clear identity is that students at this age often struggle to reconcile their own desires and dreams with those of their friends or parents. Though the influence of family is still important (Young, 1983), these students are highly influenced by their peers and want to fit in. In fact, many of their decisions are based on what their peers are doing or what their peers value, including in the area of career development.

As we discussed in Chapter 9, James Marcia (1989) elaborated on Erikson's stage of *identity versus role confusion* to look at how adolescents resolve the major life task of developing an identity. He proposed four statuses (moratorium, diffusion, foreclosure, and achievement) to describe the various ways in which adolescents form identity, and these statuses can be distinctly applied to career decision making. The four statuses are illustrated in Table 10.1.

Beyond career and identity development, social development is a major life task of adolescence. In particular, adolescents begin to develop a more keen awareness of social cues and, as a result, begin to monitor their own behavior to meet social expectations of their peer group. They can also become somewhat rebellious to adult figures in their lives and develop short-term, adolescence-limited turmoil as they are beginning to learn to negotiate conflict with others (Belsky, 2007). It is important that students at this age learn

TABLE 10.1 Marcia's Identity Statuses as Related to Careers

	Active Career Exploration	**No Career Exploration**
No Commitment to Career Choice	Moratorium	Diffusion
Committed to Career Choice	Achievement	Foreclosure

positive communication and conflict strategies as this will set the stage for positive working relationships and future career success.

Cognitive Development

As we discussed in the previous chapter, according to Piaget (1977), students in middle school are becoming more sophisticated in their thinking and are likely entering the stage of *formal operations*. At minimum, most students in grade 8 possess concrete thinking abilities. They are able to understand cause and effect and can follow sequences. Although not everyone develops formal operational thought, many students in eighth grade will show some evidence, albeit inconsistent, of their abstract thinking abilities. These are the abilities that help students understand algebraic concepts and comprehensively explain how personal experiences can affect someone later in life (e.g., understanding and predicting consequences). Additionally, abstract thinking gives adolescents new skills to use, including thinking logically, engaging in inductive and deductive reasoning, generating hypotheses, and problem solving. These skills are essential to college and career planning, as doing so requires the ability to understand one's options, research possibilities, comprehend one's own talents and abilities, and project into the future (Belsky, 2007).

Despite their advanced thinking skills, many adolescents are still quite egocentric in their thinking (Elkind, 1978). They might be able to clearly explain the consequences of a specific choice, but at the same time they may believe that they are immune to any negative outcomes (i.e., their personal fable). It is this kind of thinking that leads some students to believe that things will work out for them no matter what they do.

Beyond promoting complex academic structures and capabilities, the emergence of formal operational thought supports the ability to take another person's perspective. Perspective taking creates a critical foundation for advanced interpersonal skills such as empathy, compassion, prosocial interest, and altruism (Eisenberg et al., 1999, 1991), all of which are important for effective social interaction and positive collegial relationships in the workplace. Moreover, advanced abstract thought can promote moral development and affect career choice for adolescents who develop a strong sense of justice, an ethos of caring for others, and a propensity for activism (Belsky,

2007). Conversely, the ability to think abstractly may support critical thinking, which can manifest as students question authority and become argumentative. For students struggling academically, adolescence can become a time where they question why school is important or meaningful in their personal lives.

RELEVANT CAREER THEORIES: GOTTFREDSON, HOLLAND, AND YOUNG

Gottfredson's Theory of Circumscription and Compromise (1981, 2002) provides much insight into understanding the decision-making process in which many eighth grade students engage as they make career-related choices. Specifically, students in eighth grade would most likely fall into Gottfredson's third stage, *orientation to social valuation*. In this stage, individuals narrow career choices based on their perceived social values of particular careers. Doing so requires students to assess their own social status as well as the social status of various careers they are considering. According to Gottfredson (2002), adolescents in this stage are noticing symbols of status including cars, home, and clothing, among other material possessions. Students may begin to consider careers that will afford them the status they desire.

Beyond social status, adolescents begin to consider perceived intellectual abilities in career choice. Adolescents will consider careers that are within a tolerable level boundary, meaning the status of the career must fit within the acceptable range of careers for the individual's perceived social status. For example, a student whose parents are surgeons will most likely find a career as a fast-food restaurant manager intolerable. Similarly, a student with a single mother who is a hotel housekeeper may find a career as a physicist intolerable. Individuals circumscribe and compromise out of careers based on the social value of the career and the individual's perception of his or her social value.

With students struggling to solidify their own identities at this age, however, messages from peers can greatly influence perceptions of which careers are valuable and/or how students view themselves, although their perceptions may or may not be accurate. Gottfredson's and Piaget's theories complement each other in helping to conceptualize the unique needs of eighth grade students, particularly in regard to the development of self-concept and career decision making. We discuss ways to involve peers and address peer influence in the interventions we share later in this chapter.

John Holland's Theory of Vocational Choice (1973) also serves as an important foundation for understanding and working with eighth grade students. His emphasis on self- and career awareness as precursors to making satisfying career choices suggests that time spent helping students explore their identities and develop a realistic understanding of job requirements and characteristics can help set the stage for future career success and satisfaction. The use of assessments that target interests, abilities, and values are common with students in eighth grade, and the results of those assessments can serve as a starting point for identifying careers that are consistent with a student's personality type. More details about working with these types of assessments are presented later in this chapter.

Finally, Young's (1983) ecosystemic career concepts are particularly important both for understanding factors that can influence eighth grade students and for conceptualizing interventions relevant to those students. Young discussed both explicit and implicit career influences that can come from the school. The intentional implementation of individual, group, classroom, and school-wide career activities would reflect explicit influence exerted by the school. The implicit influences, however, can come in the form of things such as what topics are or are not addressed; what messages counselors, teachers, and other school personnel send to students regarding their future; and what opportunities are afforded all students to engage in career and self-exploration.

Young (1983) also acknowledged the role of peer (social group) and parent (family) microsystems on students' career development. Specifically, direct or indirect messages from peers and parents can be integrated into students' decision-making process. Finally, the positioning of eighth grade students in their transition to high school highlights the importance of examining mesosystemic influences. For example, the quality and extent of the relationships as well as the amount and type of communication that exists between the eighth grade school personnel and parents with the high school personnel can affect how prepared students (and their families) are for the transition to ninth grade, the important choices that must be made regarding choosing a high school curriculum, and the resulting impact those choices have on students' future career and college outcomes.

EIGHTH GRADE STUDENT CAREER DEVELOPMENT OUTCOMES

We have talked quite a bit in this book about using standards (e.g., American School Counselor Association [ASCA] Student Standards; ASCA, 2012) or grade level expectations (GLEs) as the foundation for choosing areas of focus and developing a career counseling curriculum. It is important that interventions are developed with intention. Sticking with the GLEs developed by the Missouri Center for Career Education (2006) that we have been referencing throughout this book, we share developmentally appropriate college and career-related outcomes for eighth grade students in Table 10.2.

As we discussed in Chapter 1, a multifaceted and systemic approach to college and career planning requires a focus on more than just career awareness. Things such as academic skills, interpersonal skills, and skills in self-regulation are all important to students' future career outcomes. We find each of these areas addressed throughout Missouri's academic, career, and

TABLE 10.2 Missouri GLEs for Eighth Grade

Career Development: Self and Career Awareness	
Integration of Self-Knowledge into Life and Career Plans	Develop an educational and career plan based on current interests, strengths, and limitations.
Adaptations to World of Work Changes	Identify and explore a variety of resources to aid in career exploration and planning now and in the future.
Respect for All Work	Identify personal contributions made to school and community.
Career Decision Making	Compare personal interests with information about careers and education.
Education and Career Requirements	Identify the training and education required for occupations in career paths of interest.
Personal Skills for Job Success	Assess and analyze personal, ethical, and work habit skills as they relate to individual student success.
Job-Seeking Skills	Utilize a portfolio of middle school/junior high school academic and work experience.

Academic Development	
Life-Long Learning	Consistently apply a system of study skills and test-taking strategies to promote academic success.
Self-Management for Educational Achievement	Consistently apply a self-management system to promote academic success.
Transitions	Identify the information and skills necessary to transition to high school.
Educational Planning for Life-Long Learning	Design a 4- to 6-year educational plan.

Personal/Social Development: Understanding Self, Working With Others, and Coping	
Self-Concept	Identify thoughts and feelings and how they relate to self-concept.
Balancing Life Roles	Recognize the different roles and responsibilities people play in the family, school, and community, and how those roles and responsibilities are interrelated.
Citizenship and Contribution Within a Diverse Community	Recognize personal ways for the individual to contribute as a member of the school community.
Quality Relationships	Self-assess interpersonal skills that will help maintain quality relationships.
Respect for Self and Others	Apply strategies that promote acceptance and respect of others within the global community.
Personal Responsibility in Relationships	Exhibit an awareness of personal responsibility in conflict situations.
Safe and Healthy Choices	Recognize peer influence on risk-taking behaviors and consequences.
Personal Safety of Self and Others	Apply strategies related to personal safety issues.
Coping Skills	Evaluate coping skills to manage life-changing events.

Based on the Missouri Center for Career Education (2006).

personal/social GLEs (not just in the career area). Furthermore, a clear emphasis on self-awareness, career awareness, and future planning is evident in these GLEs.

CAREER DEVELOPMENT INTERVENTIONS

Career development interventions for eighth grade students should be intentional, comprehensive, include a variety of activities and delivery methods, and involve a variety of stakeholders (ASCA, 2012; Brown, 2012). We will be sharing developmentally appropriate interventions that reflect the concepts and concerns we identified previously in the developmental and career theories and that allow school counselors to address many of the GLEs listed. The primary goal of these activities is to focus on self-awareness, career awareness, and long-term career decision making—all critical to enable students to make decisions regarding their high school curriculum. The secondary goal is to address relevant college and career readiness skills. Of further importance, novice school counselors are often surprised by how much middle school students enjoy exploring careers. Eighth grade is the pinnacle of that exploration, and students genuinely like having the opportunity to assess themselves and consider their options.

Career Counseling Curriculum

School counselors preparing classroom lessons for eighth grade students can think about that delivery system as a means for efficiently and comprehensively working with students regarding their career development needs. Ideally school counselors will be able to get into classrooms at least six times throughout the year (e.g., once a week over the course of one 6-week grading period) to administer weekly classroom lessons to eighth graders, and by partnering with teachers who can deliver supplemental lessons, they can ensure that career-related concepts are addressed comprehensively. We will present more information about teacher involvement later in this chapter. For school counselors, a three-unit approach that focuses on 1) self-assessment, 2) career awareness, and 3) decision making can be used to help them make the early career decisions requisite to their choosing a high school curriculum. A manageable approach to presenting these lessons that is consistent with Holland's theory is presented in Table 10.3.

Unit 1: Self-assessment. As reflected in many of the theories presented in the beginning of this chapter (e.g., Erikson, Marcia), students in eighth grade are working to establish their identities, which involves being able to discuss their strengths, weaknesses, interests, values, and desires for the future. While self-exploration activities are an integral part of the core counseling curriculum in grades 6 and 7, as discussed in previous chapters, a

TABLE 10.3   Sample Career Counseling Curriculum

Week	Topic	Student Product
1	Unit 1. Self-assessment. Complete and discuss interest inventory	Interest ability results
2	Unit 1. Self-assessment. Complete and discuss abilities inventory	Ability assessment results
3	Unit 1. Self-assessment. Complete and discuss values inventory and calculate personality code	Values assessment results plus overall personality code
4	Unit 2. Career awareness. Understanding personality and occupation fit	List of potential occupations that match personality code
5	Unit 2. Career awareness. Exploring occupational training requirements	List of possible postsecondary options
6	Unit 3. Decision making. Making curriculum decisions	High school curriculum choice that matches potential postsecondary plans

formal assessment of interests, abilities, and values is critical in eighth grade so that students can begin to make high school academic choices that match their future career interests. One instrument that taps into those three areas is Holland's Self-Directed Search (SDS; see Chapter 4). The SDS is a reliable and valid self-report instrument that can be used to identify a student's career personality, as defined by Holland. After completing an interest inventory, self-rating their abilities, and identifying their values, students are able to calculate their three-letter personality code.

The SDS can be completed electronically, and numerous career guidance systems used in school districts throughout the United States (e.g., Kuder, EXPLORE, and DISCOVER) have been developed based on Holland's theory. The three lessons that comprise this self-assessment unit could be conducted in a computer lab or with classroom laptop sets where students would be able to complete assessments online. Moreover, having students complete online assessments reinforces the use of technology for career decision making. Having already discussed interests, abilities, and values in grades 6 and 7, school counselors should be able to jump right in to the formal assessment process after a brief review of those constructs and the importance of self-awareness in finding a satisfying occupation.

Unit 2: Career awareness. After the self-assessment process is complete, students must be able to identify occupations that match their career personalities. By using Holland's Occupations Finder (a workbook that lists various occupations by Holland code) or other resources available in computerized career guidance systems (see Chapter 4), students can search for occupations that match their personality code. It is important to help students identify why different occupations have the codes they do so that they begin to understand the nuances that make one occupation slightly different from another similar one.

FIGURE 10.1 World of Work Map

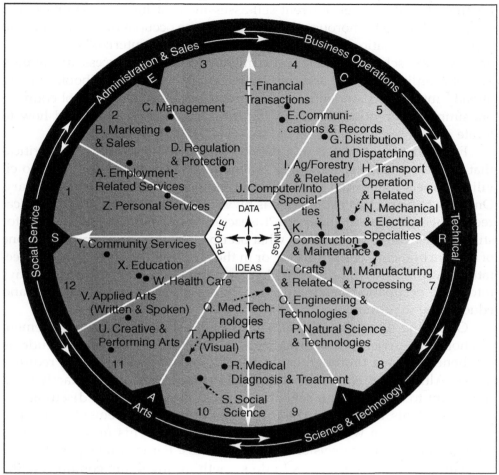

Reprinted with permission from ACT, Inc.

To facilitate students' understanding of what distinguishes one occupation from another, the *World of Work Map* (see Figure 10.1.) can be a useful visual. Using this map also can help facilitate understanding for visual learners, as they can see and measure how close or far away from each other various occupations are on the map. The placement of occupations on the map in relation to people, data, things, or ideas also can become more clear when a visual representation is used.

One approach to facilitating career awareness is to determine what students know before sharing concrete information with them. For example, school counselors can ask students to name the occupation(s) they are most interested in, and then the class can try to guess the appropriate code without looking it up. Interesting and insightful class discussion can occur as students try to explain to each other why they think one code is more appropriate than another. Evidence of formal operational thinking patterns also often emerge in these discussions, and students can learn from each other.

Once students have an idea of which occupations might be good matches for them based on their current self-assessment of interests, abilities, and values, they need to thoroughly investigate those occupations. In addition to accessing information that often is connected to computerized career guidance systems, school counselors also might have students access information available online in O*Net and the Occupational Outlook Handbook. Having already introduced students to these resources in grade 7, school counselors simply can remind them of what information is available and how to locate it.

For students interested in a possible career in the military, it is critical that they also consider how their potential military career is related to civilian careers they could have when leaving or retiring from the military. One way to begin this exploration is by visiting Careers in the Military (careersinthemilitary.com/index.cfm?fuseaction=main.home), a useful tool for students who are curious about what occupations they might pursue in one of the five branches of the military or in the National Guard. Minimal expectations would be for students to identify requisite skills, existing pathways into those occupations, and educational opportunities (such as ROTC) and educational requirements.

Given the impending transition to high school and the requirement to choose a curriculum of study before finishing eighth grade, students can benefit from a thorough exploration of occupational training requirements. Although it is unlikely that every student will know exactly what they want to do after high school, one way to approach this discussion is to ask students to identify the different training requirements for all of the occupations in which they express an interest. This information will be important in their decision-making process. For example, perhaps one student knows that she wants to do something involving computers. She knows that she will need to pursue college, but she doesn't know if she wants to get an associate's degree in programming, pursue a 4-year degree in computer science, or enter the military and become trained as a computer systems specialist. She doesn't need to decide right now—that will be one of her long-term goals. But what will be important is that she chooses a high school curriculum that will allow her to pursue as many postsecondary options as possible.

Unit 3: Decision making. Once students possess self-awareness and basic career awareness, they are in a position to make initial decisions about their long-term future and their upcoming high school curriculum choice. A psychoeducational approach is warranted, whereby school counselors review the high school curricular options to ensure that students understand the most logical postsecondary options associated with each career and college choice. In order to engage students collaboratively, a number of case scenarios could be developed for which the class would need to identify curriculum possibilities.

Another important consideration in the decision-making process relates to students who are undecided about whether or not they want to attend postsecondary school and/or what kind of postsecondary school they intend to pursue. Students might be tempted to choose a high school curriculum based on what their friends are doing or what might seem easiest to them academically. Given the importance of peers and the fact that many early adolescents believe things will work out for them no matter what they do, these scenarios are not uncommon. Students might not understand that earning a B in a weighted Honors or Advanced Placement (AP) English course would be more impressive to many colleges than earning an A in a general English course. School counselors should plan to integrate as many real-life examples as possible into classroom lessons to proactively address these issues, then they can supplement these lessons by providing students with first-hand opportunities to talk to individuals in the community and at postsecondary schools. Parents also will play a very important role in this high school curriculum decision process, and later in this chapter we will discuss more ways in which school counselors might involve and educate parents about the various career and college options available to students.

One benefit of using classroom lessons to address career development issues is that most students can benefit from similar types of information, and they can learn from each other. Nevertheless, developmentally, students will vary in their readiness to make decisions or truly understand all of the information they have acquired. School counselors cannot dismiss the importance of working individually with students in an effort to address the unique questions and concerns of each student.

Individual Interventions

Given the developmental differences that exist among young adolescents, school counselors should do what they can to ensure that each student has an accurate understanding of self and career. Starting with self-assessment, school counselors want to check in to make sure that each student understands his or her results assessment. As such, a very important part of using an instrument like the SDS is taking time to process the results with students. Similarly, once students identify potential occupations and training requirements, school counselors should make sure that their decisions are logical and well informed.

It is important to acknowledge that students' self-reported abilities may or may not be accurate indicators of their potential, and it is also important that students don't make decisions based on their own perceptions. Low self-efficacy related to skills and abilities needed for success in various occupations could lead students to rule out options unnecessarily. As such, school counselors should consider the ways in which they might supplement student self-ratings with less subjective data, and to assess and intervene regarding self-efficacy when relevant. For example, feedback from teachers, academic grades, and achievement test scores might be included in discussions with students in an effort to help them develop a comprehensive picture of their potential. Furthermore, while in the Kuder system students self-rate their abilities, the EXPLORE system generates scores in English, math, reading, and science based on student responses to items in those areas. The score report that students receive from EXPLORE explains their scores in relation to readiness for college-level coursework, and this report could be a useful tool during individual planning sessions.

One of the challenges with trying to meet individually with every student relates to school counselor caseloads. With an average caseload exceeding a 300:1 ratio (American Counseling Association, 2011), school counselors have limited time to engage in individual planning meetings with students. Yet we know this type of approach can be critical for students as they prepare for a high school transition. For example, South Carolina requires that students and their parents or guardians participate in an individual graduation plan (IGP) meeting during the eighth grade year. The purpose of these meetings is to review the students' self-assessment results and future plans, and to decide on a high school program of study. In some middle schools, the school counselors are solely responsible for conducting these meetings; in other schools, teachers and career development facilitators take the lead, under the supervision of school counselors (later we will discuss some ways that school counselors can engage teachers in this process). In any case, those IGP meetings typically run 15 to 20 minutes each, which hardly seems enough time to thoroughly engage in such an important discussion. Furthermore, the scheduling and rescheduling of those meetings can last for well over a month, leaving school counselors little time to engage in other tasks.

Classroom Curriculum Integration

Given the extensive time involved in adequately preparing students to make high school curricular decisions, school counselors should try to involve as many other stakeholders as possible. Classroom teachers can help in a number of ways. First, classroom teachers are the experts in their subject areas, and they possess knowledge of what types of subject-specific skills are needed for various occupations. They can use interactive strategies to expose students to the numerous occupations related to their subject areas (Exhibit 10.1). Also, classroom teachers can be encouraged to implement contextual learning strategies so that students are better able to understand the potential real-world application of class content, and to do so in reference to a variety of occupational choices. Examples ranging from basic arithmetic skills needed to successfully manage a cash register to advanced math skills necessary to calculate angles for a construction job or to generate complex formulas needed for accounting could be illustrated.

EXHIBIT 10.1
Helping Teachers Integrate Career Information

At one small, rural middle school in the Midwest, the eighth grade school counselor collaborated with classroom teachers to expose students to a variety of careers. At the beginning of the academic year, she attended the eighth grade teacher team meeting and shared her career development goals for the upcoming year, explaining the activities she had planned to implement and identifying areas where she felt she needed help. One of those areas was career exposure. Students had access to lots of career information online, but they were missing personal discussions about specific careers. Also, she had attempted to host a career fair the previous year, but the school is in such a rural area that it was challenging to find enough and varied speakers. She did not feel comfortable on her own trying to discuss occupations across all subject areas in a way that really helped students understand how the skills they learned in those subject areas could be applied.

To introduce the teachers more specifically to what she had in mind, she pulled out a copy of the world of work map (see Figure 10.1.). Most were not familiar with the map, so she briefly explained what it was and how the occupations were grouped. She proposed to the teachers that if they were willing to identify six occupations from the map related to their subject area and prepare brief classroom discussions about those occupations (highlighting skill application), that she would provide world of work maps for each of them and would provide them access to career information. She emphasized that she wanted them to choose at least one occupation that did not require postsecondary school, one that required vocational/technical training, and one that required a 4-year college degree. She also encouraged them to choose occupations that reflected varied career clusters as well as from different Holland codes (i.e., RIASEC) and reflecting an emphasis on data, ideas, people, and things. The goal was to help students recognize that while some subjects tend to be more highly represented in certain career clusters, others cross over many career clusters.

The school counselor also wanted the teachers to help students identify requisite occupational skills. She shared with the teachers an activity whereby they would introduce an occupation, have students locate it on the map, and then brainstorm the type and level of subject-specific skills that would be needed. By having to locate the occupation and then referencing other occupations located in proximity, students will be forced to think critically about the occupations.

(continued)

EXHIBIT 10.1 *(Continued)*
Helping Teachers Integrate Career Information

The teachers responded very positively to the idea, and each was able to spend at least 20 minutes discussing each of six occupations. They reported that students at first had difficulty locating the occupations on the map, but that over time as the students became more familiar and the teachers provided some facilitative questions (e.g., Do you think this occupation fits under data, people, ideas, or things?; Would this occupation be classified as R, I, A, S, E, or C?), they more quickly located the occupations. The teachers also reported that they personally developed a more clear conceptualization of what students were learning in their counseling classroom lessons. They appreciated that the school counselor had checked in after the first couple of sessions, and the follow-up information she had provided regarding the RIASEC codes had been very helpful to them in helping the students.

Second, classroom teachers could invite guest speakers into their classes—people who use subject-specific skills in their jobs—to share their experiences. School counselors might help to organize these speakers, maintaining a database of individuals who are willing to volunteer their time on occasion. In order to find speakers, counselors and teachers can begin by utilizing the support of community partners, local universities, and family members of students. As teachers anticipate teaching specific skill sets, they could easily contact the volunteers who could help illustrate the concepts, helping to reinforce other contextual learning and experiential strategies they might be using.

Furthermore, classroom teachers also can help students explore their strengths and weaknesses as they relate to each subject area. School counselors only have limited information about students, and reviewing report cards and achievement test results may not give an accurate picture of a student's potential. This is one opportunity, however, where teachers can unintentionally influence students in positive and negative ways regarding their future potential. The teacher who discourages a student from enrolling in algebra mainly on the basis that student has not demonstrated consistent, high achievement and not because the student is incapable, can set that student up for limited career options. Indeed, encouraging students to take rigorous courses is a critical function of teachers in preparing students for college and career readiness. School counselors can help teachers understand the impact of their feedback and can help teachers monitor their comments to provide students with helpful and constructive feedback regarding their academic futures. Helping teachers express perceptions about students' work ethics as separate from their perceptions of students' abilities can be helpful.

Finally, classroom teachers can be educated about the high school curriculum choices to the degree where they possess enough information to help students make choices. By providing them with a structured format, school counselors can rely on teachers to be collaborative partners in leading student–parent high school curriculum planning meetings. Realistically school counselors cannot meet the individual needs of students on their own, but they can provide oversight to a school-wide effort.

Fouad (1995) found moderate success for an intervention that combined many of the activities just discussed. With a focus on increasing students' awareness of careers in math and science (STEM), partnerships were developed among the school counselor, teachers, a university, parents, and individuals in the community. The intervention involved eighth grade students participating in a series of 6-week units built into core academic classes, which included general discussion of the career field (e.g., natural sciences, engineering), field trips to local businesses, guest speakers, and job shadowing opportunities. Fouad reported that a significantly higher proportion of students in the experimental group chose magnet high schools than did those in the control group. Further, there were significant differences in the type of math courses taken by minority students in the experimental versus control group, with students in the experimental group being more likely to enroll in algebra or geometry than applied math or pre-algebra.

PARTNERING WITH PARENTS AND THE COMMUNITY

We have mentioned parents a few times in this chapter, and most importantly we want to convey the importance of inviting parents/guardians to be partners in this high school curriculum decision-making process. Before they can become involved, however, parents must possess an understanding of the process and requirements. One way to avoid confusion is to give parents information more than once. For example, in a focus group of middle school parents regarding their perceptions of the school's efforts in preparing students for college and career readiness, the first author had multiple parents share the frustration of receiving eighth to ninth grade transition information in one presentation given at a meeting with over 300 parents in the school gymnasium. The parents reported feeling frustrated and overwhelmed by the amount of information and did not feel that they could help their children with the information they received. Just as it can be important to provide information to students in various ways, school counselors should consider that parents have different levels of knowledge as well as varying needs related to assisting their children in preparing for college and careers. School counselors should also consider the types of information that will be helpful to parents in assisting their children through the middle to high school transition, including information on the importance of extracurricular activities, time management, navigating increasing responsibilities, high school curriculum paths and programs, and high school registration and scheduling.

Reviewing data from a number of sources, we see that a conservative estimate of 28% of students are first-generation college students, meaning that neither of their parents attended college. Some percentage of parents in any school will likely possess little awareness of college, the requisite requirements for attending postsecondary school, or the different paths students can take to pursue various occupations. School counselors must be aware of the needs of the parents/guardians in their schools and provide relevant educational opportunities. Researchers have suggested that parental involvement is one of the most significant predictors and influencing factors of students' educational aspirations (Holcomb-McCoy, 2010) and schools need to provide support and information to assist families in making the most informed decision possible (Akos et al., 2007).

During this critical transition period, school counselors need to ensure that parents are educated about high school curriculum choices and how those choices relate to career and college options. Just like students, parents who don't accurately understand the different types of courses available (e.g., AP, honors) or how weighted grades are viewed by postsecondary schools may be uncomfortable emphasizing the most rigorous curriculum. Also, parents who don't understand requirements to enter the military may not understand that a rigorous curriculum can still be important. As school counselors help parents and students understand the benefits of taking more rigorous courses, they will need to explain how the demands of more rigorous classes will translate into the need for greater time and stress management. School counselors also should anticipate the importance of sharing information with parents about specialized options available to students, including vocational/technical training options available through high school and unique local programs such as those available at magnet or charter schools.

Parent education can occur in a number of ways. Parent workshops are a common approach, but sometimes it can be difficult for parents to attend meetings at the school. School counselors should consider alternative formats to make the information they want to share as accessible as possible, and they may have to be creative in order to reach the parents of the children in their school. For example, in one inner city school district with poor public transportation, school counselors visit community centers in housing projects. Further, publishing relevant information on the school website, sending information home in a newsletter, or partnering with local businesses to conduct breakfast or lunchtime information sessions for parents who cannot leave work are just a few ideas (see Exhibit 10.2).

A number of school counselors have been able to get local churches and other organizations to promote their workshops, and some school counselors have been able to partner with local libraries to conduct information workshops at night and on the weekends. Efforts to ensure that translating services are available are important, as more and more students in the United States come from homes where English is not the first language. The more informed parents are and the more they believe the school wants to help them, the more likely they will be to come in and ask questions. School counselors need to take the initiative to creatively reach out to parents and get them actively involved in students' career decision making.

EXHIBIT 10.2
Community Partnership for Parent Involvement

In another rural middle school, the school counselor struggled to interact face to face with parents. Although the district included individuals from all socioeconomic levels, the overwhelming majority of parents either had not graduated from high school or had achieved a high school diploma as their highest level of education. Farming and factory work were common occupations, and neither of those occupations allowed parents flexibility to come to school during the day to attend meetings. Further, although many parents would happily drive to the school to attend sporting events, few made the effort to make the often 45-minute drive to attend a meeting. The school counselor decided she needed to be creative in reaching out to parents. She believed that many parents were interested in being involved but just were stuck. Those who worked in the local factory a half mile down the road were not able to take any time off during the day—they risked their pay being docked.

The school counselor decided to pursue a collaborative partnership with the factory in order to reach out to parents who worked there. After much discussion, the factory agreed to allow the school counselor to come over during the lunch break to meet with parents in small groups or individually as necessary. The school principal was completely on board and permitted her to leave the building during the day to do this. She was able to share information about high school choices, student academic progress, career development activities, and other related information. Through this approach, the school counselor was able to disseminate career and college information to more parents than she had in the past. She found that many of the students whose parents she had talked with followed up by coming in to talk with her about their future plans and to ask questions.

FACILITATING THE EIGHTH TO NINTH GRADE TRANSITION

Although career exploration and academic advisement are essential for connecting school to the world of work for eighth grade students, another important task for school counselors is facilitating the eighth to ninth grade transition. This transition is important in regard to college and career readiness because ninth grade is a time when many students face critical decisions and challenges that can get them off track. Specifically, students need to be prepared for the greater autonomy, self-regulation demands, and responsibilities of ninth grade. With a clear understanding of what to expect in high school, students will be more successful in their transition, both academically and socially.

High school visits are a common transition intervention, and partnering with the high school is critical to developing a successful transition program. Middle school counselors can coordinate with high school counselors to provide several opportunities where parents and students can visit the high school, meet teachers, and receive instruction on how to make the transition. They also can invite ninth grade students to answer questions and talk about their own transition experiences. In addition, eighth grade teachers and school counselors can work together to cover topics that are of importance for transition success. Some possible topics include stress management, time management, academic organization, extracurricular involvement, goal setting, and more. One eighth grade counselor shared with these authors that during the eighth grade year, she and the eighth grade teaching team use *The Seven Habits of Highly Effective Teens* (Covey, 1998) to help the eighth graders develop pre-high school success skills. As part of the program they provided parent workshops to assist parents in conceptualizing how to help their children develop these skills.

Another important transition activity is to review graduation and in-state scholarship requirements. The second author recalls having many conversations with high school students who had failed one or more courses in ninth grade. Although information had been provided to them upon their arrival at the high school (e.g., graduation requirements, the importance of passing classes and credits, the fact that colleges look at ninth grade GPA), most students did not remember that information. Repetition is critical to ensuring that the message will eventually be heard, and if students can start out their high school experience with a clear understanding of how things work, perhaps more will demonstrate good academic and study skills from the start.

SUMMARY

In this chapter we have highlighted career development interventions specifically for eighth grade students. As we explained, students in eighth grade have a very important decision to make, one that could greatly impact their future. School counselors and educators must ensure that students and families are as prepared as possible to make this curricular decision. Opportunities for student self- and career exploration as well as for families and students to acquire information about college and career options will enable them to make informed decisions. The process does not end with that decision, however; once students enter ninth grade they will continue to require more and more information as they narrow down their future plans. In the next chapter we continue to look at the role of the school counselor in facilitating student career development as they enter ninth grade.

⋯❯ Test Your Knowledge

1. What developmental stage would Erikson believe most eighth grade students are in?
2. Explain the role of abstract thinking in future planning.
3. Name at least two career guidance systems you could use to assess student interests, abilities, and values.
4. Name at least two websites where students can gather occupational information.

11
• • • • •

Career Education and Counseling for Grade 9:
Focus on Academic and Work Habits
• • • • •

Much has been written about the critical nature of the ninth grade year on students' future outcomes. More and more school districts in the United States are acknowledging the need to target ninth graders via the formation of ninth grade academies, or similar initiatives, where they can provide attention to the unique needs of this group of students and help them adjust to the new academic demands of high school (McCallumore & Sparapani, 2010). With an emphasis on facilitating the transition from eighth grade and promoting academic success, these kinds of initiatives often include specific instruction in development of self-regulatory mechanisms such as study skills, goal setting, academic progress monitoring, and time management. They also prioritize teachers' relationships with students and parents (Fields, 2008).

This kind of proactive approach has helped to improve student outcomes in many schools. For example, McIntosh and White (2006) reported a reduction in the number of classes failed, fewer expulsions, and increased attendance. Further, Cook, Fowler, and Harris (2008) examined outcomes associated with students attending ninth grade academies in North Carolina. Compared to state averages, the students in ninth grade academies had lower grade level retention rates (15% versus 22%) and lower dropout rates (6.6% versus 12.5%). As we discussed earlier in this book, keeping kids in school and helping them achieve academic success can be critical to them envisioning increased career and postsecondary educational possibilities. As students experience success, they develop self-efficacy beliefs that lead them to persist even in the midst of challenges.

In ninth grade, some students realize for the first time that their academic grades affect the possibilities they have for the future. Students begin to learn the importance of setting goals, and they also acquire important study and time-management skills that will carry them through their high school careers. Ninth grade academies facilitate the development of core academic and self-regulatory skills that are critical for career and college readiness. In the absence of these kinds of programs, counselors and educators who work with ninth grade students can integrate numerous activities into their curricula in order to promote skill and knowledge development in these areas.

DEVELOPMENTAL OVERVIEW

Unless they have been retained in school, most ninth graders are around age 14 or 15. They are in a phase of life where they are trying to figure out who they are and who they want to become, and their peers play very important roles in their lives and their overall development. Below we highlight some of the more common developmental characteristics of students in ninth grade, and we later discuss relevant career and college readiness interventions based on these developmental considerations.

Psychosocial Development

Picking up with our discussion in the previous chapter, Erikson's (1963) *identity versus role confusion* stage is where most ninth grade students can be categorized. Developmentally, students who are in this stage strive to be viewed as unique and special, but at the same time want to be accepted by their peers. They want to stand out in the crowd but also to fit in. In their attempt to navigate this challenge, students often experiment with different groups of friends, clothing styles, and interests and hobbies to try to determine where they want to fit.

Further, while many ninth grade students choose classes and activities based on their own interests, others make decisions based on what their friends are doing. Similarly, students may even choose career paths and postsecondary options based on peer influence rather than personal choice. Ideally, we hope that students develop the confidence to make choices based on what *they* really like and value, but in many ways the exploration that occurs as they try to fit in with their peers can be of benefit in the long run.

During this stage, students also begin to differentiate from their families of origin, determining their own values and identifying ways that they are similar to, and different from, members of their family. Some stress and tension can result in the family system that can even manifest in academic and career advisement in school settings. For example, parents may expect their children to take courses that are aligned with the values they hold for their children's future. However, students may wish to take courses that align with a different set of values, ones that conflict with their parents' expectations.

School counselors need to be prepared to explore and understand students' and parents' expectations and help them to navigate these difficult decisions.

Recall Marcia's (1989) theory (introduced in Chapter 9). It could be argued that ninth grade students ideally should be in a moratorium status, when they are actively exploring careers without committing to anything specific. During this stage, parents and teachers may be frustrated with students' lack of commitment, so school counselors should assure these stakeholders that this is a normal transition. It is also helpful to remind students and parents that in ninth grade, there is still plenty of time for them to finalize their future decisions.

Although middle school career development interventions focus primarily on helping students explore abilities, interests, and values, it is not realistic to think that those activities alone will be sufficient in helping students finalize their career plans. Formal career development activities implemented throughout high school are designed to further assist students in developing self- and career awareness as well as narrowing down their choices. Additionally, as students interact with their peers and try out new identities and activities, they are, in fact, informally engaging in the process of exploring aspects of themselves that are very relevant to career development—they just may not realize it.

Although we all can think of success stories associated with students who foreclosed on a career choice very early (e.g., a ninth grade student, Martin, who has known forever he wanted to be a taxidermist because he has been actively involved in his family's business), there is value in encouraging exploration throughout high school. If Martin, who was an exceptional writer and avid reader in addition to doing well in his art classes, had been encouraged to explore careers in the liberal arts, would he still have decided to pursue taxidermy? Despite his talents, after exploring possible liberal arts careers Martin indeed might have decided that taxidermy was for him, or perhaps he would have identified a new potential career path.

We encourage exploration not to force students down different career paths than they initially chose, but rather to help them solidify and feel confident in their choices. We also want to help students explore options within fields. For example, a female student, Tori, wanted to work in nursing but was unsure of what type of nursing (psychiatric, neonatal, surgical). By exploring careers more thoroughly, students may be able to learn about the salient differences between related careers. Further, it is also hoped that when adolescents have opportunities to fully explore career options, they may feel greater career commitment and satisfaction in their future work lives rather than a sense of regret. Fortunately, the natural tendency for adolescents to try new things with peers as they are working to solidify their identity can provide an avenue to help them explore various career options more easily.

Cognitive Development

Anyone who has worked with students in the ninth grade knows that they have a tendency to be egocentric. Although many ninth graders are beginning to develop formal abstract thought (Piaget, 1977), they often oscillate between concrete thinking and abstraction. So, for example, while they may be able to use complex math skills and scientific theory in academic coursework, they are not always capable of thinking about their futures in a more abstract manner, particularly in regard to problem solving, generating solutions, and considering consequences of the choices they make.

Specifically, Elkind's (1978) discussion of the *personal fable* holds much relevance to career development for these students. For instance, despite possessing some abstract thinking skills and the ability to understand cause and effect, many ninth grade students believe that nothing bad will happen to them. It is this kind of thinking that leads students not to worry about their grades or about engaging in risky behavior—they refuse to believe that negative consequences could result. They also tend to be confident that things will work out for them, which can lead to apathy and procrastination regarding career and college planning as well as schoolwork.

Indeed, it is not uncommon for a student with a very low grade point average (GPA) to come in for academic advisement and proclaim the aspiration of attending Harvard and being a doctor in the future. Because students often don't make the connection between the consequences of present behavior on future options, they may unrealistically believe that their current academic standing won't matter for college and career success. Categorized according to Marcia (1989) as in a state of *identity diffusion*, these students can show little to no interest in exploring career options or planning for their future; they are the ones who will be resistant to, or ambivalent about, participating in career development interventions and often not worried about receiving low grades.

RELEVANT CAREER THEORIES: GOTTFREDSON, HOLLAND, AND SUPER

Many career counseling theories inform the types of interventions that would be useful to address the needs of ninth grade students. For these students, *self-concept* and *personality* are particularly important career constructs. In the career counseling theories presented in the following, we illustrate the connection between these constructs and career development outcomes for ninth graders.

Gottfredson's Theory of Circumscription and Compromise

Consistent with their internal struggle to develop an identity, students in ninth grade typically fall into Gottfredson's (1981, 2002) fourth stage, *orientation to internal, unique self.* During this stage, self-concepts are evolving, and students are able to articulate their beliefs regarding idealistic and realistic future careers. These beliefs reflect the careers that they have circumscribed not only based on power, sex roles, and social valuation but also based on their own *self-concept*. This includes students' beliefs about what they are capable of and their evaluation of what skills, talents, and intelligence that they have that may apply to a specific career.

For example, when he was younger, Martin (the aspiring taxidermist) may have admired his father as a taxidermist and may have thought that career took a lot of skill and strength. Later, despite his love for writing, he may have ruled out careers in the liberal arts (and writing in particular) because he believed they are not acceptable for men (orientation to gender role). At the same time he retained the possibility of being a taxidermist, because in the rural location where he lives, both his peers and family would consider that to be a very prestigious career path (orientation to social value). Now that he is older, Martin also is considering how taxidermy fits for him personally (orientation to internal, unique self).

During the fourth stage of Gottfredson's theory (1981, 2002), students take a more introspective look at their futures, determining what is and is not realistic based on how they view themselves and how accessible they perceive specific careers to be. It is not uncommon for students to abandon their most preferred or ideal occupations for less compatible, but what they perceive to be accessible, alternatives. Gottfredson (2005) refers to this situation as *compromise*, and indicates that people frequently compromise on careers due to limited or inaccurate information regarding educational requirements or pathways to pursue various careers. That is, students' inaccurate beliefs lead them to make somewhat uninformed decisions.

Continuing with Martin, because his family has been heavily involved in taxidermy, he has a very clear idea of how to enter that profession and he has a guaranteed position in the family business. Therefore, he perceives it as very accessible. Martin can easily apprentice with his family and obtain the requisite on-the-job training, and he knows that the certification requirements can be completed quickly. Martin's main interest in taxidermy relates to his love of art. He thinks he can put up with the initial hands-on work removing the animal hide—but it's creating the mold and sculpting the final product that really interests him. Martin has a talent for sculpting; he often creates carvings out of wood and sells them in his father's shop. He is unfamiliar, however, with what other careers in art might look like; he has not been exposed to other art-related occupations.

Further, although Martin could pursue other career opportunities in art, he does not believe them to be accessible to him. No one in Martin's family has completed any education beyond high school, and the idea of art school is foreign to him. Martin would not know where to start when it comes to researching, applying, enrolling, and registering for art school, and doesn't know how he would pay for school or what financial options he has. Further,

Martin's family tells him that an expensive technical degree is not necessary since he can work at the family business. They encourage and expect him to work in the family business full time when he graduates from high school. Without intervention focused on helping Martin and his family acquire more information about postsecondary school and additional career possibilities in art, Martin will likely compromise on these options because they do not appear accessible to him. He will stick with what is familiar and immediately in reach. Perhaps he will be very successful and happy being a taxidermist, but by compromising, Martin may have missed out on other opportunities that could have been equally or more satisfying to him.

Holland's Theory of Vocational Choice

Holland's theory (1973) works well in conjunction with Gottfredson's. That is, in order for students to avoid compromising on careers, they must have an accurate understanding of themselves and of careers. Holland's focus on thoroughly assessing and examining person–environment match is consistent with efforts to help students avoid compromise. As they determine their own *personality code* and examine the personality types associated with various occupations, students should develop a more accurate understanding of the connection among their interests, skills, and various occupations (see Chapters 9 and 10 for more information about Holland's theory). For this reason, self- and career exploration activities continue to be important for ninth graders.

Super's Life-Span/Life-Space Theory

According to Super (1980), students in ninth grade would probably be transitioning from the *growth stage* (typically up to age 15) into the *exploration stage*. They should have a general understanding of the world of work as well as of their interests and abilities, and should be starting to engage in activities (e.g., hobbies, job shadowing) to get more specific information about occupations in order to try to narrow down their choices. At this age, Super indicates that students should be engaged in the developmental task of *crystallization*—the process of developing a tentative career goal. Interventions spanning the types of activities associated with the growth and exploration stages would be appropriate in ninth grade to help students progress toward crystallizing their career goals.

Like Gottfredson, Super (1980) also acknowledged the importance of *self-concept* to career. According to Super, self-concept refers to how an individual pictures him- or herself in a specific role or in relationships. The development of self-concept is informed by experiences and personal reflection.

Students make career choices that are in line with their self-concepts, so as self-concepts evolve and change along with life roles, so do career goals and choices. Interventions focused on the development of self-awareness as well as an accurate understanding of interests, skills, values, and general characteristics can help students begin to articulate their self-concepts.

FACILITATING THE EIGHTH TO NINTH GRADE TRANSITION: FOLLOW-UP ACTIVITIES

In the previous chapter we talked a lot about what middle schools can do to prepare students for the transition to high school. We must remember that transition is a process, however, and that follow-up activities on the back end of the transition can be equally as important as those on the front end. Ninth grade counselors and teachers play an important role in ensuring a successful transition. Many students will adjust very quickly to ninth grade expectations, but others will struggle to find their place and feel motivated to work.

One of the biggest struggles students have when transitioning into ninth grade relates to academics. The percentage of students who fail ninth grade continues to be fairly high in many schools (McCallumore & Sparapani, 2010), and the *ninth grade bulge* is a term used to refer to the disproportionate number of students enrolled in grade 9 compared to those enrolled in grades 10 to 12. Wheelock and Miao (2005) reported 9th to 10th grade promotion rates as being much lower than promotion rates to 11th or 12th grade. Furthermore, research suggests that these ninth grade repeaters are more likely to drop out of high school than their peers who move on to 10th grade on time (Kennelly & Monrad, 2007). For this reason, an emphasis on the academic transition in ninth grade is warranted. Students who graduate from high school have increased college and career opportunities than do their peers who drop out of school.

As mentioned at the beginning of this chapter, the idea of ninth grade academies came about in response to concerns surrounding the transition to ninth grade. Even without having a formal academy, schools might be able to put into place some of the critical components of those initiatives. For example, instruction and monitoring of academic and study skills can be implemented by counselors or teachers (see the next section) or through specialized workshops. Recognizing that students might need help adjusting to different academic expectations, counselors may search for ways to build in study hall time or provide opportunities for peer tutoring, as well as providing information on homework help resources (e.g., homework help lines and helpful websites).

NINTH GRADE STUDENT CAREER DEVELOPMENT OUTCOMES

Throughout this chapter we have identified some of the main focus areas for ninth grade students with regard to college and career readiness—academic and self-regulatory skills, and self and career knowledge. How to address and evaluate outcomes in those areas in school can once again be informed by referring to the grade level expectations (GLEs) developed by the Missouri Center for Career Education (2006). Table 11.1 lists the career and academic expectancies that are directly connected to these focus areas for ninth graders.

TABLE 11.1   Missouri Ninth Grade GLEs

Career Development: Self and Career Awareness	
Integration of Self-Knowledge into Life and Career Plans	Compare current strengths and limitations with the individual's career and educational plan and adjust the plan as necessary.
Adaptations to World of Work Changes	Recognize the 16 career clusters within the six career paths as a more specific organizer for exploring and preparing for careers now and in the future.
Respect for All Work	Analyze and evaluate school and community contributions as they relate to one's career and educational plan.
Career Decision Making	Integrate career and educational information with knowledge of self and career clusters to identify occupations of interest.
Education and Career Requirements	Identify the entrance requirements and application procedures for postsecondary options.
Personal Skills for Job Success	Identify situations that would compromise ethical habits in school or work situations.
Job-Seeking Skills	Identify and refine the job seeking skills needed to apply for volunteer or part-time jobs in the community.
Academic Development	
Life-Long Learning	Review and build upon educational skills necessary to progress toward life-long learning goals.
Self-Management for Educational Achievement	Review and build upon a self-management system and adjust to increased academic demands.
Transitions	Apply information and skills necessary to transition into high school.
Educational Planning for Life-Long Learning	Monitor and revise a 4- to 6-year educational plan.

Based on the Missouri Center for Career Education (2006).

Looking closely at the GLEs, we can see parallels with many of the constructs we have discussed in this chapter. Basic self- and career-awareness activities can be designed around the career development GLEs. Additionally, the academic development GLEs lend themselves to the academic and self-regulatory skills sets we have identified as important for college and career readiness. They also connect to goal setting and future planning activities. In the following sections we share some ideas for how to address these different areas with ninth grade students.

CAREER AND COLLEGE READINESS INTERVENTIONS: COLLABORATING WITH TEACHERS

As reflected in the GLEs, interventions for ninth grade students must be developed with consideration of the importance of peers, the developmental task of establishing an identity, the relevance of self-concept, and the career development goal of crystallization. At the same time, they must address the transition-related needs of these students, specifically in relation to academic and self-regulatory skills. A proactive, collaborative approach to addressing these needs can be very manageable in a high school.

Career Counseling Curriculum

The career counseling curriculum does not need to be administered only by school counselors. In fact, a collaborative approach can help ninth grade students recognize that teachers and other school staff are all on the same page when it comes to the skills and knowledge that are important for their future success. Counselors often find it challenging to implement the counseling curriculum in a high school, but once it is developed and objectives identified, there are a few different ways that it can be implemented without detracting from students' time in other classes.

A traditional school counselor–implemented approach is one option for addressing GLEs in ninth grade. As a junior/senior high school counselor, the second author provided classroom lessons weekly to all ninth grade students. Even though students in her school were in the same building for grades 7 to 12, they still had areas of transition. The students rotated through her class opposite their physical education and health classes; in this manner they were still on a more typical middle school or junior high schedule, and it was familiar to them.

Further, she had the ability to design and implement whatever curriculum she wanted, which allowed for flexibility to accommodate student needs throughout the year. Her curriculum, based on school counseling standards and needs assessment data, addressed the importance of ninth grade and how academic skills and habits would be critical to their future success, college and career planning activities (e.g., interest inventories), and goal setting. As report cards came out and teachers reported concerns, she revisited various topics or added new ones. This approach was proactive and reactive as well as collaborative and flexible.

Another approach to implementing the counseling curriculum is to involve teachers more directly. Working together to develop the curriculum based on GLEs and student needs, school counselors and teachers can prepare units to be implemented throughout the year. Given that the content might be more familiar to school counselors, it is advised that they take the lead to ensure that everyone who will be implementing the intervention understands the content and how to present it. For example, in some ninth grade academies in Louisiana, students actually take semester-long education-for-careers courses. Although these courses are taught by classroom teachers, the counselor often oversees the curriculum. In this way, the school counselor is able to find additional time throughout the year to offer supplemental lessons.

Another way to have teachers implement the curriculum is to use teacher advisory periods. These advisory periods might be scheduled weekly, or they might be built in only during certain times of the year (e.g., every morning for 1 week each marking period). With a specific group of students to work with throughout the year, teachers can monitor student needs and seek assistance from the school counselor in modifying the curriculum if necessary. This type of approach is collaborative and efficient but does require someone monitoring for consistency to ensure all content is covered adequately.

Readiness for career decision making involves possessing self and career knowledge. Because ninth grade students often have difficulty realistically projecting what their lives might be like in the future (e.g., they imagine being a teacher who drives a fancy car and lives in a huge house), school counselors should be sure to include in their curriculum activities that help students develop a concrete understanding of occupational choices. That is, they should provide opportunities to help students understand the kind of salary they might make in various occupations as well as how far that money would stretch depending on the lifestyle they envision; this can be very beneficial to their future satisfaction. Numerous activities and resources exist to help students examine how various budgets would impact their lives and how to make informed career decisions that include the lifestyle they would like.

For example, school counselors might find the *California Career Zone* (www.cacareerzone.org/) to be a useful resource in this effort. Some states have similar online programs. This free web resource enables students to choose occupations and/or a specific salary, as well as to indicate the type of location where they envision living (e.g., small town, large city). Then they walk through choosing options related to things like housing, utilities, food, transportation, health care, social activities, and savings. An estimated budget is produced, which enables students to have a concrete understanding of how much money they would need in order to live a certain lifestyle, as well as how much money they might make in a certain occupation. Using this kind of activity can be coupled with discussions of values in order to help students to make informed career decisions.

Large Group Information Sessions

High school students need a lot of information throughout the year in order to make informed career and college decisions, and large group information sessions can be used to disseminate this type of information. Whether it is providing an overview of the graduation requirements and 4-year planning, or sharing information about job shadowing opportunities, school counselors should think about what topics might be important to discuss in person with students. Topics about which students need basic information (e.g., completing their graduation plan, how to identify educational requirements for jobs) rather than extended practice or explanation are ideal for this delivery format.

Although much of the information school counselors deliver via large groups might be available in writing in a student handbook or on a web page, for many students hearing someone talk about things and walk them through the process helps them comprehend better and allows them the opportunity to ask questions. In an ideal scenario counselors expect students to review information and come to them with questions, but only a small minority of students do this. Some do not feel comfortable approaching counselors with questions, many lack initiative, and others don't even know what to ask. By meeting them where they are developmentally, counselors might proactively facilitate their acquisition of important information. Further, providing information in numerous formats (e.g., written, oral) also can help to accommodate different learning styles.

Scheduling large group information sessions can be challenging at times, as having too large of a group will deter questions, but having too small of a group means holding more sessions. In a small high school where she worked, the second author noted that with a few exceptions (i.e., students in self-contained classrooms), all ninth grade students had the same English teacher and the same Civics teacher. She approached those teachers to inquire about the possibility of targeting students during their class time, while appreciating that those teachers likely could not afford to give up much time. Planning in advance, she and the English teacher were able to identify one day each marking period where the teacher could spend time grading papers while the counselor shared information with students. With this approach, the counselor only had a few students to reach individually (including those who had been absent) and the teacher was appreciative of the work time; the teacher stayed in the room and heard what was being shared with the students.

On that note, working closely with teachers to ensure they understand academic requirements also can be helpful, but not all teachers will be able to sit in on the discussions counselors have with students. At a large, urban school, the school counselors provided a faculty inservice training each year on student academic planning in order to promote teachers' understanding of academic paths, postsecondary preparation, in-state scholarships, and graduation plans. Details of their approach are outlined in Exhibit 11.1. Because school counselors are responsible for large numbers of students, providing teachers with information about graduation requirements and academic planning allows students to have greater access to information through all of the adults in the building.

EXHIBIT 11.1
Instructing Teachers on Academic Requirements

At West Orange High School, Mrs. Olivares, the ninth grade school counselor, along with the counseling team, presented a faculty inservice on student academic planning at the beginning of each school year. The training lasted approximately 30 minutes and was meant to serve as a refresher for faculty on academic path options and related course work, changes to graduation requirements and certificates (either legislatively or in the district), and the purpose and logistics of graduation plans (e.g., 5-year plans). By doing this, all faculty members were prepared to answer day-to-day questions from students regarding graduation requirements and academic paths. Each quarter (9 weeks), the school counselors prepared the faculty to give short, 10 to 15 minute presentations in homeroom on a topic chosen by the school counselors. Presentations included topics such as updating graduations plans, registering for courses, and reviewing transcripts to ensure academic courses taken match requirements for career paths.

Beyond the faculty inservice at the beginning of the year, Mrs. Olivares and the school counselors also designated trainings once per quarter for new faculty. In those trainings, the school counselors gave more specific, detailed information to new faculty including an overview of the developmental needs (personal/social, academic, and career) of high school students. New teachers were given information on how to best utilize the school counseling program and were given the opportunity to ask questions about their concerns of working with parents, motivating students, identifying students having personal problems, and how to deal with classroom management and conduct problems. Additionally, they were given information on how to integrate study strategies, self-regulatory time management, and other academic skills training in the daily educational curriculum.

Individual Planning

Although finding time to provide individual advising to all students in their caseloads can be challenging, school counselors need to provide opportunities for students to get some individual attention to discuss their long-term goals (American School Counselor Association [ASCA], 2012). They cannot adequately meet the unique needs of each student without finding some time to talk with them personally. The default approach seems to be to block off 3 weeks and hold back-to-back meetings with students. Although not ideal in terms of being able to provide a comprehensive counseling program and curriculum during that timeframe, that approach does allow school counselors to meet with all students within a designed period of time. Many schools have the luxury of a career counselor who has fewer general counseling responsibilities and therefore more time to focus on career planning discussions. Other school counselors need to be more creative in finding these opportunities.

During part of her counseling class time, one school counselor built in time in December where the class could work on career projects while she called them up one at a time for approximately 15 minutes each. The purpose of those individual discussions was to check in prior to the start of course registration in the spring in the hopes that registration would go more smoothly if students had thought in advance about their future plans and relevant courses. Although 15 minutes isn't much, that brief amount of time helped her provide some personalized attention to each student. For a large percentage of students, the combination of classroom activities, large group information sessions, and these brief informational meetings was sufficient to help them move forward in their career planning. During the meetings the school counselor was able to identify students who needed follow-up intervention, but those were fewer in number and therefore much more manageable to target outside of class.

Prior to meeting with each student, the school counselor asked them to be ready to answer the following general questions: What do you want to do after high school? How do you know? How certain are you? What do you know about how to reach that goal? What is your plan? What do you need from me? After hearing their initial answers, she used various probes to clarify or specify their responses. Some students came up with very well-thought out responses and others were very vague or hadn't thought about things. Their overall responses informed how she proceeded in terms of identifying relevant interventions for them, as well as when and how to involve their parents/guardians. Table 11.2 includes some of the things she was listening for during these discussions.

Another approach to individual planning involves partnering with teachers. In most schools, students in ninth grade are asked to develop a high school or graduation plan where they map out their high school courses. These plans are developed to be in line with career goals. With a little preparation, teachers can be asked to help with this process. In fact, in

TABLE 11.2   Individual Advisement Discussions

Initial Question	Listening for
What do you want to do after high school?	Has student thought about the future? Is student in *diffusion*? Does student have a specific future goal? Does student plan to graduate from high school? Does student have a specific occupational goal in mind? Is student interested in attending college?
How do you know?	What led student to the choice? Is student's choice based on peer choices? Is student's choice based on family preference? Has student *foreclosed* career choice? Has student *circumscribed or compromised* career choice? Has student explored self? Can student articulate self-concept? Has student explored career? Does student make connection between self and career? Does student have accurate career information?
How certain are you?	Use rating scale. If not completely certain, what else is student considering? What questions does student still have about choice? What would help student feel more certain with choice? (Often real and perceived barriers came up here, such as lack of information, parental pressure, etc.)
What do you know about how to reach that goal?	Does student have accurate information?
What is your plan?	Has student thought much about this? Is student ready to actively pursue the goal? Is the plan realistic? Comprehensive? Relevant?
What do you need from me?	Is student actively interested in working on goal? Are others helping the student? What interventions might I need to plan?

one Southeastern high school, teachers are responsible for holding planning conferences with all of the students in their homeroom and with their parents. Two evenings are set aside during which these sessions are scheduled. The school counselors prep the teachers, and then walk around that evening from room to room answering questions as needed. The school counselors are able to handle "make-up" sessions for anyone who could not attend during the evening. All in all the process is efficient, and the collaboration seems to work well.

Partnering With Parents

Parents/guardians play an important role in students' career outcomes. At one extreme, they can hold incredibly high aspirations for their children and limit their career options to a few acceptable, rigorous alternatives. These kind of parents are likely to want their child enrolled in every advanced placement (AP) class, encourage them to take the Scholastic Aptitude Test (SAT) every year starting in middle school, and push their kids to become involved in lots of activities. At the other extreme are parents/guardians who express very limited aspirations for their children and/or discourage careers that require much education, focusing rather on those students finding immediate employment. Often these parents just want their child to graduate, but some don't even care about high school completion and see little value in future planning. It is important that school counselors do not judge parents but, rather, try to appreciate their perspective. For example, parents may believe, based on their own experience and life knowledge, that a college education is not necessary for making a living. Counselors should be respectful while introducing other possibilities and explaining information in a sensitive manner.

The majority of parents, however, even those at the extremes, mainly want their children to be happy. They want them to find satisfaction in their future occupations and to make choices that fit for them. Many parents are well informed about career and college planning, while others have little to no information to help their children navigate this process or navigate high school. Parents can benefit just as much as students can from learning about the career and college planning process, and school counselors would be wise to involve them as much as possible. Just like students, parents are often reluctant to reach out to the school and ask for help or information. A proactive approach to disseminating information to parents and involving them in college and career planning activities can help to encourage their involvement over time.

As mentioned, involving parents in the high school planning process can be helpful in many ways. By chatting with parents and students together, counselors can examine the dynamics and listen for what messages parents send their children regarding college and careers. Further, involving parents directly ensures, in general, that they receive information, and that they have accurate information. We all know how easy it is for students unintentionally to leave out an important detail or to provide partially accurate information. For parents to be able to effectively help and reinforce school initiatives, they need to be informed.

As with students, providing information in a handbook and on a web page is always a good idea, but counselors should reach out in more ways to parents. Not all parents have access to the Internet, so technology cannot be the sole form of disseminating information to them. Some parents also do better when they have a chance to interact with someone and ask questions, as opposed to just reading information. School counselors must think of the best ways to provide these kinds of interactive opportunities. They also should remember that one-shot approaches are not likely to be effective. Just as students can benefit from receiving information in multiple formats repeated over time, parents also are more likely to understand and retain information if they are afforded different kinds of opportunities throughout their child's schooling to acquire information and ask questions.

Thinking about specific populations, school counselors might consider planning informational activities to target specific needs. For example, it is likely that some parents have helped older siblings through the college and career planning process, so their needs would differ from those of parents dealing with their first child entering high school. While some veteran parents value hearing information each year because they want to be reassured nothing has changed, for others it can be frustrating to not learn anything new. Information sessions could be advertised as beginner or advanced, for example, so that parents could make more intentional choices about what or what not to attend.

Finally, more and more families in the United States speak English as a second language. As we try to help students achieve success, we need to find ways to involve a diverse group of parents. School counselors must be conscious of the language barriers that exist and find ways to communicate effectively with parents. Providing materials in other languages and involving translators are two common ways to do this. Anticipating the unique needs of these parents is also important. Because educational systems in other countries can vary greatly from that in the United States, it is not uncommon for parents to be confused about what options are available and what expectations schools have. Providing an *Orientation to High School* or some type of similar workshop where the structure, format, and expectations are discussed can help parents understand what they can do at home to reinforce school expectations as well as to facilitate their child's learning. Similar workshops could be held regarding college and career planning in the United States.

SUMMARY

In this chapter we have highlighted career and college readiness interventions specifically for ninth grade students. A crucial year in terms of setting the stage for future opportunities, ninth grade is a time when students must really start focusing on who they want to be and what they want to do. Self-awareness, skill development, and future planning all are important. As they develop interventions and programming for these students, counselors and educators must keep in mind the developmental milestones that ninth grade students are moving through as well as the transition-related issues associated with entering ninth grade.

⋯⟩ Test Your Knowledge

1. Provide an example of a ninth grade student's career choice that illustrates your understanding of circumscription and compromise.
2. Provide an example of a statement that a ninth grade student might make reflecting his or her personal fable, and explain how that belief could affect career outcomes.
3. Define in your own words Super's notion of crystallization.

12

• • • • •

Career Education and Counseling for Grade 10: Career and College Planning

• • • • •

In the previous chapter we encouraged counselors to spend a lot of time helping ninth grade students develop the academic and self-regulatory skills (e.g., time management, academic progress monitoring, study skills) that would carry them through high school and beyond. We also encouraged counselors to help these students explore self and careers so that they could continue working to narrow down their choices. By no means are 10th graders done working on those skills or have finalized their career decisions; they still can benefit from interventions targeting those specific areas.

Nevertheless, 10th grade also is a year when counselors and educators can help students to examine the internal and external factors that affect their choices, and to start thinking more concretely about college and career planning activities. By 10th grade, students should start actively preparing for their future careers, which means narrowing their choices and engaging in activities that will help them move forward. In this chapter we share a number of ideas for helping students engage in early career and college preparation activities. As in previous chapters, we start with a review of salient developmental characteristics and career theories, and then provide recommendations for intervention.

DEVELOPMENTAL OVERVIEW

Students in 10th grade fall into the category known as mid-adolescence (ages 15–18). These students are very similar to ninth graders in many ways; they still struggle to develop an identity and their peers are very important. Additionally, many mid-adolescents are transitioning into a more advanced stage of formal operational thinking. In the following we highlight some of the more common developmental characteristics of students in 10th grade and discuss their relevance to career development.

Physical Development

By the time students reach 10th grade, many of the physical changes associated with puberty are slowing down. For the most part, these students have moved beyond what many refer to as the *awkward stage* (i.e., due to disproportionate features) and are beginning to look more like adults. Because the majority of drastic physical changes are slowing down, mid-adolescents tend to be less volatile; that is, the concerns about emotional regulation that we discussed in Chapter 9 seem to lessen. However, physical development still plays an important role in career development for these students.

Although 10th grade boys typically will experience more physical changes over the next 5 years (e.g., they might grow another few inches, develop more lean muscle, and have more noticeable facial hair growth), by 10th grade most boys are now as tall as, if not taller than, girls their age. Most also have completed one of the more embarrassing changes associated with puberty, such as the change that was so well illustrated in *The Brady Bunch* when Peter Brady had to sing—the changing voice. Increased testosterone associated with puberty causes the larynx and facial bones to grow, which results in the development of a lower voice. The process is gradual, however, and the inconsistent, cracking voice that many boys experience during that process can cause them great anxiety and embarrassment. Anyone who is able to observe boys as they develop will often notice increased confidence once they are taller than girls (or of similar height to their male peers) and once their voice has finally changed. With these types of changes, boys can start to envision the types of careers that may or may not be possible based on physical requirements.

Most girls in 10th grade have reached their adult height, and they have begun to settle in to their new body shapes. However, body image concerns are still present for many mid-adolescent girls, and some struggle with the realization that they might not be able to do some of the physical things they were good at prior to puberty. For example, Maria had been attending an arts school for ballet, and was hoping that once she adjusted to her changed body shape (i.e., wider hips, larger breasts, different weight distribution) she would be able to continue progressing toward her goal of becoming a professional ballet dancer. She was quite talented and her career path had always been clear; she had never considered other options. Although most girls are quite capable of pursuing various athletic pursuits after puberty, Maria's new body was not designed for ballet. She needed to develop a new plan and cope with the loss of her long-term dream.

Cognitive Development

According to Piaget (1969), mid-adolescents are capable of abstract and hypothetical thinking, which enables them to look into the future, predict outcomes, and consider the perspectives of others. Nevertheless, the personal fable (as noted in Chapter 11) is still very influential, and it is not uncommon for 10th graders to seemingly bounce back and forth between making healthy and unhealthy decisions. Despite cognitively being able to predict the consequences of their actions, peer influence often leads these students to engage in behaviors that they know are not in their best interests. The personal fable allows them to develop the faulty assumption that negative consequences won't happen to them. Counselors and educators should be prepared to continue challenging these students to examine the positive and negative consequences related to their choices.

As many mid-adolescents develop formal operational thinking skills, their awareness of and interest in the perspectives and experiences of others often leads, in general, to increased concern for others and a sense of personal responsibility. This is because formal abstract thought lends to an increased ability to take others' perspectives (Piaget, 1969), a necessary cognitive skill in the development of empathy and prosocial behavior (Curry, Smith, & Robinson, 2009). Students with these cognitive abilities may show an interest in engaging in volunteer work, helping underserved populations, or demonstrating an appreciation for discussions about social and global issues. For many of these students, this awareness may lead them to shift their thinking about their futures.

For example, a high school counselor was working with Tonja, who had always wanted to be an accountant like her mother. Tonja came in to see the counselor one day and asked him about starting a student organization that would focus on community service. She had talked with her older cousin over Thanksgiving about her previous spring break volunteer efforts in another state, and Tonja was intrigued and felt quite compelled to try to reach out locally. She also mentioned that maybe she wanted to think about career opportunities where she would be able to make an impact on others.

Psychosocial Development

Students in 10th grade continue to move through the *identity versus role confusion* stage (Erikson, 1963). Peers remain an important influence in their lives and in the decisions they make. For example, even though a student knows that she needs to study for her geometry test so that she can pass the class (cognitively she understands the potential consequences of going into the test unprepared and/or tired), she is easily convinced by her friends to sneak out to attend a late night party. Her decision-making process is challenging, as she attempts to balance her role as a friend wanting to fit in with her peers and her desire to be a good student and obtain a high GPA.

Students in 10th grade also frequently *experiment* with their identities, or *try on* different identities in an attempt to figure out what fits. Their self-concept is still forming (see the following discussion of Super's theory), and these experimental activities are very important to their overall development. Although parents often get concerned when their children engage in behaviors like changing the way they dress, hanging out with different peer groups, or wanting to go to a different church or no church, these behaviors are not necessarily indicative of larger concerns. They can be sometimes, but in most instances those types of behaviors simply reflect the adolescent progression through typical developmental milestones.

In their search to solidify their identity, 10th grade students often explore their values by challenging others, especially their parents. It is not uncommon for these students to openly resist or reject their parents' views during this time, and parents often view their children as argumentative or disrespectful as they do this. Many students do not possess the skills to maturely engage in discussions involving differences of opinion, and this time period offers a unique opportunity to help students be able to articulate their beliefs as well as to develop the interpersonal and conflict resolution skills that will be so critical to their future success in the workplace.

RELEVANT CAREER THEORY: SUPER AND LENT, BROWN, AND HACKETT

Interventions related to Holland and Gottfredson (see Chapter 11) continue to be very relevant for 10th grade students. In this chapter, however, we are highlighting two theories with constructs that speak specifically to the developmental challenges we already discussed. *Life roles, self-efficacy beliefs,* and *outcome expectations* are important considerations when helping 10th grade students engage in career preparation activities.

Super's Life-Span/Life-Space Theory

When we presented Super's (1980) theory in Chapter 11, we discussed the role of self-concept and the importance of helping students develop increased self-awareness. Super's discussion of life roles is very important to understanding career development and self-concept, particularly for students in 10th grade. First, according to Super, people assume various roles throughout their lives and hold many roles simultaneously. Super charted an individual's life roles through a chart known as a *Life Career Rainbow* (see Figure 12.1). The relative importance of each role (known as *role salience*) will vary, so that some roles are more important than others. In Figure 12.1, darker shading reflects increased role salience. Super identified the nine most common roles people hold as: 1) child, 2) student, 3) leisurite (i.e., time spent in leisure activities), 4) citizen, 5) worker, 6) spouse, 7) homemaker,

FIGURE 12.1   Example of a Life-Career Rainbow

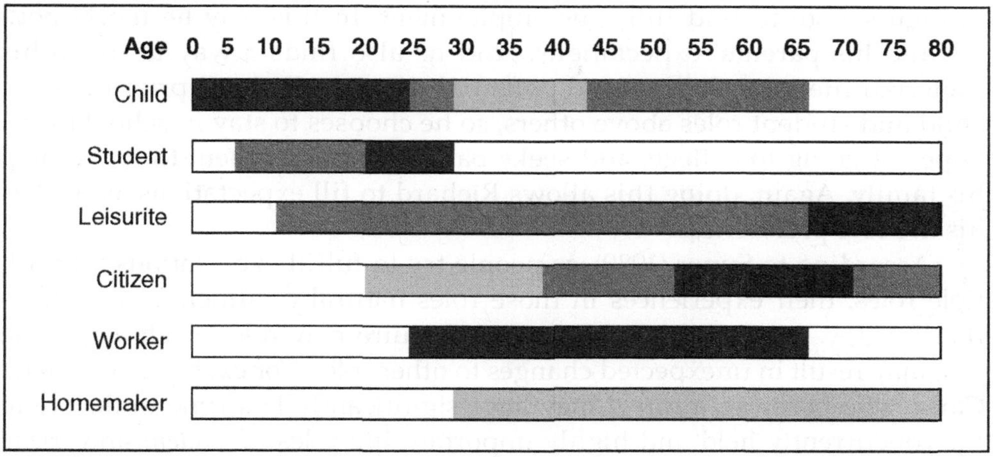

Note: Darker shading reflects increased role salience. *Adapted from Super's (1980) life-career rainbow.*

8) parent, and 9) pensioner (retired citizen). Furthermore, he acknowledged that people might identify other salient roles, such as friend or sibling, and that the length of time someone fills any given role can vary. He stated that people not only assume certain roles throughout much of their lives (e.g., a person is a child until their parents die), but also that not all people experience all roles during their lifetime.

Second, to understand life roles, Super (1980) addressed the relevance of role expectations (of the individual and of others) and the manner in which roles change over time and by situation. For example, there might be different expectations of the *child* life role depending on a person's age and/or based on cultural factors. People typically would expect a child at age 5 not to question his or her parents, but might not have the same expectations of a child who is 16 (think about the previous discussion of children exploring their own values by challenging or rejecting their parents' values). Nevertheless, some people and some cultural groups expect children to honor and respect their parents' wishes, no matter how old they are, while others allow for more independence of thought as children age. A student's perception of his or her expectations as a child may or may not differ from the expectations of others.

Major life roles for students in 10th grade tend to include child, student, friend, leisurite, citizen, and in some cases, worker. Students' personal expectations and the expectations of others inform how they approach various roles. For example, Richard prioritizes his life role as child above all others and feels an expectation to honor his parents. They also have an expectation that he honor their wishes. His parents are experiencing financial difficulties and have asked him to find a job to help bring in more income to support their family. In one possible scenario, Richard prioritizes the child and worker roles more than others, so he chooses to drop out of high school to find full-time employment. In this way he meets both his and his parents' expectations. And he also finds a way to fulfill his preferred life roles. In a second potential scenario, Richard prioritizes the child and student roles above others, so he chooses to stay in school in the hopes of going to college, and seeks part-time employment to try to help his family. Again, doing this allows Richard to fill expectations as well as his life role preferences.

According to Super (1980), as people try to fulfill expectations for multiple roles, their experiences in those roles naturally influence other roles they occupy. Some 10th grade students acquire new roles, such as parent, that may result in unexpected changes to other roles. For example, a student, Carla, who becomes a *parent* may have significantly less time to devote to the concurrently held and highly important life roles of *student* and *friend* than she had before having a baby. Carla might benefit from discussing ways to manage all of the expectations that she places upon herself related to those roles, and may need help reprioritizing her roles and developing a long-term plan.

In a different illustration of roles impacting each other, the second author recalls one particular student, Dustin, who followed the lead of his friends and found a part-time job working in a local factory. Many of the students' parents worked in this factory, and it was not uncommon for students to drop out of school at age 16 to seek full-time employment there. Shortly after obtaining the job, Dustin realized that the job was not something he wanted to do on a full-time basis or for the rest of his life. As a result, he became much more interested in school and getting his diploma so that he might have more options. Dustin kept the part-time job because he wanted to have money to fund his social activities. Despite the fact that holding a job decreased the amount of time he had available for studying, Dustin's grades started to improve, reflecting that his life role as *worker* positively impacted his role as *student* (see Figure 12.2).

Finally, the way in which people see themselves in one or more roles (i.e., their self-concept) is reflected in their life role beliefs. Examples of life role beliefs include statements such as "I enjoy learning," "I am a thoughtful friend," and "I am a dependable worker." Students develop life role beliefs by observing others, as well as through their own first-hand experience. The important role that peers play during adolescence, and the struggle students have to solidify their identities, can create much confusion with regard to their life roles, and as a result, their self-concepts. For example, because many students see positive outcomes associated with belonging to a certain group, they often prioritize the life role of friend and may make positive or negative choices (e.g., taking advanced placement classes, skipping school) based more on their friends' role expectations of them rather than basing their choices on their parents' role expectations. Students in

FIGURE 12.2 Dustin's Partial Life-Career Rainbows

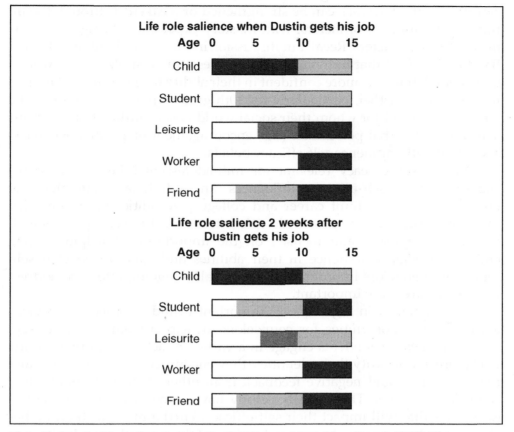

Note: Darker shading reflects increased role salience. *Adapted from Super's (1980) life-career rainbow.*

this mid-adolescent stage can benefit from opportunities to explore their life roles, and later in this chapter we provide an example of how to help them do that.

Social Cognitive Career Theory (Lent, Brown, & Hackett, 1994)

In their *Social Cognitive Career Theory* (SCCT), Lent, Brown, and Hackett (1994) explain how people develop vocational interests and make occupational choices. We focus on the former (vocational interests) in this chapter. In SCCT, Lent et al. identify the relationships among self-efficacy, outcome expectations, and personal goals. Importantly, and consistent with our focus on a student's environment and the systems in which he or she lives, they also discuss the role of personal and environmental/contextual factors in career development.

Grounded in social cognitive theory, SCCT adheres to Bandura's (1997) assertion that *self-efficacy* can be strengthened or weakened through the influence of a number of factors, with mastery experiences being one of the most influential factors. Recall our discussion in Chapter 8 about self-efficacy. Bandura believed that individuals who successfully complete tasks would, upon completion, feel more confident in their ability to perform similar tasks in the future. Further, particularly for 10th grade students, who are still a bit egocentric and for whom their social world is very influential, vicarious learning and verbal persuasion (e.g., encouragement or positive feedback) also can greatly influence self-efficacy beliefs.

Why is self-efficacy relevant for mid-adolescents? Lent et al. (1994) suggested that self-efficacy influences an individual's intentions or goals, and students limit career and college possibilities based on what they think they can or cannot do. We introduced the concept of self-efficacy in Chapter 8, and focused on the importance of helping young children develop confidence in their abilities and learn to develop self-regulatory behaviors in order to achieve goals. Ongoing efforts to address those focus areas are important.

So why revisit in high school? Importantly, mid-adolescence provides a wealth of opportunities for counselors to help students examine self-efficacy beliefs. As students engage in a variety of activities in their efforts to explore and solidify their identities, they encounter new experiences and receive positive and negative feedback from others that will inform their self-efficacy beliefs. They also hopefully have some of their own *mastery experiences* that will impact their self-efficacy. Furthermore, as their bodies change, students become increasingly aware of the strengths and limitations they might have related to their ability to fulfill the physical requirements of various careers (e.g., Maria's realization that she cannot pursue a career as a professional ballerina). As discussed in Chapter 7, many males aspire to become professional athletes. By high school, these students begin to understand how limited their opportunities are to enter professional sports based on individual talent and genetics.

Two other important constructs comprise a model that explains the development of career interests. First, Lent et al. (1994) described *outcome expectations* as the beliefs a person holds about the outcomes of engaging in certain behaviors. For example, Carla (the new teen parent) is confident she would be successful in college (high self-efficacy) and she believes that getting good grades in high school will enable her to secure a scholarship to attend college (outcome expectations). Since her family cannot afford to send her to college, a scholarship would be very important in helping her pursue her goal of attending college. Second, *personal goals* refer to an individual's plans to pursue a certain career or engage in a specific behavior (Lent et al., 1994). These goals are informed by self-efficacy beliefs and outcome

FIGURE 12.3 Carla's Goal Influences

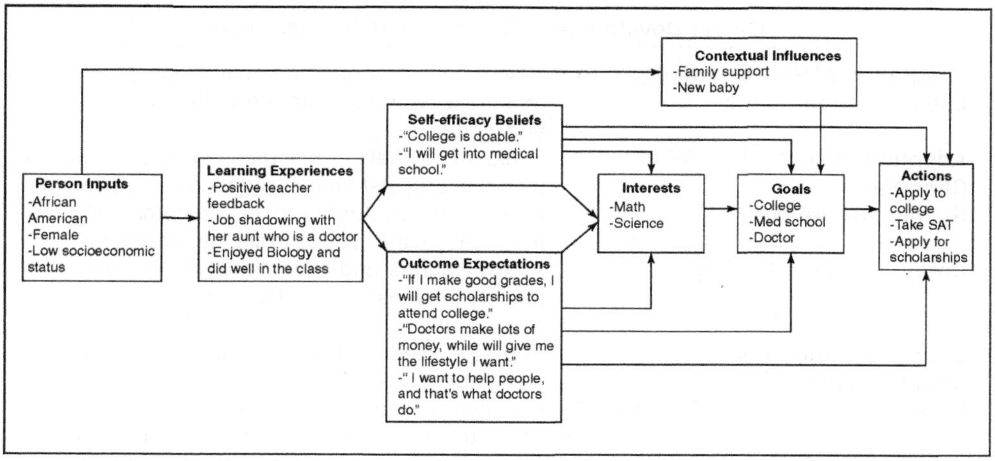

Adapted from Lent et al. (1994).

expectations (see Figure 12.3 for an illustration of the factors that influenced Carla's interests and goals of becoming a doctor), but also by contextual factors. In Carla's case, her new family responsibilities will influence her goals and the actions she takes toward pursuing them.

Notice that in Figure 12.3, one of the contextual influences in Carla's life includes her new baby. Even if Carla has high self-efficacy and outcome expectations, it is possible that factors related to being a mom and caring for her baby will deter her from successfully pursuing her goals. In this sense, SCCT acknowledges an environmental component that might warrant attention. Examining life role balance concerns could be critical to helping Carla navigate the new demands that she faces related to being a mom.

GRADE LEVEL EXPECTANCIES FOR 10TH GRADE

As we suggested for other grade levels, interventions for 10th grade students ideally should be grounded in theory and connected to grade level expectancies (GLEs). In Table 12.1 we highlight some of the Missouri Center for Career Education's (2006) career, as well as academic and personal/social, GLEs for 10th graders. Note that most of them closely correspond to the constructs we have reviewed in this chapter, things such as future planning, career goals, strengths, and balancing life roles. In the sections that follow we share examples of interventions that can be used to address many of these key areas.

TABLE 12.1 Missouri 10th Grade GLEs

Career Development: Self and Career Awareness	
Integration of Self-Knowledge into Life and Career Plans	Revisit current career and educational plan as it relates to evolving and/or new interests, strengths, and limitations.
Adaptations to World of Work Changes	Evaluate a variety of resources to aid in career exploration and planning now and in the future.
Respect for All Work	Analyze and evaluate school and community contributions as they relate to life career goals.
Career Decision Making	Analyze career and educational information to identify the most relevant resources for specific career options.
Education and Career Requirements	Apply knowledge of self to make informed decisions about postsecondary options.
Personal Skills for Job Success	Identify the steps that can be used to resolve ethical issues related to school or work situations.
Job-Seeking Skills	Compare and contrast the postsecondary application process to the job application process.
Academic Development	
Life-Long Learning	Assess and apply educational skills necessary to progress toward individual life-long learning goals.
Self-Management for Educational Achievement	Assess and apply a self-management system to meet increased academic demands.
Transitions	Self-assess and apply information to expand awareness of the relationship between high school options and postsecondary options.
Educational Planning for Life-Long Learning	Explore options and resources available to further develop personal education plans for life-long learning.
Personal/Social Development	
Self-Concept	Implement skills necessary to exhibit and maintain a positive self-concept.
Balancing Life Roles	Prioritize roles and responsibilities and implement strategies in order to balance family, school, work, and local communities.

Based on the Missouri Center for Career Education (2006).

Collaborating With Teachers and the Community to Target Future Goals

In most schools, 10th grade students have some sort of tentative program of study, grounded in a career plan and outlining the high school coursework and experiences that would facilitate them reaching their career goals. An example of this was in introduced in Chapter 10 with the individual graduation plan (IGP) used in South Carolina schools. Using these IGPs or similar plans as a foundation, school personnel can help students develop long-term goals and thoroughly examine the choices they make related to those goals, as well as the factors that influence those goals. The interventions described in the following focus on identifying and/or addressing influences to self-efficacy.

Developing and evaluating career plans. Because 10th grade students are still developing their identities and experimenting with new interests and activities, ongoing examination of their career plans is warranted. School personnel cannot assume that career plans developed at the beginning of ninth grade will remain relevant throughout high school. Opportunities to identify their talents and strengths can serve as entry points to revisit and more closely examine students' long-term career plans.

Although school and career counselors traditionally assume responsibility for working with students to develop their programs of study, teachers easily can become more involved in that process. Recall in Chapter 11 when we mentioned a high school where teachers facilitated IGP meetings. In gathering accountability data, the school counselor, Mrs. Carney, discovered that the teachers did not always feel confident facilitating those meetings and that they sometimes weren't sure how helpful they had been.

After talking with many teachers, Mrs. Carney realized that they were looking for something more concrete to help them walk students and parents through their decision-making process. She decided to provide them with a template that would allow them to help students identify and connect their strengths and goals (and that fits very well with our SCCT focus), and she provided a worksheet for them to follow as well (see Exhibit 12.1). The example in Exhibit 12.2 illustrates an abbreviated version of a teacher-led conversation using this approach.

Optimizing feedback to students (verbal persuasion). We have talked about the factors that affect self-efficacy beliefs, and adults with whom students interact can play very important roles in the formation of students' self-efficacy beliefs and future aspirations. To maximize opportunities for encouragement (verbal persuasion), school counselors can facilitate adult involvement in a number of ways.

First, school counselors can lead a faculty in-service session during which time they discuss the ways in which teacher feedback can influence student goals (review the factors that influence self-efficacy). School counselors may also provide concrete examples of how to phrase or rephrase feedback in an effort to not sound discouraging. For example, rather than a frustrated teacher saying to a student who does poorly on tests, "You'll never pass this class if you don't study for the tests," that teacher can be encouraged to provide more positive and encouraging feedback such as "You always pay attention in class but seem to do poorly on the tests—I'm wondering if we can talk about how we might help you do better on the next one." Sharing a chart like that in Table 12.2 could help teachers understand how their words can be internalized. Sometimes asking teachers to come up with statements they have made or heard, and then asking them to generate ideas for what messages students might hear, can help them to get into the mindset of their students a little better.

In addition to demonstrating to teachers how students might internalize their feedback, school counselors also can help all school personnel become more intentional about sharing feedback. We talked earlier in this

EXHIBIT 12.1
Teacher-Led Student Future Planning Conference Worksheet

Pull up the student's IGP. Review his/her career goal and ask if it is still accurate. If Yes, go to **(A)** below, if No, go to **(X)**.

(A) Ask how confident the student feels he/she is that he/she can achieve the goal: (not confident) 1 2 3 4 5 6 (very confident) 	**(X)** Ask what the new goal is what led to the change, and how much the student knows about the job requirements. Make notes here, then jump over to **(A)**: ←

(B) Ask the student what kinds of related activities (e.g., coursework, job shadowing, hobbies) he/she has engaged in this past year and list them here:

(C) Comment on the relevance of those activities in relation to the goal:

(D) Ask the student what reinforcement he/she has received related to that goal and list responses here:
- Evidence of potential (mastery experiences):
- Encouragement from parents, teachers, peers, others (verbal persuasion):

(E) Finally, develop a list of activities for this year to help the student make further progress toward his/her goal and/or to allow for some opportunities for reinforcement:

book about the need to encourage all students to consider nontraditional careers; to help more minority students, those from low socioeconomic status (SES) families, and students with disabilities consider college as a possibility; and to help females and minority students aspire to enter science, technology, engineering, and mathematics (STEM) careers. Although we

EXHIBIT 12.2
Sample IGP Meeting

Marcus, a 10th grade student, and his mother, have come to meet with his teacher for their annual career planning session. Marcus has been taking general level academic classes, thinking he will attend a 2-year college or technical school, and he has a 3.4 GPA. After engaging in introductions, Mr. Thompson walks them through the session using the template (see Exhibit 12.1) provided by the school counselor:

Mr. Thompson: So, Marcus, it looks like last year you had indicated a desire to work on computers . . . like a tech support person? Is that still something you want to do?

Marcus: Yeah, that's what I did want to do. I understand computers pretty good, so I thought that could be fun.

Mr. Thompson: Sounds like something you feel pretty confident about—like you would be good at it?

Marcus: That's right, but I have a different plan now.

Marcus's mother: He keeps changing his mind. I tell him he needs to pick something and stick with it.

Mr. Thompson: I'm sure it's difficult to see your son still trying to come up with a long-term plan. I can reassure you, however, that most kids his age are still trying out new things. The important thing is that we help him move forward in a way that will keep as many options open as possible, and we can do that today. What's your new idea, Marcus?

Marcus: I want to join the Air Force. My friend's cousin was telling me about how he is like a weatherman for the Air Force. He got all of his training there and now he gets to work with these cool computer programs to predict the weather.

Mr. Thompson: So I hear you saying that finding out about this new job through your friend's cousin got you thinking about it. (Mr. Thompson takes some time to explore what Marcus knows about the job expectations and training . . . he seems to have thought a lot about it, so Mr. Thompson proceeds to Step A on the worksheet.)

Mr. Thompson: You have done your homework and seem to have a clear idea of what is required. I'm wondering how confident you are that you could complete the requirements? If 1 = not confident and 6 = very confident . . . give me a number where you would be.

Marcus: I think a 5. I mean, I really want to do it, so I'll work hard.

(continued)

EXHIBITS 12.2 *(Continued)*
Sample IGP Meeting

Mr. Thompson: Ok, so you're pretty confident. Aside from talking with your cousin's friend, what else have you done that is related to being a weatherman? Any classes you've taken that are relevant?

Marcus: Well, the earth science I have is. I got an A in that class. I'm good with computers, too, like I said before. Nothing else I can think of.

Marcus's mother: He really hasn't done anything. He hasn't even talked to the Air Force—I know we need to do to that.

Mr. Thompson: Definitely. Before we leave today we'll try to come up with a plan. I know that, Marcus, you have done well in science and computer classes, so it makes sense that you feel pretty confident. You mentioned that your teachers have been very encouraging of your abilities as well, and that your friend's cousin was pretty confident you could do it because he and you are a lot alike, is that right?

Marcus: Yep—I can't think of any reason not to try.

Mr. Thompson (to Marcus's mother): How do you feel?

Marcus's mother: To be honest, I'm a little hesitant. I don't know much about the military, but he does seem really excited. I just want to make sure he does what needs to be done.

Mr. Thompson: Alright then . . . sounds like we need to develop a new action plan to help you move forward with this new goal. (Mr. Thompson leads them in a discussion to explore activities he should complete including things like taking the Armed Services Vocational Aptitude Battery (ASVAB), meeting with the Air Force recruiter, job shadowing with a meteorologist, signing up for advanced science classes, and so on. He also refers them back to the school counselor, just so they can make sure that the plan makes sense and nothing critical is missing.)

aren't suggesting that school personnel target some students over others, knowing how their words effect students could make a difference; thus we are encouraging them to make an intentional effort to reach out when they find opportunities.

For example, Dimitrius is an African American male from a low SES background. Neither of his parents graduated from high school, and his older sister found employment right after high school. Dimitrius is very bright and has excelled in all of his classes. He has strong academic potential to pursue college in a math or science major. Recognizing that Dimitrius might receive little information about college at home, and that he probably would need financial aid, his teachers and counselor could be very intentional and

TABLE 12.2 Examples of How Students Internalize Feedback

Feedback Statement	Message Heard	Student Action
You'll never pass the class if you don't study for the tests.	He doesn't think I can pass.	Student stops studying.
You always pay attention in class but seem to do poorly on the tests—I'm wondering if we can talk about how we might help you do better on the next one?	He thinks I can do better and is willing to work with me.	Student is willing to get tutoring and keep working.
You need to spend more time on school and less with your girlfriend.	She doesn't understand how hard I'm really trying to balance everything.	Student shuts down when teacher talks to him.
You seem to be juggling a lot of things lately and your schoolwork has dropped; would it help to talk about ways to balance everything?	She understands me and is willing to help me figure out how to bring my grades up.	Student and teacher talk, or student approaches school counselor for help.

proactive in pointing out his strengths and conveying their belief in his potential (e.g., "Your work ethic would serve you well in college—are you thinking about that?" or "I would like to see you enroll in AP Chemistry—it would be great if you could get college credit now, and I think you have a good shot"). Planting the idea of college early enough so that he would have plenty of time to enroll in requisite courses and explore financial aid options would be critical to facilitating the transition for a potential first-generation college student.

Role models and mentors (vicarious learning). Students are most influenced by individuals with whom they feel a connection based on some salient characteristic (Bandura, 1997). Those connections often are initially based on factors like race/ethnicity or gender, but sometimes students connect with certain people for other reasons. For example, lots of high school students look up to athletes who may or may not look like them, but whom they want to emulate because of their status. In any event, school counselors can work to identify individuals who can serve as mentors or role models for students and to create opportunities for them to interact. These kinds of experiences can allow for vicarious learning and verbal persuasion influences to occur.

Similar to the mentoring scenario in Exhibit 12.3, by partnering with various organizations or groups in their local community, school counselors can recruit adult mentors to pair with specific students. These kinds of arrangements can be established with local businesses, by contacting civic groups, or by soliciting parent volunteers. School counselors should be prepared to provide some information to the mentors about the purpose of the partnerships as well as how they might spend their time with the students. They also should make efforts to recruit individuals who reflect the diversity of the school population as well as nontraditional careers (e.g., male nurse).

EXHIBIT 12.3
Partnering With a College to Identify Mentors

To help promote a college-going culture, one Southeastern school part-nered with a local university to establish ongoing mentoring relation-ships. Providing monthly opportunities for lunch meetings at the school, the school counselors solicited college student volunteers whom they matched with students they thought could benefit from having a men-tor (i.e., most of these students were potential first-generation college students). Mentors were paired in order to match salient characteristics as much as possible (e.g., a Latina college student majoring in engineer-ing with a Mexican American student who excels in math and science). As the mentors talked about their backgrounds and their experiences in college, the students were able to better envision the same kinds of pos-sibilities for themselves. The mentors were encouraged to emphasize the importance of academics, to provide information and encouragement relevant to the student's career goals, and to share the things that they believed helped them be successful.

Another way to connect students with role models is through a career fair. Thoughtfully planned to include individuals who represent nontradi-tional careers, a career fair can help students recognize that people like them can succeed in any number of careers. Kolodinsky et al. (2006) discussed the positive outcomes of a career fair involving mainly females who worked in a variety of nontraditional careers. The women who served as the career role models discussed and demonstrated various aspects of their work to par-ticipants during small-group breakout sessions. Through pre-/postsurveys, the researchers found increased occupational self-efficacy among adolescent girls who attended the career fair, specifically in relation to their confidence to engage in tasks needed for various occupations.

A final way to expose students to role models is through job shadow-ing. Many students need to see or experience someone being successful in order for vicarious learning to crystallize. That is, seeing someone perform an activity may be more influential to a student's self-efficacy beliefs than simply talking with someone about his or her ability to perform an activity. Logistical concerns sometimes make organizing job-shadowing activities challenging, but school counselors can be creative in making these oppor-tunities work.

Perhaps in an ideal world, every student is provided an opportunity to participate in a meaningful job-shadowing opportunity, and with any luck he or she might have a couple of opportunities during high school to do this. The main challenge is that someone needs to coordinate these kinds of activities (e.g., identify relevant employees, match the mentor with students, coordinate schedules, address liability issues, and complete any relevant paperwork), ensure transportation is available (don't assume that all students would be able to transport themselves to and from these opportunities), and address issues related to students missing school. In schools that employ a career counselor, this type of arrangement might be very realistic. Most schools, however, are limited in staff available to organize such a comprehensive career-related initiative.

One solution to help eliminate logistical concerns related to job shadowing is to provide opportunities for students to engage in virtual job shadowing. Numerous websites (e.g., www.virtualjobshadow.com/) are available for students to learn about jobs, to hear from individuals who work in those jobs, and to capture a glimpse of what the job environment might look like. In addition to providing an option that is accessible to all students, virtual job shadowing also affords students an opportunity to explore jobs that might not be readily accessible to them. These experiences also can be completed any time of day, which means that students would not need to miss school in order to participate. Finally, when relevant, parents or counselors could participate along with students.

Mastery experiences. We will talk more about mastery experiences in the next chapter, as school personnel can facilitate opportunities for students in numerous ways. In 10th grade, however, school personnel can address self-efficacy related to academic potential by focusing on college entrance examinations. Specifically, the Preliminary Scholastic Aptitude Test (PSAT) can serve as an important factor influencing self-efficacy related to reading, writing, and math. The PSAT serves as a practice test for the Scholastic Aptitude Test (SAT) as well as an opportunity to qualify for certain scholarships and use some career planning tools (College Board, 2012). Some students start taking the actual SAT in middle school, in order to get as much exposure and practice with the real exam as possible, but for many students, that is not a financially viable option. Most students wait to take the less-expensive PSAT in their sophomore year. In this way they can get a sense of how they might do the following year on the PSAT (when they first become eligible for certain scholarship opportunities based on their scores) and later when they take the SAT.

The ACT is a similar, but slightly different, college entrance exam that students typically take in grades 11 or 12. Where the SAT assesses reading, writing, and math, the ACT assesses English, reading, math, and science skills and offers an optional writing test (ACT, 2012). Similar to the SAT, a practice test of sorts, PLAN, is available to help students estimate their future ACT scores. The test format of PLAN is identical to the ACT, but questions are a little less difficult. PLAN is meant to be taken in 10th grade.

Their experiences taking the PSAT and/or PLAN can inform students' future goals in positive and negative ways. For example, a student who does well on the PSAT might experience increased self-efficacy related to taking the SAT in the future. Anticipating that he or she might be able to get into competitive colleges, a student who does well on the PSAT may feel more motivated to put effort into academic work and/or may be inspired to investigate colleges not previously considered (due to increased self-efficacy and outcome expectations). Assuming he or she will do well, this student also might be more motivated to register for challenging high school classes. Upon receiving a good score, another student who had not really considered college but who was encouraged to take the PSAT might actively start looking at careers requiring a 4-year college degree. Some students who do not fare as well on the PSAT might be motivated to work harder in school so that they can improve their scores. Conversely, some who don't score very high may get discouraged (i.e., lower self-efficacy) and start exploring other career paths not requiring college degrees.

We encourage school counselors to use the PSAT and PLAN tests as opportunities to engage students in discussion to find out how they make sense of their scores. For instance, school counselors should clarify that students must be careful about making strong inferences based on a single test. They could explore with students things like how they felt going into the test, how much they prepared for it, and how they felt during the exam. School counselors also can emphasize that there are many things students can do to improve their scores for future tests. Building these conversations into the annual career planning meetings will ensure that parents receive the same information.

Targeted Interventions to Address Life Role Challenges

Given the number of students in 10th grade who may start to increase and/or reprioritize the number of life roles they need to balance (e.g., adding the worker role through part-time jobs, adding the parent role by having a baby), we wanted to provide an example of how school counselors might address their concerns. To focus on students currently experiencing difficulties related to life role balance, school counselors can implement small-group interventions. Nevertheless, over the course of their lives, all students will experience life role balance challenges. As such, all students potentially could benefit from engaging in similar discussions so they can develop skills to navigate similar changes in the future, and large-group or classroom-based interventions could be implemented.

Earlier in this chapter we introduced Carla, the teen mom who aspired to become a doctor. She and a few other girls in her school are all struggling with the newly acquired role of parent. Even though the students have different future goals, they can benefit from exploring their life role challenges together in a small group where they can experience peer support and a sense of universality.

One way to help students thoroughly examine the life role changes that have occurred is to have them create their own life career rainbow. These rainbows don't need to be complicated—students can simply label different bars with the life roles they assume (as in Figure 12.1) and then shade in the bars accordingly. To better illustrate the changes, students can be asked to create one rainbow to represent their life before the baby (and the acquisition of the parent role) and another to represent their life with the baby (more along the lines of Figure 12.2). To expand the rainbow, they can be asked to list the daily activities that go along with each role and/or to estimate the percent of time each day that they engage in that role.

Many students who become teenage parents may understandably feel some resentment or frustration about losing some of their youth. They may have less time with their friends or less time to focus on school, and they might start to rethink their future plans. For example, while trying to care for her baby, Carla is struggling to maintain her high academic standing in the hopes that she can still get a scholarship to attend college, but she also feels torn between prioritizing school and prioritizing her daughter. For students like Carla, creating a "reality" life role rainbow as well as a "desired" life role rainbow can encourage the identification and acknowledgment of these kinds of feelings. These rainbows also can serve as the foundation for discussing how to move forward toward pursuing future goals including examining potential barriers and brainstorming ways to navigate them.

SUMMARY

In this chapter we focused on life roles and self-efficacy as important target areas for career-related interventions. Tenth grade students should be encouraged to engage in a variety of activities so they can hone in on their talents and skills; those mastery experiences will shape their interests and goals. Further, opportunities for vicarious learning and encouragement can be provided through school-wide initiatives and connecting with the community. Counselors and educators should be intentional in their efforts to influence students' self-efficacy.

⋯❯ Test Your Knowledge

1. Explain the relationship between outcome expectations, self-efficacy, and personal goals.
2. Identify at least four life roles that most 10th graders hold.

13

•••••

Career Education and Counseling for Grade 11: Career and College Preparation

•••••

Although many students and their parents start anticipating and planning for the end of high school as far back as middle school, grade 11 is a time when most students really start to acknowledge that high school graduation is not that far away. Evidence of this shift in thinking includes students beginning to take school more seriously, worrying about being involved in enough activities to boost their college applications, and seeming eager, ready, and willing to actively engage in activities to prepare them for their future careers. Students who are still uncertain about their future plans may start to feel pressure from peers and parents to make a choice. As such, activities implemented for 11th grade students should be designed to help them narrow down or confirm their future plans and then to help them take concrete steps toward pursuing those plans. In this chapter we briefly review relevant developmental and career theories, and then focus on interventions to help them attain their career goals.

DEVELOPMENTAL OVERVIEW

Students in 11th grade have passed most major physical, cognitive, and psychosocial milestones, and their development starts to flatten out, so to speak. Therefore, developmental changes in the junior year may be more subtle than in previous grades. Most 11th grade students fall into the mid-adolescence (ages 15 to 18) category and still possess many of the characteristics discussed in the previous chapter. In particular, peer influence and abstract-thinking skills (e.g., problem-solving skills) are very important to their college and career decision-making process.

Recall our discussion of identity statuses (Marcia, 1987) in Chapter 9. As students in 11th grade are finalizing their future plans, it is not uncommon to hear them talk about pursuing options that their peers are pursuing. Relying too much on their peers' preferences can result in identity foreclosure and possible future dissatisfaction with their choices. Similarly, some students may choose the same careers as their parents or careers that fit with a family business, rather than exploring their own personal interests, aptitudes, and values before making a career decision. Further, when students engage in career exploration activities and find that they have numerous options that might make sense, it sometimes can be easier to just do what everyone else is doing. Students in a moratorium status (i.e., exploring but unable to commit; Marcia, 1987) may be more easily influenced by their peers than would students who have committed to an identity (i.e., identity achievement) and chosen a unique career path. That is, when students feel strongly about something, they can be less susceptible to influence from others.

Decisions about college (including whether or not to attend, the type of school to attend, and which particular school to attend) also are often influenced by others' opinions and choices. Both authors have worked with students who were set on attending a specific college (often based on peer or parent influence, family tradition, or because they had a good football team) without thinking about whether or not they could major in something they liked at a particular school. In essence, they foreclosed on a college choice because they didn't feel any need to explore other options.

As these students were eventually able to narrow down possible majors, they often realized that their preferred colleges did not offer those majors. These students then had to choose between attending the school they had become excited about and finding a major there that would be satisfactory, or taking a risk to branch out away from their peers and explore colleges that would allow them to pursue their career goals. For example, the first author provided career counseling and advisement to an 11th grade student, Lorena, who had decided to be a marine biologist. Lorena grew up in Florida and was a huge fan of University of Florida; thus, she had decided to pursue her college degree there. However, during an advisement session, it was discovered that University of Florida did not have a marine biology program, so Lorena was confused about whether to change her decision about her major or pursue another postsecondary option.

Whether it is choosing a career or a college, the influence of peers or other important individuals can supersede logical thinking. For example, students might be able to explain very clearly why one college might be a more logical choice than another based on their career goals or characteristics they value (e.g., religious affiliation). Yet, the idea of leaving peers behind or disappointing someone they care about can be too overwhelming for some students, and they end up making a choice that will not help them get what they want in the long run. To an outsider, their decision-making process may seem illogical.

How can students make choices and life decisions that don't match their personal goals? Even when adolescents can accurately discuss the potential consequences of their actions, they still sometimes believe that things will work out for them. In other instances, the desire to fit in and do what their peers do is just too great. For these reasons, it is important to foster autonomy and help students learn to make decisions that *they* believe to be in their best interest (even if those decisions are based on the preferences of others). We believe that decisions made in the absence of exploration (i.e., students who are in identity diffusion or foreclosure) are ones that students might question later.

We hope that very few students in 11th grade are apathetic about their future (i.e., identity diffusion), but realistically a good number of students fall into this category. Some are not ready to leave the comforts of high school, so they avoid planning. Others have a difficult time picturing themselves living a successful life, leaving them unmotivated to plan. Yet another subset of students don't envision themselves working or attending school, so they believe there is nothing to plan for. Later in this chapter we will discuss ideas for helping these students become more engaged in thinking about and preparing for their futures.

RELEVANT CAREER THEORY: LENT, BROWN, AND HACKETT (1994) AND SAVICKAS (2005)

In Chapter 12 we introduced Social Cognitive Career Theory (SCCT; Lent, Brown, & Hackett, 1994), and we elaborate on that theory in this chapter by focusing on factors that affect student *performance* on academic and career tasks. In addition, we present another theory that can be used to help students finalize their career decisions: Savickas' (2005) *Career Construction Theory*. These two theories provide the framework for interventions we review later in this chapter.

Social Cognitive Career Theory (Lent, Brown, & Hackett, 1994)

In the previous chapter we introduced Lent, Brown, and Hackett's (1994) interest model to help explain the personal and environmental factors that influence the development of career interests. Continuing with the example from the previous chapter of Carla, the teen mom who wants to become a doctor, in this chapter we review SCCT's *performance model* (see Figure 13.1). This model explains success at and persistence toward academic and career-related tasks. Notice that self-efficacy and outcome expectations continue to play important roles.

According to Lent et al. (1994), the ability/past performance box in Figure 13.1 refers to task-specific knowledge and skills that Carla has acquired. For example, by doing well in a trigonometry class, Carla develops math-related skills and strategies that will help her to achieve success in more advanced math classes. In this way, her acquired skills directly affect her

FIGURE 13.1 Carla's Task Performance Model

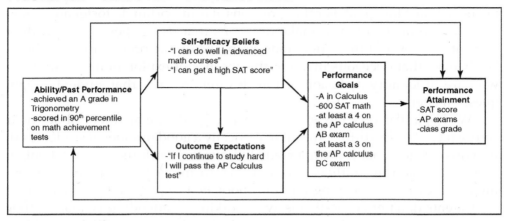

Adapted from Lent et al. (1994).

performance attainment (i.e., level of performance). As illustrated through the arrows in Figure 13.1, past performance also indirectly affects performance attainment by influencing self-efficacy and outcome expectations.

Recall from the previous chapter our discussion of how *mastery performances* can greatly influence self-efficacy beliefs; as Carla achieves success, she feels more and more confident that she has the ability to achieve success in similar tasks in the future. Further, in seeing that her study habits seem to be working, Carla's outcome expectation is that approaching future math classes as she did her trigonometry class should result in academic success. Based on her self-efficacy beliefs and outcome expectations, Carla develops performance goals. The more confidence she has in her ability to achieve success and attain desired outcomes, the more challenging goals she will set.

Persistence is an important construct in relation to the performance model. Lent et al. (1994) indicated that students who persist are more likely to achieve success in academic or career tasks (e.g., graduate from high school) than are their peers who do not persist. They believe that persistent students are probably more competent at specific tasks than are students who are not persistent. That is, students who had successful mastery experiences would naturally feel more confident in their future capabilities, and therefore they would put forth continual effort (i.e., persist) toward a goal. This sentiment holds true especially for students who encounter obstacles or barriers; to persist in the face of obstacles suggests positive and high self-efficacy beliefs and outcome expectations. Interestingly, in examining the career beliefs of inner city youth, Turner and Conkel Ziebell (2011) found that only 24% of participants believed that effort was linked to success; these students had low outcome expectations. Without knowing how their beliefs developed, SCCT would suggest that past performance would play a role.

Finally, Lent et al. (1994) discussed the importance of examining self-efficacy beliefs in relation to a person's past performance/abilities. More specifically, they articulate that both overconfidence and underconfidence in one's actual abilities can be detrimental to performance attainment. Thinking they are very capable, overconfident individuals may mistakenly believe that they do not have to put forth much effort. Further, these individuals may set unrealistic or unattainable goals, often resulting in failure because they did not possess the requisite skills or knowledge to be successful. For example, students with average or below average grades may set the goal of attending medical school, not realizing that their academic record may prohibit them from meeting admissions requirements or underestimating the amount of effort it will take to be successful in such an endeavor. As a result, high schools often try to set students up for success by requiring teacher recommendations before students can enroll in higher level or advanced placement (AP) courses.

Underconfident individuals possess similar challenges. Feeling less hopeful, these students tend to exert less effort, give up more quickly, and set less challenging goals (Lent et al., 1994). Because they have little confidence in their abilities, the anxiety that many of these students experience before engaging in tasks can prevent them from achieving success. By missing out on opportunities that would allow them to advance their skills, underconfident students often fail to reach their potential.

Savickas's Theory of Career Construction (2005)

Although a thorough discussion of Career Construction Theory is beyond the scope of this book (refer to Savickas, 2002, 2005 for more information), we want to highlight a few key aspects of this theory that are particularly relevant to working with 11th grade students. Savickas (2005) wrote, "Individuals construct their careers by imposing meaning on their vocational behavior and occupational experiences" (p. 43). Career Construction (Savickas, 2002) is a postmodern theory that is grounded in the belief that the best way to understand individuals is in the context of their environment and how they experience it, as well as by examining how they make meaning of their experiences. Further, according to Savickas, Career Construction:

> . . . views careers from a contextualist perspective, one that sees development as driven by adaptation to an environment rather than by maturation of inner structures. Viewing careers from constructionist and contextual perspectives focuses attention on interpretive processes, social interaction, and the negotiation of meaning. Careers . . . are constructed as individuals make choices that express their self-concepts and substantiate their goals in the social reality of work roles. (p. 43)

Understandably, Career Construction relies on subjective measures and qualitative assessments as opposed to objective and quantitative measures, and counselors using this approach focus on individual perceptions and stories or personal narratives (Savickas, 2005). Nevertheless, Savickas's theory complements theories such as those of Holland (1973) and Super (1980) that rely on objective, or concrete, assessments of person and/or environment. Savickas does not discount the value of examining objective assessment data (e.g., Holland codes), but rather, he believes that subjective data are necessary for truly understanding career behaviors. That is, while Savickas values Holland's RIASEC types, he cautions that those types are socially constructed categories that may or may not make sense to a client. When they use objective assessments like interest inventories, counselors who adhere to a career construction approach use the results as a starting point for discussion about things such as how their clients view their interests and experiences in relation to various occupations and how those interests evolved.

Similar to Holland (1973), Savickas (2005) defined *vocational personality* as comprised of factors like abilities, values, and interests. He also indicated that those factors are evident long before people engage in work through things like hobbies, school activities, and other leisure activities. Unlike focusing on an objective assessment of traits to identify an individual's vocational personality, using Career Construction Theory, a counselor would focus on acquiring a more subjective understanding of an individual's vocational self-concept and *life themes*. This counselor would be interested in examining how clients understand and make sense of themselves and their world, and how they find meaning in life. Savickas (2005) believes that no matter what occupation they are in or what job they hold, everyone can find ways to express themselves (i.e., their self-concept) and find meaning through their work. With this idea in mind, counselors can help high school students begin to examine self-concept and life themes through their hobbies, activities, and formal or informal work experience.

Savickas (2005) indicated that beliefs about self and life are reflections of one's purpose, and that one's purpose truly explains career behaviors. That is, people make choices that fit with who they are and who they want to be. It is through subjective assessment, where life patterns and themes emerge, that Savickas (2005) says an individual's purpose becomes elucidated. Later in this chapter we illustrate how the *Career Style Interview* introduced in Chapter 4 can be used to facilitate the process of examining purpose through self-concept and life themes.

GRADE LEVEL EXPECTANCIES (GLEs) FOR 11TH GRADE

Missouri's Center for Career Education (2006) 11th grade GLEs reflect a focus on helping students gather more information about themselves and careers in order to inform their career decisions. Consistent with the two theories we just presented, objectives related to self-assessment, goal setting, and finding meaning in work are evident in the GLEs in Table 13.1. Interventions for 11th

TABLE 13.1 Missouri 11th Grade GLEs

Career Development: Self and Career Awareness	
Integration of Self-Knowledge into Life and Career Plans	Analyze the education, training, and personal characteristics needed to achieve current life career goals and compare those characteristics with one's own characteristics.
Adaptations to World of Work Changes	Utilize a variety of resources to aid in career exploration and planning.
Respect for All Work	Identify personal contributions to a global society to be made as a result of one's life career choices.
Career Decision Making	Synthesize information gathered from a variety of sources.
Education and Career Requirements	Apply research skills to obtain information on training and education requirements for postsecondary choices.
Personal Skills for Job Success	Demonstrate the steps that can be used to resolve ethical issues related to school or work situations.
Job-Seeking Skills	Refine and utilize a portfolio which may be used for a variety of postsecondary opportunities.
Academic Development	
Life-Long Learning	Consistently utilize educational skills necessary to progress toward individual life-long learning goals.
Transitions	Increase knowledge and refine skills in preparation for the senior year and postsecondary options.

Based on the Missouri Center for Career Education (2006).

grade students should allow for concrete and experiential opportunities to engage in career-related tasks, and we illustrate this through the interventions presented in the next section.

INTERVENTIONS: COLLABORATING WITH TEACHERS

As we discussed in previous chapters, teachers can continue to play very important roles in helping 11th grade students prepare for their futures. By partnering with teachers, school counselors can expand opportunities for students to identify mastery experiences, articulate their strengths, and develop challenging performance goals. In the following we provide specific suggestions for collaborating with teachers in this regard.

Using Clubs and Activities to Facilitate Mastery Experiences

Consistent with Savickas's (2005) belief that the factors comprising vocational personality are evident in the activities in which people engage, it makes sense to find instances to help students identify strengths through their activities and hobbies. Because teachers often tend to be engaged with students as club advisors and coaches, they have frequent opportunities to monitor students and recognize students' strengths. These advisors and coaches (who are often parents or community members) may or may not, however, do anything when they notice innate abilities or talents in their students. School counselors can encourage these individuals to be proactive and intentional in identifying strengths and offering encouragement (verbal persuasion). In Exhibit 13.1 we offer an example of a teacher initiating a conversation with a student and being intentional in her use of verbal persuasion.

In Exhibit 13.1, Mrs. Talley could have very easily made a comparison between Maria's behavior in class and what she was seeing on the project. Her comment might have been something along the lines of "You were so quiet in class last year, I never expected to see you taking charge the way you are now." We all have heard many people share that kind of feedback, meant with the best of intentions but sometimes heard by the student as condescending. Rather than mention weaknesses or negative characteristics, teachers and school personnel can simply choose to highlight the positive things they are seeing, in the hopes that students internalize their feedback.

Before advisors and coaches can offer encouragement in activities, students need to get involved in activities. Classroom teachers often are in the

---

EXHIBIT 13.1
Teacher Highlights Student Strengths

The purpose of the Key Club is to foster school and community relationships. Students work all year to implement a spring activity that will serve to connect the school and community and to raise money for a designated charity. About halfway through the year the advisor, Mrs. Talley, begins to notice the leadership role that Maria is playing. She taught Maria in a History class last year, and recalls her having been very shy and reserved, but quite bright. The energy, initiative, and confidence she sees Maria displaying in this task are quite different from what she saw in class.

Mrs. Talley decides to approach Maria. She mentions how impressed she is with Maria's leadership, initiative, and assertiveness in relation to the project. Maria responds by explaining her interest in the project, talking about how she feels passionate about it because of her own personal experiences related to the charity cause as well as from her general interest in sociology. Mrs. Talley then takes the opportunity to provide encouragement and to comment on how happy she is to experience Maria's passion and how it seems this type of work might make her very happy. She expresses curiosity about Maria's future career plans.

best position to identify students' interests and strengths, and encourage their involvement in meaningful activities where they can develop or hone their talents. Teachers can quickly pick up on which students possess innate talents and which students express strong interest and persistence. With intentional effort, teachers can facilitate opportunities for mastery experiences by recommending that students join various clubs or activities. For example, math teachers might identify students whom they believe would do well on the math team or who might benefit from participating in a robotics competition. Similarly, English teachers might identify students who could do well on the debate team or in drama club.

Many students are not aware of the different clubs or activities available at school or in the community. Others might be aware, but also might be reluctant to join for any number of reasons—because none of their friends are members, because they lack self-efficacy, or because they have assumptions about what the experience might be like. A little encouragement (i.e., verbal persuasion) from teachers who can share why the activity might be beneficial or why they think the student would be a good fit can sometimes be enough to pique students' interest. As we discussed in the previous chapter, students engage in activities when they believe they can succeed and when they believe positive outcomes will result from their involvement (Lent et al., 1994). Tapping into the power of peer influence, teachers also might invite current members of different clubs and activities to talk about their experiences and the benefits of joining various organizations. This kind of information can help students more clearly envision potential outcomes of becoming involved. Simply seeing other students with whom they sense a connection or similarity to themselves can provide the impetus for them to take a risk on something new.

In addition to extracurricular activities, teachers can include mastery experiences in the classroom. For example, through a federal grant program, one school district was able to redesign all of their science classrooms and to provide learning materials that were very hands-on. In biology lab, students had the equipment and space to dissect animals, in the physics lab students worked on designing and developing models of bridges, and in chemistry class students had the equipment to run and evaluate experiments. These types of hands-on, mastery activities are helpful for the learning process, but also enable students to envision themselves doing the work of a biologist, chemist, or physicist. Teachers should be encouraged to seek the professional development and resources necessary to provide these kinds of activities.

In considering accessibility of activities, teachers and school personnel should be aware of the associated costs. It is very likely that some students do not join activities because they cannot afford to do so. Schools might consider engaging in discussions about if and how to support students who possess strong talents but who lack opportunities because of financial concerns. As we discussed in the beginning of this book, students from low socioeconomic status (SES) families often have lower aspirations because they have not had the same kinds of opportunities or exposure to career and educational options that tend to be more readily accessible to students from higher SES families. For that reason alone, it becomes all the more important to provide experiential opportunities in school when possible. Ideally, schools should have support systems (such as a student activity fund) in place to ensure accessibility of activities and clubs for all students.

Creating Resumes to Highlight Mastery Experiences

English classes are logical places for students to work on a variety of writing projects, such as resumes. In fact, because many students who are enrolled in general or lower-level English classes enter the workforce right after graduating, it is common for teachers of those English classes to include resume and cover letter writing in their curriculum. Unfortunately, for many 11th grade students who are enrolled in AP or honors classes, a resume may not be a regular part of their curriculum. We believe that all students can benefit from preparing resumes, and school counselors can partner with English teachers in this regard.

In keeping with the idea that mastery experiences and outcome expectations inform future performance goals and attainment, resume writing can be approached with an emphasis on helping students identify experiences and successes relevant to their future goals. For example, using the resume preparation form in Exhibit 13.2, a teacher could assign students to gather the background information needed to write their resume in a way that requires them to identify accomplishments and strengths. Hopefully through the process of completing this form, students will become more aware of their ability/past performance and mastery experiences.

After students compile their resume background information, school counselors could partner with the English teachers to conduct lessons during which they help students make the connections between their experiences, skills, and future goals. While the teachers could focus on helping students format and write their resumes, the school counselor can engage in targeted career discussions. Through this activity, students who might benefit from additional career development assistance could easily be identified. See Figure 13.2 for an example of how the student example in Exhibit 13.2 would translate into a resume.

To make this type of assignment appealing to English teachers, especially those teaching advanced classes, an extra component could be added that would connect back to the basic college and career readiness skills that we reviewed earlier in this book. To foster and assess critical thinking skills, the resume and an accompanying cover letter could be used as part of an assignment focusing on how well students are able to make a convincing argument. Specifically, English teachers could grade the resume and cover

EXHIBIT 13.2
Sample Resume Preparation Form

Pull out your graduation plan/program of study, and use that information as a starting point for completing this form.

1. List your career goal – the occupation would you like to pursue: *I want to be a preschool teacher*	
2a. List any paid or volunteer jobs you have held in which you did things related to that occupation: *babysit* *volunteer at the children's summer program at my church*	2b. List examples of things you accomplished in those jobs: *kept kids entertained* *monitored child's behavior* *used fun activities* *was team leader last summer*

3. List any hobbies or activities you have participated in that relate to that occupation: *I like doing crafty things and scrapbooking* *I like to play games*
4. List the school subjects/classes you completed, and the grades you received, that relate to that occupation: *parenting class – B, *art – A, chorus – A, overall GPA – 3.64*
5. List any other experiences you have had that you think are relevant to your occupational goal: *not sure*
6. Go back through what you listed above and * any items that you think would be important to include on your resume – as evidence of your potential for success in your desired occupation.

letter not only based on required format, but also on how well the student convinced the reader of his or her potential for success; that is, how well the content supported his or her career goal.

TARGETED COUNSELING INTERVENTIONS

A large number of 11th grade students usually are not quite certain about their career paths, and they might benefit from creative ways to explore

FIGURE 13.2 Resume Generated from Content in Exhibit 13.2

Ashley B. Peters

1234 MayBerry Lane
Abby Creek, WA 97825
(878) 555-4321
apeters@gmail.com

Objective
To become a preschool teacher.

Education
Abby Creek High School
Expected Graduation – May 2014
Honors Student
GPA – 3.64/4.00

Work Experience
Volunteer, Children's Summer Program   Summer 2009 and 2010
Abby Creek Church

- Served as Team Leader (2010) for a staff of four student volunteers
- Planned and set up activities for children based on predetermined themes
- Led craft activities for kids in grades 1 and 2

Babysitter   2009–present
Three families in Abby Creek (references available upon request)
- Worked with children ages 1–10
- Fed and cared for infants
- Helped one child learn to tie his shoes
- Provided educational activities for children in grades 1–5

Activities
- Abby Creek High School Chorus
- Abby Creek High School Yearbook Club
- Abby Creek High School Girl's Track

Skills
- Singing
- Art (painting)

possible options outside of the more traditional trait-and-factor approaches used in many schools. Other students in 11th grade have difficulty narrowing down college choices, or have made tentative choices of schools that don't seem to closely match their desired majors. The interventions discussed in the following could be implemented with individuals or with small groups of students who are struggling with similar career development concerns.

Narrowing Down Possible Career Paths via the Career Style Interview

As we discussed in Chapter 4, the *Career Style Interview* (Savickas, 2005) can be a useful tool for helping students examine personal interests and themes that might inform possible career options. This type of assessment can be particularly beneficial for students who have Holland code profiles that lack differentiation (i.e., their RIASEC scores are very similar across categories). When students have an aptitude for a lot of things and are interested in a lot of things, they often need extra assistance in trying to figure out how to narrow down career options. They often cannot simply answer questions like "What are you most interested in?" or "In which classes do you do the best?" The constructionist approach of the *Career Style Interview* can help noteworthy interests and skills emerge. Students who are used to answering concrete questions about their interests and abilities through assessments, like those offered through the Kuder (2006) system, sometimes are thrown off by this type of subjective interview. Nevertheless, school counselors who use the *Career Style Interview* should make sure to explain up front why they are asking certain questions and how they will use the information to help students narrow down career possibilities.

School counselors also can be creative in how they approach the *Career Style Interview*. As suggested in Chapter 4, although the interview can be conducted in person, school counselors realistically do not have time to engage in long interviews with many students. As such, they might first use an introductory session to briefly review the assessment, then they can ask the student to complete the assessment as homework to be turned in to them sometime before the two of them meet again. Students can be asked to provide responses in writing, or they might be encouraged to create a collage of images or words in response to each interview item. Sometimes students cannot generate the exact words they want to express their ideas, but they might find pictures or lyrics that very clearly capture their experiences. Allowing for flexibility in the format of the interview helps to accommodate different learning styles.

By turning in their responses in advance, students give school counselors time to review the responses and look for themes, which allows them to make the most of their next session together. The follow-up session with the student could then be devoted to reviewing the counselor's and student's interpretation, soliciting feedback from the student, and generating next steps. The example in Exhibit 13.3 illustrates a sample Career Style Interview interpretation session between a counselor and student.

EXHIBIT 13.3
Career Style Interview Interpretation Session

A student submitted the following written responses:

Role models: when I was little it was all superheroes—I always liked the idea of catching the bad guys and saving people; I also admire my grandfather—he died helping put out a fire

Books: ones by Sherlock Holmes and by James Patterson

Magazines: I don't read magazines

Leisure activities: baseball, video games, Sudoku

School subjects: History, English, PE

Mottos: Everyone gets what they deserve

Ambitions: make my grandfather proud, play baseball

Decisions (how made): I talk to people (friends or parents) to get their opinions

The counselor generated the following:

Career style—he values communication and collaborative problem solving; he expects people to take responsibility for their actions and to be held accountable

Career path—his future career likely will involve using analytical and communication skills

Interests—he appreciates the humanities, communication, and being physically active

Occupational prospects—many areas in the Law and Public Safety cluster

Guiding fiction—I will make a difference if I can help to protect others from harm

Counselor–Client Meeting (Abbreviated)

Counselor: So, I've reviewed the answers (above) you provided last week to the Career Style Interview. I have identified some patterns, but I'm wondering if anything stood out to you as you reflected on what you wrote?

Student: Not really. I didn't know what to put for some of the questions.

(continued)

EXHIBIT 13.3 *(Continued)*

Counselor: That's okay. Even when students give short responses, sometimes patterns come out. I definitely noticed some patterns for you. Would you like me to tell you what I picked up on?

Student: Sure, I'm kinda curious.

Counselor: Well, for one thing, it seemed like you connect with law enforcement and protectors—superheroes, detectives, police, firefighters. I noticed that in your role models and books, and kind of in your motto. Did you notice that at all?

Student: I hadn't, but I see what you're saying. I guess I always have liked the idea of helping make sure people are safe.

Counselor: I wonder if there are any other places in your life where that idea of protecting comes up—maybe in some of the video games you play or things you like about History?

[Counselor explores this further since student had not expanded on those items in his responses above.]

Counselor: So we've determined, then, that you have a pretty long history of being interested in these kinds of protecting and detective roles, and it crosses over many activities you engage in. Even though this wasn't really an area that you initially could narrow down as worth exploring, I'm wondering if you might want to now? We're really talking about the Law and Public Safety career cluster.

Student: Yeah—that actually sounds a lot like something that I might like.

Counselor: Well, there are a lot of different possibilities within that cluster, some that require college and others that don't. I know you also weren't sure about how much education you wanted to get, so maybe we can keep exploring your responses to see if we can make some decisions about that, too?

Student: Sure.

Counselor: Well, a few things stand out to me from your responses that I thought were worth pointing out. First is I see that you like History and English. I also know that you have a very good GPA and scored high on the PSAT. If you were to pursue something like law, which would require a 4-year college degree and a law school degree, based only on your responses, it seems like that might be interesting to you and that you would be good at that. I also notice that you like PE and baseball—being active and athletic. Your grandfather was a firefighter. Maybe

(continued)

EXHIBIT 13.3 (Continued)
Career Style Interview Interpretation Session

the idea of doing something that is pretty active physically would be more appealing—like being a firefighter or police officer. Those types of positions don't require formal college, but they do require specialized training. Finally, I see that you like detective books and you also like Sudoku puzzles. I'm thinking maybe you like figuring things out—solving problems. Becoming a police detective or something similar might appeal to you, and you could achieve that goal with or without college. I do notice that you want to play baseball, though, and I know you are pretty good. Is playing in college something you're hoping to do—have you talked with your coaches about that?

Student: I really do want to play college ball, and it sounds like I have a good chance . . . so I think I do want to try to go to college.

Counselor: So with college in mind, what do you think of my interpretations? What do you think about some of those possibilities?
[Counselor and client continue to explore career options as well as educational requirements.]

Exploring Postsecondary Options With Students Who Envision College in Their Futures

Many students in 11th grade will express their intentions to pursue postsecondary education, yet a large number will approach that decision as they do their career decisions; they will choose colleges that are familiar to them or ones that their friends plan to attend. With this awareness, school counselors should be very intentional about providing opportunities to increase students' (and their parents') awareness of the variety of postsecondary institutions that exist. They also should help students find a good match; students need to know if the institutions they are considering offer majors that match their career goals.

Students also need to consider what type of environment they might prefer or that would best support their academic and social needs. General factors such as cost, financial aid, location, class size, and religious affiliation (to name but a few) are important to explore. Students with disabilities ideally would want to explore the types of disability support services available to them on a particular campus, first-generation college students might specifically examine the general college transition programs available, and students seeking to connect with others like themselves might explore the availability of student organizations such as the Latino Student Association or the Gay/Straight Alliance.

School counselors might already have college comparison forms that students can use to record information about postsecondary institutions, but numerous worksheets also are available online. The authors conducted an online search using the phrase "college comparison worksheet" that generated a long list of resources. These types of forms could be introduced during large group sessions with students and parents/guardians and then discussed more thoroughly during individual or smaller group sessions.

Given the continued importance of peers during high school, the use of peers can be important in the college exploration process. For many students, seeing someone like them being successful (vicarious learning) can provide the impetus to persist. As such, school counselors should be conscientious about trying to secure the involvement of a group of individuals who are representative of the current student body—hopefully students will identify someone with whom they feel a connection.

For example, every high school has graduates who go on to attend a variety of postsecondary institutions, and numerous ways exist to involve them in helping future graduates explore colleges. In a more general approach, recent graduates who are doing well in college could be invited back to participate in a panel discussion. Their focus would be to 1) identify steps the current students should be taking now to prepare for college, 2) discuss their experiences in exploring and choosing colleges, and 3) talk about characteristics that have been important to their success.

For a more targeted approach, recent graduates also could be invited back to talk about their specific institutions or majors. For example, knowing that everyone experiences a setting differently, a number of graduates who are all attending the same institution could be invited back to compare and contrast their experiences at that institution. Similarly, a number of students who are majoring in the same degree areas but across different institutions could be invited to discuss their experiences across those different schools. Additionally, a group of graduates who are now first-generation college students could participate in an informational workshop for students and their parents. The possibilities are endless for how targeted opportunities could be set up involving the use of peers and the needs of numerous populations could be addressed in this manner. To ensure accessibility and to enable new topics to be presented each year, school counselors might consider preserving these kinds of workshops and discussions electronically, either as webinars that can be posted on the school website or as DVDs that can be checked out for viewing at home. They also should consider ways in which they can accommodate the needs of parents who do not speak English.

Helping All Students and Their Families "Visit" Colleges

Students and their families can probably best learn about colleges by visiting them; there is nothing like walking around a campus and interacting with people to truly get a sense of what it might be like to be a student there. During the spring of the junior year and the summer following that year, many students participate in college tours and visits. Postsecondary schools all have various options (ranging from weekend events to afternoon tours) for orienting prospective students and their families to campus and their programs. By discussing these visits proactively with students and their families, school counselors can provide suggestions for how to maximize the visit and gather important information that may or may not be included in the planned activities. Visiting schools can be expensive, however, and not realistic for many families.

In order to increase accessibility to postsecondary schools that may not be geographically close, school counselors can encourage the use of virtual tours. Websites like www.campustours.com or www.ecampustours.com provide access to information about schools across the United States. An online search using the phrase "college virtual tour" will pull up links to other similar sites that can assist students in identifying and exploring schools based on a variety of factors (e.g., location, religious affiliation). Many postsecondary institutions have virtual tour links on their own websites as well, so school counselors could help students access those links directly. In preparing students and families for viewing the virtual tours, school counselors can suggest they have the college comparison worksheets handy so they can make notes and list questions that may not have been answered.

Assigning Summer Homework

The summer before the senior year of high school might be considered one of the most important in terms of career development, especially for students who plan to attend college. School counselors can encourage students and their families to take full advantage of the summer months to complete tasks and participate in activities that will help them be prepared to submit college applications in the fall. We already discussed the importance of college visits, and the summer months are a good time for students and their families to visit any schools they are still considering. As they are gathering final comparison information about prospective schools, students also can be encouraged to create a list of application deadlines and required materials for the application process.

Regarding the application process, many postsecondary institutions require some sort of application essay, and its importance varies from school to school. In addition to hosting a workshop on application essays during the school year in conjunction with the English teachers, school counselors can encourage students to prepare draft essays over the summer. If they come back to school at the start of their senior year with drafts, they can seek feedback early, leaving time for revisions before applications are due.

Finally, all students can benefit from focusing on building their resumes over the summer through work and/or volunteer experiences. Students who are preparing to attend college might get a part-time job to help save some money for college. They also could use paid or volunteer work to gain valuable experience related to their future career plans. Similarly, individuals who plan to enter the workforce after college could start looking for employment that would boost their potential for finding a good job upon graduation.

SUMMARY

In this chapter we focused on mastery experiences as a critical focus of career-related interventions. Eleventh grade students should be encouraged to engage in a variety of activities so they can hone in on their talents and skills; their mastery experiences will shape their interests and goals. Further, opportunities for vicarious learning and encouragement can be provided through school-wide initiatives and connections with peers and the community. Counselors and educators should be intentional in their efforts to influence students' self-efficacy by helping them identify and develop their strengths and make connections to future goals.

⋯❯ Test Your Knowledge

1. Discuss which students might benefit from something like the *Career Style Interview* and explain why.
2. Compare and contrast Lent, Brown, and Hackett's (1994) performance model with the interest model discussed in the previous chapter. Explain how these models jointly explain career choice and behavior for students in mid-adolescence.

14
•••••
_____

Career Education and Counseling for Grade 12: Postsecondary Transitions

•••••

A student's senior year of high school can bring about many conflicting emotions, including excitement, fear, sadness, hope, and even apathy. Some students would prefer to remain in high school forever rather than face the unknowns and responsibilities of the real world, while others can't escape fast enough. No matter how students feel, in order to be successful after high school, they all need to spend some time during their senior year focusing on their future careers. In this chapter we discuss factors important to their postsecondary transition as well as interventions that could be implemented to help them move forward.

DEVELOPMENTAL OVERVIEW

Students in 12th grade still fall cleanly into Erikson's (1963) *identity versus role confusion* stage. Although many of them can pretty clearly articulate their interests and abilities and identify future career goals, a large majority of students are uncertain about who they are and who they want to become. The importance of peers and the experimentation with various roles that we discussed in previous chapters continues into and beyond the senior year of high school.

Further, as students move closer to finishing high school, a sense of urgency to make decisions can set in. This urgency can come not only from parents putting pressure on them to make decisions, but also from their own competitiveness to keep up with peers who solidify their decisions more quickly than they do, as well as from the reality that decisions about college are, to some degree, time limited. Unfortunately this kind of pressure can lead some students to make decisions in haste and based on the interests and values of others rather than their own desires.

Peer relationships continue to play important roles, and romantic relationships also take on more prominence as students often consider future plans with their partners in mind. Many students limit their future options based on friends or romantic partners, prioritizing their relationships over their own dreams or desires. These are the students who choose to live at home and either work or attend a local college because their friends/partner plans to stay in town, or the students who choose to attend a college only because their friends/partner is doing so. The idea of leaving behind a support system or significant other can be overwhelming to students who may naturally be a little scared about moving forward into something unknown. By making decisions that will allow them to have a familiar face or support system, students' choices may not feel as scary.

In addition to the typical pressures associated with graduating, students who are in their senior year of high school experience one specific milestone that can affect their decision making; they reach the age of consent. Many adolescents start to exert their independence during high school, especially as they secure driver's licenses and part-time employment. By the senior year and as they get closer to age 18, many students start to feel more comfortable expressing their own opinions and making decisions that their parents may or may not support. It is not uncommon to hear students and parents talk about changes in their relationships that involve more arguments. As students struggle to break away, parents do what they can to regain control.

The confusion that many high school seniors experience related to their identities, their independence, their relationships, and their future suggests that interventions targeting 12th grade students should be designed to help them and their parents navigate this transition to life after high school. Activities to further allow students to gain self-awareness, identify their values, and make decisions with future goals in mind will be discussed later in this chapter. Additionally, suggestions for working with parents to help them appreciate and cope with the uncertainty of their children's futures will be shared.

RELEVANT CAREER THEORY: SAVICKAS (2005) AND BROWN (1996)

In this chapter we expand on Savickas's Theory of Career Construction (2005), which we introduced in Chapter 13, to discuss how it explains career development behaviors. We also introduce another career theory, Brown's *Values-Based Theory* (1996). Brown discussed the ways in which values, which have cognitive and emotional components, influence career goals and behaviors. These two theories provide the framework for interventions we review later in this chapter.

Savickas's Theory of Career Construction (2005)

In the previous chapter, we discussed how Savickas's theory could be useful for working with students who have difficulty narrowing down career options based only on trait and factor approaches. Through the identification of a construct called *career adaptability,* the Theory of Career Construction also helps to explain the career-related behaviors that students engage in over time.

Similar to Super's Life-Span Life-Space theory (1980), in the Theory of Career Construction, Savickas (2005) discussed five developmental stages: growth, exploration, establishment, management, and disengagement. The growth and exploration stages are relevant for P–12 students, and most 12th grade students would be in the exploration stage. Successful completion of each stage leads to greater likelihood of success for task completion in future stages. Savickas indicated that to successfully transition from task to task, individuals must possess *career adaptability.*

According to Savickas (2005), career adaptability is "a psychosocial construct that denotes an individual's readiness and resources for coping with current and imminent vocational development tasks, occupational transitions, and personal traumas" (p. 51). It allows people to implement their self-concept and regulate their behavior. Savickas identified four dimensions of career adaptability as: 1) concern, 2) control, 3) curiosity, and 4) confidence.

Career concern refers to an individual's interest in his or her future (Savickas, 2005). In addition to recognizing that planning for future activities is important, understanding the connection between past and current experiences and behaviors and future goals is critical to successfully navigate career development tasks. Savickas believes that optimism is also important in fostering a concern for the future. Individuals who are pessimistic about future outcomes are more likely to exhibit what Savickas refers to as *career indifference.*

According to Savickas (2005), *career control* refers to individuals believing that it is their responsibility to construct their careers. Savickas emphasizes that in both individualistic and collectivistic cultures, individuals still can control their careers; it is not as much about making decisions independently as it is about feeling that you have some level of control over your choice. Choosing to take into consideration the opinions of others, such as family, still reflects control. For some people, career options may be limited (e.g., everyone in your family expects you to be a doctor), but personal control exists in an individual's ability to make that limited choice meaningful and personal (e.g., meeting your parents' wishes of you becoming a doctor, but choosing to become a pediatrician because you want to help kids as opposed to being a dermatologist like your dad). *Career indecision* is the opposite of career control. People have a difficult time putting energy into making career decisions if deep down they do not believe that the outcome will be within their control.

Career curiosity refers to being inquisitive about people and work (Savickas, 2005). Curiosity leads people to seek out self and occupational knowledge and also to be willing to try new things. Savickas did not identify a specific term to refer to a lack of career curiosity, but he indicated that people who are not curious tend to lack accurate information about themselves and the world of work. As such, these individuals might develop unrealistic plans or expectations.

Finally, *career confidence* refers to one's sense of self-efficacy about planning and carrying out a course of action to implement their career choices (Savickas, 2005). Concepts like mastery experiences, from Social Cognitive Career Theory (Lent, Brown, & Hackett, 1994), are particularly useful in understanding career confidence. Savickas explained that a lack of career confidence results in *career inhibition*; people who are inhibited often lack the courage to try new things or fail to persist when challenged.

In a nutshell, school counselors should want students to be concerned about their future and feel a sense of control over it. They also should hope that students demonstrate curiosity about and a willingness to explore themselves and careers, and feel confident in their ability to achieve their goals. By identifying where students fall on these four dimensions, school counselors can identify relevant interventions to target any of the dimensions that are low.

Brown's Values-Based Theory (2002)

Duane Brown's (2002) theory focuses on the importance of a person's values in his or her career decision making. Brown explained that values are what we use to evaluate our and others' actions; they are those things that are important to us and that influence our behavior and goals. As such, values that we prioritize inform our occupational choices. When our occupations do not match our values, over time we become dissatisfied. School counselors proactively can help students identify and consider values as they are making important life decisions.

When discussing values, Brown (2002) not only includes what he considers to be work values—things such as helping others or being able to use one's creativity—but he also includes cultural values like collectivism versus individualism. Brown indicated that values can be examined through standardized assessment instruments like the *Life Values Inventory* (Brown & Crace, 2002; see Chapter 4), or through more informal assessments such as card sorts or checklists. Many of the computerized career guidance programs widely used by schools also have a values exploration component. Once values are identified, counseling sessions can be used to help students explore career and college choices that would match prioritized values and also to integrate interests, abilities, and values into their future decisions. Interventions we present later in this chapter will demonstrate a focus on values.

GRADE LEVEL EXPECTANCIES (GLEs) FOR 12TH GRADE

The Missouri Center for Career Education (2006) 12th grade GLEs (see Table 14.1) reflect a focus on helping students to apply the skills and knowledge they have developed throughout their schooling. Interventions for 12th grade students should allow them opportunities to review and reflect on the information they have gathered about themselves and careers; to set concrete goals that match their interests, abilities, and values; and to complete initial steps toward achieving those goals.

COUNSELING AND EDUCATIONAL INTERVENTIONS

Skills and knowledge needed for successful postsecondary transitions are highlighted in the interventions we present in the following. In this section, we share interventions targeting both students and parents. We also focus on interventions that are grounded in the two theories we presented earlier in this chapter.

TABLE 14.1 Missouri 12th Grade GLEs

Career Development: Self and Career Awareness	
Integration of Self-Knowledge into Life and Career Plans	Utilize knowledge of the world of work; personal interests; and strengths and limitations to develop short- and long-term postsecondary plans.
Adaptations to World of Work Changes	Utilize knowledge of career exploration and planning to adapt new career and educational opportunities as the world of work changes.
Respect for All Work	Respect all work as important, valuable, and necessary in maintaining a global society.
Career Decision Making	Utilize career and educational information in career decision making.
Education and Career Requirements	Know and understand the levels of training and education required for life career goals.
Personal Skills for Job Success	Apply personal, ethical, and work habit skills that contribute to job success.
Job-Seeking Skills	Utilize appropriate job-seeking skills to obtain employment.
Academic Development	
Life-Long Learning	Achieve educational levels necessary to reach, maintain, and continue with individual life-long learning goals.
Transitions	Utilize the achievement and performance skills necessary to transition to postsecondary options.

Based on the Missouri Center for Career Education (2006).

Summer Interventions

As noted in Chapter 13, having homework (e.g., write draft college application essays) between the junior and senior year is one way to ensure that students are staying on track toward their career and college readiness goals. Another option is to hold formal events, such as workshops for parents and students. During these events students can receive information about writing college application essays, interviewing for jobs, and other topics. One school counselor, Mrs. Hinote, ran a summer program called "Seize the Day" (Exhibit 14.1).

EXHIBIT 14.1
Seize the Day Summer Program for High School Seniors

Seize the Day was a 2-day career and college readiness summer program developed by Mrs. Hinote to help students between their junior and senior years develop skills and make informed decisions about their postsecondary options. Partnering with the community, she was able to run the program for little to no expense. Volunteer community members who had expertise in many of the content areas served as guest speakers for the seminar sessions. Further, local restaurants donated breakfast and lunch. She was able to offer a variety of seminars, and students could choose the seminars most relevant to their postsecondary plans. For example, some of the seminar topics included essay writing, financial literacy, using technology to search college admissions information, participating in volunteer service, preparing a resume, and developing college study skills.

Financial presentations were provided for a range of monetary issues including opening bank accounts, saving money, using credit wisely, understanding the difference between a credit card and debit card, and navigating college financial aid. These presentations were provided through a local bank and credit union.

In a college planning seminar, students were given the opportunity to create timelines for their senior year that document deadlines for relevant activities including but not limited to things such as attending college fairs, taking the Scholastic Aptitude Test (SAT), submitting college applications, and submitting financial aid forms. In the career readiness seminars, students were given information about the types of communication skills that employers are looking for, and they participated in games and activities that demonstrated these skills. In the job interviewing seminar, students learned about and role-played interviewing skills. They also could sign up to participate in mock interviews with community members. Although parents were not included in this activity, the format could be changed to an evening program and parents could be invited to participate.

Teachers Helping Students Become "Concerned" About Their Futures

As students get closer and closer to graduation, many find it easier and often preferable to avoid making decisions rather than face the difficult choices they have ahead of them. Further, by not thinking about their life after high school, they can put off dealing with the conflicting feelings they have about their futures. Teachers can help students consider their futures through class assignments, which can be less intimidating and sometimes easier to do than if they were just asked to talk about their plans.

Although 12th grade students might be enrolled in a variety of English classes, a common assignment could be put into place to help them practice their writing skills and think about their futures. By having students write an autobiography that would reflect their life at age 25 or 30, teachers can encourage students to dream big. By collaborating with teachers in this endeavor, school counselors can help to design the assignment in a way that will require students to articulate important things like what they will be doing, how they got there, what their strengths are, and other accomplishments that came along the way.

After reviewing the student papers, school counselors could use the information in a couple of ways. For example, they could identify any students who appear to be lacking concern about their future; that is, those who cannot envision any specific future. Additionally, they can look for consistency between the futures articulated in the students' papers and the behaviors the students are engaging in currently: Are they doing the things they would need to do now in order to achieve that future? Finally, school counselors can pay attention to the process students describe, looking for signs of potential barriers the students anticipate. Interventions could be designed accordingly to address identified needs.

Focusing on Values to Address Career Indecision

Examining values can be helpful for students struggling with career indecision. Whether their indecision relates to choosing a career path or making a final college choice, students need to have some sense of control over their future (Savickas, 2002). As we discussed previously, pressure from peers, partners, or family may lead some students to feel like they have no say about their futures. These students can benefit from understanding the ways in which they DO have control. When working with a student who is struggling with indecision, or is lacking a sense of control over his or her future, a school counselor can administer the *Life Values Inventory* (Brown & Crace, 2002). The following case (Exhibit 14.2) illustrates how this kind of assessment can be useful in these situations.

EXHIBIT 14.2
Using the Life Values Inventory With a Student

A school counselor, Carole, has been working with Dimitrius, a 12th grade student, for the past 3 years as he has explored his future plans. He has completed honors coursework and has a 3.48 GPA. Dimitrius is an African American male and the youngest of four children; his older sisters have all completed 2-year degrees. He is the son of an auto mechanic and secretary, and lives in a lower-middle class suburban neighborhood. Dimitrius has been dating his girlfriend for the past 2 years and hopes to marry her.

In their recent sessions, Carole has noticed that Dimitrius seems less excited about his initial plans to attend a 4-year college to study mechanical engineering. Having worked alongside his dad for many years, Dimitrius became excited when he learned about the possibility of contributing to the design of cars. He had been encouraged throughout high school by his math and science teachers, and has identified a number of scholarships geared to help students like him enter science, technology, engineering, and math (STEM) fields.

When discussing his plans recently, Carole learned that Dimitrius was feeling pressure from his family to attend school close to home, and from his girlfriend to not move away. He indicated that his girlfriend threatened to break up with him if he chose to move away. His family doesn't understand why he needs to pursue a 4-year degree when everyone else has been successful attending the local technical college. Dimitrius was struggling because he really wants to pursue engineering but also does not want to disappoint the people who are important to him. As they talked, it became apparent that Dimitrius was feeling resentful that others were limiting his future options. He didn't think that he had much of a choice, especially given his girlfriend's ultimatum to break up with him if he moves away. Carole thought that a values inventory might be something that could help him to explore this challenge a little more concretely.

After he completed the *Life Values Inventory*, they discovered that his highest rated values were belonging (being accepted by others and feeling included), interdependence (following family expectations), and achievement (challenging oneself). Carole discussed and normalized the internal conflict that is resulting from his conflicting values. They also talked about how he felt about the results, if he agreed with the priority order, and if he wanted to maintain that priority order for the future. Carole helped Dimitrius to realize that he had a choice of whether or not to place value on his family and girlfriend's opinions—that he had some control over how much he allowed others to influence his future. Once he realized the degree to which he could exert control over his future, they were able to brainstorm ways to help him fulfill both his achievement and belonging values while trying to pursue mechanical engineering.

Notice how Carole (in Exhibit 14.2) was able to help Dimitrius prioritize his values. In discussing what was important to him, he was able to realize that the control he had in this situation was more in relation to how he made his decisions than what those decisions actually were. After realizing that he did have some control and was able to accept his responsibility to make a choice, Dimitrius was able to move forward exploring solutions to his dilemma.

Counselors also can use a focus on values to help students narrow down college choices. If a student is trying to decide between two schools and is feeling stuck, sometimes bringing things back to core values can make a difference. For example, if the schools are fairly comparable in terms of the quality of a particular program, exploring things like size, organizations, or the religious affiliation may help a student make a final decision. Further, perhaps a student is trying to choose between two schools that are different mainly in terms of distance from their home. If the student values independence and wants to gain further autonomy, perhaps choosing the school that is farther away might afford him or her more opportunities to be independent. Rather than focus so much on the details, sometimes a broader focus on values can make decisions easier.

Encouraging College Curiosity: It's Not Too Late

Although possessing accurate information about the world of work and one's self is critical to informed decision making, for high school seniors that might not be enough. It is equally important that students acquire accurate knowledge of a transitional experience—attending college. Many students enter their senior year still uncertain if they want to attend college or not quite clear about the differences between 2- and 4-year colleges. Although ideally students would have explored schools and visited colleges prior to their senior year, many avoid doing so until the last minute. School counselors can help those in need of a crash course and can provide them with information in time to make decisions before they miss application deadlines.

The first thing school counselors can do is to remind students of opportunities to visit colleges, virtually or in person. We talked about this in Chapter 13, as ideally students would start visiting schools *no later than* grade 11 or the summer in between 11th and 12th grades. Reminders can be made over school announcements and placed on the school counseling website. Individual students may need to meet with their school counselor for in-person reminders and career advisement.

School counselors can involve peers in the process of sharing information about colleges (see Exhibit 14.3). Additionally, school counselors can take advantage of opportunities to heavily promote existing activities and events that might be in place. For example, fall is a time when college recruiters and admissions counselors are making rounds to high schools to meet with

EXHIBIT 14.3
Sharing College Information Through Peer Interventions

One high school counselor organized a week-long lunchtime sharing session. She set aside separate lunch tables with information and
brochures about various colleges, posted a college banner at the table,
and asked students who had attended in-person visits during the past
year to talk about what they saw and experienced. These students also
were able to field specific questions from other students. Some of the
students shared pictures that they took when they were on campus as
well as pictures of the surrounding community (before they visited,
the school counselor had encouraged them to take pictures to bring
back for sharing). Students who had not been able to visit those colleges
or who wanted other perspectives about the college were able to sit at
a different table each day during lunch to learn about multiple schools
throughout the week.

prospective students. School counselors should ensure that notices about
these upcoming meetings are widely disseminated (e.g., morning announcements, website, school newsletter) to students and parents. Ideally, they
should also identify students who express curiosity but who need more information before finalizing their plans. Personal invitations sent to students
encouraging them to attend can sometimes increase the probability they will
attend. For these students, one-on-one conversations with individuals who
can provide first-hand information about the schools can be very valuable.

Finally, college fairs are commonly held during the early fall semester, organized either by individual schools, school districts, or local communities.
These fairs provide opportunities for students and their families to gather information from a variety of schools, learn what majors and special programs
they offer, and talk to recruiters and admissions counselors. As they would
with the other opportunities already discussed, school counselors can target
specific 12th grade students who need more information about colleges in order to narrow down their plans, encouraging them and their families to participate. For these students in particular, follow-up conversations with school
counselors can be useful to help them process what they learned and weigh
pros and cons of their options in relation to their career goals.

Addressing Career Inhibition Through Peer Support

Earlier in this book we discussed the different rates at which students apply
to and attend college, with certain populations (e.g., Latinos) being underrepresented. We have talked a lot in this text about the role that beliefs and

self-efficacy can play in career development behaviors. Many students will complete high school with all of requirements that will enable them to pursue college, and they will also engage in many relevant preparatory activities (e.g., such as visiting colleges). When it comes to submitting a college application, however, some students do not follow through because they lack the confidence in their ability to be successful. This lack of confidence can be particularly true for students who would be the first in their family to attend college. These potential first-generation college students can use a lot of support and encouragement as they engage in the process of applying to college, and opportunities for peer support and encouragement can help to increase their self-efficacy about this process. The state of South Carolina has provided a unique opportunity to address this lack of confidence and attempt to increase the number of students who apply to college (see Exhibit 14.4).

EXHIBIT 14.4
College Application Day Event

A large number of high schools in South Carolina organize College Application Day events during the month of October (The Riley Institute at Furman University, 2012). The main purpose of these days is to assist first-generation students or others who might not typically apply to college to successfully complete their online college applications. High schools are, however, encouraged to provide opportunities for all seniors. School counselors, in collaboration with volunteers and staff from the South Carolina Commission on Higher Education, assist students with the online application process. In the 2 years since its inception, the number of high schools participating increased from 12 to 121, and the number of public high school seniors in South Carolina participating increasedfrom 1,000 to 20,000 (The Riley Institute at Furman University, 2012).

At one high school, school counseling staff and volunteers made themselves available all day in the computer lab to assist students. Teachers agreed to come in to help during their planning periods, as the school believed that students would appreciate seeing familiar faces there to provide encouragement. Agreements were made with classroom teachers to permit students to leave specific classes in order to participate, and students were permitted to come in before and after school or during lunch or other free times. Comments heard from students throughout the day supported the idea that many students felt less intimidated knowing that help was available, that many students would not have completed applications at home on their own because they didn't know how to start and were afraid to ask for help, and that students were glad to know that lots of other students were confused about the process.

Creating a vicarious learning opportunity, school counselors also might consider involving former graduates in a college application day process. By inviting diverse students who were able to successfully navigate the college application process and who are attending college to assist with college application days, school counselors can provide role models for a variety of students. These student volunteers can help to normalize the fears or uncertainty that many of the seniors might be experiencing, as well as provide encouragement through sharing their own successes.

Assisting Students Not Pursuing Postsecondary School

Students who do not have postsecondary education plans need assistance in developing career-related skills. School counselors can use classroom time to provide instruction and support for things like resume writing, crafting cover letters, developing interview skills, and approaching the job search process. One creative way to provide this assistance for students is to recruit local community partners and form a mock interview committee. Students can develop their resumes and cover letters and the mock interview committee can set up interviews with students. Appropriate interview attire also should be discussed with students and resources provided (if possible) to help them look their best. For example, one inner city school in an economically disadvantaged area provides a clothing donation closet where students are loaned shirts, ties, dresses and other interview appropriate clothing when they go on job interviews

Interventions to Foster Parent–Student Relationships

As we mentioned earlier in this chapter, parents and students often experience tension as students try to separate themselves and parents try to keep them close. For many parents, especially those who have had very strong and comfortable relationships with their children, this tension can be heartbreaking and confusing. They may begin to catastrophize, fearing that their teenager will move out after graduation and never want to come home. The tendency of some parents in these situations will be to exert greater control, setting and enforcing stricter rules. Other parents will give up, afraid that if they push too hard they will lose the relationship they have with their teenager.

Although everyone was an adolescent at some point, it can be challenging to take oneself back to that age. Arguably, adolescents today have different challenges to face than their parents did at that same age. Furthermore, some adolescents are preparing for very different kinds of postsecondary plans than their parents did (e.g., first-generation college students), so it can be difficult for their parents to really know what they are experiencing. Understandably, parents can benefit from information to help them understand what their adolescents are going through.

One thing school counselors might do is offer parent workshops or information via a newsletter regarding adolescent development. Important topics to address would include information about identity development and peer relationships. By providing examples of the range of ways that adolescents interact with peers and family and experiment with and explore new identities (see Exhibit 14.5), school counselors can help to normalize what parents might be experiencing. Specific examples related to preparing for graduation and leaving home can be provided, along with concrete suggestions for what parents can do to support their adolescents throughout that process.

Parents also can benefit from information about issues specific to career and college development. The second author vividly recalls working with many parents who experienced extreme stress because their adolescent was planning to start college with an undeclared major. A lot of parents, even those who did attend college, have unrealistic expectations that their adolescents must know *exactly* what they want well before they graduate from

---

EXHIBIT 14.5
Engaging Parents and Students in a Values Comparison

One of the things that many parents struggle most with is acknowledging that their children may not adopt the same values that they did. At the core of many parent–adolescent arguments is a difference in values. One high school counselor found himself addressing these kinds of issues a lot with parents, and he developed a way to help parents and students get to the core issues. He developed a list of values that he found commonly came up when working with adolescents—things like making money, being respected, having a sense of control, fitting in. He gave this list to students and their parents, asking them to fill it out by rating the values that were important to them personally, then asking them to rate as if they were each other.

Engaging them in discussion, the school counselor was quickly able to identify similarities and differences. Helping people identify commonalities can go a long way toward building relationships, so in discussing the results with them, the school counselor would focus on pointing out those things they had in common. He then would move on to discuss the differences as well as the assumptions they had about each other, specifically examining the accuracy of their assumptions as well as how their assumptions played out in their relationship. Although school counselors are not family counselors and do not have the time or expertise to engage in family counseling sessions, this school counselor found that he could be quite effective in helping to make inroads during a 30-minute meeting following this basic approach. He would encourage them to continue focusing on the things that they did agree on, and offered them suggestions for how to address differences.

high school. Providing them with data that are available can sometimes help alleviate their concerns. For example, school counselors could share that approximately 80% of students enter college without a declared major, and that 50% of college students who do enter with a specific major will change their major at least once (Ronan, 2005). They also could talk about the types of programs that are available at most colleges to help students explore and choose a major—things such as first-year seminar courses, career exploration courses, and academic advisors. The fact that these types of services exist suggests a great need among college students for career exploration.

Just like students value their peers, sometimes parents are more receptive to hearing from their peers. School counselors can organize panel discussions involving parents of recent graduates. During these sessions, the parents can discuss their experiences—including challenges and successes—as well as their adolescents' experiences. Parents often just want to know that their children fit into a norm, so to speak, and the more schools can help them understand what is typical and common, the less pressure they might put on their adolescents to make decisions before they are developmentally ready to do so.

A final way that school counselors can help parents of 12th graders is to provide them with suggestions about how they might talk with their adolescents. Many adolescents will say that adults don't listen to them, that they always try to tell them what to do. By understanding that what their adolescents probably want most is to be heard and supported, parents can approach conversations with them differently than they might have in the past. School counselors can offer case studies, engage in role-play demonstrations, and provide verbiage that parents might use to convey empathy and support before they challenge or question.

Teaching Parents and Students About Financial Literacy

Whether students are college bound or not, teaching them and their parents about finances is a critical step in their transition from high school student to young adult. Abundant evidence exists that Americans are in chronic debt and that the economy has caused difficulties for many families. Specifically, in 2011 there were over 800,000 home foreclosures in the United States (Veiga, 2012) and in 2010 over 1.5 million Americans filed for bankruptcy (Dugas, 2010). Furthermore, the average credit card holder has approximately $6,500 in credit card debt and 1 in 10 consumers have 10 or more credit cards (Economy Watch, 2011).

It is important that regardless of the type of school in which they work (i.e., inner city, private, public), school counselors need to understand that students and parents may not comprehend the core principles of financial independence. Also, depending on their own financial status and experiences, parents may have a limited understanding of common financial challenges people experience. Conducting a joint parent–student workshop on financial literacy is one way to educate families and promote conversation about money. Three major pieces of information that should be covered are 1) how to create a budget, 2) problems with credit card debt, and 3) creating an emergency fund.

Creating a budget may be a new life skill for both parents and students. Moreover, according to a survey of 16 to 18 year olds by Charles Schwab (2011), only 35% of teens knew how to balance a checkbook or check the accuracy of a bank statement. Given how important these skills are, it is critical to help parents and teens talk about money including how to create a budget, how to balance a checkbook, and how to avoid spending pitfalls. One interesting approach for teaching budgeting involves using a simulation program, such as the Budget Challenge program that can be done on computer (www.budgetchallenge.com). In the Budget Challenge simulation, students are assigned a job, salary, and options such as the types of services they wish to purchase (e.g., having cable, owning a car, having a cell phone), where to bank and a choice of bank accounts (checking, savings, etc.), and retirement savings options. Students and parents can learn the value of savings and how to create financial growth over time.

According to Charles Schwab (2011), only 31% of teens understand credit card interest and fees. One resource for teaching how credit cards work is the *House of Cards Credit Card Project* (Espana, Fegette, Islip, Sampson, & Walker, 2004). This comprehensive lesson packet is free, downloadable, and covers credit card interest, how to calculate compound interest, credit card amortization, and how to calculate an average daily balance.

The third financial literacy component that should be covered is the importance of an emergency fund. Students and parents should consider the types of emergencies and occasional expenses that young adults commonly encounter (e.g., extra college expenses, car repairs, deposits on housing and utilities). Next, students and parents should consider how large the emergency fund needs to be and should devise a plan to set money aside weekly until that amount is achieved. In general, an emergency fund should cover necessary expenses (food, shelter) for several months in the event that income is lost.

CELEBRATING THE HIGH SCHOOL TRANSITION

As has been evident throughout this book, the milestone of leaving high school and transitioning to career or college is one of life's major moments. As we have cautioned, this postsecondary transition period is an important time to identify students who may need extra support (e.g., first-generation college students, students with disabilities, English language learners) and connect them to resources. However, it also is a time to celebrate (in ways that are befitting to each unique school community) students' accomplishments.

For example, at a private school in Florida, the senior counselor hangs a pennant in the school cafeteria for every college that a student in the senior class has committed to attend. By the end of each school year, the cafeteria is full of the different colleges' pennants. At a high school for pregnant and parenting teens, the graduation ceremony includes the teen mother walking across the stage with her child, honoring the work and commitment of getting through high school and being a parent. During graduation at a high school near a military post, the ROTC color guard does a presentation and all students who have chosen to go into the military are honored during the ceremony. Many schools around the country have formal celebrations for students making this critical transition. School counselors should determine what types of celebrations are appropriate for their populations and consider ways to positively send students forward into their postsecondary futures.

SUMMARY

In this chapter we focused on helping high school seniors prepare for their transitions to college or the workforce. These students should be provided with concrete opportunities to explore self, make connections between self and career, and develop confidence in their ability to direct their futures. Their parents are important partners as they navigate the postsecondary transition, and school counselors and educators should consider the various ways in which they can educate and involve parents.

••▶ Test Your Knowledge

1. Name and define the four dimensions of career adaptability.
2. Explain the connection between Lent, Brown, and Hackett's (1994) Social Cognitive Career Theory and Savickas's Theory of Career Construction.
3. List three components of financial literacy training.

•••••

Appendices

Appendices

A
• • • • •

National Career Development Association Minimum Competencies for Multicultural Career Counseling and Development

• • • • •

(This document replaces the 1997 Career Counseling Competencies)
Approved by the NCDA Board—August 2009

INTRODUCTION

The purpose of the multicultural career counseling and development competencies is to ensure that all individuals practicing in, or training for practice in, the career counseling and development field are aware of the expectation that we, as professionals, will practice in ways that promote the career development and functioning of individuals of all backgrounds. Promotion and advocacy of career development for individuals is ensured regardless of age, culture, mental/physical ability, ethnicity, race, nationality, religion/spirituality, gender, gender identity, sexual orientation, marital/partnership status, military or civilian status, language preference, socioeconomic status, any other characteristics not specifically relevant to job performance, in accordance with NCDA and American Counseling Association (ACA) policy. Further, they will provide guidance to those in the career counseling and development field regarding appropriate practice with regard to clients of a different background than their own. Finally, implementation of these competencies for the field should provide the public with the assurance that they can expect career counseling and development professionals to function in a manner that facilitates their career development, regardless of the client's/student's background.

If you believe that you need assistance with performing at these minimum levels, or would like to further develop your skills in these areas, please visit the NCDA website (www.ncda.org) for contact information regarding sources for increasing your competence in dealing with individuals with different cultural backgrounds than yourself.

For those seeking a designation of competency, NCDA offers the Master Career Counselor and Master Career Development Professional Special Memberships. Visit www.ncda.org for more information.

THE MULTICULTURAL CAREER PROFESSIONAL

Career Development Theory

- understands the strengths and limitations of career theory and utilizes theories that are appropriate for the population being served.

Individual and Group Counseling Skills

- is aware of his/her own cultural beliefs and assumptions and incorporates that awareness into his/her decision making about interactions with clients/students and other career professionals.
- continues to develop his/her individual and group counseling skills in order to enhance his/her ability to respond appropriately to individuals from diverse populations.
- is cognizant when working with groups of the group demographics and monitors these to ensure appropriate respect and confidentiality is maintained.

Individual/Group Assessment

- understands the psychometric properties of the assessments he/she is using in order to effectively select and administer assessments, and interpret and use results with the appropriate limitations and cautions.

Information, Resources, and Technology

- regularly evaluates the information, resources, and use of technology to determine that these tools are sensitive to the needs of diverse populations amending and/or individualizing for each client as required.

- provides resources in multiple formats to ensure that clients/students are able to benefit from needed information.
- provides targeted and sensitive support for clients/students in using the information, resources, and technology.

Program Promotion, Management, and Implementation

- incorporates appropriate guidelines, research, and experience in developing, implementing, and managing programs and services for diverse populations.
- utilizes the principles of program evaluation to design and obtain feedback from relevant stakeholders in the continuous improvement of programs and services, paying special attention to feedback regarding specific needs of the population being served.
- applies his/her knowledge of multicultural issues in dealings with other professionals and trainees to ensure the creation of a culturally-sensitive environment for all clients.

Coaching, Consultation, and Performance Improvement

- engages in coaching, consultation, and performance improvement activities with appropriate training and incorporates knowledge of multicultural attitudes, beliefs, skills and values.
- seeks awareness and understanding about how to best match diverse clients/students with suitably culturally sensitive employers.

Supervision

- gains knowledge of and engages in evidence-based supervision, pursues educational and training activities on a regular and ongoing basis inclusive of both counseling and supervision topics. Further, is aware of his/her limitations, cultural biases and personal values and seeks professional consultative assistance as necessary.
- infuses multicultural/diversity contexts into his/her training and supervision practices, makes supervisees aware of the ethical standards and responsibilities of the profession, and trains supervisees to develop relevant multicultural knowledge and skills.

Ethical/Legal Issues

- continuously updates his/her knowledge of multicultural and diversity issues and research and applies new knowledge as required.
- employs his/her knowledge and experience of multicultural ethical and legal issues within a professional framework to enhance the functioning of his/her organization and the image of the profession.
- uses supervision and professional consultations effectively when faced with an ethical or legal issue related to diversity, to ensure he/she provides high-quality services for every client/student.

Research/Evaluation

- designs and implements culturally appropriate research studies with regards to research design, instrument selection, and other pertinent population-specific issues.

NCDA Headquarters
305 N. Beech Circle
Broken Arrow, OK 74012
918/663-7060 Toll-free 866-FOR-NCDA
Fax: 918/663-7058
www.ncda.org

B

•••••

Career Counselor Assessment
and Evaluation Competencies

•••••

*Adopted by the National Career Development Association
on January 10, 2010 and Association for Assessment
in Counseling and Education on March 20, 2010*

The purpose of these competencies is to provide a description of the knowledge and skills that career counselors must demonstrate in the areas of assessment and evaluation. Because effectiveness in assessment and evaluation is critical to effective career counseling, these competencies are critical for career counselor practice and service to students, clients, and other customers.

The competencies can be used by counselors as a guide in the development and evaluation of workshops, inservice, and other continuing education opportunities, as well as to evaluate their own professional development, and by counselor educators as a guide in the development and evaluation of career counselor preparation programs.

Competent career counselors strive to meet each of the eight numbered competencies and exhibit the specific knowledge, understandings, and skills listed under each competency.

CAREER COUNSELORS ARE SKILLED IN

Competency 1. choosing assessment strategies. *Career counselors . . .*

a. can describe the nature and use of different types of formal and informal assessments, including questionnaires, checklists, interviews, inventories, tests, observations, surveys, and performance assessments, and they work with individuals skilled in clinical assessment.

b. can specify the types of information most readily obtained from different assessment approaches.

c. can identity the type of information needed to assist the client and select the assessment strategy accordingly.

d. are familiar with resources for critically evaluating each type of assessment and can use the resources to choose appropriate assessment strategies.

e. are able to advise and assist organizations, such as educational institutions and governmental agencies, in choosing appropriate assessment strategies.

f. use only those assessments for which they are properly and professionally trained.

Competency 2. identifying, accessing, and evaluating the most commonly used assessment instruments. *Career counselors . . .*

a. know which assessment areas are most commonly assessed in career counseling, such as ability, skills, personality, preference work style, career thoughts and barriers, work values, and interests, including alternate formats.

b. know the factors by which assessment instruments should be evaluated, including developmental procedures, target audience, purpose, validity, utility, norms, reliability and measurement error, score reporting method, cost, and consequences of use.

c. obtain and evaluate information about the quality of career assessment instruments used.

d. use the highest quality instruments available with their students, clients, or customers.

Competency 3. using the techniques of administration and methods of scoring assessment instruments. *Career counselors . . .*

a. implement appropriate administration procedures, including administration using computers.

   b. follow strict standardized administration procedures as dictated by the directions and resulting interpretation.
   c. modify administration of assessments to accommodate individual differences consistent with publisher recommendations and current statements of professional practice.
   d. provide consultation, information, and training to others who assist with administration and scoring and follow the guidance of others who are more extensively trained.

Competency 4. interpreting and reporting assessment results.
Career counselors . . .
   a. can explain scores that are commonly reported, interpret a confidence interval for an individual score based on a standard error of measurement, and always consider the impreciseness of assessment results.
   b. evaluate the appropriateness of a norm group when interpreting the scores of an individual or a group.
   c. are skilled in communicating assessment information to the client and others, including peers, supervisors and the public.
   d. evaluate their own strengths and limitations in the use of assessment instruments and in assessing clients with disabilities or linguistic or cultural differences.
   e. know how to identify professionals with appropriate training and experience for consultation.
   f. follow the legal and ethical principles regarding confidentiality and disclosure of assessment information, and recognize the need to abide by professional credentialing and ethical standards on the protection and use of assessments.

Competency 5. using assessment results in decision making.
Career counselors . . .
   a. recognize the limitations of using a single score in making an educational or career decision and know how to access multiple sources of information to improve decisions.
   b. evaluate their own expertise for making decisions based on assessment results, and also the limitations of conclusions provided by others, including the reliability and validity of computer-assisted assessment interpretations.
   c. determine whether the available technical evidence is adequate to support the intended use of an assessment result for decision

making, particularly when that use has not been recommended by the developer of the assessment instrument.

d. can evaluate the consequences of assessment-related decisions and avoid actions that would have unintended negative consequences.

Competency 6. producing, interpreting, and presenting statistical information about assessment results. *Career counselors . . .*

a. can describe data (e.g., test scores, grades, demographic information) by forming frequency distributions, preparing tables, drawing graphs, and calculating descriptive indices of central tendency, variability, and relationship.

b. can compare a score from an assessment instrument with an existing distribution, describe the placement of a score within a normal distribution, and draw appropriate inferences.

c. interpret statistics used to describe characteristics of assessment instruments, especially reliability coefficients, validity studies, and standard errors of measurement.

d. can use computers for data management, statistical analysis, and production of tables and graphs for reporting and interpreting results.

Competency 7. engaging in professionally responsible assessment and evaluation practices. *Career counselors . . .*

a. act in accordance with ACA's Code of Ethics and Standards of Practice and NCDA's Ethical Guidelines.

b. adhere to professional codes and standards, including the Code of Fair Testing Practices in Education, to evaluate counseling practices involving assessments.

c. understand test fairness and avoid the selection of biased assessment instruments and biased uses of assessment results.

d. do not violate the legal and ethical principles and practices regarding test security, reproducing copyrighted materials, and unsupervised use of assessment instruments that are not intended for self-administration.

e. obtain and maintain available credentialing that demonstrates their skills in assessment and evaluation and update their skills on a regular basis.

Competency 8. using assessment results and other data to evaluate career programs and interventions. *Career counselors . . .*

a. collect data to determine the impact of the career development activities on clients.
b. use appropriate statistics when comparing groups, making predictions, and drawing conclusions about career programs and strategies.
c. use evaluation results to improve current practices or implement more successful techniques to assist the client.
d. can explain evaluation results to relevant persons, colleagues, agencies, and other stakeholders.

DEFINITION OF TERMS

Competencies describe knowledge, understanding, and skills that a career counselor must possess to perform assessment and evaluation activities effectively.

Assessment is the systematic gathering of information for decision making about individuals, groups, programs, or processes. Assessment targets include abilities, achievements, personality variables, aptitudes, attitudes, preferences, interests, values, demographics, beliefs, and other characteristics. Assessment procedures include, but are not limited to, standardized and nonstandardized tests, questionnaires, inventories, checklists, observations, portfolios, performance assessments, rating scales, surveys, interviews, card sorts, and other measurement techniques.

Evaluation is the collection and interpretation of information to make judgments about individuals, programs, or processes that lead to decisions and future actions.

Committee:

Cheri Butler (NCDA, Chair), Belinda McCharen (NCDA, Chair), Janet Wall (AACE/NCDA, Chair), Rick Balkin (AACE), Lori Ellison (AACE), Chester Robinson (AACE), Brian Taber (NCDA), Pat Nellor Wickwire (AACE)

C
•••••

ASCA National Standards for Students

•••••

ACADEMIC DEVELOPMENT

ASCA National Standards for academic development guide school counseling programs to implement strategies and activities to support and maximize each student's ability to learn.

Standard A: Students will acquire the attitudes, knowledge and skills that contribute to effective learning in school and across the life span.

A:A1 Improve Academic Self-Concept
A:A1.1 Articulate feelings of competence and confidence as learners
A:A1.2 Display a positive interest in learning
A:A1.3 Take pride in work and achievement
A:A1.4 Accept mistakes as essential to the learning process
A:A1.5 Identify attitudes and behaviors that lead to successful learning

A:A2 Acquire Skills for Improving Learning
A:A2.1 Apply time-management and task-management skills
A:A2.2 Demonstrate how effort and persistence positively affect learning
A:A2.3 Use communications skills to know when and how to ask for help when needed
A:A2.4 Apply knowledge and learning styles to positively influence school performance

A:A3 Achieve School Success
A:A3.1 Take responsibility for their actions
A:A3.2 Demonstrate the ability to work independently, as well as the ability to work cooperatively with other students

A:A3.3 Develop a broad range of interests and abilities
A:A3.4 Demonstrate dependability, productivity and initiative
A:A3.5 Share knowledge

Standard B: Students will complete school with the academic preparation essential to choose from a wide range of substantial post secondary options, including college.

A:B1 Improve Learning
A:B1.1 Demonstrate the motivation to achieve individual potential
A:B1.2 Learn and apply critical-thinking skills
A:B1.3 Apply the study skills necessary for academic success at each level
A:B1.4 Seek information and support from faculty, staff, family and peers
A:B1.5 Organize and apply academic information from a variety of sources
A:B1.6 Use knowledge of learning styles to positively influence school performance
A:B1.7 Become a self-directed and independent learner

A:B2 Plan to Achieve Goals
A:B2.1 Establish challenging academic goals in elementary, middle/junior high and high school
A:B2.2 Use assessment results in educational planning
A:B2.3 Develop and implement annual plan of study to maximize academic ability and achievement
A:B2.4 Apply knowledge of aptitudes and interests to goal setting
A:B2.5 Use problem-solving and decision-making skills to assess progress toward educational goals
A:B2.6 Understand the relationship between classroom performance and success in school
A:B2.7 Identify postsecondary options consistent with interests, achievement, aptitude and abilities

STANDARD C: Students will understand the relationship of academics to the world of work and to life at home and in the community.

A:C1 Relate School to Life Experiences
A:C1.1 Demonstrate the ability to balance school, studies, extracurricular activities, leisure time and family life
A:C1.2 Seek co-curricular and community experiences to enhance the school experience
A:C1.3 Understand the relationship between learning and work
A:C1.4 Demonstrate an understanding of the value of lifelong learning as essential to seeking, obtaining and maintaining life goals

A:C1.5 Understand that school success is the preparation to make the transition from student to community member

A:C1.6 Understand how school success and academic achievement enhance future career and vocational opportunities

CAREER DEVELOPMENT

ASCA National Standards for career development guide school counseling programs to provide the foundation for the acquisition of skills, attitudes and knowledge that enable students to make a successful transition from school to the world of work, and from job to job across the life span.

Standard A: Students will acquire the skills to investigate the world of work in relation to knowledge of self and to make informed career decisions.

C:A1 Develop Career Awareness

C:A1.1 Develop skills to locate, evaluate and interpret career information

C:A1.2 Learn about the variety of traditional and nontraditional occupations

C:A1.3. Develop an awareness of personal abilities, skills, interests and motivations

C:A1.4 Learn how to interact and work cooperatively in teams

C:A1.5 Learn to make decisions

C:A1.6 Learn how to set goals

C:A1.7 Understand the importance of planning

C:A1.8 Pursue and develop competency in areas of interest

C:A1.9 Develop hobbies and vocational interests

C:A1.10 Balance between work and leisure time

C:A2 Develop Employment Readiness

C:A2.1 Acquire employability skills such as working on a team, problem-solving and organizational skills

C:A2.2 Apply job readiness skills to seek employment opportunities

C:A2.3 Demonstrate knowledge about the changing workplace

C:A2.4 Learn about the rights and responsibilities of employers and employees

C:A2.5 Learn to respect individual uniqueness in the workplace

C:A2.6 Learn how to write a résumé

C:A2.7 Develop a positive attitude toward work and learning

C:A2.8 Understand the importance of responsibility, dependability, punctuality, integrity and effort in the workplace

C:A2.9 Utilize time- and task-management skills

Standard B: Students will employ strategies to achieve future career goals with success and satisfaction.

C:B1 Acquire Career Information

C:B1.1 Apply decision-making skills to career planning, course selection and career transition

C:B1.2 Identify personal skills, interests, and abilities and relate them to current career choice

C:B1.3 Demonstrate knowledge of the career-planning process

C:B1.4 Know the various ways in which occupations can be classified

C:B1.5 Use research and information resources to obtain career information

C:B1.6 Learn to use the Internet to access career-planning information

C:B1.7 Describe traditional and nontraditional career choices and how they relate to career choice

C:B1.8 Understand how changing economic and societal needs influence employment trends and future training

C:B2 Identify Career Goals

C:B2.1 Demonstrate awareness of the education and training needed to achieve career goals

C:B2.2 Assess and modify their educational plan to support career

C:B2.3 Use employability and job readiness skills in internship, mentoring, shadowing and/or other work experience

C:B2.4 Select course work that is related to career interests

C:B2.5 Maintain a career-planning portfolio

Standard C: Students will understand the relationship between personal qualities, education, training and the world of work.

C:C1 Acquire Knowledge to Achieve Career Goals

C:C1.1 Understand the relationship between educational achievement and career success

C:C1.2 Explain how work can help to achieve personal success and satisfaction

C:C1.3 Identify personal preferences and interests influencing career choice and success

C:C1.4 Understand that the changing workplace requires lifelong learning and acquiring new skills

C:C1.5 Describe the effect of work on lifestyle

C:C1.6 Understand the importance of equity and access in career choice

C:C1.7 Understand that work is an important and satisfying means of personal expression

C:C2 Apply Skills to Achieve Career Goals
C:C2.1 Demonstrate how interests, abilities and achievement relate to achieving personal, social, educational and career goals
C:C2.2 Learn how to use conflict management skills with peers and adults
C:C2.3 Learn to work cooperatively with others as a team member
C:C2.4 Apply academic and employment readiness skills in work-based learning situations such as internships, shadowing and/or mentoring experiences

PERSONAL/SOCIAL DEVELOPMENT

ASCA National Standards for personal/social development guide school counseling programs to provide the foundation for personal and social growth as students' progress through school and into adulthood.

Standard A: Students will acquire the knowledge, attitudes and interpersonal skills to help them understand and respect self and others.

PS:A1 Acquire Self-Knowledge
PS:A1.1 Develop positive attitudes toward self as a unique and worthy person
PS:A1.2 Identify values, attitudes and beliefs
PS:A1.3 Learn the goal-setting process
PS:A1.4 Understand change is a part of growth
PS:A1.5 Identify and express feelings
PS:A1.6 Distinguish between appropriate and inappropriate behavior
PS:A1.7 Recognize personal boundaries, rights and privacy needs
PS:A1.8 Understand the need for self-control and how to practice it
PS:A1.9 Demonstrate cooperative behavior in groups
PS:A1.10 Identify personal strengths and assets
PS:A1.11 Identify and discuss changing personal and social roles
PS:A1.12 Identify and recognize changing family roles

PS:A2 Acquire Interpersonal Skills
PS:A2.1 Recognize that everyone has rights and responsibilities
PS:A2.2 Respect alternative points of view
PS:A2.3 Recognize, accept, respect and appreciate individual differences
PS:A2.4 Recognize, accept and appreciate ethnic and cultural diversity
PS:A2.5 Recognize and respect differences in various family configurations
PS:A2.6 Use effective communications skills
PS:A2.7 Know that communication involves speaking, listening and nonverbal behavior
PS:A2.8 Learn how to make and keep friends

Standard B: Students will make decisions, set goals, and take necessary action to achieve goals.

PS:B1 Self-knowledge Application

PS:B1.1 Use a decision-making and problem-solving model

PS:B1.2 Understand consequences of decisions and choices

PS:B1.3 Identify alternative solutions to a problem

PS:B1.4 Develop effective coping skills for dealing with problems

PS:B1.5 Demonstrate when, where and how to seek help for solving problems and making decisions

PS:B1.6 Know how to apply conflict resolution skills

PS:B1.7 Demonstrate a respect and appreciation for individual and cultural differences

PS:B1.8 Know when peer pressure is influencing a decision

PS:B1.9 Identify long- and short-term goals

PS:B1.10 Identify alternative ways of achieving goals

PS:B1.11 Use persistence and perseverance in acquiring knowledge and skills

PS:B1.12 Develop an action plan to set and achieve realistic goals

Standard C: Students will understand safety and survival skills.

PS:C1 Acquire Personal Safety Skills

PS:C1.1 Demonstrate knowledge of personal information (i.e., telephone number, home address, emergency contact)

PS:C1.2 Learn about the relationship between rules, laws, safety and the protection of rights of the individual

PS:C1.3 Learn about the differences between appropriate and inappropriate physical contact

PS:C1.4 Demonstrate the ability to set boundaries, rights and personal privacy

PS:C1.5 Differentiate between situations requiring peer support and situations requiring adult professional help

PS:C1.6 Identify resource people in the school and community, and know how to seek their help

PS:C1.7 Apply effective problem-solving and decision-making skills to make safe and healthy choices

PS:C1.8 Learn about the emotional and physical dangers of substance use and abuse

PS:C1.9 Learn how to cope with peer pressure

PS:C1.10 Learn techniques for managing stress and conflict

PS:C1.11 Learn coping skills for managing life events

D
• • • • •

National Career Development Guidelines (NCDG) Framework: Understanding the NCDG Framework
• • • • •

DOMAINS AND GOALS

Domains, goals and indicators organize the NCDG framework. The **three domains**: Personal Social Development (PS), Educational Achievement and Lifelong Learning (ED) and Career Management (CM) describe content. Under each domain are **goals** (eleven in total). The goals define broad areas of career development competency.

PERSONAL SOCIAL DEVELOPMENT DOMAIN

- GOAL PS1 Develop understanding of self to build and maintain a positive self-concept.
- GOAL PS2 Develop positive interpersonal skills including respect for diversity.
- GOAL PS3 Integrate growth and change into your career development.
- GOAL PS4 Balance personal, leisure, community, learner, family and work roles.

EDUCATIONAL ACHIEVEMENT AND LIFELONG-LEARNING DOMAIN

- GOAL ED1 Attain educational achievement and performance levels needed to reach your personal and career goals.
- GOAL ED2 Participate in ongoing, lifelong-learning experiences to enhance your ability to function effectively in a diverse and changing economy.

CAREER MANAGEMENT DOMAIN

- GOAL CM1 Create and manage a career plan that meets your career goals.
- GOAL CM2 Use a process of decision making as one component of career development.
- GOAL CM3 Use accurate, current and unbiased career information during career planning and management.
- GOAL CM4 Master academic, occupational and general employability skills in order to obtain, create, maintain and/or advance your employment.
- GOAL CM5 Integrate changing employment trends, societal needs, and economic conditions into your career plans.

INDICATORS AND LEARNING STAGES

Under each goal in the framework are indicators of mastery that highlight the knowledge and skills needed to achieve that goal. Each indicator is presented in **three learning stages** derived from *Bloom's Taxonomy*: knowledge acquisition, application, and reflection. The stages describe learning competency. They are not tied to an individual's age or level of education.

Knowledge Acquisition (K). Youth and adults at the knowledge acquisition stage expand knowledge awareness and build comprehension. They can recall, recognize, describe, identify, clarify, discuss, explain, summarize, query, investigate and compile new information about the knowledge.

Application (A). Youth and adults at the application stage apply acquired knowledge to situations and to self. They seek out ways to use the knowledge. For example, they can demonstrate, employ, perform, illustrate and solve problems related to the knowledge.

Reflection (R). Youth and adults at the reflection stage analyze, synthesize, judge, assess and evaluate knowledge in accord with their own goals, values and beliefs. They decide whether or not to integrate the acquired knowledge into their ongoing response to situations and adjust their behavior accordingly.

CODING SYSTEM

The NCDG framework has a simple **coding system** to identify domains, goals, indicators, and learning stages. The coding system makes it easy for you to use the NCDG for program development and to track activities by goal, learning stage, and indicator. However, you do **not** need to know or include the codes to use the NCDG framework.

Domains

- PS—Personal Social Development
- ED—Educational Achievement and Lifelong Learning
- CM—Career Management

Goals

Coded by domain and then numerically.

- For example, under the Personal Social Development domain:
- Goal PS1: Develop understanding of yourself to build and maintain a positive self-concept.
- Goal PS2: Develop positive interpersonal skills including respect for diversity.

Indicators and Learning Stages

Coded by domain, goal, learning stage and then numerically.

Learning Stages:

- K—Knowledge Acquisition
- A—Application
- R—Reflection

For example, the second indicator under the first goal of the Personal Social Development domain:

- PS1.K2 Identify your abilities, strengths, skills, and talents.
- PS1.A2 Demonstrate use of your abilities, strengths, skills, and talents.
- PS1.R2 Assess the impact of your abilities, strengths, skills, and talents on your career development.

If you have questions about the NCDG framework, in general, or its technical development, please contact the National Training Support Center (703.416.1840).

Personal Social Development Domain

Goal PS1	Develop Understanding of Yourself to Build and Maintain a Positive Self-Concept.
PS1.K1	Identify your interests, likes, and dislikes.
PS1.A1	Demonstrate behavior and decisions that reflect your interests, likes; and dislikes.
PS1.R1	Assess how your interests and preferences are reflected in your career goals.
PS1.K2	Identify your abilities, strengths, skills, and talents.
PS1.A2	Demonstrate use of your abilities, strengths, skills, and talents.
PS1.R2	Assess the impact of your abilities, strengths, skills, and talents on your career development.
PS1.K3	Identify your positive personal characteristics (e.g., honesty, dependability, responsibility, integrity, and loyalty).
PS1.A3	Give examples of when you demonstrated positive personal characteristics (e.g., honesty, dependability, responsibility, integrity, and loyalty).
PS1.R3	Assess the impact of your positive personal characteristics (e.g., honesty, dependability, responsibility, integrity, and loyalty) on your career development.
PS1.K4	Identify your work values/needs.
PS1.A4	Demonstrate behavior and decisions that reflect your work values/needs.
PS1.R4	Assess how your work values/needs are reflected in your career goals.
PS1.K5	Describe aspects of your self-concept.
PS1.A5	Demonstrate a positive self-concept through your behaviors and attitudes.
PS1.R5	Analyze the positive and negative aspects of your self-concept.
PS1.K6	Identify behaviors and experiences that help to build and maintain a positive self-concept.
PS1.A6	Show how you have adopted behaviors and sought experiences that build and maintain a positive self-concept.
PS1.R6	Evaluate the effect of your behaviors and experiences on building and maintaining a positive self-concept.
PS1.K7	Recognize that situations, attitudes, and the behaviors of others affect your self-concept.
PS1.A7	Give personal examples of specific situations, attitudes, and behaviors of others that affected your self-concept.
PS1.R7	Evaluate the effect of situations, attitudes, and the behaviors of others on your self-concept.
PS1.K8	Recognize that your behaviors and attitudes affect the self-concept of others.
PS1.A8	Show how you have adopted behaviors and attitudes to positively affect the self-concept of others.
PS1.R8	Analyze how your behaviors and attitudes might affect the self-concept of others.
PS1.K9	Recognize that your self-concept can affect educational achievement (i.e., performance) and/or success at work.
PS1.A9	Show how aspects of your self-concept could positively or negatively affect educational achievement (i.e., performance) and/or success at work.

(continued)

Goal PS1	**Develop Understanding of Yourself to Build and Maintain a Positive Self-Concept.** (*Continued*)
PS1.R9	Assess how your self-concept affects your educational achievement (performance) and/or success at work.
PS1.K10	Recognize that educational achievement (performance) and/or success at work can affect your self-concept.
PS1.A10	Give personal examples of how educational achievement (performance) and/or success at work affected your self-concept.
PS1.R10	Assess how your educational achievement (performance) and/or success at work affect your self-concept.

Goal PS2	**Develop Positive Interpersonal Skills Including Respect for Diversity.**
PS2.K1	Identify effective communication skills.
PS2.A1	Demonstrate effective communication skills.
PS2.R1	Evaluate your use of effective communication skills.
PS2.K2	Recognize the benefits of interacting with others in a way that is honest, fair, helpful, and respectful.
PS2.A2	Demonstrate that you interact with others in a way that is honest, fair, helpful, and respectful.
PS2.R2	Assess the degree to which you interact with others in a way that is honest, fair, helpful, and respectful.
PS2.K3	Identify positive social skills (e.g., good manners and showing gratitude).
PS2.A3	Demonstrate the ability to use positive social skills (e.g., good manners and showing gratitude).
PS2.R3	Evaluate how your positive social skills (e.g., good manners and showing gratitude) contribute to effective interactions with others.
PS2.K4	Identify ways to get along well with others and work effectively with them in groups.
PS2.A4	Demonstrate the ability to get along well with others and work effectively with them in groups.
PS2.R4	Evaluate your ability to work effectively with others in groups.
PS2.K5	Describe conflict resolution skills.
PS2.A5	Demonstrate the ability to resolve conflicts and to negotiate acceptable solutions.
PS2.R5	Analyze the success of your conflict resolution skills.
PS2.K6	Recognize the difference between appropriate and inappropriate behavior in specific school, social, and work situations.
PS2.A6	Give examples of times when your behavior was appropriate and times when your behavior was inappropriate in specific school, social, and work situations.
PS2.R6	Assess the consequences of appropriate or inappropriate behavior in specific school, social, and work situations.
PS2.K7	Identify sources of outside pressure that affect you.
PS2.A7	Demonstrate the ability to handle outside pressure on you.
PS2.R7	Analyze the impact of outside pressure on your behavior.

(*continued*)

Goal PS2	**Develop Positive Interpersonal Skills Including Respect for Diversity.** *(Continued)*
PS2.K8	Recognize that you should accept responsibility for your behavior.
PS2.A8	Demonstrate that you accept responsibility for your behavior.
PS2.R8	Assess the degree to which you accept personal responsibility for your behavior.
PS2.K9	Recognize that you should have knowledge about, respect for, be open to, and appreciate all kinds of human diversity.
PS2.A9	Demonstrate knowledge about, respect for, openness to, and appreciation for all kinds of human diversity.
PS2.R9	Assess how you show respect for all kinds of human diversity.
PS2.K10	Recognize that the ability to interact positively with diverse groups of people may contribute to learning and academic achievement.
PS2.A10	Show how the ability to interact positively with diverse groups of people may contribute to learning and academic achievement.
PS2.R10	Analyze the impact of your ability to interact positively with diverse groups of people on your learning and academic achievement.
PS2.K11	Recognize that the ability to interact positively with diverse groups of people is often essential to maintain employment.
PS2.A11	Explain how the ability to interact positively with diverse groups of people is often essential to maintain employment.
PS2.R11	Analyze the impact of your ability to interact positively with diverse groups of people on your employment.
Goal PS3	**Integrate Personal Growth and Change into your Career Development.**
PS3.K1	Recognize that you will experience growth and changes in mind and body throughout life that will impact on your career development.
PS3.A1	Give examples of how you have grown and changed (e.g., physically, emotionally, socially, and intellectually).
PS3.R1	Analyze the results of your growth and changes throughout life to determine areas of growth for the future.
PS3.K2	Identify good health habits (e.g., good nutrition and constructive ways to manage stress).
PS3.A2	Demonstrate how you have adopted good health habits.
PS3.R2	Assess the impact of your health habits on your career development.
PS3.K3	Recognize that your motivations and aspirations are likely to change with time and circumstances.
PS3.A3	Give examples of how your personal motivations and aspirations have changed with time and circumstances.
PS3.R3	Assess how changes in your motivations and aspirations over time have affected your career development.
PS3.K4	Recognize that external events often cause life changes.
PS3.A4	Give examples of external events that have caused life changes for you.
PS3.R4	Assess your strategies for managing life changes caused by external events.

(continued)

Goal PS3	Integrate Personal Growth and Change into your Career Development. *(Continued)*
PS3.K5	Identify situations (e.g., problems at school or work) in which you might need assistance from people or other resources.
PS3.A5	Demonstrate the ability to seek assistance (e.g., with problems at school or work) from appropriate resources including other people.
PS3.R5	Assess the effectiveness of your strategies for getting assistance (e.g., with problems at school or work) from appropriate resources including other people.
PS3.K6	Recognize the importance of adaptability and flexibility when initiating or responding to change.
PS3.A6	Demonstrate adaptability and flexibility when initiating or responding to change.
PS3.R6	Analyze how effectively you respond to change and/or initiate change.
Goal PS4	**Balance Personal, Leisure, Community, Learner, Family, and Work Roles.**
PS4.K1	Recognize that you have many life roles (e.g., personal, leisure, community, learner, family, and work roles).
PS4.A1	Give examples that demonstrate your life roles including personal, leisure, community, learner, family, and work roles.
PS4.R1	Assess the impact of your life roles on career goals.
PS4.K2	Recognize that you must balance life roles and that there are many ways to do it.
PS4.A2	Show how you are balancing your life roles.
PS4.R2	Analyze how specific life role changes would affect the attainment of your career goals.
PS4.K3	Describe the concept of lifestyle.
PS4.A3	Give examples of decisions, factors, and circumstances that affect your current lifestyle.
PS4.R3	Analyze how specific lifestyle changes would affect the attainment of your career goals.
PS4.K4	Recognize that your life roles and your lifestyle are connected.
PS4.A4	Show how your life roles and your lifestyle are connected.
PS4.R4	Assess how changes in your life roles would affect your lifestyle.

Educational Achievement and Lifelong Learning Domain

Goal ED1	Attain Educational Achievement and Performance Levels Needed to Reach your Personal and Career Goals.
ED1.K1	Recognize the importance of educational achievement and performance to the attainment of personal and career goals.
ED1.A1	Demonstrate educational achievement and performance levels needed to attain your personal and career goals.
ED1.R1	Evaluate how well you have attained educational achievement and performance levels needed to reach your personal and career goals.
ED1.K2	Identify strategies for improving educational achievement and performance.

(continued)

Goal ED1	**Attain Educational Achievement and Performance Levels Needed to Reach your Personal and Career Goals.** *(Continued)*
ED1.A2	Demonstrate strategies you are using to improve educational achievement and performance.
ED1.R2	Analyze your educational achievement and performance strategies to create a plan for growth and improvement.
ED1.K3	Describe study skills and learning habits that promote educational achievement and performance.
ED1.A3	Demonstrate acquisition of study skills and learning habits that promote educational achievement and performance.
ED1.R3	Evaluate your study skills and learning habits to develop a plan for improving them.
ED1.K4	Identify your learning style.
ED1.A4	Show how you are using learning style information to improve educational achievement and performance.
ED1.R4	Analyze your learning style to develop behaviors to maximize educational achievement and performance.
ED1.K5	Describe the importance of having a plan to improve educational achievement and performance.
ED1.A5	Show that you have a plan to improve educational achievement and performance.
ED1.R5	Evaluate the results of your plan for improving educational achievement and performance.
ED1.K6	Describe how personal attitudes and behaviors can impact educational achievement and performance.
ED1.A6	Exhibit attitudes and behaviors that support educational achievement and performance.
ED1.R6	Assess how well your attitudes and behaviors promote educational achievement and performance.
ED1.K7	Recognize that your educational achievement and performance can lead to many workplace options.
ED1.A7	Show how your educational achievement and performance can expand your workplace options.
ED1.R7	Assess how well your educational achievement and performance will transfer to the workplace.
ED1.K8	Recognize that the ability to acquire and use information contributes to educational achievement and performance.
ED1.A8	Show how the ability to acquire and use information has affected your educational achievement and performance.
ED1.R8	Assess your ability to acquire and use information in order to improve educational achievement and performance.
Goal ED2	**Participate in Ongoing, Lifelong Learning Experiences to Enhance your Ability to Function Effectively in a Diverse and Changing Economy.**
ED2.K1	Recognize that changes in the economy require you to acquire and update knowledge and skills throughout life.

(continued)

Goal ED2	**Participate in Ongoing, Lifelong Learning Experiences to Enhance your Ability to Function Effectively in a Diverse and Changing Economy.** *(Continued)*
ED2.A1	Show how lifelong learning is helping you function effectively in a diverse and changing economy.
ED2.R1	Judge whether or not you have the knowledge and skills necessary to function effectively in a diverse and changing economy.
ED2.K2	Recognize that viewing yourself as a learner affects your identity.
ED2.A2	Show how being a learner affects your identity.
ED2.R2	Analyze how specific learning experiences have affected your identity.
ED2.K3	Recognize the importance of being an independent learner and taking responsibility for your learning.
ED2.A3	Demonstrate that you are an independent learner.
ED2.R3	Assess how well you function as an independent learner.
ED2.K4	Describe the requirements for transition from one learning level to the next (e.g., middle school to high school, high school to postsecondary).
ED2.A4	Demonstrate the knowledge and skills necessary for transition from one learning level to the next (e.g., middle to high school, high school to postsecondary).
ED2.R4	Analyze how your knowledge and skills affect your transition from one learning level to the next (e.g., middle school to high school, high school to postsecondary).
ED2.K5	Identify types of ongoing learning experiences available to you (e.g., two- and four-year colleges, technical schools, apprenticeships, the military on-line courses, and on-the-job training).
ED2.A5	Show how you are preparing to participate in ongoing learning experiences (e.g., two- and four-year colleges, technical schools, apprenticeships, the military, on-line courses, and on-the-job training).
ED2.R5	Assess how participation in ongoing learning experiences (e.g., two- and four-year colleges, technical schools, apprenticeships, the military, on-line courses, and on-the-job training) affects your personal and career goals.
ED2.K6	Identify specific education/training programs (e.g., high school career paths and courses, college majors, and apprenticeship programs).
ED2.A6	Demonstrate participation in specific education/training programs (e.g., high school career paths and courses, college majors, and apprenticeship programs) that help you function effectively in a diverse and changing economy.
ED2.R6	Evaluate how participation in specific education/training programs (e.g., high school career paths and courses, college majors, and apprenticeship programs) affects your ability to function effectively in a diverse and changing economy.
ED2.K7	Describe informal learning experiences that contribute to lifelong learning.
ED2.A7	Demonstrate participation in informal learning experiences.
ED2.R7	Assess, throughout your life, how well you integrate both formal and informal learning experiences

Career Management Domain

Goal CM1	Create and Manage a Career Plan that Meets your Career Goals.
CM1.K1	Recognize that career planning to attain your career goals is a lifelong process.
CM1.A1	Give examples of how you use career-planning strategies to attain your career goals.
CM1.R1	Assess how well your career planning strategies facilitate reaching your career goals.
CM1.K2	Describe how to develop a career plan (e.g., steps and content).
CM1.A2	Develop a career plan to meet your career goals.
CM1.R2	Analyze your career plan and make adjustments to reflect ongoing career management needs.
CM1.K3	Identify your short-term and long-term career goals (e.g., education, employment, and lifestyle goals).
CM1.A3	Demonstrate actions taken to attain your short-term and long-term career goals (e.g., education, employment, and lifestyle goals).
CM1.R3	Re-examine your career goals and adjust as needed.
CM1.K4	Identify skills and personal traits needed to manage your career (e.g., resiliency, self-efficacy, ability to identify trends and changes, and flexibility).
CM1.A4	Demonstrate career management skills and personal traits (e.g., resiliency, self-efficacy, ability to identify trends and changes, and flexibility).
CM1.R4	Evaluate your career management skills and personal traits (e.g., resiliency, self-efficacy, ability to identify trends and changes, and flexibility).
CM1.K5	Recognize that changes in you and the world of work can affect your career plans.
CM1.A5	Give examples of how changes in you and the world of work have caused you to adjust your career plans.
CM1.R5	Evaluate how well you integrate changes in you and the world of work into your career plans.
Goal CM2	Use a Process of Decision Making as One Component of Career Development.
CM2.K1	Describe your decision-making style (e.g., risk taker, cautious).
CM2.A1	Give examples of past decisions that demonstrate your decision-making style.
CM2.R1	Evaluate the effectiveness of your decision-making style.
CM2.K2	Identify the steps in one model of decision-making.
CM2.A2	Demonstrate the use of a decision-making model.
CM2.R2	Assess what decision-making model(s) work best for you.
CM2.K3	Describe how information (e.g., about you, the economy, and education programs) can improve your decision-making.
CM2.A3	Demonstrate use of information (e.g., about you, the economy, and education programs) in making decisions.
CM2.R3	Assess how well you use information (e.g., about you, the economy, and education programs) to make decisions.

(continued)

Goal CM2	**Use a Process of Decision Making as One Component of Career Development.** (*Continued*)
CM2.K4	Identify alternative options and potential consequences for a specific decision.
CM2.A4	Show how exploring options affected a decision you made.
CM2.R4	Assess how well you explore options when making decisions.
CM2.K5	Recognize that your personal priorities, culture, beliefs, and work values can affect your decision-making.
CM2.A5	Show how personal priorities, culture, beliefs, and work values are reflected in your decisions.
CM2.R5	Evaluate the effect of personal priorities, culture, beliefs, and work values in your decision-making.
CM2.K6	Describe how education, work, and family experiences might impact your decisions.
CM2.A6	Give specific examples of how your education, work, and family experiences have influenced your decisions.
CM2.R6	Assess the impact of your education, work, and family experiences on decisions.
CM2.K7	Describe how biases and stereotypes can limit decisions.
CM2.A7	Give specific examples of how biases and stereotypes affected your decisions.
CM2.R7	Analyze the ways you could manage biases and stereotypes when making decisions.
CM2.K8	Recognize that chance can play a role in decision-making.
CM2.A8	Give examples of times when chance played a role in your decision-making.
CM2.R8	Evaluate the impact of chance on past decisions.
CM2.K9	Recognize that decision-making often involves compromise.
CM2.A9	Give examples of compromises you might have to make in career decision-making.
CM2.R9	Analyze the effectiveness of your approach to making compromises.
Goal CM3	**Use Accurate, Current, and Unbiased Career Information During Career Planning and Management.**
CM3.K1	Describe the importance of career information to your career planning.
CM3.A1	Show how career information has been important in your plans and how it can be used in future plans.
CM3.R1	Assess the impact of career information on your plans and refine plans so that they reflect accurate, current, and unbiased career information.
CM3.K2	Recognize that career information includes occupational, education and training, employment, and economic information and that there is a range of career information resources available.
CM3.A2	Demonstrate the ability to use different types of career information resources (i.e., occupational, educational, economic, and employment) to support career planning.
CM3.R2	Evaluate how well you integrate occupational, educational, economic, and employment information into the management of your career.

(*continued*)

Goal CM3	**Use Accurate, Current, and Unbiased Career Information During Career Planning and Management.** (*Continued*)
CM3.K3	Recognize that the quality of career information resource content varies (e.g., accuracy, bias, and how up-to-date and complete it is).
CM3.A3	Show how selected examples of career information are biased, out-of-date, incomplete, or inaccurate
CM3.R3	Judge the quality of the career information resources you plan to use in terms of accuracy, bias, and how up-to-date and complete it is.
CM3.K4	Identify several ways to classify occupations.
CM3.A4	Give examples of how occupational classification systems can be used in career planning.
CM3.R4	Assess which occupational classification system is most helpful to your career planning.
CM3.K5	Identify occupations that you might consider without regard to your gender, race, culture, or ability.
CM3.A5	Demonstrate openness to considering occupations that you might view as nontraditional (i.e., relative to your gender, race, culture, or ability).
CM3.R5	Assess your openness to considering non-traditional occupations in your career management.
CM3.K6	Identify the advantages and disadvantages of being employed in a non-traditional occupation.
CM3.A6	Make decisions for yourself about being employed in a non-traditional occupation.
CM3.R6	Assess the impact of your decisions about being employed in a non-traditional occupation.
Goal CM4	**Master Academic, Occupational, and General Employability Skills in Order to Obtain, Create, Maintain, and/or Advance your Employment.**
CM4.K1	Describe academic, occupational, and general employability skills.
CM4.A1	Demonstrate the ability to use your academic, occupational, and general employability skills to obtain or create, maintain, and advance your employment.
CM4.R1	Assess your academic, occupational, and general employability skills and enhance them as needed for your employment.
CM4.K2	Identify job seeking skills such as the ability to: write a resume and cover letter, complete a job application, interview for a job, and find and pursue employment leads.
CM4.A2	Demonstrate the following job seeking skills: the ability to write a resume and cover letter, complete a job application, interview for a job, and find and pursue employment leads.
CM4.R2	Evaluate your ability to: write a resume and cover letter, complete a job application, interview for a job, and find and pursue employment leads.
CM4.K3	Recognize that a variety of general employability skills and personal qualities (e.g., critical thinking, problem solving, resource, information, and technology management, interpersonal skills, honesty, and dependability) are important to success in school and employment.

(*continued*)

Goal CM4	**Master Academic, Occupational, and General Employability Skills in Order to Obtain, Create, Maintain, and/or Advance your Employment.** (*Continued*)
CM4.A3	Demonstrate attainment of general employability skills and personal qualities needed to be successful in school and employment (e.g., critical thinking, problem solving, resource, information, and technology management, inter-personal skills, honesty, and dependability).
CM4.R3	Evaluate your general employability skills and personal qualities (e.g., critical thinking, problem solving, resource, information, and technology management, interpersonal skills, honesty, and dependability).
CM4.K4	Recognize that many skills are transferable from one occupation to another.
CM4.A4	Show how your skills are transferable from one occupation to another.
CM4.R4	Analyze the impact of your transferable skills on your career options.
CM4.K5	Recognize that your geographic mobility impacts on your employability.
CM4.A5	Make decisions for yourself regarding geographic mobility.
CM4.R5	Analyze the impact of your decisions about geographic mobility on your career goals.
CM4.K6	Identify the advantages and challenges of self-employment.
CM4.A6	Make decisions for yourself about self-employment.
CM4.R6	Assess the impact of your decision regarding self-employment on your career goals.
CM4.K7	Identify ways to be proactive in marketing yourself for a job.
CM4.A7	Demonstrate skills that show how you can market yourself in the workplace.
CM4.R7	Evaluate how well you have marketed yourself in the workplace.
Goal CM5	**Integrate Changing Employment Trends, Societal Needs, and Economic Conditions into your Career Plans.**
CM5.K1	Identify societal needs that affect your career plans.
CM5.A1	Show how you are prepared to respond to changing societal needs in your career management.
CM5.R1	Evaluate the results of your career management relative to changing societal needs.
CM5.K2	Identify economic conditions that affect your career plans.
CM5.A2	Show how you are prepared to respond to changing economic conditions in your career management.
CM5.R2	Evaluate the results of your career management relative to changing economic conditions.
CM5.K3	Identify employment trends that affect your career plans.
CM5.A3	Show how you are prepared to respond to changing employment trends in your career management.
CM5.R3	Evaluate the results of your career management relative to changes in employment trends.

E

•••••

Missouri Comprehensive Guidance and Counseling Program Career Development Grade Level Expectations

•••••

Big Idea 7: CD 7 Applying Career Exploration and Planning Skills in the Achievement of Life Career Goals

K-12 CONCEPTS	GRADE K GLEs	GRADE 1 GLEs	GRADE 2 GLEs
Integration of Self-Knowledge into Life and Career Plans	Identify likes and dislikes at home and school.	Identify strengths and interests at home and school.	Identify new activities and interests to explore.
Adaptations to World of Work Changes	Identify workers in the school and in families related to the six career paths.	Identify workers in the local community related to the six career paths	Identify the academic skills necessary for workers in the six career paths.
Respect for All Work	Recognize that all work is important.	Explain the importance of jobs in the family and school.	Explain the importance of jobs and workers in the community.

Big Idea 8: Knowing Where and How to obtain Information About the World of Work and Postsecondary Training/Education

K-12 CONCEPTS	GRADE K GLEs	GRADE 1 GLEs	GRADE 2 GLEs
Career Decision Making	Identify roles and responsibilities of family members in the world of work.	Identify and compare roles and responsibilities of workers within the school.	Identify and compare roles and responsibilities of workers within the community.
Education and Career Requirements	Identify the skills family members use in their work.	Identify the skills needed by workers in the school.	Identify the skills needed by workers in the community.

Big Idea 9: Applying Employment Readiness Skills and the Skills for On-the-Job Success

K-12 CONCEPTS	GRADE K GLEs	GRADE 1 GLEs	GRADE 2 GLEs
Personal Skills for Job Success	Identify personal and ethical skills needed to work coopera- tively with others in a group at school.	Identify and develop personal, ethical, and work habit skills needed for school success.	Identify personal, ethical, and work habit skills needed for workers in the community.
Job Seeking Skills	Identify helper jobs that are available in the classroom.	Understand how helper jobs are assigned in the classroom.	Identify and apply the steps to obtain helper jobs within the classroom.

Big Idea 7: CD 7 Applying Career Exploration and Planning Skills in the Achievement of Life Career Goals

K-12 CONCEPTS	GRADE 3 GLEs	GRADE 4 GLEs	GRADE 5 GLEs
Integration of Self- Knowledge into Life and Career Plans	Identify and apply the steps to setting short-term and long- term, personal, and educational goals.	Compare interests and strengths with those of workers in the local community.	Compare interests and strengths with those of work- ers in the global community.
Adaptations to World of Work Changes	Compare and con- trast the academic skills required of workers in the six career paths.	Identify school and community re- sources available for exploration of the six career paths.	Describe occupa- tional changes that have occurred over time within the six career paths.
Respect for All Work	Recognize the contributions made by all workers to the school and community.	Recognize the con- tributions of all jobs to the community.	Describe the self-satisfaction that comes from completing a work responsibility.

Big Idea 8: Knowing Where and How to Obtain Information About the World of Work and Post secondary Training/Education

K-12 CONCEPTS	GRADE 3 GLEs	GRADE 4 GLEs	GRADE 5 GLEs
Career Decision Making	Explain what work- ers do and need to know in various careers.	Relate current stu- dent learning to each of the six career paths.	Compare and con- trast the roles and responsibilities of workers within the six career paths.
Education and Career Requirements	Gather information regarding training and education for a variety of careers.	Outline the training and educational requirements for a variety of careers.	Compare and con- trast the training and educational require- ments for a variety of careers.

Big Idea 9: Applying Employment Readiness Skills and the Skills for On-the-Job Success

K-12 CONCEPTS	GRADE 3 GLEs	GRADE 4 GLEs	GRADE 5 GLEs
Personal Skills for Job Success	Compare personal, ethical, and work habit skills needed for school success with those of workers in the community.	Demonstrate personal and ethical skills needed to work with diverse groups of people.	Apply personal, ethical, and work habit skills needed for success in any school or work environment.
Job Seeking Skills	Identify and apply the steps to obtain helper jobs within the school.	Identify the components of a portfolio.	Identify the skills needed to develop a portfolio.

Big Idea 7: CD 7 Applying Career Exploration and Planning Skills in the Achievement of Life Career Goals

K-12 CONCEPTS	GRADE 6 GLEs	GRADE 7 GLEs	GRADE 8 GLEs
Integration of Self-Knowledge into Life and Career Plans	Use current interests, strengths, and limitations to guide individual career exploration.	Use current interests, strengths, and limitations to guide career exploration and educational planning.	Develop an educational and career plan based on current interests, strengths, and limitations.
Adaptations to World of Work Changes	Recognize the career path concept as an organizer for exploring and preparing for careers now and in the future.	Be aware of occupations and careers as they relate to career paths, personal interests, and aptitudes.	Identify and explore a variety of resources to aid in career exploration and planning now and in the future.
Respect for All Work	Identify males and females in non-traditional work roles.	Recognize the relevance of all work and workers, and their existence in a global society.	Identify personal contributions made to school and community.

Big Idea 8: Knowing Where and How to Obtain Information About the World of Work and Postsecondary Training/Education

K-12 CONCEPTS	GRADE 6 GLEs	GRADE 7 GLEs	GRADE 8 GLEs
Career Decision Making	Evaluate career and educational information resources.	Utilize career and educational information to explore career paths of interest.	Compare personal interests with information about careers and education.
Education and Career Requirements	Compare different types of post-secondary training and education as they relate to career choices.	Utilize a variety of resources to obtain information about the levels of training and education required for various occupations.	Identify the training and education required for occupations in career paths of interest.

Big Idea 9: Applying Employment Readiness Skills and the Skills for On-the-Job Success

K-12 CONCEPTS	GRADE 6 GLEs	GRADE 7 GLEs	GRADE 8 GLEs
Personal Skills for Job Success	Assess and analyze personal, ethical, and work habit skills as they relate to individual student success.	Utilize information about personal, ethical, and work habit skills to enhance individual student success.	Evaluate personal, ethical, and work habit skills as they relate to achieving the student's educational career plan.
Job Seeking Skills	Develop a resume of work experiences for home and school.	Identify and demonstrate basic job seeking skills of interviewing and completing applications.	Utilize a portfolio of middle school/junior high school academic and work experience.

Big Idea 7: CD 7 Applying Career Exploration and Planning Skills in the Achievement of Life Career Goals

K-12 CONCEPTS	GRADE 9 GLEs	GRADE 10 GLEs	GRADE 11 GLEs	GRADE 12 GLEs
Integration of Self-Knowledge into Life and Career Plans	Compare current strengths and limitations with the individual's career and educational plan and adjust the plan as necessary	Revisit current career and educational plan as it relates to evolving and/or new interests, strengths, and limitations.	Analyze the education, training, and personal characteristics needed to achieve current life career goals and compare those characteristics with one's own characteristics.	Utilize knowledge of the world of work; personal interests; and strengths and limitations to develop short- and long-term post-secondary plans.
Adaptations to World of Work Changes	Recognize the sixteen (16) career clusters within the six career paths as a more specific organizer for exploring and preparing for careers now and in the future.	Evaluate a variety of resources to aid in career exploration and planning now and in the future.	Utilize a variety of resources to aid in career exploration and planning.	Utilize knowledge of career exploration and planning to adapt new career and educational opportunities as the world of work changes.
Respect for All Work	Analyze and evaluate school and community contributions as they relate to one's career and educational plan.	Analyze and evaluate school and community contributions as they relate to life career goals.	Identify personal contributions to a global society to be made as a result of one's life career choices.	Respect all work as important, valuable, and necessary in maintaining a global society.

**Big Idea 8: Knowing Where and How to Obtain Information
About the World of Work and Post secondary Training/Education**

K-12 CONCEPTS	GRADE 9 GLEs	GRADE 10 GLEs	GRADE 11 GLEs	GRADE 12 GLEs
Career Decision Making	Integrate career and educational information with knowledge of self and career clusters to identify occupations of interest.	Analyze career and educational information to identify the most relevant resources for specific career options.	Synthesize information gathered from a variety of sources.	Utilize career and educational information in career decision-making
Education and Career Requirements	Identify the entrance requirements and application procedures for post-secondary options.	Apply knowledge of self to make informed decisions about post-secondary options.	Apply research skills to obtain information on training and education requirements for post-secondary choices.	Know and understand the levels of training and education required for life career goals.

**Big Idea 9: Applying Employment Readiness Skills and the Skills
for On-the-Job Success**

K-12 CONCEPTS	GRADE 9 GLEs	GRADE 10 GLEs	GRADE 11 GLEs	GRADE 12 GLEs
Personal Skills for Job Success	Identify situations which would compromise ethical habits in school or work situations.	Identify the steps which can be used to resolve ethical issues related to school or work situations.	Demonstrate the steps which can be used to resolve ethical issues related to school or work situations.	Apply personal, ethical, and work habit skills, that contribute to job success.
Job Seeking Skills	Identify and refine the job-seeking skills needed to apply for volunteer or part-time jobs in the community.	Compare and contrast the post-secondary application process to the job application process.	Refine and utilize a portfolio which may be used for a variety of post-secondary opportunities.	Utilize appropriate job-seeking skills to obtain employment.

References

ACT. (2011). *DISCOVER Career planning program.* Iowa City, IA: Author.

ACT. (2012). *EXPLORE.* Iowa City, IA: Author.

ACT, Inc. (2012). *Description of the ACT.* Retrieved from http://www.actstudent.org/testprep/descriptions/index.html

ACT, Inc. (2008). *The forgotten middle: Ensuring that all students are on target for college and career readiness before high school* (Policy brief). Iowa City, IA: Author.

Association for Career and Technical Education. (2010). *What is career ready?* Alexandria, VA: Author.

Akos, P., Lambie, G., Milsom, A., & Gilbert, K. (2007). Early adolescents' aspirations and academic tracking: An exploratory investigation. *Professional School Counseling, 11*(1), 57–64. doi:10.5330/PSC.n.2010-11.57

Akos, P., Niles, S. G., Miller, E. M., & Erford, B. T. (2011). Promoting educational and career planning in schools. In B. T. Erford (Ed.), *Transforming the school counseling profession.* (3rd ed.) (pp. 202–221). Upper Saddle River, NJ: Pearson.

Alexander, N. P. (2000). *Early childhood workshops that work! The essential guide to successful training and workshops.* Beltsville, MD: Gryphon House.

Alliman-Brissett, A. E., Turner, S. L., & Skovholt, T. M. (2004). Parent support and African American adolescents' career self-efficacy. *Professional School Counseling 7*(3), 124–132.

Amaram, D. I. (2010). The gender pay gap: Review and update. *China-USA Business Review, 9*(6), 51–58.

American Counseling Association. (2005). *2005 code of ethics.* Retrieved from http://www.counseling.org/resources/codeofethics/TP/home/ct2.aspx

American Counseling Association. (2011). *United States student to counselor ratios for elementary and secondary schools.* Retrieved from http://www.counseling.org/PublicPolicy/ACA_Ratio_Chart_2011_Overall.pdf

American Psychological Association, Task Force on the Sexualization of Girls. (2007). *Report of the APA Task Force on the Sexualization of Girls.* Retrieved from www.apa.org/pi/wpo/sexualization.html

American School Counselor Association. (2004). *ASCA student standards.* Alexandria, VA: Author.

American School Counselor Association. (2005). *The ASCA national model: A framework for school counseling programs.* (2nd ed.). Alexandria, VA: Author.

American School Counselor Association. (2010). *Ethical standards for school counselors.* Retrieved from http://www.schoolcounselor.org/files/EthicalStandards2010.pdf

American School Counselor Association. (2012). *The ASCA national model: A framework for school counseling programs.* (3rd ed.). Alexandria, VA: Author.

Americans with Disabilities Act of 1990, 42 U.S.C. 12101 et seq. (Pub. L No. 101-336).

Amundson, N. E., & Penner, K. (1998). Parent involved career exploration. *The Career Development Quarterly, 47*(2), 135–144. doi:10.1002/j.2161-0045.1998.tb00547.x

Association for Career and Technical Education (2011). *What is 'career ready?'* Retrieved from Association for Career and Technical Education website: http://www.acteonline.org/uploadedFiles/Publications_and_Online_Media/files/Career_Readiness_Paper.pdf

Auger, R. W., Blackhurst, A. E., & Wahl, K. H. (2005). The development of elementary aged children's career aspirations and expectations. *Professional School Counseling, 8*(4), 322–329.

Aune, E. (1991). A transition model for postsecondary-bound students with learning disabilities. *Learning Disabilities Research & Practice, 6,* 177–187.

Ausubel, D. P. (1954). *Theory and problems of adolescent development.* New York, NY: Grune & Stratton.

Bailey, D. F., Getch, Y. Q., & Chen-Hayes, S. F. (2007). Achievement advocacy for all students through transformative school counseling programs. In B. T. Erford (Ed.), *Transforming the school counseling profession.* (2nd ed.) (pp. 98–120). Upper Saddle River, NJ: Pearson.

Bandura, A. (1977). *Social learning theory.* Englewood Cliffs, NJ: Prentice Hall.

Bandura, A. (1986). *Social foundations of thought and action: A social cognitive theory.* Englewood Cliffs, NJ: Prentice Hall.

Bandura, A. (1997). *Self-efficacy: The exercise of control.* New York, NY: Freeman.

Bandura, A., Barbaranelli, C., Caprara, G. V., & Pastorelli, C. (1996). Multifaceted impact of self-efficacy beliefs on academic functioning. *Child Development, 67*(3), 1206–1222. doi:10.2307/1131888

Barker, J. & Satcher, J. (2000). School counselors' perceptions of required workplace skills and career development competencies. *Professional School Counseling, 4*(2), 134–139.

Bayer Corporation. (2012). Bayer facts of science education XV: A view from the gatekeepers—STEM department chairs at America's Top 200 research universities on female and underrepresented minority undergraduate STEM students. *Journal of Science Education Technology, 21,* 317–324. doi: 10.1007/s10956-012-9364-1

Becker, R. L. (2000). *Reading-Free Vocational Interest Inventory-2 (R-FVII:2).* Columbus, OH: Elbern Publications.

Bell, N. E. (2011). *Graduate enrollment and degrees: 2000–2010. The CGS/GRE Survey of Graduate Enrollment and Degrees is jointly sponsored by: Council of Graduate Schools Graduate Record Examinations Board.* Retrieved online from http://www.cgsnet.org/ckfinder/userfiles/files/R_ED2010.pdf

Belsky, J. (2007). *Experiencing the lifespan.* New York, NY: Worth Publishers.

Bennet, G. K., Seashore, H. G., & Wesman, A. G. (1990). *Differential Aptitude Test.* San Antonio, TX: Pearson Assessments.

Blackhurst, A. E., & Auger, R. W. (2008). Precursors to the gender gap in college enrollment: Children's aspirations and expectations for their futures. *Professional School Counseling, 11*(3), 149–158. doi:10.5330/PSC.n.2010-11.149

Blackhurst, A. E., Auger, R. W., & Wahl, K. H. (2003). Children's perceptions of vocational preparation requirements. *Professional School Counseling, 7*(2), 58–67.

Bloom, B. S., Engelhart, M. D., Furst, E. J., Hill, W. H., & Krathwohl, D. R. (1956). *Taxonomy of educational objectives: The classification of educational goals.* New York, NY: David McKay Company, Inc.

Boden, K. (2011). Perceived academic preparedness of first-generation Latino college students. *Journal of Hispanic Higher Education, 10*(2), 96–106. doi:10.1177/1538192711402211

Bourdieu, P. (1977). *Outline of a theory of practice.* Cambridge, UK: Cambridge University Press.

Bowen, M. (1976). Theory in the practice of psychotherapy. In P. J. Guerin (Ed.), *Family therapy.* New York, NY: Gardner.

Brandon, E. (2006, September). *Better yet, no tuition. U. S. News & World Report.* Retrieved from http://www.usnews.com/usnews/biztech/articles/060910/18free.htm

Briggs, K. C., & Briggs Myers, I. (2004). *The Myers-Briggs type indicator.* Palo Alto, CA: Consulting Psychologists Press.

Brock, T. (2010). Young adults and higher education: Barriers and breakthroughs to success. *Future of Children, 20*(1), 109–132.

Bronfenbrenner, U. (1977). Toward an experimental ecology of human development. *American Psychologist, 32,* 513–531. doi:10.1037/0003-066X.32.7.513

Bronfenbrenner, U. (1979). *The ecology of human development.* Cambridge, MA: Harvard University Press.

Brown, C. & Lavish, L. A. (2006). Career assessment with Native Americans: Role salience and career decision-making self-efficacy. *Journal of Career Assessment, 14*(1), 116–129.

Brown, D. (1996). Brown's values-based, holistic model of career and life-role choices and satisfaction. In D. Brown, L. Brooks, & Associates (Eds.), *Career choice and development* (pp. 337–372). San Francisco, CA: Jossey-Bass.

Brown, D. (2002). The role of work values and cultural values in occupational choice, satisfaction, and success: A theoretical statement. In D. Brown & Associates (Eds.), *Career choice and development* (4th ed.) (pp. 465–509). San Francisco, CA: Jossey-Bass.

Brown, D. (2012). *Career information, career counseling, and career development* (10th ed.). Boston, MA: Pearson.

Brown, D., & Crace, R. K. (2002). *Life Values Inventory.* Williamsburg, VA: Applied Psychology Resources.

Budget Challenge. (2012). Retrieved from the Budget Challenge website at http://www.budgetchallenge.com/HowItWorks.aspx

Burtnett, F. (2011). Defining the role of graduate education: An ACA interview with Debra Stewart, president of the Council of Graduate Schools. *Counseling Today, 54*(2), 44–45.

California Career Resource Network. (n.d.). *California career zone.* Retrieved from www.cacareerzone.org

Campbell, D. (1992). *Campbell interest and skill survey.* San Antonio, TX: Pearson Assessments.

Carnevale, A. P., Rose, S. J., & Cheah, B. (2011). *The college payoff: Education, occupations, lifetime earnings.* Retrieved from the Georgetown University Public Policy Institute, Center on Education and the Workforce website: http://cew.georgetown.edu/collegepayoff/

Carnevale, A. P., Smith, N., & Strohl, J. (2010). *Help wanted: Projections of jobs and education requirements through 2018.* Retrieved from the Georgetown University Public Policy Institute, Center on Education and the Workforce website: http://cew.georgetown.edu/jobs2018/

Carter, M., & Curtis, D. (1994). *Training teachers: A harvest of theory and practice.* St. Paul, MN: Redleaf Press.

Carty, K. (2010). *Trajectories of Black men from baccalaureate degree attainment through career transition* (Doctoral dissertation). Retrieved from ProQuest Dissertations and Theses database. (UMI No. 3410469)

Caster, T. R. (1984). The young child's play and social and emotional development. In T. D. Yawkey & A. D. Pellegrini (Eds.), *Child's play and play therapy* (pp. 17–29). Lancaster, PA: Technomic Publishing Co., Inc.

Center for the Study of Education Policy, Illinois State University. (2005). *Improving chances for college success for low income and minority high school students.* Retrieved from Illinois State University, Center for the Study of Education Policy website: http://centereducationpolicy.illinoisstate.edu/initiatives/collegesuccess/finalreport.pdf

Center on Education Policy. (2010). *Improving achievement for the growing Latino population is critical to the nation's future* (Student Achievement Policy Brief #3: Latino Students). Washington, DC: Author.

Charles Schwab, Inc. (2011). *Charles Schwab 2011 teens & money survey findings: Insights into money attitudes, behaviors and expectations of 16–18 year olds.* Retrieved online from http://www.channelone.com/pdf/generationmoney/teens-and-money-surveyfindings.pdf

Choate, L. H., & Curry, J. (2009). Addressing the sexualization of girls through comprehensive programs, advocacy and systemic change: Implications for professional school counselors. *Professional School Counseling, 12*(3), 213–221. doi:10.5330/PSC.n.2010-12.213

College Board. (2012). *About the PSAT/ NMSQT.* Retrieved from the College Board website: http://www.collegeboard.com/student/testing/psat/about.html

Conley, D. (2007). *Toward a more comprehensive conception of college readiness. Educational Policy Improvement Center.* Retrieved from: http://www.s4s.org/upload/Gates-College%20Readiness.pdf

Connolly, P. (1998). *Racism, gender identities and young children: Social relations in a multi-ethnic inner-city primary school.* London: Routledge.

Cook, C., Fowler, H., & Harris, T. (2008). *Ninth grade academies: Easing the transition to high school.* Raleigh, NC: North Carolina Department of Public Instruction.

Council for Accreditation of Counseling and Related Educational Programs. (2009). *2009 Standards.* Alexandria, VA: Author.

Covey, S. (1998). *The 7 habits of highly effective teens.* New York, NY: Fireside.

Crow, L. D., & Crow, A. (1965). Adolescent development and adjustment (2nd ed.). New York, NY: McGraw-Hill Inc.

Curry, J. (2010). Addressing the spiritual needs of African American students: Implications for school counselors. *Journal of Negro Education, 79*(3), 405–415.

Curry, J., Belser, C. T., & Binns, I. C. (2013). Integrating post-secondary college and career options in the middle school curriculum: Considerations for teachers. *Middle School Journal, 44*(3), 26–32.

Curry, J., & Bickmore, D. (2012). School counselor induction and the importance of mattering. *Professional School Counseling, 15*(3), 110–122. doi:10.5330/PSC.n.2012-15.110

Curry, J., & Choate, L. (2010). The oversexualization of young adolescent girls: Implications for Middle Grades Educators. *Middle School Journal, 42*(1), 6–15.

Curry, J., & Choate, L. (2012). Building bridges to address issues of gender: School leaders' role in promoting equity. In C. Boske (Ed.), *The anatomy of bridge leadership in US public schools: Expanding the boundaries for social justice discourse* (pp. 91–116). Charlotte, NC: Information Age Publishing.

Curry, J., & Lambie, G. W. (2007). Enhancing school counselor accountability: The large group guidance portfolio. *Professional School Counseling, 11*(2), 145–148. doi:10.5330/PSC.n.2010-11.145

Curry, J., Smith, H., & Robinson, E. H. (2009). The development and manifestation of altruistic caring: A qualitative inquiry. *Counseling and Values, 54*, 2–16.

Dalke, C. (1993). Making a successful transition from high school to college: A model program. In S. A. Vogel & P. B. Adelman (Eds.), *Success for college students with disabilities* (pp. 57–80). New York, NY: Springer Verlag.

Department of Defense. (2004). *Armed Services Vocational Aptitude Battery.* Washington, DC: Author.

Diamond, K. E., Spiegel-McGill, P., & Hanrahan, P. (1988). Planning for school transition: An ecological-developmental approach. *Journal of the Division for Early Childhood, 12,* 245–252.

Dickinson, D. L., & Verbeek, R. L. (2002). Wage differentials between college graduates with and without LD. *Journal of Learning Disabilities, 35,* 175–185.

Diekman, A. B., Brown, E. R., Johnston, A. M., & Clark, E. K. (2010). Seeking congruity between goals and roles: A new look at why women opt out of science, technology, engineering and mathematics careers. *Psychological Science.* doi:10.11777/0956797610377342

Diekman, A. B., Clark, E. K., Johnston, A. M., Brown, E. R., & Steinberg, M. (2011). Malleability in communal goals and beliefs influences attraction to STEM careers: Evidence for a goal congruity perspective. *Journal of Personality and Social Psychology, 101*(5), 902–918. doi:10.1037/a0025199

Dolan, T. G. (2008). Minority students and college success: Challenges and solutions. *Education Digest: Essential Readings Condensed for Quick Review, 73*(7), 27–30.

Dugas, C. (2010, March 3). More consumers file for bankruptcy protection. *USA Today.* Retrieved from USA Today website: http://usatoday30.usatoday.com/money/economy/2010-03-03-bankruptcy03_ST_N.htm

Durodoye, B. A., & Bodley, G. (1997). Career development issues for ethnic minority college students. *College Student Journal, 31*(1), 27–32.

Economy Watch. (2011, May 23). *9 Alarming U.S. consumer debt statistics.* Retrieved online from the Business Insider website: http://articles.businessinsider.com/2011-05-23/markets/30101275_1_consumer-debt-credit-cards-student-loans#ixzz2E1Prmcqz

Education Week. (2011, July 7). Special education. *Education Week.* Retrieved from http://www.edweek.org/ew/issues/special-education/

Eisenberg, N., Guthrie, I. K., Murphy, B. C., Shepard, S. A., Cumberland, A., & Carlo, G. (1999). Consistency and development of prosocial dispositions: A longitudinal study. *Child Development, 70*(6), 1360–1372. doi:10.1111/1467-8624.00100

Eisenberg, N., Miller, P. A., Shell, R., McNalley, S., & Shea, C. (1991). Prosocial development in adolescence: A longitudinal study. *Developmental Psychology, 27*(5), 849–858. doi:10.1037/0012-1649.27.5.849

Elkind, D. (1978). Understanding the young adolescent. *Adolescence, 13*(49), 127–134.

Ellis, B. (2011, November 16). *Delaying retirement: 80 is the new 65.* Retrieved online from CNN Money http://money.cnn.com/2011/11/16/retirement/age/index.htm

Erikson, E. H. (1963). *Childhood and society* (2nd ed.). New York, NY: Norton.

Espana, S., Fegette, K., Islip, B., Sampson, J., & Walker, M. (2004). *House of cards: Credit card project.* Retrieved online from http://www.wafbla.org/wpcontent/uploads/2011/12/Economics-House-of-CR-Cards.pdf

Ferguson, L. R. (1970). *Personality development.* Belmont, CA: Brooks/Cole Publishing.

Fernandez-Ballesteros, R., Diez-Nicolas, J., Caprara, G. V., Barbaranelli, C., & Bandura, A. (2002). Determinants and structural relation of personal efficacy to collective efficacy. *Applied Psychology: An International Review, 51*(1), 107–125. doi:10.1111/1464-0597.00081

Fields, G. M. (2008). *Reinventing 9th grade: Academics through personalization.* International Rexford, NY: Center for Leadership in Education.

Flexer, R. W., Simmons, T. J., Luft, P., & Baer, R. M. (2005). *Transition planning for secondary students with disabilities* (2nd ed.). Upper Saddle River, NJ: Pearson.

Fouad, N. A. (1995). Career linking: An intervention to promote math and science career awareness. *Journal of Counseling & Development, 73,* 527–534.

Frank, L. K. (1982). Play in personality development. In G. L. Landreth (Ed.), *Play therapy: Dynamics of the process of counseling with children* (pp. 19–32). Springfield, IL: Thomas.

Fredrickson, B. L., & Roberts, T-A. (1997). Objectification theory: Toward understanding women's lived experiences and mental health risks. *Psychology of Women Quarterly, 21*(2), 173–206. doi:10.1111/j.1471-6402.1997.tb00108.x

Gardner, H. (1983). *Frames of mind: The theory of multiple intelligences.* New York, NY: Basic Books.

Gardner, H. (2004). *Frames of mind: The theory of multiple intelligences.* New York, NY: Basic Books.

Gibbons, M. M., & Borders, L. D. (2010). A measure of college-going self-efficacy for middle school students. *Professional School Counseling, 13,* 234–243.

Gibson, D. M. (2005). The use of genograms in career counseling with elementary, middle, and high school students. *The Career Development Quarterly, 53*(4), 353–362. doi:10.1002/j.2161-0045.2005.tb00666.x

Gibson, D. M. (2012). *Using career genograms in K-12 settings.* Retrieved from the National Career Development Association website: http://associationdatabase.com/aws/NCDA/pt/sd/news_article/5473/_PARENT/layout_details/false

Gibson, R. L., & Mitchell, M. H. (2006). *Introduction to career counseling for the 21st century.* Upper Saddle River, NJ: Pearson.

Gibson, R. L., & Mitchell, M. H. (2008). *Introduction to counseling and guidance* (7th ed.). Upper Saddle River, NJ: Pearson.

Goodman, R. D., & West-Olatunji, C. A. (2010). Educational hegemony, traumatic stress, and African American and Latino American students. *Journal of Multicultural Counseling and Development, 38*(3), 176–186. doi:10.1002/j.2161-1912.2010.tb00125.x

Gottfredson, L. S. (1981). Circumscription and compromise: A developmental theory of occupational aspirations. *Journal of Counseling Psychology, 28*(6), 545–579. doi:10.1037/0022-0167.28.6.545

Gottfredson, L. S. (2002). Gottfredson's theory of circumscription, compromise, and self-creation. In D. Brown (Ed.), *Career choice and development* (4th ed.) (pp. 85–148). San Francisco: Jossey-Bass.

Gottfredson, L. S. (2005). Applying Gottfredson's theory of circumscription and compromise in career guidance and counseling. In S. D. Brown & R. W. Lent (Eds.), *Career development and counseling: Putting theory and research to work* (pp. 71–100). Hoboken, NJ: John Wiley & Sons.

Graves, M. (1996). *Planning around children's interests: The teacher's idea book 2.* Ypsilanti, MI: High/Scope Press.

Greene, M. J. (2006). Helping build lives: Career and life development of gifted and talented students. *Professional School Counseling, 10*(1), 34–42.

Griffith, A. L. (2010). Persistence of women and minorities in STEM field majors: Is it the school that matters? *Economics of Education Review, 29,* 911–922. doi:10.1016/j.econedurev.2010.06.010

Gushue, G. V., Scanlan, K. R. L., Pantzer, K. M., & Clarke, C. P. (2006). The relationship of career decision-making self-efficacy, vocational identity, and career exploration behavior in African American high school students. *Journal of Career Development, 33*(1), 19–28. doi:10.1177/0894845305283004

Hagner, D., & Salomone, P. R. (1989). Issues in career decision making for workers with developmental disabilities. *The Career Development Quarterly, 38,* 148–159.

Hall, A. S. (2003). Expanding academic and career self-efficacy: A family systems framework. *Journal of Counseling & Development, 81*(1), 33–39. doi:10.1002/j.1556-6678.2003.tb00222.x

Hall, G. S. (1904). *Adolescence.* New York, NY: Appleton.

Hansen, R., Johnston, J., Krieshok, T., & Wong, S. C. (2012). *Missouri Occupational Card Sort.* Columbia, MO: University of Missouri.

Hart Research Associates. (2005). *Rising to the challenge: Are high school graduates prepared for college and work? A study of recent high school graduates, college instructors, and employers.* Retrieved from Achieve, Inc. website: http://www.achieve.org/files/pollreport_0.pdf

Harter, S. (1999). *The construction of the self: A developmental perspective.* New York, NY: Guilford Press.

Havighurst, R. J. (1972). *Developmental tasks and education* (3rd ed.). New York, NY: David McKay Company, Inc.

Heinrich, R., Molenda, M., Russell, J. D., & Smaldino, S. E. (1996). *Instructional media and technologies for learning.* Englewood Cliffs, NJ: Merrill.

Helwig, A. A. (1998). Occupational aspirations of a longitudinal sample from second to sixth grade. *Journal of Career Development, 24*(4), 247–266. doi:10.1023/A:1025085830778

Henderson, C. (1999). *1999 college freshmen with disabilities statistical year 1998: A biennial statistical profile.* Washington, DC: American Council on Education, HEATH Resource.

Herr, E. L., Cramer, S. H., & Niles, S. G. (2004). *Career guidance and counseling through the lifespan: Systematic approaches* (6th ed.). Boston, MA: Pearson.

Hindley, C. B. (1983). Psychological changes in adolescence related to physical changes. In W. Everaerd, C. B. Hindley, A. Bot, & J. J. van der Werff ten Bosch (Eds.), *Development in adolescence: Psychological, social and biological aspects* (pp. 28–48). Boston, MA: Martinus Nijhoff Publishers.

Hoffman, L. L., Jackson, A. P., & Smith, S. A. (2005). Career barriers among Native American students living on reservations. *Journal of Career Development, 32*(1), 31–45. doi:10.1177/0894845305277038

Holcomb-McCoy, C. (2010). Involving low income parents and parents of color in college readiness activities: An exploratory study. *Professional School Counseling, 14*(1), 115–124.

Holcomb-McCoy, C., & Chen-Hayes, S. F. (2007). Multiculturally competent school counselors: Affirming diversity by challenging oppression. In B. T. Erford (Ed.), *Transforming the school counseling profession* (2nd ed.) (pp. 74–97). Upper Saddle River, NJ: Pearson.

Holcomb-McCoy, C., & Chen-Hayes, S. F. (2011). Culturally competent school counselors: Affirming diversity by challenging oppression. In B. T. Erford (Ed.), *Transforming the school counseling profession* (3rd ed.) (pp. 90–109). Upper Saddle River, NJ: Pearson.

Holland, J. L. (1973). *Making vocational choices: A theory of careers.* Englewod Cliffs, NJ: Prentice Hall, Inc.

Holland, J. L. (1994). *Self-directed search.* Lutz, FL: Psychological Assessment Resources, Inc.

Holland, J. L. (1997). *Making vocational choices: A theory of vocational personalities and work environments* (3rd ed.). Odessa, FL: Psychological Assessment Resources.

Holland, J. L., Daiger, D. C., & Power, P. G. (1980). *My vocational situation.* Palo Alto, CA: Consulting Psychologists Press.

Hoover, N. (2007). *Cultural disparities of SAT scores and the influence on higher education opportunities for African American and Latino students* (Master's thesis). Retrieved from ERIC database. (ED499158)

Hossler, D., Schmit, J., & Vesper, N. (1999). *Going to college: How social, economic and educational factors influence the decisions students make.* Baltimore, MD: The Johns Hopkins University Press.

Ivers, N. N., Milsom, A., & Newsome, D. W. (2012). Using Gottfredson's theory of circumscription and compromise to improve Latino students' school success. *Career Development Quarterly, 60,* 231–242.

Ivey, A., Ivey, M., Myers, J., & Sweeney, T. (2005). *Developmental counseling and therapy: promoting wellness over the lifespan.* Boston, MA: Lahaska Press.

Jackson, A. P., & Turner, S. (2004). Counseling and psychotherapy with Native Americans. In T. Smith (Ed.), *Practicing Multiculturalism* (pp. 215–233). Boston, MA: Allyn & Bacon.

Janiga, S. J., & Costenbader, V. (2002). The transition from high school to postsecondary education for students with learning disabilities: A survey of college service coordinators. *Journal of Learning Disabilities, 35,* 462–468.

Jalongo, M. R., & Isenberg, J. P. (2004). *Exploring your role: A practitioner's introduction to early childhood education* (2nd ed.). Upper Saddle River, NJ: Pearson.

Johnson, L. S. (2000). The relevance of school to career: A study in student awareness. *Journal of Career Development, 26*(4), 263–276. doi:10.1177/089484530002600403

Jones, L. K. (2009). *The career key.* Hood River, OR: Career Key, Inc.

Jones, L. K. (2011). *Holland's six personality types.* Retrieved from The Career Key website: http://www.careerkey.org/asp/your_personality/hollands_6_personalitys.asp

Kelty, R., Kleykamp, M., & Segal, D. R. (2010). The military and the transition to adulthood. *Future of Children, 20*(1), 181–207.

Kemp, C., & Carter, M. (2000). Demonstration of classroom survival skills in kindergarten: A five-year transition study of children with intellectual disabilities. *Educational Psychology, 20,* 393–411. doi:10.1080/713663756

Kennelly, L. & Monrad, M. (2007). *Easing the transition to high school: Research and best practices designed to support high school learning.* Washington, DC: National High School Center.

Kimmel, M. S. (2005). *Manhood in America: A cultural history* (2nd ed.). Oxford, NY: Oxford University Press.

Knowdell, R. L. (2005). *Career values card sort.* San Jose, CA: Career Research & Testing, Inc.

Koebler, J. (2012, April 11). White house report: More women need to study STEM. *U.S. News.* Retrieved online http://www.usnews.com/news/blogs/stem-education/2012/04/11/white-house-report-more-women-need-to-study-stem

Kohlberg, L. (1981). *The philosophy of moral development.* San Francisco, CA: Harper & Row.

Kolodinsky, P., Schroder, V., Montopoli, G., McLean, S., Mangan, P. A., & Pederson, W. (2006). The career fair as a vehicle for enhancing occupational self-efficacy. *Professional School Counseling, 10,* 161–167.

Krieshok, T. S., & Black, M. D. (2009). Assessment and counseling competencies and responsibilities: A checklist for counselors. In E. A. Whitfield, R. W. Feller, & C. Wood (Eds.), *A counselor's guide to career assessment instruments* (5th ed.) (pp. 61–68). Broken Arrow, OK: National Career Development Association.

Krumboltz, J. D. (1994). *Career beliefs inventory.* Menlo Park, CA: Mind Garden, Inc.

Krumboltz, J. D., Mitchell, A. M. & Jones, G. B. (1976). A social learning theory of career selection. *The Counseling Psychologist, 6,* 71–81.

Kuder, F. (2006). *Kuder career planning system.* Adel, IA: Kuder, Inc.

Lacey, T. A., & Wright, B. (2009). Occupational employment projections to 2018. *Monthly Labor Review,* 82–123.

Landreth, G. L. (1982). Children communicate through play. In G. L Landreth (Ed.), *Play therapy: Dynamics of the process of counseling with children* (pp. 45–46). Springfield, IL: Thomas.

Legum, H. L., & Hoare, C. H. (2004). Impact of a career intervention on at-risk middle school students' career maturity levels, academic achievement, and self-esteem. *Professional School Counseling, 8*(2), 148–155.

Lent, R. W., Brown, S. D., & Hackett, G. (1994). Toward a unifying social cognitive theory of career and academic interest, choice, and performance. *Journal of Vocational Behavior, 45*, 79–122.

Levin, D. E., & Kilbourne, J. (2008). *So sexy so soon: The new sexualized childhood and what parents can do to protect their kids.* New York, NY: Ballantine.

Levin, H., Belfield, C., Muennig, P. & Rouse, C. (2007). *The costs and benefits of an excellent education for all of America's children.* Retrieved from Alliance on Education website http://www.all4ed.org/publication_material/research/costsbenefits_exed

Levine, M. P., & Smolak, L. (2002). Body image development in adolescence. In T. F. Cash & T. Pruzinsky (Eds.), *Body image: A handbook of theory, research, and clinical practice* (pp. 74–82). New York, NY: The Guilford Press.

Lewin, T. (2006, July 9). At colleges, women are leaving men in the dust. *The New York Times.* Retrieved from http://www.nytimes.com/2006/07/09/education/09college.html?pagewanted=all

Long, J. (1999). *School-to-work transitions with Native American Indians: Implications for counselors.* Retrieved from ERIC database. (ED444787)

Lucas, M. S. (1993). Personal, social, academic, and career problems expressed by minority college students. *Journal of Multicultural Counseling & Development, 21*(1), 2–13. doi:10.1002/j.2161-1912.1993.tb00578.x

Luzer, D. (2011, February 15). How students get remediation. *Washington Monthly.* Retrieved from http://www.washingtonmonthly.com/college_guide/blog/how_students_get_remediated.php?page=all&print=true

Maddux, J. E. (2002). Self-efficacy: The power of believing you can. In C. R. Snyder & S. J. Lopez (Eds.), *Handbook of positive psychology* (pp. 277–287). Oxford: University Press.

Madriaga, M., Hanson, K., Heaton, C., Kay, H., Newitt, S., & Walker, A. (2010). Confronting similar challenges? Disabled and non-disabled students' learning and assessment experiences. *Studies in Higher Education, 35*(6), 647–658. doi:10.1080/03075070903222633

Marcia, J. E. (1987). The identity status approach to the study of ego identity development. In T. Honess & K. Yardley (Eds.), *Self and identity: Perspectives across the lifespan* (pp. 161–171). New York, NY: Routledge.

Marcia, J. E. (1989). Identity and intervention. *Journal of Adolescence, 12*(4), 401–410. doi:10.1016/0140-1971(89)90063-8

Martin, P. J., & Robinson, S. G. (2011). Transforming the school counseling profession. In B. T. Erford (Ed.), *Transforming the school counseling profession* (pp. 1–18). Upper Saddle River, NJ: Pearson.

Marvasti, J. A. (1997). Ericksonian play therapy. In K. O'Connor & L. M. Braverman (Eds.), *Play therapy theory and practice: A comparative presentation* (pp. 285–309). New York, NY: John Wiley & Sons, Inc.

Masten, A. S., & Reed, M. J. (2002). Resilience in development. In C. R. Snyder & S. J. Lopez (Eds.), *Handbook of positive psychology* (pp. 74–88). Oxford: University Press.

McCallumore, K. M., & Sparapani, E. F. (2010). The importance of the ninth grade on high school graduation rates and student success in high school. *Education, 130*(3), 447–456.

McIntosh, J., & White, S. (2006). Building for freshman success: High schools working as professional learning communities. *American Secondary Education, 34* (2), 40–49.

McMahon, L. (1992). *The handbook of play therapy.* New York, NY: Routledge.

Mihesuah, J. K. (2004). Graduating indigenous students by confronting the academic environment. In D. A. Mihesuah & A. C. Wilson (Eds.), *Indigenizing the academy: Transforming scholarship and empowering communities* (pp. 191–199). Lincoln, NE: University of Nebraska.

Mijares, A. (2007). *Defining college readiness.* Retrieved from College Board website: http://www.edsource.org/assets/files/convening/CollegeBoard_brief.pdf

Miller, M. (2009). *Teaching for a new world: Preparing high school educators to deliver college- and career-ready instruction.* Retrieved from ERIC database. (ED507351)

Miller, P. W. (2008). The gender pay gap in the US: Does sector make a difference? *Journal of Labor Research, 30*(1), 52–74.

Miller, P. W. (2009). The gender pay gap in the US: Does sector make a difference? *Journal of Labor Research, 30*(1), 52–74. doi:10.1007/s12122-008-9050-5

Milsom, A. (2007). Interventions to assist students with disabilities through school transitions. *Professional School Counseling, 10*(3), 273–278.

Milsom, A., Akos, P., & Thompson, M. (2004). A psychoeducational group approach to postsecondary transition planning for students with learning disabilities. *Journal for Specialists in Group Work, 29,* 395–411.

Milsom, A., & Dietz, L. (2009). Defining college readiness for students with learning disabilities: A Delphi study. *Professional School Counseling, 12,* 315–323.

Milsom, A., & Hartley, M. T. (2005). Assisting students with learning disabilities transitioning to college: What school counselors should know. *Professional School Counseling, 8,* 436–441.

Missouri Center for Career Education. (2006). *Missouri Comprehensive Guidance Program Content Standards Grade Level Expectations (GLE).* Retrieved from http://www.missouricareereducation.org/project/guidegle

Missouri Comprehensive Guidance Program. (2006). *Content Standards Grade Level Expectations (GLE) Strand CD: Career Development.* Retrieved from http://www.missouricareereducation.org/doc/guidegle/GLE_Career.pdf

Muennig, P., & Fahs, M. (2001). The cost effectiveness of public post-secondary education subsidies. *Preventive Medicine, 32,* 156–162. doi:10.1006/pmed.2000.0790

Murnen, S. K., Smolak, L., Mills, J. A., & Good, L. (2003). Thin, sexy women and strong, muscular men: Grade school children's responses to objectified images of women and men. *Sex Roles, 49,* 427–437. doi:10.1023/A:1025868320206

Myers, J. E., Sweeney, T. J., & Witmer, J. M. (2000). The wheel of wellness counseling for wellness: A holistic model for treatment planning. *Journal of Counseling & Development, 78*(3), 251–266. doi:10.1002/j.1556-6676.2000.tb01906.x

National Association of State Directors of Career and Technical Education consortium. (2012). *The 16 career clusters.* Retrieved from http://www.careertech.org/career-clusters/glance/careerclusters.html

National Career Development Association. (2009). *The National Career Development Association minimum competencies for multicultural career counseling and development.* Retrieved from http://ncda.org/aws/NCDA/pt/sp/guidelines

National Center for Education Statistics. (2011). *2008-2009 baccalaureate and beyond longitudinal study (B&B:08/09).* Washington, DC: U.S. Department of Education.

National Financial Educators Council. (n.d.). *Financial literacy definition.* Retrieved from National Financial Educators Council website: http://www.financialeducatorscouncil.org/financial-literacy-definition.html

National Math and Science Initiative. (2011). *The STEM crisis.* Retrieved from http://www.nationalmathandscience.org/solutions/challenges.

National Poverty Center. (2011). *Poverty in the United States: Frequently asked questions.* Retrieved from The University of Michigan Gerald Ford Policy Center website: http://www.npc.umich.edu/poverty/.

Nelson, R. C. (1982). Elementary school counseling with unstructured play media. In G. L Landreth (Ed.), *Play therapy: Dynamics of the process of counseling with children* (pp. 259–264). Springfield, IL: Thomas.

Niles, S. G., & Harris-Bowlesbey, J. (2009). *Career development interventions in the 21st century* (3rd ed.). Upper Saddle River, NJ: Merrill.

O'Brien, K. M., Dukstein, R. D., Jackson, S. L., Tomlinson, M. J., & Kamatuka, N. A. (1999). Broadening career horizons for students in at-risk environments. *The Career Development Quarterly, 47*(3), 215–229. doi:10.1002/j.2161-0045.1999.tb00732.x

Orthner. (2012). *CareerStart: A proven approach to middle-school success.* Retrieved from http://www.learnnc.org/lp/pages/7260

Parris, G. P., Owens, D., Johnson, T., Grbevski, S., & Holbert-Quince, J. (2010). Addressing the career development needs of high-achieving African American high school students: Implications for counselors. *Journal for the Education of the Gifted, 33*(3), 417–436.

Parsons, F. (1909). *Choosing a vocation.* Boston, MA: Houghton Mifflin.

Patton, W., & Creed, P. (2007). The relationship between career variables and occupational aspirations and expectations for Australian high school adolescents. *Journal of Career Development, 34*(2), 127–148. doi:10.1177/0894845307307471

Pellegrini, A. D. (1984). Children's play and language: Infancy through early childhood. In T. D. Yawkey & A. D. Pellegrini (Eds.), *Child's play and play therapy* (pp. 45–58). Lancaster, PA: Technomic Publishing Co., Inc.

Peterson, G. W., Sampson, J. P. Jr., & Reardon, R. (1991). *Career development and services: A cognitive approach.* Pacific Grove, CA: Brooks/Cole.

Phillips, P. (1990). A self-advocacy plan for high school students with learning disabilities: A comparative case study analysis of students', teachers', and parents' perceptions of program effects. *Journal of Learning Disabilities, 23*, 466–471.

Piaget, J. (1965). *The moral judgment of the child.* New York, NY: Free Press.

Piaget, J. (1969). The intellectual development of the adolescent. In G. Caplan & S. Lebovici (Eds.), *Adolescence: Psychosocial perspectives* (pp. 22–26). New York, NY: Basic Books, Inc.

Piaget, J. (1977). *The development of thought: Equilibration of cognitive structure.* New York, NY: Viking Press.

Ponec, D. L. (1997). *African-American females: A theory of educational aspiration.* Retrieved from ERIC database. (ED415457)

Porfeli, E. J., Hartung, P. J., & Vondracek, F. W. (2008). Children's vocational development: A research rationale. *The Career Development Quarterly, 57*(1), 25–37. doi:10.1002/j.2161-0045.2008.tb00163.x

Radcliffe, R., & Bos, B. (2011). Mentoring approaches to create a college-going culture for at-risk secondary level students. *American Secondary Education, 39*, 86–107.

Raphael, S. (2004). *The socioeconomic status of black males: The increasing importance of incarceration* (Unpublished manuscript). Goldman School of Public Policy, University of California, Berkley.

Remley, T. P., & Herlihy, B. (2007). *Ethical, legal, and professional issues in counseling* (2nd ed.). Upper Saddle River, NJ: Pearson.

Reynolds, A. L., Sodano, S. M., Ecklund, T. R., & Guyker, W. (2012). Dimensions of acculturation in Native American college students. *Measurement and Evaluation in Counseling and Development, 45*(2), 101–112. doi:10.1177/0748175611428330

Roach, R. (2006). Survey: American girls aren't interested in STEM careers. *Diverse Issues in Higher Education, 23*(4), 54.

Rock, E., & Leff, E. H. (2011). The professional school counselor and students with disabilities. In B. T. Erford (Ed.), *Transforming the school counseling profession* (3rd ed.) (pp. 314–341). Upper Saddle River, NJ: Pearson.

Ronan, G. B. (2005, November 29). College freshmen face major dilemma. *MSNBC News.* Retrieved from http://www.msnbc.msn.com/id/10154383/ns/business-personal_finance/t/college-freshmen-face-major-dilemma/#.UJgoNoU88a0

Rumrill, P. D., & Roessler, R. T. (1999). New directions in vocational rehabilitation: A "career development" perspective on "closure." *Journal of Rehabilitation, 65*, 26–30.

Sampson, J. P. Jr., Peterson, G. W., Lenz, J. G., Reardon, R. C., & Saunders, D. E. (1996). *Career thoughts inventory.* Odessa, FL: Psychological Assessment Resources, Inc.

Savickas, M. L. (1998). Career style assessment and counseling. In T. Sweeney (Ed.), *Adlerian counseling: A practitioner's approach* (4th ed.) (pp. 329–360). Philadelphia, PA: Accelerated Development Press.

Savickas, M. L. (2002). Career construction: A developmental theory of vocational behavior. In D. Brown & Associated (Eds.), *Career choice and development* (4th ed.) (pp. 149–205). San Francisco, CA: Jossey-Bass.

Savickas, M. L. (2005). The theory and practice of career construction. In S. D. Brown & R. W. Lent (Eds.), *Career development and counseling: Putting theory and research to work* (pp. 42–70). Hoboken, NJ: John Wiley & Sons, Inc.

Schneider, M., & Yin, L. (2011). *The high cost of low graduation rates: How much does dropping out of college really cost?* Retrieved from the American Institutes for Research website: http://www.air.org/focus area/education/index.cfm?fa=view Content&content_id=1404

Schultheiss, D. E. P. (2008). Current status and future agenda for the theory, research, and practice of childhood career development. *The Career Development Quarterly, 57*(1), 7–24. doi:10.1002/j.2161-0045.2008.tb00162.x

Schultheiss, D. E., Palma, T. V., & Manzi, A. J. (2005). Career development in middle childhood: A qualitative inquiry. *The Career Development Quarterly, 53*, 246–262.

Seidenberg, P. L. (1987). *The unrealized potential: College preparation for secondary learning disabled students. A guide for secondary school administrators, faculty and parents.* Retreved from ERIC database. (ED289336)

Shaffer, D. R. (2009). *Social and personality development* (6th ed.). Belmont, CA: Wadsworth.

Sharf, R. S. (2006). *Applying career development theory to counseling* (4th ed.). Belmont, CA: Thomson.

Shutiva, C. L. (2001). *Career and academic guidance for American Indian and Alaska Native youth.* ERIC digest. ERIC Clearinghouse on rural education and small schools.

Simmons, C. H., & Sands-Dudelczyk, K. (1983). Children helping peers: Altruism and preschool environment. *The Journal of Psychology, 115*(2), 203–207. doi:10.1080/002 23980.1983.9915437

Stanton, A. L., Parsa, A., & Austenfeld, J. L. (2002). The adaptive potential of coping through emotional approach. In C. R. Snyder & S. J. Lopez (Eds.), *Handbook of Positive Psychology* (pp. 148–158). Oxford: University Press.

Stout, J. G., Dasgupta, N., Hunsinger, M., & McManus, M. A. (2011). STEMing the tide: Using ingroup experts to inoculate women's self-concept in science, technology, engineering, and mathematics (STEM). *Journal of Personality and Social Psychology, 100*(2), 255–270. doi:10.1037/a0021385

Strauss, V. (2011, August 17). 2011 ACT scores show problems with college readiness. *The Washington Post.* Retrieved online from http://www.washingtonpost. com/blogs/answer-sheet/post/2011-act-scores-show-problems-with-college-readiness/2011/08/16/gIQABKu4JJ_blog.html

Strong, E. K. Jr. (2004) *Strong interest inventory.* Palo Alto, CA: Consulting Psychologists Press.

Super, D. E. (1953). A theory of vocational development. *American Psychologist, 8*, 185–190.

Super, D. E. (1980). A life-span, life-space approach to career development. *Journal of Vocational Behavior, 16*(3), 282–298. doi:10.1016/0001-8791(80)90056-1

Super, D. E., Thompson, A. S., Lindeman, R. H., Jordan, J. P., & Myers, R. A. (1984). *Career development inventory.* Palo Alto, CA: Consulting Psychologists Press.

Talent Assessment, Inc. (2000). *Pictorial inventory of careers.* Jacksonville, FL: Author.

Taningco, M. T. (2008). *Latinos in STEM professions: Understanding challenges and opportunities for next steps. A qualitative study using stakeholder interviews.* Washington, DC: The Tomas River Policy Institute. Retrieved from the Education Resources Information Center online. (ED502064).

Taylor, K. M., & Betz, N. E. (1983). *Career decision making self-efficacy scale.* Menlo Parl, CA: Mind Garden, Inc.

The Center for Public Education. (2009). *Special education: A better perspective.* Retrieved online The Center for Public Education website: http://www.centerforpubliceducation.org/Main-Menu/Evaluating-performance/Special-education-At-a-glance/Special-education-A-better-perspective-full-report.html

The Chronicle of Higher Education. (2011). *Almanac of higher education 2011.* Retrieved from The Chronicle of Higher Education website: http://chronicle.com/section/Almanac-of-Higher-Education/536/

The Opportunity Agenda. (2010). *The state of opportunity in America.* Retrieved from The Opportunity Agenda website: http://opportunityagenda.org/stateofopportunity

The Riley Institute at Furman University. (2012). *College application month.* Retrieved from http://riley.furman.edu/sites/default/files/docs/CEPLClearinghouseCollegeApplicationMonth5.25.12.pdf

Tomatzky, L. G., Macias, E. E., Jenkins, D., & Solis, C. (2006). *Access and Achievement: Building educational and career pathways for Latinos in advanced technology. Report on a national study of Latino access to postsecondary education and careers in information technology.* The Tomas Rivera Policy Institute. Retrieved from ERIC database. (ED502061)

Turner, S., & Lapan, R. T. (2002). Career self-efficacy and perceptions of parent support in adolescent career development. *The Career Development Quarterly, 51*(1), 44–55. doi:10.1002/j.2161-0045.2002.tb00591.x

Turner, S. L. & Conkel, J. L. (2010). Evaluation of a career development skills intervention with adolescents living in an inner city. *Journal of Counseling & Development, 88,* 457–465.

Turner, S. L., Conkel, J., Starkey, M. T., & Landgraf, R. (2010). Relationships among middle-school adolescents' vocational skills, motivational approaches, and interests. *The Career Development Quarterly, 59,* 154–168. doi:10.1002/j.2161-0045.2010.tb00059.x

Turner, S. L., Trotter, M. J., Lapan, R. T., Czajka, K. A., Yang, P., & Brissett, A. E. A. (2006). Vocational skills and outcomes among Native American adolescents: A test of the integrative contextual model of career development. *The Career Development Quarterly, 54*(3), 216–226. doi:10.1002/j.2161-0045.2006.tb00153.x

U.S. Census Bureau, Statistical Abstract of the United States. (2011). *Educational attainment by race, Hispanic origin, and sex: 1970-2009.* Retrieved from http://www.census.gov/compendia/statab/2011/tables/11s0225.pdf

U.S. Department of Commerce, U. S. Census Bureau. (2006). *American Community survey. Ethnicity and ancestry branch.* Retrieved from http://www.census.gov/acs/www/

U.S. Department of Education. (2004). *NCLB overview: Executive summary. Archived file.* Retrieved from http://www2.ed.gov/nclb/overview/intro/execsumm.html.

U.S. Department of Education. (2009, November 26). U.S. Department Of Education endorses STEM initiatives.*GovMonitor: Public Sector News & information.* Retrieved from http://www.thegovmonitor.com/world_news/united_states/u-s-department-of-education-endorses-stem-initiatives-16770.html.

U.S. Department of Education. (2010, March). *A blueprint for reform: The reauthorization of the elementary and secondary education act.* Retrieved from http://www2.ed.gov/policy/elsec/leg/blueprint/publicationtoc.html

U.S. Department of Education, National Center for Education Statistics. (2008). *The condition of education 2008: Family characteristics of 5–17 year old.* (Indicator 7-2012). Retrieved from http://nces.ed.gov/programs/coe/indicator_fch.asp

U.S. Department of Education, National Center for Education Statistics. (2010). *The condition of education 2010: Racial/ethnic enrollment in public schools.* Retrieved from http://nces.ed.gov/programs/coe/indicator_1er.asp

U.S. Department of Education, National Center for Education Statistics. (2011). *Digest of Education Statistics, 2010.*(NCES 2011-015). Retrieved from http://nces.ed.gov/fastfacts/display.asp?id=59

U.S. Department of Labor, Bureau of Labor Statistics. (2010). *Persons with a disability: Labor force characteristics - 2009.* (USDL-10-1172). Retrieved from http://www.bls.gov/news.release/archives/disabl_08252010.pdf

U.S. Department of Labor, Bureau of Labor Statistics. (2011a). *College enrollment and work activity of 2010 high school graduates.* (USDL-12-0716). Retrieved from http://www.bls.gov/news.release/pdf/hsgec.pdf

U.S. Department of Labor, Bureau of Labor Statistics. (2011b). *Employment status of the civilian noninstitutional population by age, sex, and race.* Retrieved from http://www.bls.gov/cps/cpsaat03.htm

U.S. Department of Labor, Bureau of Labor Statistics. (2011c). *Employment status of the civilian noninstitutional population 16 to 24 years of age by school enrollment, age, sex, race, Hispanic or Latino ethnicity, and educational attainment.* Retrieved from http://www.bls.gov/web/empsit/cpseea16.pdf

Usinger, J. (2005). Parent/guardian visualization of career and academic future of seventh graders enrolled in low-achieving schools. *The Career Development Quarterly, 53*(3), 234–245. doi:10.1002/j.2161-0045.2005.tb00993.x

Veiga, A. (2012, August 9). *Number of homes facing foreclosure rose in July: Lenders placed more homes on foreclosure path in July, but repossessions decline.* Retrieved from the Yahoo! Finance website http://finance.yahoo.com/news/number-homes-facing-foreclosure-rose-040831645.html

Vygotsky, L. S. (1978). Mind in society: *The development of higher mental processes.* Cambridge, MA: Harvard University Press.

Wadsworth, J., Milsom, A., & Cocco, K. (2004). Career development for adolescents and young adults with mental retardation. *Professional School Counseling, 8,* 141–147.

Wagner, M., Newman, L., Cameto, R., Garza, N., and Levine, P. (2005). *After high school: A first look at the postschool experiences of youth with disabilities. A Report from the National Longitudinal Transition Study-2 (NLTS2).* Menlo Park, CA: SRI International. Retrieved July 9, 2008 from: www.nlts2.org/reports/2005_04/nlts2_report_2005_04_complete.pdf.

Walker, T., Pearson, F., & Murrell, P. (2010). Quality of effort and career preparation differences between African American and White community college students. *Community College Journal of Research and Practice, 34*(9), 738–754. doi:10.1080/10668920902917450

Walker, T. L., & Tracey, T. J. G. (2012). Perceptions of occupational prestige: Differences between African American and White college students. *Journal of Vocational Behavior, 80,* 76–81. doi:10.1016/j.jvb.2011.06.003

Watson, M., & McMahon, M. (2008). Children's career development: Metaphorical images of theory, research, and practice. *The Career Development Quarterly, 57*(1), 75–83. doi:10.1002/j.2161-0045.2008.tb00167.x

Wells, R. R. (1997). *The native American experience in higher education: Turning around the cycle of failure II.* ERIC Database. (ED414108)

Wertheim, E., Freeman, E., & Trinder, M. (2012). Enhancing relationships in school communities: Promoting cooperative conflict resolution and respect for cultural diversity in schools. In D. Bretherton & N. Balvin (Eds.), *Peace Psychology in Australia* (pp. 139–160). doi:10.1007/978-1-4614-1403-2_9

West-Olatunji, C. A., Baker, J. C., & Brooks, M. (2006). African American adolescent males: Giving voice to their educational experiences. *Multicultural Perspectives, 8*(4), 3–9. doi:10.1207/s15327892mcp0804_2

West-Olatunji, C., Shure, L., Garrett, M. T., Conwill, W., & Rivera, E. T. (2008). Rite of passage programs as effective tools for fostering resilience among low-income African American male adolescents. *The Journal of Humanistic Counseling, Education and Development, 47*(2), 131–143. doi:10.1002/j.2161-1939.2008.tb00053.x

West-Olatunji, C., Shure, L., Pringle, R., Adams, T., Lewis, D., & Cholewa, B. (2010). Exploring how school counselors position low-income African American girls as mathematics and science learners. *Professional School Counseling, 13*(3), 184–195. doi:10.5330/PSC.n.2010-13.184

Wettig, H. H. G., Franke, U., & Fjordbak, B. S. (2006). Evaluating the effectiveness of theraplay. In C. E. Schaefer & H. G. Kaduson (Eds.), *Contemporary play therapy* (pp. 103–135). New York, NY: Guilford Press.

Wheelock, A., & Miao, J. (2005). The ninth-grade bottleneck: An enrollment bulge in a transition year that demands careful attention and action. *School Administrator, 62*(3), 36–40.

White House. (2011). *Winning the future: President Obama's budget.* Retrieved from the White House website: http://www.whitehouse.gov/winning-the-future/education

Whitfield, E. A., Feller, R. W., & Wood, C. (Eds.) (2009). *A counselor's guide to career assessment instruments* (5th ed.). Broken Arrow, OK: National Career Development Association.

Wright, L. L. (2010). *Social, demographic, and institutional effects on African American graduation rates in U. S. colleges and universities* (Doctoral dissertation). Retrieved from ProQuest Dissertations and Theses database. (UMI No. 3417790)

Yawkey, T. D., & Diantoniis, J. M. (1984). Relationships between child's play and cognitive development and learning in infancy birth through age eight. In T. D. Yawkey & A. D. Pellegrini (Eds.), *Child's play and play therapy* (pp. 31–44). Lancaster, PA: Technomic Publishing Co., Inc.

Young, R. A. (1983). Career development of adolescents: An ecological perspective. *Journal of Youth and Adolescence, 12*(5), 401–417. doi:10.1007/BF02088723

Young, R. A., Paseluikho, M. A., & Valach, L. (1997). The role of emotion in the construction of career in parent-adolescent conversations. *Journal of Counseling & Development, 76*(1), 36–44. doi:10.1002/j.1556-6676.1997.tb02374.x

Author Index

• • • • •

Subject Index